KEY TEXTS

KEY TEXTS
Classic Studies in the History of Ideas

THE PHILOSOPHICAL THEORY OF THE STATE AND RELATED ESSAYS

Bernard Bosanquet

Edited by
Gerald F. Gaus and William Sweet

ST. AUGUSTINE'S PRESS
SOUTH BEND, INDIANA
2001

This edition published by St. Augustine's Press, 2001

St. Augustine's Press
South Bend, Indiana
USA

ISBN 1-890318-65-5

Introduction, annotation and index
© Gerald F. Gaus and William Sweet, 2001

Manufactured in the United States of America.

Library of Congress Cataloging-in-Publication Data

Bosanquet, Bernard, 1848–1923
    The philosophical theory of the state and related essays /
    Bernard Bosanquet ; edited by Gerald F. Gaus and William
    Sweet
        p.   cm
    Originally published: London ; New York : Macmillan, 1899
    Includes bibliographical references and index.
    ISBN 1-890318-65-5 (alk. paper)
    1. State, The—Philosophy. 2. Political science—Philosophy.
    I. Gaus, Gerald F. II. Sweet, William. III. Title.

    JC223.B79   1999
    320.1'01—dc21   99–045575
                                                      CIP

∞ *The paper used in this publication meets the minimum*
requirements of the American National Standard for
Information Sciences – Permanence of Paper for Printed
Materials, ANSI Z39.48-1984.

CONTENTS

Related Essays

EDITORS' INTRODUCTION

The best introduction to an author is typically the author's work itself. All the same, Bernard Bosanquet's political writings have frequently been the object of misunderstanding and misrepresentation, and some preliminary remarks are likely to be useful. In this Introduction, we give a brief outline of the background to, and character of, Bosanquet's political thought: a short biographical sketch, an outline of some of the major philosophical and political movements in nineteenth and early twentieth century Britain (e.g., utilitarianism, Spencerian natural rights theory, British Idealism, Fabian Socialism and the New Liberalism), a summary of the epistemological and metaphysical background to Bosanquet's political theory, some comments on his influence on later political philosophy, and a guide to further reading.

LIFE

Bernard Bosanquet was born on July 14, 1848 in Rock Hall (near Alnwick), Northumberland, England. He was the youngest of five sons of the Reverend R. W. Bosanquet; his mother was the latter's second wife, Caroline (MacDowall). Many of the Bosanquet children rose to prominence. Bernard's eldest brother, Charles, was one of the founders of the London Charity Organization Society and its first Secretary. Another brother, Day, was an Admiral in the Royal Navy and served as Governor of South Australia (1909–1914). Yet another, Holford, was a mathematician and physicist, an accomplished musician, and a barrister of Lincoln's Inn in London.

Bosanquet studied at Harrow (1862–1867) and at Balliol College, Oxford (1867–1870), where he became influenced by the idealist "German" philosophy of Kant and Hegel, principally through the work of Benjamin Jowett, Edward Caird and T.H. Green. Described by Green as "the most gifted man of his generation,"[1] Bosanquet received first class

---

[1] *Bernard Bosanquet and his Friends*, ed. J.H. Muirhead (London: G. Allen & Unwin,

honours in classical moderations (1868) and *literae humaniores* (1870) and, upon graduation, was elected to a Fellowship of University College, Oxford. As Fellow (1870–1881), Bosanquet taught the history of logic, Greek history, and the history of moral philosophy, but published little.

Following the death of his father, Bosanquet received a small inheritance and, in 1881, left for London. Here, he became involved in adult education and social work through the Charity Organisation Society, the London Ethical Society, and the short-lived London School of Ethics and Social Philosophy (1897–1900). During this time he met and married (in 1895) Helen Dendy, an activist in social reform, who was later a member of, and largely wrote the Majority report for, the Royal Commission on the Poor Laws (1905–1909).[2] While in London, Bosanquet also engaged in philosophical work, and many of his major publications date from this time. Some of them – such as *The Philosophical Theory of the State* and *Psychology of the Moral Self* – were developed from lectures that he gave in public university extension courses.

At the age of fifty-five, Bosanquet briefly returned to professorial life, as Professor of Moral Philosophy at the University of St. Andrews in Scotland (1903–1908), but his health was not good and he found that he had too little time for writing. He retired to Oxshott, Surrey, though he remained active in social policy and philosophical research. In 1910, Bosanquet was elected Gifford Lecturer for 1911–1912 in the University of Edinburgh. These lectures – *The Principle of Individuality and Value* and *The Value and Destiny of the Individual* – provide the most developed statement of his metaphysical views.

Bosanquet's later work focused on themes arising out of his Gifford lectures, but is nevertheless remarkable for its range. He was especially interested in the "new philosophies" discussed in Europe and America, and he was among the first philosophers in the Anglo-American world to discuss the work of Edmund Husserl, Benedetto Croce, Giovanni Gentile and Émile Durkheim. Bosanquet's books, articles, and letters

---

1935), p. 19.
[2]See A.M. McBriar, *An Edwardian Mixed Doubles: The Bosanquets versus the Webbs; A Study in British Social Policy* (Oxford: Clarendon Press, 1987), p. 282ff.

demonstrate his desire to find common ground among philosophers of various traditions, rather than dwell on what separates them.

At the time of his death, on February 8, 1923, Bosanquet was arguably "the most popular and the most influential of the English idealists."[3] He was the author or editor of more than twenty books and some one hundred and fifty articles, ranging over logic, aesthetics, epistemology, social and public policy, psychology, metaphysics, ethics and political philosophy. For his contributions to philosophy and to social work, he was made a Fellow of the British Academy in 1907, and received honorary degrees from Glasgow, Birmingham, Durham, and St. Andrews. Although F.H. Bradley is today far better known in philosophical circles, in his obituary in *The Times*, Bosanquet was said to have been "the central figure of British philosophy for an entire generation."[4]

FEATURES OF NINETEENTH CENTURY POLITICAL THOUGHT

Bosanquet's political philosophy was both a response to, and a continuation of, nineteenth century thought. It was a response to naturalist ethical and political theories, such as that of Herbert Spencer, and to the utilitarian positivism of Jeremy Bentham and John Stuart Mill. It was also a continuation of earlier idealist philosophy – of that found in T.H. Green and, more generally, of a tradition which Bosanquet traced through Fichte, Hegel, Kant and Rousseau, back to Aristotle and Plato. But it also constituted an alternative to some of the currents then present in British social thought which advocated extensive state intervention in social life – particularly that represented by the Fabian Society and in the work of the "New Liberals," J.A. Hobson and L.T. Hobhouse.

The Utilitarians and Spencer

The utilitarians Jeremy Bentham (1748–1832) and John Stuart Mill (1806–1873), and the natural rights theorist, Herbert Spencer (1820–1903), are now often seen as defending quite distinct philosophical positions. However, at the time, each saw in the other important affinities

---

[3] J.H. Randall, Jr., "Idealistic Social Philosophy and Bernard Bosanquet," in *The Career of Philosophy*, 3 vols., (New York: Columbia University Press, 1977), vol. 3, pp. 97–130, p. 114.

[4] Quoted in Muirhead, *Friends*, p. 19.

(e.g., in method and concerning the functioning of the mind), and their work has been said to reflect similar principles that aim at protecting or maximizing political liberty. In reaction to the social problems of late eighteenth and nineteenth century society, they advocated reform of the legal system, extensive freedom of contract, and self government. This, they believed, would favour both the economic development of the community, and the personal development of the individual.

"Negative" liberty and law. The conception of liberty found in these authors is virtually unchanged from that found at the beginning of the liberal tradition, in Hobbes.[5] It is fundamentally what Isaiah Berlin has called "negative" liberty.[6] On this view, liberty is the absence of interference with one's actions. In *On Liberty*, for example, Mill defines "liberty" (in much the same way as Hobbes, and echoed in Locke, Bentham and Spencer) as "doing what one desires" or as "pursuing our own good in our own way," understanding that the individuals themselves (best) determine their own good.[7] Consequently, as far as one is not hindered in the pursuit of the good by others in society, one has liberty and is "free."

For the utilitarians and Spencer alike, liberty was a basic good; law, therefore, as a restriction of liberty, was a *prima facie* evil that requires justification. Although Mill is often seen as presaging later nineteenth century views of "positive liberty," even in his later writings (such as the *Chapters on Socialism*), he did not see human freedom as being significantly enhanced through widespread use of the law.

Psychological associationism. This "negative" account of liberty and law was allied with a view of the nature of the individual that reflected a psychological associationism indebted to David Hartley and David

---

[5]There, liberty is described as "the absence of external impediments of motion," and one is free when "in those things, which by his strength and wit he is able to do, [he] is not hindered to do what he has a will to do." See Thomas Hobbes, *Leviathan,* ed. C.B. MacPherson (Harmondsworth: Penguin Books, 1985), Pt. II, ch. xxi, pp. 261–262.

[6]Isaiah Berlin, *Two Concepts of Liberty* (Oxford: Clarendon Press, 1958), pp. 6ff.

[7]See Mill, *On Liberty,* ch. v, para. 5 (In *Essays on Politics and Society,* in *The Collected Works of John Stuart Mill,* vol. XVIII, ed. J.M. Robson [Toronto: University of Toronto Press, 1977], pp. 213–310, p. 293); ch. i, para. 13 (*Works,* p. 226); ch. iv, para. 4 (*Works,* p. 226); ch. v, para. 17 (*Works,* p. 305).

Hume. According to associationism, consciousness can be explained by understanding the relations among mental states (e.g., perceptions, thought) in terms of laws governing the association of ideas. Bentham's analysis of "habit" (which is essential to his understanding of political society) and Mill's "hedonism" particularly exhibit associationist presuppositions. Because pleasure and pain are objective states that can be measured in terms of their intensity, duration, certainty, proximity, fecundity and purity, Bentham held that there can be both an impartial determination of the amount of pleasure of an activity or state, and a comparison of pleasures among persons.

Moral individualism and self-interest. Associationism is closely connected to what is typically referred to as "individualism": the human person is seen as the basic unit in the social sphere; groups or collectivities are simply aggregations of individual "atoms." As Bentham famously remarks, "the community is a fictitious body;"[8] it is but "a sum of the interests of the several members who compose it."[9] Though Spencer advocated an "organic" view of society, he too believed that society is simply an aggregate of individuals,[10] and that "human nature" was just "the aggregate of men's instincts and sentiments" which, over time, would become adapted to social existence.[11] The utilitarians and the Spencerians also held that individuals exhibit a natural rational self-interest – a psychological egoism – and that human action is motivated by a desire to maximize one's own good.[12] Consistent with their view of

---

[8]Bentham, *An Introduction to the Principles of Morals and Legislation*, ed. J.H. Burns and H.L.A. Hart (London: Athlone Press, 1970), Chap. I, sec. 4 (p. 12).

[9]Ibid. One finds the same view in Mill's *A System of Logic: Ratiocinative and Inductive*: "Human beings in society have no properties but those which are derived from, and which may be resolved into, the laws of the nature of individual men." *The Collected Works of John Stuart Mill*, ed. J.M. Robson (Toronto: University of Toronto Press, 1963), vol. VIII, p. 879.

[10]See, for example, *First Principles* (London: Williams and Norgate, 1862), ch. 10, sect. 85.

[11]See *Social Statics, or, The Conditions Essential to Human Happiness Specified, and the First of them Developed* (1851), (London: Williams and Norgate, 1868), p. 252.

[12]See "Remarks on Bentham's Philosophy," (1833) *in Essays on Ethics, Religion and Society*, in *The Collected Works of John Stuart Mill*, ed. J.M. Robson (Toronto: University of Toronto Press, 1965), vol. X, pp. 3–18, p. 14; see also "Bentham (1838)" in *Works*,

the nature of the individual and with associationist psychology, Bentham and Mill espoused a "moral individualism." This individualism is evident in their calculus of value, based on pleasures and pains (which can exist only in individuals) and in their emphases on autonomy. As Mill maintained, individuals themselves are "the final judge" of their "own concerns," and that "[o]ver himself, over his own body and mind, the individual is sovereign."[13]

Spencer followed Bentham and Mill, and their recognition of the value of personal liberty. Nevertheless, he parted company with the utilitarians when it came to elaborating the implications of this "moral individualism." Whereas the utilitarians were suspicious of the idea of "natural, inalienable rights" – Bentham referred to the doctrine of natural rights as "anarchical" and as "nonsense"[14] – Spencer argued that the natural growth of an organism required "liberty," and that everyone had basic rights to liberty "in virtue of their constitutions" as human beings.[15] (These rights, which Spencer saw as essential to social progress, included rights to life, liberty, property, free speech, and the right "to ignore the state.") The sole function of government was the policing and protection of individual rights; education, religion, the economy, and care for the sick or indigent were not to be undertaken by the state – this is a consequence of Spencer's "law of equal freedom," that "Every man has freedom to do all that he wills, provided he infringes not the equal freedom of any other man."[16] Thus, Spencer also rejected the arguments of the early utilitarians on the justification of law and authority and on the origin of rights.

J.S. Mill's ambiguous position. Although in many respects J.S. Mill – the dominant figure in mid-nineteenth-century English philosophy – belongs to the empiricist, individualist tradition, his thought also manifests important features that link him to late nineteenth-century thinkers, including Bosanquet. Mill's individualism, for instance, is moderated by

---

vol. X, pp. 75–115.

[13] *On Liberty*, ch. iv, para. 4 (*Works*, p. 276); ch. i, para. 9 (*Works*, p. 223).

[14] See *Anarchical Fallacies*, in *The Works of Jeremy Bentham*, ed. John Bowring (Edinburgh: Tait, 1838–1843), vol. II, pp. 491–534.

[15] *Social Statics*, p. 77.

[16] Ibid., p. 103.

his belief that social life was essential to the development of the moral sentiments and to the realization of the individual.[17] Mill was also greatly influenced by continental thinkers, such as Alexis de Tocqueville, Auguste Comte and, especially Wilhelm von Humboldt. The influence of the last is particularly obvious in the crucial third chapter of *On Liberty*, which defends a perfectionist ideal of the multifaceted and harmonious development of human capacities. As L.T. Hobhouse was to recognise, Mill is here introducing a theme that becomes central to later liberal theorists such as Green.[18]

The Origins of British Idealism

Although British philosophy in the middle decades of the nineteenth century was dominated by empiricism, psychological associationism, metaphysical and moral individualism, and utilitarianism, there were challenges to it. Drawing on the writings of G.W.F. Hegel and Immanuel Kant and, to a lesser degree, of J.F. Fichte and J-J. Rousseau, T.H. Green (1836–1882) and Edward Caird (1835–1908) offered particularly detailed responses to the empiricist approach; the views they developed came to be representative of what is now called "British Idealism." According to J.H. Muirhead, idealism has had a place in philosophical thought in Britain since the time of Berkeley and the Cambridge Platonists of the seventeenth century,[19] but the idealism that came to be prominent by the latter half of the nineteenth century is particularly indebted to four distinct, but related "movements."

Cultural studies. Later idealism was importantly influenced by early nineteenth-century studies in aesthetics, literary criticism, and the analysis of culture – particularly in the work of Samuel T. Coleridge (1772–1834). Coleridge was influenced by Kant and Friedrich Schelling

---

[17]*Utilitarianism*, ch. 3, para. 10 (In *Essays on Ethics, Religion and Society*, in *The Collected Works of John Stuart Mill*, ed. J.M. Robson, vol. X, pp. 203–259, p. 231).

[18]See here Gerald F. Gaus, *The Modern Liberal Theory of Man* (New York: St. Martin's, 1983). On Hobhouse's evaluation of the roles of Mill and Green in the development of liberalism, see his *Liberalism* (London: Williams and Norgate, 1911; Oxford: Oxford University Press, 1964).

[19]J.H. Muirhead, *The Platonic Tradition in Anglo-Saxon Philosophy; Studies in the History of Idealism in England* (London: Allen and Unwin, 1931).

(1775–1854) and, in turn, influenced Thomas Arnold, Master of Rugby School, where T.H. Green was a student from 1850 to 1855.

Biblical studies. At approximately the same time, German theological and biblical criticism, principally that of David Strauss, Ferdinand Bauer, W.M.L. De Wette, and members of the Tübingen school (who were largely influenced by Hegel), came to be read and commented on in Britain. By the early 1860s, this influence had found root at Oxford among the "Broad Churchmen" such as Benjamin Jowett (1817–1893), A.P. Stanley, Rowland Williams, Mark Pattison and H.B. Wilson. Jowett was the tutor of T.H. Green and Edward Caird.

"German" philosophy. Gradually, the writings of Hegel and Kant themselves (and, to a lesser, but not inconsiderable extent, R.H. Lotze [1817–1881]) influenced British philosophers – though the extent of their influence has recently been a matter of some debate. Hegel's impact was initially in the area of logic, though later idealists were influenced by his aesthetics and political philosophy. By the 1860s, with the writings of J.F. Ferrier (1808–1864) on metaphysics and J.H. Stirling's (1820–1909) *The Secret of Hegel* (1865), idealist "German" philosophy was established at Oxford and the major Scottish universities of Glasgow, Edinburgh, and St. Andrews.

Classical Greek studies. The general attitude towards Hegel and Kant was, however, far from uncritical, and a considerable role in the development of idealism in nineteenth-century Britain was also played by the study of classical Greek philosophy. Basic philosophical education at Oxford at the time focused on texts from Greek and Roman authors, and many idealists came to Hegel largely as an interpreter of the Greeks.

With figures such as Caird and Jowett in place at the leading universities in Britain, idealism's dominance grew exponentially, particularly in metaphysics, religion,[20] and social and political philosophy. By the late 1870s, idealism was one of the major "schools" of thought in education

---

[20]For some, the "turn to idealism" was seen as a way to address scepticism and the attacks on religion emanating from empiricism and the development of evolutionary science, but its relation to religious belief was, at best, an uneasy one. Though many of the principal British idealists (e.g., Green, Bosanquet, F.H. Bradley, and Henry Jones) were from clerical homes or were initially destined for the ministry, they came to distance themselves from orthodox religious belief.

and in the intellectual community. For the next fifty years it had a central (though not undisputed) place.

T.H. Green and Idealist Thought

The best known figures of the first generation of philosophical idealists were T.H. Green, Edward Caird, and Caird's brother, John – though, in political philosophy, Green had pride of place. Fellow and tutor at Balliol College, Oxford, and, later, Whyte's Professor of Moral Philosophy, Green was also active in educational reform and in university and civic politics. His influence on students was enormous, and they, in turn, became leading figures not only in the universities, but in the civil service, social reform, journalism, and the clergy. Green's two major works, *Prolegomena to Ethics*[21] and *Lectures on the Principles of Political Obligation*[22] were, however, left incomplete at his death. Because of this, it is sometimes difficult to be certain what his most considered views might be, and this is reflected in the different approaches to social reform that his students came to advocate.

Green was concerned about what he considered to be an uncritical complacency in Hegel's political thought, and the presence of Kant remains strong in Green's epistemology and ethics. Nevertheless, Green was undoubtedly influenced by Hegel. Green's theory of the eternal consciousness is certainly Hegelian,[23] and he also exhibited an opposition to individualism and purely hedonistic conceptions of the good, arguing that humans manifest an impulse to development and to self-realisation, and that "the perfection of human character"[24] constituted the moral goal.

We witness here the importance of the "impulse to coherence" or completion, which characterises idealist metaphysics and epistemology (discussed below), and particularly the conception of the self. The self,

---

[21]*Prolegomena to Ethics* (1883), 5th edn (Oxford: Clarendon Press, 1906).

[22]*Lectures on the Principles of Political Obligation*, with preface by Bernard Bosanquet (London: Longmans, Green, 1895); cf. *T.H. Green: Lectures on the Principles of Political Obligation, and Other Writings*, ed. Paul Harris and John Morrow (Cambridge: Cambridge University Press, 1986).

[23]See Green, *Prolegomena*, especially Book I on "eternal consciousness." See also A. Quinton, "Absolute Idealism," *Proceedings of the British Academy*, 57 (1971): 303–29.

[24]*Prolegomena*, sect. 247 (p. 293).

Green argues, is a system of content, and reason is an impulse towards completion and unity. Thus, self-satisfaction – as opposed to the satisfaction of discrete desires – requires the development of our capacities into a coherent whole. Green held that this "perfection" could be approximated by individuals only within a social context; this was the "common good" and constituted the moral end. But this common good was also each individual's good, and it is this, Green thought, that provides the substantive element lacking in Kantian ethics.[25] Nevertheless, and in keeping with both his Christianity and his interest in Kantian philosophy, Green emphasised the importance of the individual as an "end in itself." (This focus on the human individual is also central to his metaphysics and epistemology.) Green held that the human person was an organised, finite centre of experience, which is conscious of itself as an object to itself. Yet the individual was also a social being, and awareness of oneself as an individual could occur only through others. One's moral and civic responsibilities were determined by finding "the duties of one's station."[26]

For philosophical – and also for political – reasons, Green insisted that rights could be ascribed to persons only within a social context and in view of "the good,"[27] and that "a right against society, as such, is an im-

---

[25]Green wrote "The only reason why a man should not be used by other men as a means to their ends is that he should use himself as a means to an end which is really his and theirs at once." *Lectures on the Principles of Political Obligation*, sect. 155 (p. 159); cf. *T.H. Green: Lectures on the Principles of Political Obligation, and Other Writings*, ed. Harris and Morrow, p. 120.

[26]*Prolegomena*, sect 183; cf. 313, 338. Though this notion is most often associated with Green's student, F.H. Bradley (in *Ethical Studies* [1876], 2nd edn [Oxford: Oxford University Press, 1927], Essay V), it is unclear whether this locution was first employed by him. See William Sweet, *Idealism and Rights* (Lanham, MD: University Press of America, 1997), p. 65, n. 8.

[27]For Green, "[a] right is a power claimed and recognized as contributory to a common good." Green, *Lectures on the Principles of Political Obligation*, sect. 99 (p. 110); see *T.H. Green: Lectures on the Principles of Political Obligation, and Other Writings*, ed. Harris and Morrow, p. 79. On Green's theory of rights, see Ann R. Cacoullos, *Thomas Hill Green: Philosopher of Rights* (New York: Twayne Publishers, 1974); Peter P. Nicholson. *The Political Philosophy of the British Idealists: Selected Studies* (Cambridge: Cambridge University Press, 1990), pp. 83–95.

possibility."[28] Nevertheless, commentators sympathetic to Green's liberalism have stressed his concern for the individual. Indeed, his apparent suspicion of the Hegelian dictum that the state has been – or actually is – a realisation of freedom, and his comment that rights can exist independently of the state,[29] have been said by some to allow for a robust theory of individual rights.

By his own example, Green applied his moral and political philosophy to the political realm. As part of the first generation of Oxford faculty to marry and establish families, Green became involved in the community and, especially, in the temperance movement,[30] which he saw as the only bulwark to impede an evil which not only destroyed people's lives, but contributed to broad social disruption. Moral and social improvement, however, also required education and training, and this, in turn, suggested a more positive role for the state. This, along with his critique of laissez faire has led many to view him as one of the main inspirations of the reformist "New Liberals."

Economic Reform, Fabian Socialism and the New Liberalism
By the mid-nineteenth century, concern for poverty and "the social problem" was growing. Much debate centred around the adequacy of The New Poor Law of 1834 which, while established on a national basis, was administered locally. There were reformers who wished to bring the Poor Law up to date, but also those who rejected it altogether – both from the "right" (such as the Spencerian "Liberty and Property Defence League") and from the "left."

Beginning in 1869 in England, regional volunteer Charity Organisation Societies (COS) – non-sectarian philanthropic groups, in partnership with the state – were established to provide additional support to the poor. Another important (though at first less successful) response was initiated by (General) William Booth (1829–1912), a Methodist

---

[28]Green, *Lectures on the Principles of Political Obligation*, sect. 141 (p. 145); see *T.H. Green: Lectures on the Principles of Political Obligation, and Other Writings*, ed. Harris and Morrow, p. 110

[29]Ibid.

[30]Many of Green's speeches on temperance and on educational reform may be found in Volume 5 of the *Collected Works of T.H. Green*, ed. Peter Nicholson (Bristol: Thoemmes Press, 1998).

minister who founded what became The Salvation Army in 1878. The COS sought to separate the "undeserving" from the deserving poor by its use of individual casework, but it gradually abandoned a purely individualist analysis of social problems.[31] Octavia Hill (1838–1912), one of the founders of the London COS, initiated a number of housing projects in slum areas and established programmes for the education and training of social workers. Toynbee Hall, started by former students of Green in 1884, was the first "university settlement" house. Its objective was to attempt to narrow the gap between social classes by having those with money and education live and work among and with the poor.

One group who rejected the Poor Law altogether was the Fabian Society. Founded in 1883, it included a number of progressive reformers, such as Sidney and Beatrice Webb, Annie Besant, Sidney Ball, G.B. Shaw, H.G. Wells, and Bertrand Russell. The Fabians were not a political party; many of them were associated with the radical wing of the Liberal Party and, later, Labour, but they also had allies in the Conservative Party. The major causes of economic poverty were, the Fabians held, structural and not the fault of the individuals concerned. Social change, therefore, must occur through legislation and economic reform, which the Fabians sought to encourage through lobbying and the publication of tracts and manifestos which proposed a moderate non-revolutionary, non-Marxist economic socialism. Although many of its ideas paralleled those advocated by Green, the Society developed quite independently of his influence.

The Fabians saw their views on social policy as being at odds with those of the Charity Organisation Society. The opposition between these groups was, in part, over strategy, but, at base, the conflict was theoretical – primarily over the Fabian conviction that the role of individual character was less central in cases of poverty than general, structural, concerns. (This issue lies at the root of Bosanquet's essay, "The Antithesis between Individualism and Socialism Philosophically Considered," reprinted in this volume, pp. 324–46).

---

[31] See Jose Harris, *Private Lives, Public Spirit: A Social History of Britain, 1870–1914* (Oxford: Oxford University Press, 1993).

Issues of economic inequality and social progress were also on the agenda of a group of activists, politicians, and journalists, called the "New Liberals." Influenced by Mill and by the evolutionary theories of Darwin, Huxley and Spencer, the New Liberals also accepted many "idealist" presuppositions about the relation of the individual to the state. They were especially influential in the reformist policies discussed during the Liberal governments of 1908–1914, and in later Labour politics. Though the New Liberals kept close to the radical liberal traditions of the late nineteenth century, they argued that the emphasis on "negative liberty" and restrictions on government intervention threatened both the stability of society and the dignity of the impoverished class. For the New Liberals, like the Fabians, government must take an active role in social reform through a graduated taxation system and restrictions on private property.

L.T. Hobhouse (1864–1929) – perhaps the most prominent of the New Liberals – was greatly influenced by Green, whose "organicism" or harmonic conception of society he adopted.[32] For many years a journalist and writer, he was the first professor of sociology at the University of London. Hobhouse was an economic radical (see his *The Labour Movement* [1893]) and sympathetic to Sidney Ball's "collectivism" – though he never joined the Labour Party. Hobhouse understood himself to be developing Mill's later views, arguing that:

> Liberalism is the belief that society can safely be founded on...[the] self-directing power of personality, that it is only on this foundation that a true community can be built, and that so established its foundations are so deep and so wide that there is no limit that we can place to the extent of the building. Liberty then becomes not so much a right of the individual as a necessity of society.[33]

On practical matters his views were similar to the Fabians (e.g., concerning the provision of old age pensions, minimum wage, and the provision of meals for school children). Despite his admiration for Green, Hobhouse attacked later idealist political thought as vague, overly theoretical, and potentially conservative and oppressive, and he is the author

---

[32]Hobhouse, *Liberalism* [1964], pp. 69, 72–3.

[33]Ibid., p. 66.

of the classical critique of idealist political philosophy, *The Metaphysical Theory of the State* (1918).

The Second Generation of Idealists

By the mid 1880s the idealist movement was strong, and the influence of Green and Caird had given rise to a second generation of idealists. Bosanquet and, with him, David Ritchie (1853–1903), Henry Jones (1852–1922), William Wallace (1843–1897), F.H. Bradley (1846–1924), and John Watson (1847–1939),[34] continued to address the earlier empiricist and associationist views of Bain, Bentham, Spencer, and Mill, but also sought to develop and defend the conclusions of the "first generation" of idealists.

There were, in fact, several different currents within idealism; a principal division was that between "absolute" (with which Bosanquet is associated, along with Bradley) and "personalist" idealism (e.g., that of Andrew Seth Pringle-Pattison, J.M.E. McTaggart, and W.R. Sorley). The central differences between the two concerned the understanding of human nature and place of the divine. Though their disagreement bore largely on religious matters (e.g., the personality of a divine being and the existence of an individual "afterlife"), it also had ethical and political implications. One also finds idealists who were sympathetic to utilitarianism or Darwinism (Ritchie), and others who were opposed to the work of the COS (Jones) – and there were differences among idealists as well on such issues as the principle of ethical value, aesthetic theory, and on the nature and justification of punishment. There seems, however, to have been some agreement among the idealists concerning such political issues as the basis of political obligation, the social character of human personality, the importance of a common good, and the nature of rights.

Still, idealism was neither dominant nor monolithic. The Oxford "pragmatist" F.C.S. Schiller was angered by the influence of Bosan-

---

[34]David Ritchie, *Natural Rights: A Criticism of Some Political and Ethical Conceptions* (London: S. Sonnenschein, 1895); William Wallace, *Lectures and Essays on Natural Theology and Ethics*, Edited, with a biographical introduction, by Edward Caird (Oxford: Clarendon Press, 1898); Henry Jones, *The Working Faith of the Social Reformer and Other Essays* (London, Macmillan, 1910); F.H. Bradley, *Ethical Studies* (London: H.S. King, 1876), 2nd edn, (Oxford: Oxford University Press, 1927); John Watson, *The State in Peace and War* (Glasgow: J. Maclehose and sons, 1919).

quet's and Bradley's idealism, and was the principal author of a spoof of the philosophical journal, *Mind*, where, on the frontispiece, one found a blank page with the caption "The Portrait of Its Immanence, the Absolute."[35] At Cambridge University, Henry Sidgwick continued the utilitarian tradition and, by the turn of the century, his younger colleagues, Bertrand Russell and G.E. Moore, had begun a series of systematic attacks on idealist thought. That the opposition to idealism was motivated as much by personality as philosophical argument is suggested by C.D. Broad's comment that Green had turned more undergraduates into prigs than Sidgwick ever turned into philosophers.[36]

Like Green before them, Bosanquet and his idealist contemporaries were active in political and social affairs; their political philosophies reflected this practical work. As noted earlier, Bosanquet's wife, Helen, was an influential social reformer in her own right. R.B. Haldane entered the British Parliament in 1885, later becoming Lord Chancellor under both Liberal (1912–15) and Labour (1924) governments. Similarly, while Professor of Philosophy at Glasgow (1894–1922), Henry Jones was engaged in civic politics, in educational reform and, during the first world war, canvassed in support of recruitment and against opposition to the Asquith government.

BOSANQUET'S PHILOSOPHICAL AND POLITICAL IDEALISM
Coherence and Idealist Thought
A principal feature of idealism was its emphasis on unity and coherence.[37] For Bosanquet, as for Green, philosophy in its various guises has

---

[35]See F.C.S. Schiller, *Mind! A Unique Review of Ancient and Modern Philosophy*, ed. A. Troglodyte [pseud.] with the cooperation of The Absolute and others (London: Williams and Norgate, 1901).

[36]C.D. Broad, *Five Types of Ethical Theory* (London: Kegan Paul, Trench and Trubner, 1930), p. 144. See William James' remark, in *Essays in Radical Empiricism* (New York: Longmans, Green, 1912), that "Certainly, to my personal knowledge, all Hegelians are not prigs, but I somehow feel as if all prigs ought to end, if developed, by becoming Hegelians" (p. 277).

[37]For a fuller treatment, see Gerald Gaus, "Green, Bosanquet and the Philosophy of Coherence" in *The Routledge History of Philosophy*, S.G. Shanker and G.H.R. Parkinson general editors, vol. 7, *The Nineteenth Century*, ed. C.L. Ten (London: Routledge, 1994), pp. 408–36.

completion and harmony as its goals: epistemology, metaphysics, ethics and political philosophy all reflect the search for coherence and comprehensiveness.

On the idealist view, human beings are not simply natural objects and, therefore, not just subject to desire, but to reason. In contrast to empiricists like Hobbes, reason is not understood as essentially calculative – a matter of "adding and subtracting, of the consequences of general names agreed upon for the marking and signifying of thoughts."[38] The "inherent nature of reason," Bosanquet argues, is "the absolute demand for totality and consistency,"[39] and involves a "*nisus*" or "impulse to the whole."[40] Idealists were thus led to a coherence theory of knowledge; to know something is for it to be related to, and to cohere with, the rest of one's beliefs or experiences. This notion of coherence, however, goes considerably beyond requirements of formal consistency.[41] It includes connectedness among beliefs and a richness of content; "The truth is the whole."[42]

Absolute Idealism

For Bosanquet, complete coherence is "the Absolute" – involving the systematization and completion of finite minds. "The general formula of the Absolute," Bosanquet writes, is "the transmutation and rearrangement of particular experiences, and also the contents of individual minds, by inclusion in a more complete whole of experience...."[43] Being complete and harmonious, it is ultimate reality.

This Absolute is not, however, anything separate or over and above finite things or appearances, but the totality or full realisation of them. For Bosanquet, it is a system in which all things are arranged and understood in their multiple relations to one another. The "real," then, is not what is

---

[38]*Leviathan*, p. 111 (Part I, ch. 5, para. 2).

[39] Bosanquet, *The Value and Destiny of the Individual* (London: Macmillan, 1913), p. 8.

[40]Bosanquet, *Value and Destiny*, p. 7; Bosanquet, *Some Suggestions in Ethics* (London: Macmillan, 1918), p. 130.

[41]Bosanquet, *Logic, or the Morphology of Knowledge* (Oxford: Clarendon Press, 1888; 2nd edn, Oxford: Clarendon Press, 1911), vol. 2, ch. viii.

[42]Bosanquet, *Logic* (1888), vol. 2, p. 204.

[43]Bosanquet, *The Principle of Individuality and Value* (London: Macmillan, 1912) p. 373.

actual, but what is complete and coherent, just as the standard of what is rational – knowledge and truth – is completeness and coherence. It is in this sense alone that one should understand the idealist dictum that "the real is the rational." For Bosanquet, the Absolute is immanent in each finite individual as the whole life of an organism is in every part, and it serves as a kind of *telos*. Human consciousness is dependent upon this "whole," and its own realisation or development as "self-conscious" is thereby also a realisation of the Absolute.

In his studies in metaphysics, the Absolute is also described as a "concrete universal." It is concrete so far as it exists only in and through particular things, and it is universal so far as it is complete, comprehensive, wholly determinate and self-sufficient.[44] Thus, "human," "justice," "number," and "triangle," are not concrete, but abstract, universals; we come closer to what Bosanquet has in mind by a "concrete universal" when we think of objects like a work of art. Because of its self-sufficiency and completeness, Bosanquet calls the Absolute an individual and the principle of individuality. This has several important implications – principally that, since the Absolute alone is real, complete, and self-sufficient, all finite things (including human persons) are only partly individual, concrete and real. Still, Bosanquet did not claim that nature or the finite individual did not exist, and he asserts that, in some respects, not only is nature independent of mind, but it actually determines mind (e.g., so far as mind is a product of the process of evolution).

Absolute Idealism and Political Philosophy
Though Bosanquet's political philosophy reflects his absolute idealism, the term "the Absolute" does not have an explicit role in his discussion of political and social issues, and some have argued that his political thought can stand independently of a theory of the Absolute.[45] Bosanquet appears to have first contemplated writing on ethics and political philosophy in the early 1870s, but this was apparently forestalled by the publication, in 1876, of F.H. Bradley's *Ethical Studies*.[46] No doubt Bo-

---

[44]Ibid., p. 69.

[45]See, for example, A.J.M. Milne, *The Social Philosophy of English Idealism* (London: Allen and Unwin, 1962).

[46]Upon hearing of the publication of *Ethical Studies*, Bosanquet wrote that "the book I

sanquet also felt that what he would write would be similar to that found in Green's political theory which, he later remarked, "in many points I follow very closely" (see below p. 2). (It is interesting, however, that in July 1876 Green pressed Bosanquet to write something on the subject.)[47] Certainly, one finds an affinity between Green and Bosanquet concerning the desire to preserve the importance of the individual and to recognise the central role of the community, and Bosanquet's views on the moral development of the human individual and on limiting the state from directly promoting morality clearly reflect both his own reading of Kant and the Kantian influences on Green.

Although Bosanquet discusses such questions as the nature of the state and the relation of the individual to the community in his metaphysics, the main source for his political thought is *The Philosophical Theory of the State* (1899; 4th edn, 1923) – though many of his ideas are developed in the dozens of articles and essays he wrote for professional academic journals, for the Charity Organisation Society, and for the popular press. His metaphysical idealism is revealed in his claim that social relations and institutions are not ultimately material phenomena, but best understood as existing at the level of human consciousness. Bosanquet's views here also reflect principles found in the work of his teachers and colleagues and he traces their origin back to Aristotle and Plato. Although Bosanquet is frequently held to be especially indebted to Hegel, one should not overstate this. At the beginning of his philosophical career, Bosanquet wrote that Kant and Hegel were "the great masters who sketched the plan,"[48] but he added that his greatest master was Plato and that there was "no sound political philosophy which is not an embodiment of Plato's" (p. 50 below). Not only was one of Bosanquet's first works *A Companion to Plato's Republic for English Readers* (1895), but he described his theory as "classical" (p. 17 below).

Although closely related to his metaphysics and epistemology, Bosanquet's political thought also benefitted from his analysis of events of the

---

was to write must wait, perhaps forever," Muirhead, *Friends*, p. 37

[47]See Green's letter to Bosanquet, dated 8 July 1876, in *Collected Works of T.H. Green*, ed. Peter Nicholson (Bristol: Thoemmes Press, 1998), vol. 5, p. 465.

[48]Muirhead, *Friends*, p. 21.

latter part of nineteenth and the early twentieth centuries, from his own background in social welfare, and from the opportunity to respond to the criticisms of his work. Nevertheless, his views develop many elements that one finds in earlier idealism. The key concepts here are (1) the description of society as organic, (2) the theory of the general will and (3) the analysis of the state and political obligation.

Bosanquet's Organicism

For Bosanquet, society is an "organism"[49] or a "whole of parts": it is a system containing the persons that compose it.[50] It is, however, crucial to keep in mind here Bosanquet's insistence that "it takes all sorts to make a world [or organism]."[51] A "true co-operative structure," he argues, "is never characterised by repetition, but always by identity in difference; it is the relation not of a screw to an exactly similar screw, but of the screw to the nut into which it fastens" (p. 80 below).[52] A social organism, then, is a system of interlocking wills or minds, each implying the others. It is a "macrocosm constituted by microcosms."[53]

The General Will

Central to his view of society are the doctrines of the common good and "my station and its duties,"[54] and both depend on his psychological account of the general or real will. Green himself suggested the link between the common good and the general will in his *Lectures on the Principles of Political Obligation*, where he remarked that "the truth" latent in Rousseau's doctrine of the general will is that "an interest in the common good is the ground of political society."[55] Bosanquet acknowl-

---

[49]Bosanquet, "Hegel's Theory of the Political Organism," *Mind* n.s. 7 (1898): 1–14.

[50]Bosanquet, *Principle of Individuality*, p. 37.

[51]Ibid, p. 29; Bosanquet, *Social and International Ideals* (London: Macmillan, 1917), p. 133.

[52]See also Bosanquet, "The Relation of Sociology to Philosophy," in his *Science and Philosophy* (London: Allen and Unwin, 1927), p. 243; *Value and Destiny*, pp. 49–50.

[53]Bosanquet, *Principle of Individuality*, p. 38.

[54]Though Bosanquet uses this expression frequently (e.g., "The Kingdom of God on Earth," in his *Essays and Addresses* [London, Swan Sonnenschein, 1889], pp. 108–130, p. 116), it is clearly an allusion to the ethical view described in Essay V of Bradley's *Ethical Studies*, op. cit. See note 26, p. xvi above.

[55]Green, *Lectures on the Principles of Political Obligation,* sect. 109, (p. 98); see *T. H.*

edges that he follows Green very closely on such matters, but believes that his own exploration of the general or "real" will was an important advance on Green (p. 2 below). Following Rousseau as well, Bosanquet characterises the general will as the will of the entire society so far as it aims at the common good (p. 124 below). But just what sort of 'will" can a whole society share?

As noted above, Bosanquet rejects the associationist view of the self and, in his *Psychology of the Moral Self* (the relevant chapter from which is included in this volume pp. 294–304), he develops a new account of the organization of the mind. "Every individual mind, in so far as it thinks and acts in definite schemes or contexts, is a structure of appercipient systems or organized dispositions" (p. 172 below).[56] Such a system, Bosanquet writes, is a

> set of ideas, bound together by a common rule or scheme, which dictates the point of view from which perception will take place, so far as the system in question is active. And without some "apperception," some point of view in the mind which enables the new-comer to be classed, there cannot be perception at all....A child calls an orange a "ball"; a Polynesian calls a horse a "pig." These are the nearest "heads" or rules of apperception under which the new perception can be brought (p. 167 below).

A person organizes his experience in terms of these "schemes of attention"; as different situations arise, one mass will arise to prominence in consciousness, leaving the others inert (p. 167 below). The self or mind is a multiplicity of such systems.

Now, Bosanquet goes on to argue, those participating in the same social institution or social group – those who share a common life – possess similar appercipient systems and have minds which are similarly organized; it is this which constitutes their common mind and will – the general will (p. 302 below). Note that at this point Bosanquet depends not simply on coherence – on a fitting together of different minds into a broader unity – but on similarity of organization. It is not entirely clear

---

Green: Lectures on the Principles of Political Obligation, eds. Harris and Morrow, p. 70.

[56] See pp. 301 below (p. 42 of *Psychology of the Moral Self* [London: Macmillan, 1897]). See also John W. Chapman, *Rousseau – Totalitarian or Liberal?* (New York: Columbia University Press, 1956), pp. 128ff.

how this principle of social life as based of similarity of organization coheres with that of organic unity (pp. 72–73 below), but it does at least allow Bosanquet to argue that a general will and a community sharing a common life are correlative. Consequently, those sharing no common life – such as humanity as a whole – cannot possess a general will.[57]

The general will, Bosanquet holds, is our "real will," and is to be contrasted with our "actual will." But what is this "general" will? Bosanquet replies:

> In order to obtain a full statement of what we will, what we want at any moment must at least be corrected and amended by what we want at all other moments; and this cannot be done without also correcting and amending it so as to harmonise with what others want, which involves the application of the same process to them (p. 133).

A fully coherent self and will, which took into account our interest in the common good, would, then, be very different from a self and will that had not undergone this process of rational reconstruction. That the former is more real than the latter follows directly from the idealist claim that the criterion of reality is coherence – that with greater coherence is more real. And this "common good" is not only a shared good, but each person's individual good – "the existence and the perfection of human personality."

Because the general will is not simply a common volition but a system of interconnected volitions, only the entire system truly manifests the general will. And because the general will is primarily a coherent system of volitions, a person reveals the general will, not by attempting an overall social judgment about what is to be done, but by manifesting a will that meshes with others. This shows again the importance of the ethic of "my station and its duties" in Bosanquet's social philosophy.

Society and the State
Bosanquet's account of the common good and the general will forms the basis for his theory of the state. Like Rousseau, Bosanquet saw society as "a moral and collective body" (p. 113 below) permeated by this general will[58] – or, what he says is the same thing, by "dominant ideas."[59]

---

[57] Bosanquet, *Social and International Ideals*, pp. 271–301.

[58] See here William Sweet, "Bernard Bosanquet and The Development of Rousseau's

On Bosanquet's view, the state "includes the entire hierarchy of institutions by which life is determined, from the family to the trade, and from the trade to the Church and the University" (p. 156 below). Such institutions are systems of similarly and correlatively organized minds; the state is a system of those systems; its aim is coherence among these institutions. There is, then, no "irreconcilable opposition" between society and the state (p. 169 below).

Bosanquet did not see his views on social and political philosophy as far from those expressed by his teacher Green and his colleagues Ritchie, Wallace, and Bradley. Still, he has been accused of employing a more expansive use of the term "state," which gave rise to the criticism that he failed or refused to distinguish it from society and its institutions – and it is this that Hobhouse and MacIver considered to be "the central fallacy of the metaphysical theory of the state."[60] Bosanquet's response here is detailed in the Introduction to the Second edition of *The Philosophical Theory of the State* (pp. 17–46 below) and, more particularly, in his exchange of letters with R.M. MacIver, (pp. 312–23 below). As one sees from these texts, his view is that society and the state are ultimately distinct.[61] One can, for example, speak of social action, which is entirely different from both political and private activity and, where political action is inappropriate or fails, Bosanquet emphasizes that an important role can be played by volunteer work.[62]

Although the state employs compulsion and restraint, its role is "positive" in that it provides the material conditions for liberty, the function-

---

Idea of the General Will," *L'homme et la nature – Man and Nature*, vol. X (1991): 179–197.

[59] See Bosanquet's article, "The Reality of the General Will," *International Journal of Ethics*, IV (1893–1894), p. 311; reprinted in his *Aspects of the Social Problem* (London: Macmillan, 1895), p. 325.

[60] Hobhouse, *The Metaphysical Theory of the State; a Criticism* (London: G. Allen & Unwin, 1918), p. 77; R.M. MacIver, *Community* (London: Macmillan, 1917), Appendix B, "A Criticism of the Neo-Hegelian Identification of Society and the State," pp. 425–33; cf. MacIver, "Society and State," *Philosophical Review* XX (1911): 30–45.

[61] See p. 45 below and also *Principle of Individuality*, p. 311.

[62] See Stefan Collini, "Hobhouse, Bosanquet and State," *Past and Present,* vol. 72 (1976): 86–111, p. 95.

ing of social institutions, and the development of individual moral character. There is no incompatibility between liberty and the law. Moreover, since individuals are necessarily social beings, their rights are neither absolute nor inalienable, but reflect the "station" or "positions" they hold in the community.[63] Strictly speaking, as with Green, there can be no rights against the state. Nevertheless, Bosanquet acknowledged that, where social institutions were fundamentally corrupt, even though there was no right to rebellion, there could be a duty to resist (p. 201 below).

Bosanquet was, however, generally hesitant about endorsing state policies intended to articulate the general will: "our life is probably more rational than our opinions."[64] This does not mean that Bosanquet opposes the reform of institutions, but it does imply that such reform is best worked out by the participants who engage in the common life that comprises those institutions. Moreover, Bosanquet is very impressed by the way in which inadequate knowledge of institutions and ways of life lead to reforms with deleterious consequences, such as poor relief that produces dependency.[65] To be sure, Bosanquet does not embrace what he calls "administrative nihilism," i.e., refusal ever to employ conscious policy to further the common good.[66] The "distinctive sphere" of State agency "is rightly described as the hindrance of hindrances of good life" (pp. 21, 189ff. below). However, Bosanquet was an adamant critic of economic socialism, precisely because it sought to impose a conscious plan on society. In contrast to economic individualism, economic socialism, he charged, seeks to substitute a mechanical, contrived, unity for the organic unity of society. He saw his own view as a kind of

[63]For a more complete discussion of Bosanquet's theory of rights, see Sweet, *Idealism*, especially chapter 2.

[64]*Principle of Individuality*, p. 218.

[65]*Essays and Addresses* (London: Swan Sonnenschein, 1889), pp. 3ff, 45ff.; "Character and its Bearing on Social Causation," in Bosanquet's *Aspects of the Social Problem*, pp. 103–117).

[66]Bosanquet, "Socialism and Natural Selection" in *Aspects of the Social Problem*, p. 301. See also "Liberty and Legislation" in his *The Civilization of Christendom* (London: Swan Sonnenschein, 1893), pp. 358–83 and below, pp. 25, 92.

"moral socialism" and held that, if this could be made the basis of an economic socialism, it would be "heaven."[67]

How far could law and the state go? Bosanquet's answer can be seen particularly in his essays dealing with the work of the Charity Organisation Society and various university extension organisations. He argued that the state may act "positively" in providing individuals with the means for moral action (p. 189 below), even if it cannot itself act morally or directly promote a moral end.[68] As examples here, Bosanquet mentions building schools in order to help combat illiteracy, and controlling the sale of liquor to limit alcohol abuse – though he argues against a state attempting to guarantee full employment or providing housing for everyone. The key factor here is whether the state, by acting, works against its purpose of favouring the conditions for the development of individual character and, hence, the full realisation of human personality (pp. 185–86 below). Still, while he did not hold that there were any a priori restrictions on state action, he believed that there were a number of practical conditions that could limit it.

Bosanquet insisted that, while law was necessary to the promotion of the common good, it could not make a person good, and that, for practical reasons, social progress could often be better achieved by volunteer action; this is defended and discussed in a number of essays, such as that defending the Majority Report of the Poor Law Commission, "Idealism in Social Work" (pp. 358–69 in this volume). In social work, Bosanquet holds that one must "individualise the case," and automatic appeal to a State agency "to solve a problem by brute force" is, he thought, a "very poor" response to a situation.[69] It is this emphasis on the importance of the development of individual moral character that led many of Bosanquet's critics, including Hobson and Hobhouse, to view the COS position on the Poor Law and, by extension, Bosanquet himself, as individu-

---

[67] See "The Antithesis between Individualism and Socialism," pp. 324–46 below.

[68] See p. 25 below. While Bosanquet allows that society and the state can 'act' and while they can encourage the moral activity of others, neither is, strictly speaking, a moral agent.

[69] See "The Affinity of Philosophy and Casework," in his *Social and International Ideals*, pp. 161–182, pp. 164–167.

alistic, moralistic and condescending, and as engaged in acts of mere charity and philanthropy rather than mutual support and responsibility.

INFLUENCE AND GENERAL ASSESSMENT

Bosanquet's political thought has clearly suffered from neglect. Some have argued that his work is unoriginal, and, in keeping with his general tendency to look for common ground among philosophers, rather than to accentuate their differences, Bosanquet himself did not consider that there was a wide gap separating his views from his fellow idealists – particularly, Green and Bradley. Nevertheless, Bosanquet did not simply repeat or apply earlier idealist political thinking. Bradley did not provide a political philosophy, and his ethical views are often distinct from Bosanquet's. Green's political theory is also clearly less developed than that of Bosanquet – though this is not surprising. The principal works of Green were, as noted earlier, published posthumously, following his death at the age of forty-six; Bosanquet, on the other hand, lived until seventy-five, and *The Philosophical Theory of the State* went through four editions by the time of his death. The central if not unique place of Bosanquet's analysis within British idealism is confirmed by the dubious honour of being the target of Hobhouse's *The Metaphysical Theory of the State*.[70]

No doubt another of the principal reasons for the undervaluing of Bosanquet's political thought is that his philosophical style is sometimes uninviting to a modern audience. His prose does not have the philosophical sharpness of Bradley's – though this is largely because his audience was as often the professional in social work or the politician, as the academic philosopher – and, as he himself admitted, he usually rushed his books.[71] Bosanquet's association with the Majority members of the Royal Commission on the Poor Laws – who have often mistakenly or inaccurately been represented as conservative, in contrast to the more popular and crusading views of the Fabian minority – and the subse-

---

[70] Bosanquet's comment: "I don't think I shall read it – I don't feel I learn much from him, and books are expensive since the war began; and time is not cheap" (Muirhead, *Friends*, p. 21).

[71] Muirhead, *Friends*, p. 131.

quent criticisms of Hobhouse, MacIver, Hobson, and Russell, among others, are also factors. Finally, idealism, as a general philosophical approach, went into eclipse after the 1920s,[72] and it is perhaps not incidental to this decline in influence that the three leading figures in later British idealism, Bosanquet, F.H. Bradley and J.M.E. McTaggart, died within three years of one another.

Recent studies have, however, pointed out that Bosanquet was an active Liberal and, in the second decade of the twentieth century, supported the Labour Party.[73] More substantively, it is clear that Bosanquet adopted many of the ideals of the liberal tradition. He emphasised the importance of autonomy and self-government (which, for Bosanquet, implied representative, democratic rule), was concerned to promote the improvement of character and the self-realisation of the individual human person, and saw that limits must be imposed on the state to prevent it from interfering with this development (p. 186 below).

---

[72]Still, despite the apparently rapid shift away from idealism in philosophy and political thought in Britain, it did not vanish altogether. There was a "third generation" of idealists or idealist–influenced philosophers, which included R.G. Collingwood (1889–1943), C.E.M. Joad (1891–1953), A.C. Ewing (1899–1973), G.R.E. Mure (1893–1979), C.A. Campbell (1897–1974), Michael Oakeshott (1901–1990) and Dorothy Emmet (1904–); these and others had an important place in philosophy through the middle decades of the twentieth century. The British idealists also had a significant impact in English-language philosophy in Canada (with John Watson [1847–1939] and Rupert Lodge [1886–1961]), in the United States (with George Holmes Howison [1834–1917], Josiah Royce [1855–1916], Evander Bradley McGilvary [1864–1953], W.E. Hocking [1873–1966], Elijah Jordan [1875–1953], Gustavus Watts Cunningham [1881–1968], and Brand Blanshard [1892–1987]), in Australia (with W.R. Boyce–Gibson [1869–1935], Sir William Mitchell [1861–1962], and John Anderson [1893– 1962]), in South Africa (with R.F.A. Hoernlé [1880–1943] and Jan Christian Smuts [1870–1950]), and in India (with Surendranath Dasgupta [1885–1952], Sarvepalli Radhakrishnan [1888–1975], J.C.P. d'Andrade [1888–1949], and P.T. Raju [1904–1992]). There is, moreover, a continuation and revival of British idealism today, that can be seen in the work of Errol E. Harris (1908–), Nicholas Rescher (1928–), Leslie Armour (1931–), Timothy Sprigge (1932–), and their students. While the conclusions of these authors often became less and less homogeneous with those of their predecessors, their principal concerns (such as the rejection of naturalism, materialism and various forms of reductionism, and the insistence on a greater recognition of the role of "mind" in the understanding of social and political reality) remained constant.

[73]See McBriar, *An Edwardian Mixed Doubles*, p. 8; Sweet, *Idealism*, pp. 233–234.

Moreover, Bosanquet's combination of a thoroughgoing organicist view of society, with a strong defense of economic individualism, provides a unique contribution to the development of "non-individualist" liberal thought in the late nineteenth and early twentieth centuries. The essay on the "The Antithesis Between Individualism and Socialism Philosophically Considered" (pp. 324–46 in this volume) provides what might be described as a "communitarian" defense of economic individualism.

There are certainly a number of tensions in Bosanquet's thought – particularly concerning the adequacy of his account of the distinction between society and the state, and his ability to reconcile his Kantian and Hegelian tendencies, for example concerning the value of the "finite individual." Again, many contemporary liberals, like the Fabians of his time, would challenge Bosanquet's tendency to emphasize the primacy of the will over circumstance in dealing with welfare support – though it is important to recognise that his reasons for this are more strategic than metaphysical. Furthermore, given Bosanquet's reluctance to embrace the "guild socialism" of G.D.H. Cole and the "pluralism" of Ernest Barker, one may well ask whether his idealism is compatible with modern liberal pluralism.

Nevertheless, when one reviews Bosanquet's political thought in its context, especially in light of his metaphysics, epistemology and his practical work, some of these tensions seem less marked. As suggested above, some of Bosanquet's views appear to be close to contemporary communitarianism though, perhaps, they might also be seen as representative of an alternative to both communitarianism and classical liberalism. In a period in which liberals are faulted for ignoring or for failing to appreciate fully the social embededness of the human individual, then, his idealist political philosophy may well be inviting.

The late John Plamenatz once remarked that *The Philosophical Theory of the State* was the last great work by an English political theorist. Indeed, despite the many criticisms of Bosanquet's political philosophy, even the critic Adam Ulam has noted that *The Philosophical Theory of the State* "has a comprehensiveness and an awareness of conflicting political and philosophical opinions which give it a supreme importance in modern political thought. Bosanquet is both a political theorist and a political analyst."[74] It is our hope that, in presenting this new edition, another generation of political theorists will become acquainted with this important achievement of twentieth-century political thinking.

---

[74] Adam Ulam, *The Philosophical Foundations of English Socialism* (Cambridge, MA: Harvard University Press, 1951), p. 60.

In addition to books and articles referred to in this Introduction, readers might consult the following:

Bosanquet, Bernard, *The Collected Works of Bernard Bosanquet*. Edited by William Sweet. 20 volumes. Bristol: Thoemmes Press, 1999. Volume 1 contains a comprehensive bibliography of Bosanquet's books, articles, and reviews.

Bosanquet, Helen. *Bernard Bosanquet: A Short Account of his Life*. London: Macmillan, 1924.

Bradley, James. "Hegel in Britain: A Brief History of British Commentary and Attitudes." *The Heythrop Journal*, vol. 20 (1979): 1–24; 163–182.

Collini, Stefan. "Hobhouse, Bosanquet and the State: Philosophical Idealism and Political Argument in England: 1880–1918." *Past and Present*, vol. 72 (1976): 86–111.

Den Otter, Sandra M. *British Idealism and Social Explanation: A Study in Late Victorian Thought*. Oxford: Clarendon Press, 1996.

Gaus, Gerald. "Green, Bosanquet and the Philosophy of Coherence." In *The Routledge History of Philosophy*, Volume 7 – *The Nineteenth Century*, Edited by C.L. Ten. London: Routledge, 1994, 408–36.

Gaus, Gerald. *The Modern Liberal Theory of Man*. New York: St. Martin's, 1983.

Harris, Frederick Philip. *The Neo-Idealist Political Theory: Its Continuity with the British Tradition*. New York: King's Crown Press, 1944.

Houang, François. *Le néo-hegelianisme en Angleterre: la philosophie de Bernard Bosanquet (1848–1923)*. Paris: Vrin, 1954.

Laski, Harold and A.D. Lindsay. "Bosanquet's Theory of the General Will." *Proceedings of the Aristotelian Society*, n.s. supp. vol. VIII (1928): 31–61.

Meadowcroft, James. *Conceptualizing the State: Innovation and Dispute in British Political Thought*. Oxford: Clarendon Press, 1995.

Milne, A.J.M. *The Social Philosophy of English Idealism*. London: Allen & Unwin, 1962.

Morrow, John. "Ancestors, Legacies and Traditions: British Idealism in the History of Political Thought,. *History of Political Thought*, vol. 6 (1985): 491–515.

Muirhead, J.H. *The Platonic Tradition in Anglo-Saxon Philosophy; Studies in the History of Idealism in England*. London: Allen and Unwin, 1931.

Nicholson, Peter P. *The Political Philosophy of the British Idealists: Selected Studies*. Cambridge: Cambridge University Press, 1990.

Pfannenstill, Bertil. *Bernard Bosanquet's Philosophy of the State*. (und: Hakan Ohlsson, 1936.

Primoratz, Igor. "The Word 'Liberty' on the Chains of Galley-Slaves: Bosanquet's Theory of the General Will." *History of Political Thought*, vol. 15 (1994): 249–267.

Robbins, Peter. *The British Hegelians: 1875–1925*. New York: Garland, 1982.

Russell, Bertrand, C. Delisle Burns and G.D.H. Cole. "The Nature of the State in its External Relations." *Proceedings of the Aristotelian Society*, n.s. vol. XVI (1915–1916): 290–310. (A round table, with a discussion of Bosanquet's theory of international politics.)

Sabine, George. "Bosanquet's Theory of the Real Will." *Philosophical Review*, vol. XXXII (1923): 633–651.

Sweet, William. *Idealism and Rights*. Lanham, MD: University Press of America, 1997.

Sweet, William. "Was Bosanquet a Hegelian?" *Bulletin of the Hegel Society of Great Britain*, vol. 31 (1995): 39–60.

Vincent, Andrew and Raymond Plant. *Philosophy, Politics and Citizenship: the Life and Thought of the British Idealists*. Oxford: B. Blackwell, 1984.

Willis, Kirk. "The Introduction and Critical Reception of Hegelian Thought in Britain 1830–1900." *Victorian Studies*, vol. 32 (1988): 85–111.

ABOUT THIS EDITION

The text of *The Philosophical Theory of the State* has been edited from the fourth edition (Macmillan, 1923). Some errors from this edition have been corrected and the text has been modified to conform to contemporary standards in punctuation and presentation. The editors have added notes to assist contemporary readers. Editors' notes, and their additions to Bosanquet's notes, appear in square brackets. The editors have also provided short introductions to each of the related essays, explaining their relevance to *The Philosophical Theory of the State*. Throughout, our aim has been to produce a volume accessible to contemporary readers.

ACKNOWLEDGMENTS

The editors would like to express their appreciation for Victoria Parkinson's assistance in preparing this edition. Ms. Parkinson was of tremendous help in tracking down some of Bosanquet's more obscure references. Ms. Parkinson was also responsible for the index. We are also most grateful to Andrea Gaus for final layout design and copyediting. The editors would also like to thank Jane Williamson of Thoemmes Press for her interest in the project, as well as Paula Callan, Humanities librarian at the Queensland University of Technology for her reference assistance. Gerald Gaus would like to express his deep thanks to John W. Chapman, who (long ago, now) convinced him that *The Philosophical Theory of the State* is one the century's great works in political theory. Will Sweet would like, as well, to acknowledge Peter Nicholson, Colin Tyler, and Leslie Armour for their advice and continued support, and the financial support of the University Council for Research, St. Francis Xavier University.

The Philosophical Theory of the State

To

CHARLES STEWART LOCH

PREFACE

The present work is an attempt to express what I take to be the fundamental ideas of a true social philosophy. I have criticised and interpreted the doctrines of certain well-known thinkers only with the view of setting these ideas in the clearest light. This is the whole purpose of the book; and I have intentionally abstained from practical applications, except by way of illustration. It is my conviction, indeed, that a better understanding of fundamental principles would very greatly contribute to the more rational handling of practical problems. But this better understanding is only to be attained, as it seems to me, by a thorough examination of ideas, apart from the associations of practical issues about which a fierce party spirit has been aroused. And, moreover, it is my belief that the influence of the ideas here maintained upon practical discussion, would be, in a certain sense, to detach it from philosophical theory. The principles which I advocate would destroy so many party prejudices, would put the mind in possession of so many clues to fact, that practical "social" issues would in consequence be considered as problems of life and mind, to be treated only with intimate experience, and by methods adequate to their subtlety. The result would be that such discussions would be regarded, if one may use the expression, more respectfully, and would acquire an independence and completeness worthy of their importance. The work of the social reformer should no more be regarded as a mere appendix to social theory than that of the doctor is regarded as a mere appendix to physiology. Such a division of labour is, of course, no hindrance to the interchange of facts and ideas between theory and practice. On the contrary, it tends to promote such an interchange, by increasing the supply on either side, and improving the intellectual communication between them.

It will occur to philosophical readers that the essence of the theory here presented is to be found not merely in Plato and in Aristotle, but in very many modern writers, more especially in Hegel, T.H. Green,

Bradley,[1] and Wallace.[2] And they may be inclined to doubt the justification for a further work on the same lines by one who can hardly expect to improve upon the writings of such predecessors.

On this point I should like to make a brief explanation. To begin with, it is a truism that every generation needs to be addressed in its own language; and I might even plead that the greatness of a tradition justifies some urgency in calling attention to it. But further, as regards T.H. Green in particular, whom in many points I follow very closely, I had two special reasons for desiring to express myself independently. One of these is to be found in my attempt to apply the conceptions of recent psychology to the theory of State coercion and of the Real or General Will, and to explain the relation of Social Philosophy to Sociological Psychology. For a short discussion of the Imitation Theory, which the purpose of the present work would not permit me to include in it, I may refer to a paper which will shortly appear in *Mind*.[3]

My other reason lay in the conviction that the time has gone by for the scrupulous caution which Green displayed in estimating the value of the State to its members. I have referred to this subject in the body of my work (ch. x); but I desire to emphasise my belief that our growing experience of all social "classes" proves the essentials of happiness and character to be the same throughout the social whole. Scepticism on this point is the product, I am convinced, of defective social experience. Indeed, it seems worth while to observe that the attention which is now rightly paid to such disadvantages, affecting the poorer classes of citizens, as it may be possible to remedy, has given rise to a serious confusion. The zeal of the advocate has led him to slander his client. In proving that under such and such conditions it would be no wonder if "the poor" were bad, he forgets to observe that in fact they are generally just

---

[1]See especially the chapter in [F.H. Bradley] *Ethical Studies* [(London: Henry S. King & Co., 1876; 2nd edn, Oxford, 1927)] entitled "My Station and its Duties."

[2]See *Lectures and Essays* [*of the late Professor W. Wallace* (Oxford: Clarendon Press, 1898)], especially p. 213, "Our Natural Rights," and p. 427, "The Relation of Fichte and Hegel to Socialism."

[3]*Mind*, vol. VIII, [(1899)] pp. 167[−175], "Social Automatism and the Imitation Theory." [Note added in] 1919.

as good as other people. The all-important distinction between a poor home and a bad home is neglected. And yet it seems probable that, omitting the definitely criminal quarters, there is no larger proportion of bad homes among the poor than among the rich. Such terms as "den" and "slum" are too freely used, with an affectation of intimacy, for homes in which thousands of respectable citizens reside. Our democratic age will be remarkable to posterity for having dimmed the time-honoured belief in the virtues of the poor. There was cant, no doubt, in the older doctrine, but it was not so far from the fact as the opposite cant of to-day; and it is time that the truth in it should be revived.

I must repeat that these remarks are not intended to be controversial. There is nothing in them which serious men of all schools may not accept. They are meant to defend my attitude in treating the Real Will, and Freedom in the greater Self, as matters of universal concern, and not merely as hopes and fancies cherished by "educated" persons. Indeed, although it would be churlish for a student to disparage literary education, it must never be forgotten that, as things are to-day, the citizens who live by handicraft possess a valuable element of brain-culture, which is on the whole denied to the literary class. Whatever, therefore, may be wanting in the following pages, it is not, I think, the relation of their subject-matter to the general life of peoples.

The social student should shun mere optimism; but he should not be afraid to make the most of that which he studies. It is an unfortunate result of the semi-practical aims which naturally influence social philosophers, that they are apt throughout to take up an indifferent, if not a hostile, attitude to their given object. They hardly believe in actual society as a botanist believes in plants, or a biologist in vital processes. And hence, social theory comes off badly. No student can really appreciate an object for which he is always apologising. There is a touch of this attitude in all the principal writers, except Hegel and Bradley, and therefore, as I venture to think, they partly fail to seize the greatness and ideality of life in its commonest actual phases. It is in no spirit of obscurantism, and with no thought of resisting the march of a true social logic, that some take up a different position. They are convinced that an actual living society is an infinitely higher creature than a steam-engine, a plant, or an animal; and that the best of their ideas are not too good to be employed in analysing it. Those who cannot be enthusiastic in the study of society as it is, would not be so in the study of a better society if they had it. "Here or nowhere is your America."

BERNARD BOSANQUET

CATERHAM, *March*, 1899

PREFACE TO THE SECOND EDITION

The present edition contains a new Introduction, defining my attitude towards movements in European thought which have declared their nature more distinctly in the interval since the first publication of my work. A few alterations have also been made in the text and notes, and the opening of ch. viii has been rewritten. With regard to pressing social questions, I have maintained, as before, an uncontroversial position, though I have found it inevitably necessary to illustrate some or my contentions by references to social experience.

BERNARD BOSANQUET

OXSHOTT, *Nov.* 12, 1909

PREFACE TO THE THIRD EDITION

In the twenty years since the first publication of this book every theory of the State has been severely tested. Criticism, suggested by historical events, has attacked the writer's views among others as attributing an unreal uniqueness and a fictitious sovereignty to the State. And it has thus become difficult even for the writer himself to bear steadily in mind that the original intention of the book was neither to magnify the State nor to decry it, but to explain how its functions flow from its nature, and, most certainly, to emphasise their inherent limitations. Such a discrimination is to-day more necessary than ever. A cry has arisen for the limitation of sovereignty, by pluralism at home and by monism abroad, which proves, on examination, to involve on the contrary a just demand for deeper unity and higher organising achievement in both directions. And again, these very demands and necessities reawaken the time-honoured problem concerning the limits of State intervention. There is little, we recognise now as always, with which the State must not in some sense busy itself. But the precise *modus operandi* – the avoidance of routine bureaucracy and of mechanical collectivism – remains all-important. And here the general principle, which a social theory proposes,[4] maintains itself, I believe, through all changes of actual problems. It is never more imperative than when the word "nationalisation" is mentioned. The present work has never been controversial in matters of social or industrial detail, but it has always claimed freedom of illustration; and I would venture to suggest that in any discussion regarding the nationalisation of an industry, the true issue, at once of principle and of practice, turns on the possibility of creating an administration which shall fulfil the requirements of personal responsibility, invention, initiative, and energy.[5] For it is these, and not self-interest, as both sides are too apt to assume, which form the spur and the delight of what is known as private enterprise, and which ordinary bureaucracy destroys.

The use which I have made in the Introduction of Miss Follett's *The New State*[6] is sufficient proof of the debt which I owe to its author. And I desire to take this opportunity of alluding to an older book, *Spinoza's Political and Ethical Philosophy*[7] by Dr R.A. Duff. In this very valuable work the author seems to me to be singularly successful where he insists on all that side of Spinoza's philosophy which depends on the Jus Naturae[8] as one with Potentia, to which Green, perhaps, hardly assigned its full significance. For this natural Jus or Potentia – so Dr Duff elucidates Spinoza's conception – is for every natural object and so for man, its God-given rule of existence and claim to a place in the universe. Here is the point of Spinoza's well-known doctrine that man's natural appetites and passions are not to be censured but to be studied. For these passions form both the necessity of the State and its condition. It is through the efficient and educational handling of them, the arduous task whose prog-

---

[4]See Introd. to 2nd edn, sect. 2, and ch. viii, sect. v.

[5]See Lord Haldane's evidence on the training of Government servants before the Sankey Coal Commission, and cf. Marshall, *Industry and Trade*, 1919, p. 850, "Nature and Limitations of the Constructive Work of a Democratic Government in Regard to Industry."

[6][London: Longmans, Green and Co., 1918.]

[7]See below, footnote 9.

[8][*jus naturae*: law of nature.]

ress history records, that the State develops its civil right, which is, like the natural right out of which it springs, a form of power, the power which comes of bringing all desires into unity. Thus, sovereignty and the truly absolute State are existences de facto, practical creations. They exist by actual growth and accomplishment, as the author of *The New State* assures us, though like everything else they have an essence of their own, and you cannot have just as much or as little of them as you may choose. "There[9] is no human being who is willing to live without it [the State]." But he who is not willing to live without it, must also will all the conditions that go to its efficiency, else he must live without it. For even the State "is a natural object, with laws of its own existence" [Spinoza]. You may constitute a State, or you may not. But you cannot constitute a State, and give it, or withhold from it, what powers you please.

"These[10] powers which are reserved from the State's control are not really limits, or limitations of a power which it might have had with advantage to itself, but simply the essential conditions on which all sovereignty rests" [i.e. these essential conditions exclude the possession of those powers by the sovereign]. In this sense sovereignty and absolutism are limited. They are limited by being what they are and not something else.

The same work reminds us[11] that the principle that the civil rule and moral laws *which are binding upon a citizen in private life*[12] are not binding upon a State in its dealings with other States comes originally not from "the Germans" but from Machiavelli. Spinoza adopts it, pointing out that things which are very completely different cannot be governed by the same laws. But of course he does not hold that the State is bound by no laws. It is under "law to God," the law of its own nature, and can act well or badly, according to this law. Spinoza, then, in using the above language never meant to deny what is understood by the

---

[9]*Spinoza's Political and Ethical Philosophy* [Glasgow: J. Maclehose and Sons, 1903], p. 274.

[10][Ibid.,] p. 473: the "powers" in question are freedom of thought, speech and religion.

[11][Ibid.,] p. 453 ff.

[12]My italics. This is the essential point. See the note on Sidgwick, p. 37.

moral responsibility of the State. What he meant is essentially what is pointed out below,[13] that you gain nothing in the way of guidance by comparing its task with that of a private person, but you may cause confusion. It seems, however, to be a matter on which the progress of civilisation has a considerable bearing. The difference diminishes, between circumstances which condition the State and those which condition the individual, as a context of international obligations, reinforced by a recognised authority, comes into being. But here as elsewhere, in the language of *The New State*, sovereignty must be an actual growth.

Mr Hirst,[14] author of *Self and Neighbour*, has written a very different book from that of Dr Duff, and it is perhaps permissible to wish that Dr Duff's assistance, acknowledged in the Preface, had been extended further than to the revision of the proofs. I do not propose to refer to his criticisms of absolutist metaphysic, which do not specifically touch the present work. But it seems necessary to mention his defective conception of the good or real will. He shows, indeed, in my judgment, a sound instinct when he rejects at starting the popular antithesis of egoism and altruism; but, so far as I can see, he falls a victim to the same formula at a slightly higher level, in the bare notion of community or love as such. This bare notion of unity between myself and my neighbour, an impartial unity, he insists, involving equality of regard, *not* an aspect inherent in all union of man with nature and with God, is all that can be regarded as the content of the common good, the object of the good will.

The reason of this abstraction appears to me to lie in a failure to grasp what great thinkers on society have understood under their different forms of expression, by the good or real will, the impulse of self-conservation or self-satisfaction, as the self-developing aspiration towards a system of living which is the realisation of all capacities in and for all. He fails to grasp this, I feel it necessary to observe, for the fault is much too common, because of the slightness and rapidity of the survey which he devotes to the great philosophers of the past, giving himself no opportunity for exercising true interpretative ability. He might have gained the required understanding from Plato or Aristotle from

---

[13]Introd. to 2nd edn, p. 37 and p. 284.
[14][Francis Wrigley Hirst (1873–1953).]

Spinoza – he could have no better guide than Dr Duff – or from Hegel, from any adequate appreciation of Kant, and certainly from Green. But as it is, that which Spinoza called the intellectual love of God, the fundamental impulse of the good and universal will, which nearly every great thinker on society has in some way made the root of his conception, has escaped the author's grasp altogether. To find the values in which, and in the will for which, mankind are one, he has no principle in his hands but the bare name of love or community or interpersonal experience. The absolutely disastrous consequence of this misconception appears on pp. 113–4, where it becomes clear that the ghost of the "ego" and the "alter" is not really laid. "For only as good resides in the will can collision of goods be escaped. And we do not think that the interests of 'ego' and 'alter' can ever be reconciled, or any satisfactory solution of the ethical problem secured, if even such things as knowledge, or art, or pleasure, be regarded as components or ingredients of 'the good'."

His difficulty lies, I gather, in a notion into which I am afraid that Dr Rashdall has helped to mislead him, that the supreme spiritual values imply inequalities of enjoyment, while inequalities of enjoyment are fatal to "community" (cf. p. 99). The real doctrine of shareable goods is thus quite obscured for him. It does not occur to him that inequality in their case loses its depreciatory meaning, because the augmentation of their enjoyment by anyone tends not to the diminution but to the augmentation of their enjoyment by everyone. And in a considerable degree this character is communicated by them even to their material instruments. I really do not think that it is necessary to say anything more, unless to point out that, if I understand him right, the principle of equality, which has wrought this mutilation of the conception of common good, having done all this mischief is itself discarded in the end, and unity is seen after all to lie in a common good which excludes it (pp. 274–5).

In the third edition several pages have been added to the Introduction, some footnotes have been inserted, dated 1919, and the Index has been enlarged. I avoid, so far as possible, re-writing the text. I think it fairer to the reader to give him the means of following the development of a writer's thought together with its reasons.

It is possible that *The New State* may owe a little, in its treatment of the Neighbourhood group, to the last chapter of the present work. I mention the point here only in order to acknowledge that, if so, the idea has but returned home. For, in its special emphasis, it came to me through contact in London with Dr Stanton Coit, who brought it, I believe, from social work in New York.

BERNARD BOSANQUET

OXSHOTT, *November*, 1919

CONTENTS

INTRODUCTION TO THE SECOND EDITION[1]

I. [THE THREE LINES OF CRITICISM]

Since the present work was first published, it has become apparent in many ways that the wealth of new experiences which modern life brings with it is tending to obscure the definite outlines of such a theory as is here advocated. There are three directions in particular in which the classical theory of the State might appear to be undermined; and it will be well to say a word on each of them. The philosophy of political society, in view of modern phenomena and modern investigations, is held to be too narrow and rigid, too negative, and too intellectualist.

1. *It is held to be too narrow and too rigid*

Too narrow, because the analysis which applies easily to the City-state, and with some reinterpretation to the Nation-state, is held to be inapplicable to the varied gradation of communities with which modern life makes us acquainted – to a man's membership in the Empire composed of free dominions, or in the European concert of nations, or in the Parliament of man, the federation of the world; not to speak of the hierarchy of societies in which we are involved within the boundaries of the Nation-state itself. The idea of the Nation-state, it may be thought, might even come to lose its distinctiveness and supremacy through the impossibility of determining in which of several concentric communities its peculiar prerogatives lay. There might be a return, on other lines, to medieval conditions, which scarcely admitted of a truly independent sovereign State. Again, the theory may appear too rigid, because the strict democratic account of self-government is most readily understood as applied to the exercise of power, if not necessarily by primary assemblies, at least through elected representative bodies, not merely in the case of Parliament, but in local administration on the one hand and Imperial organisation on the other. But tendencies and phenomena are now visible which suggest that elected representative bodies may not be in

---

[1] [1st edn, 1899; 2nd edn, 1910; 3rd edn, 1920; 4th edn, 1923.]

every case the preferable type of organs of the general will, whether in the microcosm of municipal administration, or in the macrocosm of the Empire or the Federation.[2]

(i) In dealing with the suggestion of narrowness, I would begin by calling attention to that argument of the present work which treats of the State as the ultimate and absolute power of adjustment, and as necessarily, therefore, single in respect to every individual,[3] and also to the point of view[4] which refers the difficulty of recognising what we call the State in the large-scale characteristics of modern phenomena, simply to the tendency not to see the wood for the trees; so that our analysis is hard to verify just because it is so true, and is really much more applicable, because there is much more for it to apply to, in the case of modern experience, than in that of the lesser and more clear-cut objects from which it was originally drawn. We are thus led to see more plainly the true character of the State as a source of pervading adjustments and an idea-force holding together a complex hierarchy of groups, and not itself a separable thing like the monarch, or the "government," or the local body, with which we are tempted to identify it. And I would further illustrate the problem by reference to the late Professor Maitland's delightful Introduction to his translation of Gierke's *Political Theories of the Middle Age[s]*.[5] The position there sketched by him, according to which the real or general will is present in its degree in every co-operating group of human beings, is one with which the theory of the State is fully in accord. Where two or three are gathered together with any degree of common experience and co-operation, there is *pro tanto*[6] a general will. The uniqueness of the general will of the State, and the necessity that it should be unique, is an additional and peculiar feature, depending on the

---

[2] [Bosanquet often referred to society as a "macrocosm constituted by microcosms" – an organism constituted by other organisms, or a system constituted by subsystems. See *The Principle of Individuality and Value* (London: Macmillan, 1912), p. 38.]

[3] Ch. viii, sect. 3.

[4] Ch. x, sect. 6.

[5] [F.W. Maitland, "Translator's Introduction" to Otto Gierke, *Political Theories of the Middle Ages*, trans., F.W. Maitland] (Cambridge: Cambridge University Press, 1900), pp. xi, xli-ii.

[6] [*pro tanto*: to the extent of; so far.]

necessity referred to above, that an absolute power should be single in reference to each individual. How far even the absolute power of any one group in relation to individuals within it may be interfered with by constitutional tradition or by a conflict of authorities (as, e.g., the conflict between a State and the Federal Government in the U.S.A.), or by International Courts or Leagues, is a question of degree and detail. It must be remembered that our theory does not place Sovereignty in any determinate person or body of persons, but only in the working of the system of institutions as a whole.[7] There is therefore no technical difficulty in the modification of the Nation-state towards larger forms of authoritative co-operation, so long as it is made clear to what system of authorities every separate human being is subject in respect of the ultimate adjustment or claims upon him. And it would seem that there must always be at least a machinery for making this clear (like the Court which interprets the constitution of the U.S.A.), if civilised life is to be possible. The all-important point is that the recognition of the Real or General Will should be maintained. And this, as we have seen above, it is the tendency of recent legal theory to sustain as the recognition of an actual fact.

(ii) The question of rigidity may be treated more briefly. It is plain from what has been said above and from the whole trend of our theory, that the administrative expression of the general will is not necessarily confined to *ad hoc* elective bodies, but may take any efficient and convenient shape[8] without violation of the theory of democratic self-government. It is impossible to lay down in detail any indispensable form even for the supreme direction of affairs, the manner of which varies very greatly between States which may be supposed to be in principle equally free and democratic. As in all practical matters, the first necessity is *bona fides*, which means in this case a genuine intention throughout society to make the institutions express the best will of the people. It is always through a complex of institutions, and never through

---

[7]Ch. v, sect. 4; ch. x, sect. 8.

[8]See ch. x sect. 8, on the tendency to one-man administration in the U.S.A. The question is raised in another form by the substitution of "statutory" committees for purely elective *ad hoc* authorities.

the mere voices of a crowd, that a people's freedom finds utterance; and every complex of institutions must be criticised on its own merits as an expression of freedom. Parliamentary government, in one shape or another, seems hardly likely to be superseded as the normal form for civilised peoples. But the example of the English judiciary, which, I imagine, is generally approved, suffices to show that for certain functions a very high degree of independence is desirable in the social interest, and that even responsibility – the indispensable guarantee of freedom – may mean rather the inevitable effect of publicity than immediate subordination to a popular body. These observations are made simply in the interest of maintaining the concreteness and adaptability of our theory. There is at present an enthusiasm for the study of group-life at first-hand, and for practical amelioration of it, which, partly under the influence of such criticisms as have just been noticed, tends to submerge the interest of strict political theory. But for a true comprehension of group-life it will always be necessary to refer its inward and spiritual side to something like the general will, and its outward and visible form to a complex of institutions, and thereby to set its outward and inward aspect in their true relation to each other and to the social unity.

2. *The theory of the state is held to be too negative*

(i) This objection is directed against the principle, drawn from Kant, and identical with that adopted by Green,[9] which is defended in the present work. The principle rests on the obvious truth that the distinctive action of the State cannot be *in pari materia*[10] with the positive end of the social whole, but is, qua distinctive, confined to dealing with external acts in the sense in which all that can be dealt with by compulsion is external.[11] From this follows the doctrine that the distinctive province of the

---

[9][Thomas Hill Green (1836–1882).]

[10][*in pari materia*: a legal term meaning "upon the same matter or subject." Statutes taken *in pari materia* are to be construed and interpreted together. Bosanquet's point here is that the distinctive goal of the state is not the same subject as the end of the social whole; it is a specialised end, dealing with external acts only.]

[11]Ch. viii, sects. 4–5. The view is analogous to Kant's doctrine that our action with a view to perfection (moral excellence) is confined to our own case, while for others we are restricted to the attempt to secure happiness (command of externals). This view is taken by [Edward] Caird to belong to Kant's individualism (*A Critical Account of the Philosophy*

State is rightly described as the hindrance to hindrances of good life. The use of spiritual influences in a spiritual form is only open *per accidens*[12] to State agency, while the promotion of spiritual ends by external means, and, pre-eminently, by external means in which compulsion is operative, is only possible through very delicate and indirect methods.

(ii) We have here the same peculiarly modern difficulty, describable as not being able to see the wood for the trees, which was referred to in the previous section. State activity has bewilderingly increased and multiplied its shapes and organs. Though there are some things that the modern State, as compared with the ancient city, rules out of its purview, such as religion and fine art, yet on the whole it probably plays a greater part in life than the City-state in its prime; so much more is known today about desirable outward conditions; so many more claims for the regulation of outward life are publicly recognised.

But this big bulking of the modern State in our eyes makes it all the more important to be clear as to its truly distinctive powers and functions. The harder the distinction is to make, the more disastrous it is to fail in making it. If nobody expected much from the State, there would be no danger; but when all eyes are turned to it, it is fatal not to understand precisely the conditions of its interference.

(iii) The error lies, on both sides, in an insufficient appreciation of what is involved in man's social being. Between visible activities backed by the force of the State, and the narrowest self-assertion, equally visible, of the separate, or would-be separate, human person, the whole social development – the development, that is, of man's universal

---

of Kant [Glasgow: James Maclehose, 1877], ii, pp. 396–7.) And no doubt it is true that the perfection of others cannot be finally separated from our own, and that social influences may be the means of grace (T.H. Green, *Prolegomena to Ethics*, ed. A.C. Bradley [Oxford: Clarendon Press, 1890], sect. 100 [pp. 113–115]). But it remains true also, as Caird has in effect pointed out (loc. cit., p. 550) with reference to Kant's view of the moral education of humanity, that the attempt to promote excellence or perfection through external dealings can only succeed by an indirect method. [Edward Caird (1835–1908), was one of the "Scottish Hegelians." The book to which Bosanquet refers is a distinctively Hegelian reading of Kant].

[12][*per accidens*: by accident, not following by the nature of state agency.]

nature, of which these are merely extreme limiting cases – fails to obtain due recognition.

(α) The one party credits the individual – the supposed self-existent isolable being – with all that does not emanate from the formal procedure of the political group as such; and thus, setting down, for example, art and religion as "individual" activities and concerns, has a certain justification for alleging that the individual is the end to which society (at most, the argument should run, the direct machinery of politics) is a means.[13]

(β) The other, rightly aware that the deepest and loftiest achievements of man do not belong to the particular human being in his repellent isolation, and, like its antagonist, recognising only two opposites – society as the State, and the man at his minimum as the individual, naturally claims for the State the glamour which belongs to the highest self-expression by which man transcends his isolation. I do not say that poetry and philosophy are actually treated as a product of political activity; but I do say that the fascination attaching to all that is "social" – all that springs from the co-operation and the sympathies of human beings – is habitually attached and restricted to that legal and political form of co-operation which we call the State.

Between the two parties, the profounder meaning of the term "social" goes unrecognised. We thus lose a great and important truth, that which Aristotle expressed in the position he gave to Theoria[14] as the quintessence and consecration of the social whole. We then take as representative conceptions the State and the atomic individual respectively, and

---

[13]See p. 106ff below.

[14][Bosanquet provides a more detailed discussion of his view of *theoria* in Appendix II to Lecture X of *The Principle of Individuality and Value* (London: Macmillan, 1912). Bosanquet writes that: "Theoretical wisdom is always one and the same, and strictly speaking it is divine; it studies no production of instruments for the good of mankind; it cannot strictly be said to aim at the special good of mankind; it does not specially concern itself with man, or at all with one group of creatures rather than another. Its object of study or contemplation is rather what is above and beyond man...more especially, it occupies itself with the nature of God." (p. 400). Bosanquet views contemplation in the forms of art, poetry and religion as instances of *theoria*. W.F.R. Hardie notes Bosanquet's interpretation in *Aristotle's Ethical Theory*, 2nd edn, (Oxford: Clarendon Press, 1980), p. 340.]

thus forfeit all possibility of understanding the nature of an activity which is neither semi-political on the one hand, nor "individualistic" on the other; and any reference to the negative conditions of legislative and administrative operations we are therefore inclined to regard as blasphemy against man's social possibilities as a whole.

(iv) But if we take the point of view just suggested, we can conceive how the working of the State proper, as society armed with force, has in it a negative element, without being driven by a false antithesis to ascribe all fertile and positive achievement to "individualistic" factors. The true terminology would be to take the ultimate achievements we have referred to as the fullest examples of true social activity, understanding that they are at once ultra-social as being above all compulsory group arrangements, and ultra-individual as being beyond the aspect of exclusiveness, which, however falsely, clings to the current conception of individuality. It is easy to grasp that in the profoundest sense it is this ultra-social and also ultra-individual level of life which represents the highest fulfilment at once of society and of the individual. And below it, but belonging to the same general line of progress, is the whole enormous complex of "social" co-operation, which is associated with the State in very various degrees of indirectness. And both of these belong, strictly speaking, neither to the State, nor yet to the private person who hugs his privateness.

If we apprehend the phenomena in this light, a degree of negativity in State action follows at once from its being that form of social self-expression which is inevitably mixed with compulsion.

(α) To begin with the simplest point, which is really decisive of the whole question. It is absolutely certain that morality and religion cannot be enforced by the State. The thing is a contradiction in terms. This case must not be disregarded because it is so familiar. It means that the most powerful of all social and human motives cannot be directly controlled or moulded by the public power as such. It may be urged that they can be "promoted"; but that is another question, and falls within what we shall say below.[15]

---

[15]See p. 25.

To illustrate the absurdities that spring from disregarding this truth, we may notice the pessimistic complaint that the basis of society as now arranged is not ethical, in the sense that material success does not correspond to moral merit and social service. Now to make this a complaint depends upon ignoring the necessary opposition between the nature of the power of the State and the nature of the good life which is its ultimate end. To attempt to assign material success in proportion to true merit and social service would be flatly self-contradictory. Material success belongs to a certain sort of career which displays a certain definite sort of capacity and utility. The distribution of it depends, on the whole, upon the principle "the tools to him who can use them," which is on the whole, under any and every possible economic system, a socially useful principle. But no one will be blind enough to deny that if we are to speak of the truest and greatest social service, the first rank belongs to the great poets or the great religious teachers. And the suggested apportionment would have the effect that these men would be crushed with colossal fortunes, or, under any system, with great material responsibilities, which would at once be fatal to their special form of life, and would also probably have disastrous effects on society. The relation of external means to spiritual ends is much more subtle than this; and even the rashest devotee of mere ethical justice must surely be revolted by the idea that the best – the spiritually strongest – is to have the easiest and pleasantest lot.[16] If we look at the analogous case of physical strength, we ourselves should scorn to adopt the principle assumed in the complaint, supposing us to be apportioning burdens for a mountain climb or a campaign. The fact that the goodness of the best has a certain deep underlying relation to external success,[17] in as far as goodness is the nature of things, further demonstrates the subtlety of the problem, but does not justify the direct relation desiderated by the complaint.[18]

---

[16]This idea is the basis of the complaint I am discussing. If the doctrine were that the greatest success is the heaviest burden and *therefore* belongs to the spiritually best, that would rest on an opposite principle, akin to the one to which I am now appealing.

[17]See previous note. Goodness certainly exercises material power, but not necessarily in the way of *personal* success.

[18]The paradox may be illustrated by the fate of the founder of Christianity. We see, there, the two extremes united, the immediate apparent failure of the best, along with the great-

(β) Further, then, every negative, of course, has a positive side; and the fact that the action of the State, being confined to externals,[19] cannot directly promote its spiritual end, does not mean what has been called administrative nihilism. The problem is one familiar in various degrees throughout the whole of life, especially to all who are or make themselves responsible for the lives of others. It is that of the evocation of spiritual good by dealing with external circumstance; and the solution of the problem is in general terms that such evocation must be indirect. We are aware of the dangers of parasitism,[20] and of the subtle and easily disconcerted nature of those external conditions – we may take as examples bodily health, comfortable homes, effective income – which are most akin to spiritual goods, and are therefore the least capable of being maintained by the agency of compulsion.[21] All this experience gives rise, in the minds of those who most fully appreciate it, to the paradox of social reform, in which practical necessity corroborates our theory of the State. Perhaps I may quote from a writing in which I have dealt with the matter more in detail. "Our common purpose is the excellence of human souls: the only means to this purpose which as social reformers we can handle lies in legal provisions and acts of public and private administration, which cannot directly affect anything at all except external circumstances. Our purpose, therefore, can only be promoted indirectly, and for that reason, the greatest skill and the finest adjustment are needed in the handling of projects of reform. Simply to *do* in every case what you desire to *see done* is a policy that frustrates itself."[22]

(γ) Finally, this position may be illustrated by the general de facto relation of the content of State action in the way of social amelioration to what I have here called social action in contrast to the action of the State. As I have pointed out elsewhere in greater detail,[23] and as the most ex-

---

est material influence that any individual in history has ever exerted.

[19] In the special sense explained, ch. viii, sect. 4.

[20] Ch. ii, sect. 2, iii.

[21] Ch. viii, sect. 5.

[22] *The Social Criterion* (London: J. Blackwood, 1907).

[23] ["Individual and Social Reform,"] *Essays and Addresses*, 2nd edn, (London: Swan Sonnenschien, 1891), pp. 24–47. (In the language which I now think more correct, Individual as used in that essay = pure social, and "Social" = social mixed with compulsion.)

treme of recent proposals for the increase of State action admit and maintain,[24] the content of legislation and administration with a view to the public good, the inventive, experimental, creative element, is almost entirely supplied by one or other of the forms of social action which are not due to the initiative of the State. The relation on the whole is like that by which a tree makes its wood, or a living body deposits its skeleton. The work of the State is de facto for the most part "endorsement" or "taking over" – setting its *imprimatur*, the seal of its force, on what more flexible activities or the mere progress of life have wrought out in long years of adventurous experiment or silent growth. True social work, independent of the public power, is the laboratory of social invention. The taking over of social inventions by the State is something like the taking over of a private business by a limited company, and there are analogous results for good and evil. The introduction of State socialism would be a gigantic taking over of this kind. We are not now discussing the advantages or disadvantages on the whole of such taking over on the large scale. We are only pointing out that in detail the normal course of improvement starts from origination by pure social invention, and passes subsequently, if at all, into adoption by the State. Of course it is not meant that the representatives of the State are incapable of invention and adaptation. But there is a mass of experience to corroborate the plain theoretical inference that what is distinctive and normal in State action, as it cannot be the direct enforcement of good life, so is not primarily the power of invention, adaptation, fine adjustment in the promotion of it.

See also [my] paper in the *Sociological Review*, [vol. 2,] April, (1909), [pp. 109–26,] "The Majority Report of the Poor Law Commission, 1909."

[24]"Minority Report of Poor Law Commission, 1909," xii, E. There are innumerable examples in social work of the relation in question. Such are Case papers, Children's Care Committees (I have shown the history of this example, and its significance, at length in the paper in the *Sociological Review*), health visiting, friendly visiting, residential homes for the feeble-minded, vacation schools for children, workmen's dwellings, labour colonies. Each of these has behind it a long and interesting history of pure social effort and invention well worth writing down in a more specialised work than the present. [Bosanquet was a critic of the minority report, which supported more radical forms of welfare provision. Sidney and Beatrice Webb were the force behind the minority report; Helen and Bernard Bosanquet endorsed the majority view.]

(δ) It is not denied that the organs of State can learn and borrow the methods of indirect self-subordination to spiritual ends. The gist of our whole contention is that these methods are just what it has to learn, and to rely upon, so far as it passes beyond the nature of the "Rechtsstaat"[25] – the mere maintenance of an order according to law. This necessity is imposed upon it by the same characteristic which is its *raison d'être*, the need for the expression of the end of life through force as well as in spiritual form, and the harder it is to discern this factor amid the wealth of the functions which it assumes to-day, the more fatal it is to fail in discerning it. The end of the State, we repeat, is assuredly good life or the excellence of souls; but for a power which deals primarily with the compulsory arrangement of externals, and for all of us so far as in our degree we have power over externals affecting others, the only path to that end lies in very fine adjustments directed to eliciting what *ex hypothesi*[26] they cannot produce.[27]

3. *The theory of the State is held to be too intellectualist*

The philosophical crusade against "intellectualism" cannot be properly dealt with as an annexe to another subject. But it is undoubtedly affecting the theory of the State, and so far we must indicate an attitude towards it.

(i) A great movement, we may briefly suggest, seems to have fused itself with a great fallacy. Europe is full to-day of the ethical and democratic demand for real progress, guided by the actual interests and emotions of mankind; for a future to be moulded by and for humanity.[28]

---

[25] [A *Rechtsstaat* is a legal state – a state whose actions are based solely on law.]

[26] [*ex hypothesi*: by hypothesis.]

[27] I might be challenged on the great example of elementary education. Surely here, it might be urged, the State has originated, and rightly made universal by compulsion, a vast positive spiritual good. I am most unwilling to seem in any degree, even the slightest, to disparage our public education. But I suppose it did begin by standardising to a very commonplace standard, "an education contrived by clerks for a nation of working-men," and is very slowly being dragged into the right path by public protest, social experiment, and, no doubt, the energy of the best officials. The vast blunders of our early public hygiene, which the promoters of a new (or old) type of city are just attempting to remedy, are another striking case.

[28] The force of this movement, for bad as well as for good, must be apparent to anyone who so much as glances at the literary matter exposed for sale in a Continental town.

With it there comes from many quarters, supported by strange alliances, a distrust of the highly intellectual consciousness. We have had it from Schopenhauer, imported from the east, in John Henry Newman, and in Mr Kidd, no less than in Professor William James and H. Bergson.[29] Now a movement like this, of course, is not founded on a mere illusion. It is based, and feels itself to be based, on something essential, and something which has, say, since Rousseau, been gaining ground, in the self-recognition of humanity. There is in it something of an insurrection of the powers of earth against an intellectual Olympus, of the revolution portrayed by Victor Hugo, in which Jupiter was to kneel before Pan.[30] But its value for theory must depend on its interpreters. And in one crucial point – a technical but fundamental point – the most prominent of them have led it into an impasse, the great fallacy of which I spoke.[31]

(ii) In the first edition of this book I already called attention to the extraordinary treatment of identity and difference by the imitation theorists; a treatment having at least a pronounced tendency to split identity from difference, repetition from novelty, imitation from invention; with the result of setting up a barrier between the normal intellectual process and such activities as progress and creativeness. Since that time the tendency has become more emphatic, and wide acceptance has been ac-

---

[29]It must be remembered that Mr F.H. Bradley, in the *Principles of Logic* (Oxford: Oxford University Press, 1883), indicated the need for some such suspicion. [F.H. Bradley (1846–1924) was a leading British Idealist; Arthur Schopenhauer (1788–1860) insisted that consciousness is simply an instrument of our will; Cardinal J.H. Newman (1801–1890) also criticized intellectualist views of consciousness, stressing the role of faith. Benjamin Kidd (1858–1916) was known for his *Theory of Social Evolution* (1884); William James (1842–1910) was an American philosopher and psychologist, and was one of the founders of American pragmatism; Henri Bergson (1849–1941) was a French philosopher who arrived at views similar to James' on some matters, especially regarding the nature of science; both analyse consciousness and will in some detail.]

[30]Compare Kant's attitude to Rousseau, ch. ix, sect. 2 below, and see Victor Hugo, I believe in the *Légende des Siècles*: "Je suis Pan – Jupiter, aux genoux." [Victor Hugo (1802–1885), author of *Les Misérables*, was an prominent French literary figure in the nineteenth century.]

[31]The fallacy lies in the notion that the principle of the intelligence is abstraction and bare identity. Pragmatism, as a world-movement, I take to be the popular mind revolting against the results of this error, and, while retaining it, correcting them by a counter-error.

corded to a philosophy which rests upon the assumption that the intelligence has for its province only what is covered by the principle of identity construed as tautology;[32] that life, novelty, creativeness, are incompatible with its nature, and, that intelligence, consequently, is powerless to identify itself with freedom or with creative progress.

(iii) We are thus brought into the presence of a curious form of agnosticism. Life, volition, immediate experience become, as it were, a Kantian thing-in-itself. For in as far as mind finds articulate utterance or expression it departs – so the argument runs – from its self-complete and concrete being. And like all Agnosticism, this readily turns to pessimism. For pessimism is at hand whenever we are led to suppose that the

---

[32]In M. Bergson's philosophy this attitude is plainly fundamental. It is true that philosophy for him would escape from the narrowness of science, but in doing so, and in seeking its intuition it would also escape from the essential principle of the intelligence. *Essai sur les données immédiates de la conscience* (Paris: F. Alcan, 1889), p. 158: "Le principe de l'identité est la loi absolue de notre conscience," *L'Évolution Créatrice* (Paris: F. Alcan, 1907), p. 218: "L'intelligence a pour fonction essentielle de lier le même au même, et il n'y a d'entièrement adaptable au cadres de nôtre intelligence que les faits qui se repètent." The language plainly echoes that of M. Tarde (see e.g. *Les Lois de l'imitation*, 14), and it is obvious that M. Bergson, at least only looks for identity in difference in the immediate experience which he calls *durée*. Professor William James, in *A Pluralistic Universe*, [(The Hibbert lectures of 1909) (London: Longman's, Green & Co., 1909)] practically adopts Bergson's phraseology and point of view, actually attributing a logic of identity, in the sense of eristic tautology, to Mr Bradley (ibid., p. 211) though well aware of Hegel's usage (ibid., ch. iii), to which it is surely plain that Mr Bradley assents. It is interesting to compare the culmination of this view, reiterated by Bergson, with the outcome of an organic conception of identity. The doctrine constantly repeated in *Évolution Créatrice* is that "L'intelligence est charactérisée par une incomprehension naturelle de la vie" (p. 179). Put beside this, e.g., Caird's *Philosophy of Kant*, ii. 530 [loc. cit., note 11]: "So far from its being true that an organic unity is something which we cannot understand it would be nearer the truth to say that we can understand nothing else," cf. Hegel, [*The Logic of Hegel*, trans., William Wallace, 2nd edn (Oxford: Clarendon Press, 1892) translated from the *Encyclopedia of Philosophical Science*] p. 216.

It may be interesting on the whole subject of this Introduction to cite Hegel's general judgment. "All the charges of narrowness, hardness, meaninglessness, which are so often directed against thought from the quarters of feeling and immediate perception, rest on the perverse assumption that thought acts only as a faculty of abstract identification" (Hegel, 1892, loc. cit., sect. 115).

determinate is the derivative and the secondary, and that the best experience and the true inwardness of life are unutterable.

The effect of such an attitude on the theory of the State is easy to see. We may contrast it, for example, with the tone of Hegel's words. "It is just freedom that is the self of thought; one who repudiates thought and talks of freedom knows not what he is saying."[33] This is because what thought means for him is just identity realised in difference;[34] the breaking down of barriers, the fusion of inner and outer, old and new, oneself and the other. But if an immediate experience of which intelligence is a secondary phenomenon, is set up as the thing-in-itself, then all explicit organisation is discredited and degraded. The difficulty is not so much that social analysis is enlarged by tracing back the social interests and feelings to instincts which have a long biological history behind them. Plato would not have objected to this, and in fact does a good deal of it himself. It is rather that in this analysis[35] a great deal of the actual content of social – still more of supersocial – life, simply disappears. We are left with a foundation which has no superstructure.

All this fatal alternative, not the analysis of instinct and emotion, but the omission of organised ideas from the analysis of the social mind, springs, technically speaking, from the postulate that identity is the principle of the intelligence, together with the conception of identity as tautology, or as one with the similarity presented in repetition. Instead of believing that "ideas have hands and feet," we are taught to conceive of them as static systems, which can only represent what is alive by entering into a rapid succession like that of the pictures in a cinematograph. Whatever is not tautological becomes *ex hypothesi* irrational.

---

[33]Cited ch. ix, sect. 2, below.

[34][The idea of "identity in difference" is the core of Bosanquet's notion of a concrete universal. Whereas an "abstract universal" is a common feature that we have uncovered in many different things, a concrete universal is a whole or universal that arises out of systematic relation of concrete or specific things.]

[35]Mr [William] McDougall's *Introduction to Social Psychology*, [(London: Methuen, 1908)] for example, is full of interest, and traces the origin of many types of feeling and activity which, in a sense, appear in human society. But the actual structure of a society is simply not there at all.

(iv) If we abandon that indispensable postulate, the alternative between reason and the true inner life falls to the ground. An idea may be held, as the greatest thinkers have held it, to be the intensest and the most concrete just because the most highly organised phase of mental concentration, which maintains in its complex the interest and emotion due to its content. And the realisation of an idea is the essence of what we mean by volition; and therefore we have in the State at once a conception which serves as an adjustment of all adjustments, and also, in this conception, a standing will.

I believe that it could be shown that views of the type here advocated not only give the truest interpretation of social forces and processes, but have in the recent past proved the most fruitful guide and inspiration of social improvement. I hope to establish this more completely in a future work; but it seems desirable to take this opportunity of drawing attention to such an expression as that of Professor William James,[36] "a rationalistic philosophy that indeed may call itself religious, but that keeps out of all definite touch with concrete facts and joys and sorrows." I do not think that the chapter from which this sentence is taken could have been written by any man who had at all reflected on the nature of social work and the influences that have inspired it in the English-speaking world during the past half-century.[37]

I am convinced, then, that the ancient theory of the State can only be strengthened and amplified by the wealth of modern experience. And little as the present work can claim to deal with the whole province of recent State development and activity, I believe that, resting on a tradi-

---

[36][William James,] *Pragmatism* [:*A New Name for some Old Ways of Thinking* (New York: Longman's, Green, 1907)], Lecture I. T.H. Green is mentioned in this connection.

[37]There is more human nature and insight into human experience in the *Prolegomena to Ethics*, [loc. cit., note 11] than in any philosophical writing of similar or later date, except Mr Bradley's *Ethical Studies*, [(London: Henry S. King, 1876); see p. 2, note 1, above for full reference] and its influence on practice has been enormous. It is an extraordinary thing that hostile critics like Professor James never at all commit themselves, except by the most fragmentary reference, to deal with any actual human achievement or utterance; while those whom they criticise deal, one might fairly say, with nothing else. Before dealing with the absolute, for instance, why not deal with society? It is a problem of the same type, but nearer current experience, and we find in the critic no mention of it.

tion derived from thinkers who have been the sanest and profoundest students of civilised life, it affords a serviceable clue to the interpretation of such developments.

II. How the Theory Stands in 1919

1. *"Then all the old things were true"*
This is the overwhelming impression which the events of the last five years have left upon my mind. So far as it is possible for facts to affirm ideas, all the simple truths which we learned in our youth are brought home to us afresh to-day. It *is*, then, only spiritual good that is real and stable; earthly and material aims *are* delusive and dangerous, and the root of strife. This is the obvious and simple explanation of what has been happening. By spiritual goods we mean such as can, by material goods such as cannot, be shared by others without our portion being diminished. An immense fabric of civilisation, with its pride and policy mainly directed upon material prosperity, invited, according to all that our teachers have told us, disaster proportional to its magnitude. It would have been absurd, on general grounds, to prophesy in detail and as with certainty. There were counter-influences, as there are to-day. And the evil might have confined itself to the more subtle and enduring shapes in which it is always with us. But, in fact, the hazard was recognised in principle; and no one, as it seems to me, should have been seriously astonished when the calamity burst upon us. If there was any truth in the higher things which Christian and Pagan alike had professed to believe, we were walking *per ignes suppositos*.[38] The overwhelming impression, I repeat, has been "Why, all the old simple things are true"; frightfully and incredibly true.

Therefore nothing seemed and seems more astonishing than the amazement and resentment which the course of events has evoked in

---

[38]The author has discussed problems relating to the State in the light of events since 1914 in "Patriotism in the Perfect State," (in *The International Crisis*, Milford, 1915) in several essays in *Social and International Ideals* (London: Macmillan, 1917), especially "On the Function of the State in Promoting the Unity of Mankind," and "The Wisdom of Naaman's Servants," and in *Some Suggestions in Ethics* (London: Macmillan, 1918). See Index on War. [*per ignes supposito*: literally, through an illusory fire.]

many minds. Without any ridiculous pretension to superiority of foresight, it still seems natural to exclaim, "Why, did you not know it must
come, one way or another?" And therefore the setting to work, like an
African medicine-man in an epidemic, to smell out and denounce the individuals whose witchcraft is responsible for the mischief, presents itself
not only as a theoretical error but as a moral evasion. For the black
magic is in all of us.

> In tragic life, God wot,
> No villain need be! passions spin the plot,
> We are betrayed by what is false within.[39]

No doubt there are plenty of bad people, and some nations have de-
luded themselves, it would seem, with especial thoroughness. But there
are not enough "bad" people or nations to account for the evil. It is much
more truly the simple and natural result of ordinary people like ourselves
co-operating unintelligently in our commonplace aims. Unintelligently –
because these aims have a sound and necessary side; but the mischief
comes from our translating them in practice into purposes which make
our gain another's loss. Our natural interests and innate patriotism will
by themselves mislead us. They need some inspiration and some discipline to make the world safe for humanity. It is not the State, nor Sovereignty, nor merely the Germans nor the Kaiser, who made the war.[40] It is
all of us, pursuing our mingled aims, which take no account of others,
and which, apart from due subordination of means to ends, must lead us
into collision. Under the influence of material aims you can misuse and
misinterpret the State, as you can the family or the shop. But *abusus non
tollit usum.*[41]

---

[39][From Meredith's *Modern Love* (1862) st. 43. George Meredith (1828–1909) was an
English poet and novelist.]

[40][In a famous attack on Bosanquet's theory, L.T. Hobhouse insisted that the Hegelian-
inspired view of the state was an underlying cause of German militarism and World War
I. See Hobhouse, *The Metaphysical Theory of the State* (London: Allen and Unwin,
1918).]

[41][*abusus non tollit usum*: abuse is no argument against proper use.]

2. *The State and War*

The theory of the State,[42] as I understand it, is primarily the outcome of Greek life and thought, and has found its most congenial soil in English and American experience.[43] It is true that a great genius in Germany was beforehand with us in appreciating Greek political ideas and in divining those which English life was destined to intensify. But their further growth is due to thinkers versed in Anglo-Saxon self-government, or inspired by the Italian *risorgimento*.[44]

I will set down shortly and positively how I understand the matter, not spending words on controversy. For after all it is the positive that signifies, and must in the end be decisive.

What I take the theory to tell us[45] is first of all that States are diverse embodiments of the human spirit, in groups territorially determined through historical trial and failure. They are members of an ethical family of nations – so Plato and Hegel affirm at least of the European complex, which naturally filled their view. They are characterised – it is Mazzini's[46] well-known doctrine – by individual missions[47] or functions in which each state proffers its characteristic contribution to human life.

---

[42]This phrase has been objected to, as if it indicated a solipsism of the State. Such an interpretation appears to me to be a mere grammatical blunder. The idiom is one which indicates that a term is being used strictly in accordance with its connotation; and it is remarkable that those who object to it impute to the State characteristics opposed to its connotation.

[43]Miss Follett's *The New State*, [(London: Longman's, Green, 1918)] to which I shall refer largely in what follows, does much to corroborate this assertion. [Mary Parker Follett (1868–1933) was an American social reformer, who today is interpreted as a theorist of management. Follett criticised hierarchical organizations, lines of authority and competition, endorsing integrated, participatory forms of decision making.]

[44][*Risorgimento*: meaning "rising again," was the name for the nationalist movement for Italian unification that resulted in the Kingdom of Italy in 1861.]

[45]This passage is almost reproduced from ["The Function of the State in Promoting the Unity of Mankind," in] *Social and International Ideals*, [London: Macmillan, 1917], p. 275.

[46][Giuseppe Mazzini (1805–1872) was an Italian liberal nationalist, a champion of the *Risorgimento* and a republican.]

[47]It is also the word which I have used to describe the ethical unity of a Nation-state. P. 283 below.

It follows then that each of them has an analogous task within its territory as allotted by history, and so T.H. Green insists;[48] and the more completely each of them attains its proper object of giving free scope to the capacities of all persons within its territory, the easier it is for other States to do so. Obviously they are units in a world-wide co-operation. It is the essence of the theory that they must be so.

Sovereignty is a feature inherent in a genuine whole. It cannot be given or taken.

> The individual is sovereign over himself as far as he unifies the heterogeneous elements of his nature. Two people are sovereign over themselves in as far as they are capable of making one out of two. A group is sovereign over itself as far as it is capable of creating one out of several or many. A state is sovereign only as it has the power of creating one in which all are. Sovereignty is the power engendered by a complete interdependence becoming conscious of itself.[49]

It is a phenomenon of group life, and you cannot understand it by any other experience.

On these premises it is ridiculous to ask if sovereignty and the state are favourable to war. Plato already pointed out that war springs from that disease of the state which leads to policies of expansion. In order to reinforce the organisation of rights by other states, the main thing which each has to do is to perfect its own. Dissatisfied elements at home are the mainspring of cupidity abroad.[50]

On this question of the ultimate relation of the state to war a curious contradiction of thought prevails. There is a desire at once to depreciate the personality and influence of the state, and to exalt its moral responsibility. But the two are inseparable, and must vary together. It is plain where the truth lies. Our theory insists on the will and personality of the

---

[48][Thomas Hill Green, *Lectures on the*] *Principles of Political Obligation*, [with preface by Bernard Bosanquet (London: Longmans, Green, 1895), sect. 165.] p. 170.

[49]Follett, *The New State*, [loc. cit., note 43] p. 271.

[50]Cf J.W. Headlam in *Westminster Gazette*, July 31, 1917. *The Frankfurter Zeitung* on Herr von Bethmann-Hollweg: "There were always the great parties behind the throne, the agrarian fearful for their financial future, the military dreading the criticism of the Reichstag and the nation, the courtiers and intriguers with high protection behind them who had to be appeased and satisfied."

state, and with them on its moral responsibility. A state, like an individual, is responsible in respect of its functions and relations, and is bound, of course, so far as is consistent with its responsibilities or consequential upon them, to seek peace and ensue it. But what seems to me strangely neglected, in the parallel between the state and the law-abiding individual, is the possible posit of a state as a conscientious objector. Hitherto, indeed, the parallel has not held. Unquestionably in the absence of effective international law the right has had to be defended by force. But grant the basis of the parallel. What is the consequence?

As the individual must ultimately follow his conscience to the end, so the state, if it is to be morally responsible, must follow its own. It is the guardian of moral interests, and must be faithful to its duty. Merely suppose – and under some subtle disguise, some momentary intrigue, I cannot hold it inconceivable – a powerful self-styled league of nations agreeing to enforce or connive at some practice on the moral level of the slave-trade. Is it not plain that a liberty-loving nation would be bound to resist it to the last drop of its blood? It is always a possibility, in a word, though we trust a vanishing possibility, that the claims of mere life may at some certain time and place collide with the claims of a better life. Then every being and agency that is truly human, individual or collective, knows what it has to do. I believe in the League of Nations as the hope and refuge of mankind; but I do not believe that any moral being can divest itself of moral responsibility, or limit that responsibility's *ultima ratio*.[51]

What is however all-important in a theory of the state is to distinguish its moral obligations from those of the individual. And it is, I think, the attention which was paid in the present work[52] to this essential aspect of the problem that gave rise to an idea that I was denying the moral responsibility of the state. But, in reality, I was pleading in favour of the distinct recognition of the responsibility of every moral being, in accordance with its position and capacities, against an argument, formulated

---

[51][*Ultima ratio*: last resource.]

[52]See [below] p. 285ff.

by a high authority, which appeared to disregard this distinction, and so to neglect the essence of the problem.[53]

---

[53]It is a fortunate chance that the actual argument referred to has just been republished as the first of two essays by Henry Sidgwick [1838–1900] on *National and International Right and Wrong*, with a preface by Lord Bryce (London: George Allen & Unwin, 1919). Of course the discussion is interesting and suggestive. But except at the close of the first essay, where the idea of trusteeship is for a moment touched upon, the essence of the question appears to me, I confess, to escape consideration. The language employed is calculated to suggest that public morality is the total morality of statesmen's lives, and private morality that of the lives of other persons, and that political theory has maintained statesmen to be exempt, in their total lives, from those standards of morality which are accepted by other persons. Reiterated expressions such as "the exemption of the statesman from moral restraint in his conduct" (p. 26) appear intended, with a really regrettable sophistry, to insist on this impression. It was in criticism of this argument, though without mention of the essay, which was before me in some journal to which I have lost the reference, that I paid detailed attention in ch. xi, sect. 7 to the distinction between the kinds of action possible for a state and for any one man or woman respectively. They are not in the least *in pari materia*, [see note 10] and to suggest that they are so with respect to the conduct of the representative of a state when acting on its behalf, seeing that he has at every step to consider not his but its resources, abilities, and enormous context of varied obligations, certain to be in some degrees and respects inconsistent with each other, seems to me, I confess, to be simply darkening counsel.

It should be noted that Sidgwick, in the end, gives away the whole case against departures from ordinary morality, as such, in public action, by admitting that they are justifiable if and when demanded by the general welfare of mankind, and objectionable only when committed on behalf of sectional interests, having of course the nation-state in mind. A readiness to adopt this point of view is characteristic, as his argument plainly states, of utilitarianism, for which moral rules are nothing but a means to the happiness of mankind. To most of us, therefore, the conflict of moral obligations and the inevitable sacrifice of some among them, appears a more and not a less serious matter than it does to him. For *we* think that what we are accustomed to call moral goodness is a good thing in itself. Nevertheless, we observe that his doctrine recognises, although, one must say it, crudely and clumsily, a consideration which, as we have seen in the text, is irrefragable. No man in any position can do and leave undone precisely what he would like, so to speak, to do and not to do, if he were free to give full effect to his customary moral ideas. Everyone knows that he must not tell all truths (compare [Robert Browning's] *The Ring and the Book*, "How look a brother in the face and say–") nor endeavour to right all wrongs, nor carry out all promises. "…Though it were to his own hindrance?" Yes, but even so there are limits. Every man, not to speak of every great organisation, involves others, and must take account of the consequences of his acts. And in acting for a huge organisation, whether political or other, these limitations on veracity, justice, and good

The fact is, that obloquy has been drawn upon the theory of the state in particular, by the exaggerated application to it, no doubt often in sinister interests, of a principle which is universal, and has no special concern with the state or with international politics. It is the principle of the conflict of duties, and it applies to all modes of life without exception, but with peculiar emphasis to all great organisations and to all operations on a large scale. To say that the interests of the state justify everything in the way of departures from current personal morality is of course sheer nonsense. Nothing justifies everything; but on the other hand, we fall equally into nonsense if we forget that everything justifies something. A woman who becomes pregnant has rights which she had not before. A coal miner, who would give me half his coal if I were his neighbour and starved with cold, will back his organisation in keeping the whole country shivering. Both Free Trader and Protectionist will advocate measures which spell ruin to individuals, whom, if they could, they would compensate at their personal expense. Hardly any reform or improvement can be undertaken which will not injure somebody, whom its advocates would admit themselves bound in morality to see unhurt if it were possible, which it is not, to do so.

It is futile to urge self-sacrifice in such cases in order that individuals may be spared. The reply comes at once, "I can do no other. It is not I who would be sacrificed; it is my mates, my class, the good cause, the unity and welfare of mankind so far as we grasp it and are working for it. In these great operations of great organisations some individuals must be injured. Our duty to the cause conflicts with our personal duty to them, and is superior to it."[54] The principle is recognised of course throughout the whole of private life. Duties are relative to positions; I

---

faith (I take Sidgwick's cases) become more and more imperative. All we can use for our guide, and all we really need, is devotion to supreme values, common sense, and bona-fides. [*The Ring and the Book* by Robert Browning is an over 20,000-line poem, published from 1868 to 1869; it is based on a Roman murder trial.]

[54]The verification has come sooner and more clearly than I could have expected in the great railway strike. What I urge with all possible emphasis is that the right moral should be drawn. It is *not* that the railwaymen are in principle wrong; it is, that if you think they *can* be right, you are barred from saying that the state which goes to war *must* be wrong. [Note added in] October, 1919.

may not and must not do what you must and may. It is quite right to say that the aim should never be sectional but always controlled by a regard for the welfare of mankind. But this makes no difference of principle to the conflict of duties. There is no doubt some harm, some breach of moral obligation, which it will save us from committing. But there will always be much that the conflict of obligations renders inevitable. The cause of the conflict lies in the many-sidedness of life, and the inability of any moral being, whether person or organism, to do justice to all its sides at once. The collision of duties will not be removed by the recognition of so general an aim as the welfare of humanity. The ultimate differences rest on *bona-fide* convictions, which represent true and genuine aspects, of the nature of that welfare and the next steps to its achievement. The fundamental rule of morality is to be equal to the situation; but no finite being can be completely equal to any situation.

Returning to the case of the state, we may consider the unification of Italy. No one would deny that here the aim was in harmony with the general happiness of mankind if not directly consisting in it. But this did not prevent a conflict of duties in which things were done which were repugnant, so to speak, to the customary private consciences of the doers, but which, I take it, they did not on the whole wish undone.[55]

The problem is one inherent in human life, and it is foolish to make capital out of it either in favour of the state or against it. What is necessary is to distinguish carefully the position and true functions of all moral beings, but especially of powerful organisations, and to strive that no more harm may be done than is inevitable. We shall remember that the moral burden laid upon their agents is terrible, and if it were possible to strike a balance in such things, it is likely that even in private morality, in courage, in strenuousness, truth-telling of the deepest kind, gener-

---

[55]Persano [the Sardinian Admiral] sent his Diary in MS. to Azeglio [Sardinian ex-minister and envoy to Bologna] and asked his advice on publishing it. Azeglio referred to Cavour's saying, "If we did for ourselves what we are doing for Italy, we should be sad blackguards," and begged Persano to let his secrets be secrets, saying that since the partition of Poland no confession of such "colossal blackguardism had been published by any public man." [Charles Alan] Fyffe, *History of Modern Europe* [(New York: H. Holt and Company, 1896) ch.] ii, [p.] 292 note.

osity, sympathy, devotion to humanity, they would be found greatly to surpass the common run of mankind.

3. *The State and Pluralism*

"In the face of the growth of Syndicalism in every direction – it is no longer venturesome to assert that the state is dead."

This quotation from an unnamed author opens the treatment of pluralism in the most sane and brilliant of recent works on political theory.[56] I preface a brief reference to the views developed in this treatise by an observation which vindicates for our doctrine the right to hold itself continuous with them.

The authoress sympathises with the reaction of the pluralists "against the sovereignty which our legal theory postulates,"[57] otherwise spoken of as the Austinian conception of sovereignty. This, she agrees with the pluralists, and, in this sense, the conception of the absolute monistic state, must go. But I do not think that the writers whom she has in mind – her own judgment I believe to be sound – are thoroughly aware of the diametrical and fundamental contrast between Austinian sovereignty,[58] the sovereignty that is contemplated by legal experts, and the sovereignty contemplated by such a theory as ours. Their history and character are altogether discrepant. Austinian sovereignty is based on the idea of force; sovereignty in our sense is based on the will of the whole.[59] "Sovereignty resides only in the organised whole acting qua organised whole."[60] Therefore it is only absolute in as far as the groups contribute to it, and we have a perfect right to such developments of the conception of sovereignty as appear in the work I am referring to. And for my part I

---

[56]Follett, *The New State*, [loc. cit., note 43; p. 258].

[57]Ibid., p. 272.

[58][John Austin (1790–1859) was an English jurist and legal scholar; his command theory of the law – according to which laws are commands of the sovereign – was a forerunner of modern day positivism, which clearly demarcates law from custom, morality and sentiment. See Austin's *The Province of Jurisprudence Determined* (1832) with an introduction by H.L.A. Hart (London: Weidenfeld and Nicolson, 1954).]

[59]"Will not force is the basis of the state" is T.H. Green's well-known principle. [Lecture G (sects. 113–136), *Principles of Political Obligation*, loc. cit., note 48].

[60]P. 253 below.

propose to claim them as elucidations of my doctrine, without in the least impeaching the author's unquestionable originality.

Sound political theory, in her eyes, must be founded on the psychological understanding of group-life, an understanding which, when acquired, will take shape in a new knowledge and practice of the art of living together – an art, she considers, which as yet can hardly be said to exist. The analogy of the herd or crowd, the influence of imitation, the communication or recognition of similarities, throw no light at all on the true social group, which is always an affair of the integration of differences, and may be typified, not by a herd or crowd, but by a first-rate committee, which genuinely busies itself in creating ideas through co-operative contributions of thought, and not by compromise. For compromise means surrender and diminution of ideas; but integration or creation means the inclusion of what all have to offer in a more complete conception which becomes the collective will.

Thus the social unit is still the individual; but the individual, the bearer of the will, is not given at starting, not anyone you can find and refer back to; he is the member of the group, determined by his relations, and evoked in his creative activities. He is, to use an old expression, not a datum but a problem. The aim of politics is to find and realise the individual.

What, then, is sovereignty? "The sovereignty of the people is that which they actually create."[61]

Five people produce a collective idea, a collective will. That will becomes at once an imperative upon those five people. It is not an imperative upon anyone else. On the other hand no one else can make imperatives for those five people. It has been generated by the social process, which is a self-sufficing all-inclusive process. The same process which creates the collective will creates at the same time the imperative of the collective will. It is absolutely impossible to give self-government. No one has the right to give it; no one has the power to give it. Group A *allows* group B to govern itself? This is an empty permission unless B has *learned how* to govern itself. Self-government must always be grown.[62]

---

[61] Follett, *The New State*, p. 274.
[62] Ibid., p. 275.

Political philosophers talk of the state, but there is no state till we make it.[63] The philosophy of the matter is found in William James' recognition that states of consciousness can separate and combine themselves freely and keep their identity unchanged while forming part of simultaneous fields of experience of wider scope.[64] Each individual is not only himself but the state.

This conception leads up to the doctrine of – not the *unified* but – the *unifying* state. Granting the intense importance of neighbourhood groups and occupational groups, to which a detailed treatment is devoted, yet the unifying force cannot possibly stop when these are reached. The power developed within the group does not cease with the formation of the group.[65] It must carry you on to a unify*ing* sovereignty.

In considering any form of "Functionalism" we have to remember that functions – even all a man's functions taken one by one – do not exhaust a man's nature without remainder. "The State will never get the whole of a man by his trying to divide himself into parts." "The State cannot be composed of groups, because no group, nor any number of groups, can contain the whole of me, and the ideal State demands the whole of me." "My group uses me, and the whole of me is still left to give to the whole" – "vocational representation does not deal with men, it deals with masons and doctors." – "The whole of every man must go into his citizenship."[66]

> The true State must gather up every interest within itself. It must take over many loyalties and find how it can make them one. I have all these different allegiances. I should indeed lead a divided and therefore uninteresting life if I could not unify them.... The true state has my devotion because it gathers up into itself the various sides of me, is the symbol of my multiple self, is my multiple self brought to significance, to self-realisation. If you leave me with my plural selves you leave me in desolate places, my soul

---

[63] Ibid., p. 265.

[64] Ibid., pp. 264, 266. Cp. e.g., James, *A Pluralistic Universe*, [loc. cit., note 32] pp. 290–2. The author, if I understand her right, judges Hegel more justly than James did; and see F.H. Bradley, *Essays on Truth and Reality* [Oxford: Clarendon Press, 1914], p. 152.

[65] Follett, *The New State*, p. 285.

[66] Ibid., p. 291.

craving its meanings and its home. The home of my soul is in the State.[67]

The leading thought is that one organisation, one loyalty or sovereignty, within another, is not deducted from the latter, but enters into its foundation.[68] As an organisation and co-ordination of groups – primarily neighbourhood and occupational groups – the state becomes not less than it was before, but more and greater. Sovereignty is not a concession; it is a growth of inherent power. The form of organisation, indeed, has yet to work itself out. Democracy binds us to no rigid shape. Only the idea of the crowd is wholly a thing of the past. Some form of Federalism is strongly advocated by the author. But the citizen is to be directly a member of the state as such, not merely of a federated group. The constituent groups are not simply to replace the individuals, as bare particulars, operating by a majority, though now a majority of groups. We shall need a new individualism, vitalised through the groups. The member of a state will not be the unit of a crowd whether of persons or of groups, but the full individual, the many-sided activity, revealed and realised in the system of groups.

4. *The State and the League*

And the same principle demands, in the same spirit, the World-state or the League of Nations. The unifying activity cannot cease with the state, as it could not cease with the group. On such a principle, the hesitation which rightly accompanied the vision of a supreme and central force, levelling down the individualities of nations,[69] no longer has a *locus standi*;[70] the secret is integration of differences as opposed to the generalisation of similarities. The support of a thorough communal will throughout the participant countries is, as I have maintained before,[71] the presupposition or rather the essence and daily self-renewing genesis of a

---

[67]Ibid., p. 312.

[68]Cf. [Bosanquet] *Social and International Ideals*, [loc. cit., note 45], p. 281.

[69]Ibid., pp. 286, 292.

[70][*Locus standi* is a legal term referring to a "recognised position," an acknowledged right or claim, or a right to intervene, according to law. Prior to the First World War, some British parliamentarians held that Britain had a *locus standi* if Germany attacked France through Belgium.]

[71]Loc. cit.

world-will. On such a foundation, or as far as we can presume its beginning – for like all sovereignty it must be an actual growth – we may go forward with confidence. With such expectations we may say of the League of Nations what I said of it while the world's destiny still appeared to hang in the balance, words which I will venture to quote in the present context, as a summary of what springs from the theory of the present work in the year 1919.

Nationalism and Internationalism[72]

We see it so constantly; two ideas, both excellent, both, indeed, necessary. Yet in times of excitement they are set against each other, and instead of reinforcing each other, as of course, they ought, they become "Like two spent swimmers, that do cling together, and choke their art."[73]

It is heart-breaking to a student, whose business it is to see connexions, especially if he is under impeachment, however he may resent it, that he has championed the one to the rejection of the other.

And it is so simple. It is only to note how ideas grow; how they push forth the flower and fruit that were in them all along. Our nation, our country, our state – England, say; what has it always stood for to those who loved it right? For more things than I can tell; but for these at least, honesty, justice, liberty. Of course, we were stupid and ignorant, and often we thought that we alone stood for these; and, so thinking, we sinned, and took their name in vain. But for all that, we stood for them; we helped Greece and Italy, and admitted that we wronged America. "England" has always meant the cause of humanity; so has every nation, so far as it saw and fought for a true good. All saw the good differently; in the house of humanity are many mansions; but all saw some of it, not in themselves alone, and knew darkly that they were there to see it and to champion it.

Well; things are getting clearer now, and England begins to mean more definitely what it has always meant. Our best men and the world's best men throughout our crusaders' league tell us, "You must learn to accept limitations; to put up with things you may not like, and with more perhaps than you now anticipate." Of course, they are right, and those, if any, who think with me will follow them to the end. It is only to see and follow what England has always meant – honesty, justice, liberty; did we ever se-

---

[72]Published in the *Westminster Gazette*, August 20, 1918.

[73][Shakespeare, *Macbeth*, act 1, scene 2.]

riously mean that they were for us and for none else? Surely, never.

And now to be English means at least to belong to the British Commonwealth. It means, that is, all it ever did mean, and that, too; not less, but so infinitely more. To be Australian, too, and Canadian, and all them; they too mean to belong to the British Commonwealth, and they too mean all they meant before, and more, infinitely more.

And the further vistas open out, all expansions of the same meaning; to belong to the British Commonwealth will mean belonging to the League of Humanity; the great values and qualities are to display themselves and to show their full bearing for mankind. Is all this hostile to "the State"? Where did the question come from, "What is man's soul for?" and the answer, "To live well"? From the first great book on the State, did it not? Not the soul of Greek or Jew, but the soul of *man*. Sovereignty will find it hard to accept limitations? Hard, very likely; Sovereignty is there to do hard things. To find your own soul, in helping the soul of man; both of them are hard things; but easier together, surely, than apart. Are they in antagonism? I think not.

5. *Two reservations concerning* The New State

Finally, before parting with *The New State* two points appear to me to demand attention.

(i) The relative distinction between society and state is, I think, inherent and permanent. Society will always possess a stern and negative side, in which law will present itself as compulsion, however successfully a triumphant vitality may disguise and appear to supersede it. However much we may ameliorate the operations of criminal law, yet definitely to check the definite bad will as such, by a reaction expressly directed against it, that is, by punishment for punishment's sake,[74] will always be a civic necessity. And within the luxuriance of the highest social individuality there must always be, if its basis is to be healthy, the clear and iron will to determinate good and justice, which the legal and political fabric of the state will exist to sustain and to defend.

(ii) In the enthusiasm for the "new" art of living together something is not emphasised, which probably was so obvious to the author as not to demand notice, but which to my mind is fundamental. It is that social

---

[74]See *Some Suggestions in Ethics*, [London: Macmillan, 1918], ch. viii, "On the Growing Repugnance to Punishment."

life presupposes a guide and criterion beyond its current activities. No training in group-life will dispense with a direction of the social mind to the positive values which are not diminished by sharing; to beauty that is, to truth, and to religion. Aristotle was surely right when he made religion the ultimate aim and quintessence of civic life, and it is only devotion to these supreme values that can guide desire aright, and keep patriotism clean and sweet.[75]

The author, striving I think with some success to be all things to all men, goes far in disclaiming mysticism (to which the mind of the jurist is particularly averse), and in applying the name of psychology rather than metaphysic to the study of real unities. And all this may be simply a question of convenience in expression, so long as we do not forget, what I am sure that she remembers, that life for and in the supreme positive values is the safeguard of patriotism and the criterion of the social will, because it is the only source of abiding satisfaction, and the only sure preventive of cupidity.

---

[75]Cf. below, p. 292; *Social and International Ideals*, [loc. cit., note 45] p. 16; *The International Crisis*, [loc. cit., note 38] p. 132; and *The Principle of Individuality and Value*, [loc. cit., note 14] Lecture X, Appendix ii, "On the Perfecting of the Soul in Aristotle's Ethics."

THE PHILOSOPHICAL THEORY
OF THE STATE

CHAPTER I

RISE AND CONDITIONS
OF THE PHILOSOPHICAL THEORY OF THE STATE

1. First, it will be well to indicate, in a very few words what is implied in a "philosophical theory," as distinguished from theories which make no claim to be philosophical. The primary difference is that a philosophical treatment is the study of something as a whole and for its own sake. In a certain sense it may be compared to the gaze of a child or of an artist. It deals, that is, with the total and unbroken effect of its object. It desires to ascertain what a thing is, what is its full characteristic and being, its achievement in the general act of the world. History, explanation, analysis into cause and conditions, have value for it only in so far as they contribute to the intelligent estimation of the fullest nature and capabilities of the real individual whole which is under investigation. We all know that a flower is one thing for the geometrician, another for the chemist, another for the botanist, and another, again, for the artist. Now, philosophy can of course make no pretension to cope with any one of the specialists on his own ground. But the general nature of the task imposed upon it is this: aiding itself, so far as possible, by the trained vision of all specialists, to make some attempt to see the full significance of the flower as a word or letter in the great book of the world. And this we call studying it, as it is, and for its own sake, without reservation or presupposition. It is assumed, then, for the purpose of a philosophical treatment, that everything, and more particularly in this case the political life of man, has a nature of its own, which is worthy of investigation on its own merits and for its own sake. How its phases come into being, or what causes or conditions have played a part in its growth, are other questions well worthy of investigation. But the philosophical problem is rather to see our object as it is and to learn what it is, to estimate, so to

47

speak, its kind and degree of self-maintenance in the world, than to trace its history or to analyse its causation.

Yet such phrases as "what it is" and "for its own sake" must not mislead us. They do not mean that the nature of any reality which we experience can be appreciated in isolation from the general world of life and knowledge. On the contrary, they imply that when fully and fairly considered from the most thoroughly adequate point of view, our subject-matter will reveal its true position and relations with reference to all else that man can do and can know. This position and these relations constitute its rank or significance in the totality of experience, and this value or significance – in the present case, what the form of life in question enables man to do and to become – is just what we mean by its nature "in itself," or its full and complete nature, or its significance when thoroughly studied "for its own sake" from an adequate point of view. Further illustrations of the distinction between an adequate point of view and partial or limited modes of consideration, and of the relations between the former and the latter, will be found in the following chapter.

2. In a certain sense it would be true to say that wherever men have lived there has always been a "State." That is to say, there has been some association or corporation, larger than the family, and acknowledging no power superior to itself. But it is obvious that the experience of a State in this general sense of the word is not co-extensive with true political experience, and that something much more definite than this is necessary to awaken curiosity as to the nature and value of the community in which man finds himself to be a member.

Such curiosity has been awakened and sustained principally if not exclusively by two kindred types of associated life – the City-state of ancient Greece, and the Nation-state of the modern world. It will throw light on the nature of our subject if we glance rapidly at the characteristics to which it is due that political philosophy began in connection with the former, and revived in connection with the latter.

In considering the Greek city-states in connection with the birth of political philosophy, there are three points which press upon our attention: (α) the type of experience which they presented; (β) the type of mind which that experience implied; and (γ) the type of interpretation which such a mind elicited from such an experience.

(α) A Greek city-state presented a marked contrast to the modes of human association which prevailed in the non-Greek world. It differed from them above all things by its distinct individuality. No doubt there was a recognisable character in the life and conduct of Egypt or of Assyria, of Phoenicia or of Israel. But the community which has a youth, a maturity, and a decadence, as distinct as those of a single human being, and very nearly as self-conscious; which has a tone and spirit as recognisable in the words and bearing of its members as those of a character in a play; and which expresses its mind in the various regions of human action and endurance much as an artist expresses his individuality in the creations of his genius – such a community had existed, before the beginnings of the modern world, in the Greek City-state, and in the Greek City-state alone. A political consciousness in the strict sense was a necessary factor in the experience of such a commonwealth. The demand for "autonomy" – government by one's own law – and for "isonomy" – government according to equal law – though far from being always satisfied, was inherent in the Greek nature; and its strenuousness was evinced by the throes of revolution and the labours of legislation which were shaking the world of Greece at the dawn of history. The very instrument of all political action was invented, so far as we can see, by the Greeks. The simple device by which an orderly vote is taken, and the minority acquiesce in the will of the majority as if it had been their own – an invention no less definite than that of the lever or the wheel – is found for the first time as an everyday method of decision in Greek political life.

(β) Such a type of experience implies a corresponding type of mind. It is not surprising that science and philosophy should owe their birth to the genius from which politics sprang. For politics is the expression of reason in the relations that bind man to man, as science and philosophy are the expression of it in the relations which link together man's whole experience. The mind which can recognise itself practically in the order of the commonwealth, can recognise itself theoretically in the order of nature. And ultimately, though not at first (for curiosity is awakened by objects perceived in space and time before attention is turned to the very hinge and centre of man's own being), science passes into philosophy; and mind, and conduct, and the political consciousness, are themselves made objects of speculation. It has become a commonplace that this transference of curiosity from the outer to the inner – really, that is, from the partial to total world – took shape in the work of Socrates, who invested with the greatness of his own intelligence and character a movement which the needs of the age had rendered inevitable. And thus there arose the ethical and political philosophy of Plato and Aristotle, the successors of Socrates, just at the time when the distinctive political life of Greece was beginning to decay.

(γ) This philosophy, like all genuine philosophy, was an interpretation of the experience presented to it; and in this case the interpretation was due to minds which were themselves a part of the phenomena on which they reflected. Such minds, hostile as they may feel themselves to the spirit of the age, and however passionately they may cry out for reform or for revolution, are none the less its representatives; and their interpretation, though it may modify and even mutilate the phenomena, will nevertheless be found to throw the central forces and principles of the time into the clearest light. So Plato's negative treatment of the family, and of other elements which seem essential to Greek civilisation, was no bar to his grasping, and representing with unequalled force, the central principle of the life around him. The fundamental idea of Greek political philosophy, as we find it in Plato and Aristotle, is that the human mind can only attain its full and proper life in a community of minds, or more strictly in a community pervaded by a single mind, uttering itself consistently though differently in the life and action of every member of the community. This conception is otherwise expressed by such phrases as "the State is natural," i.e. is a growth or evolution, apart from which the end implied in man's origin cannot be attained; "the State is prior to the individual," i.e. there is a principle or condition underlying the life of the human individual, which will not admit of that life becoming what it has in it to be, unless the full sphere or arena which is constituted by the life of the State is realised in fact. The whole is summed up in the famous expression of Aristotle "Man is a creature formed for the life of the City-state." The working out of this idea, as we find it in Plato's commonwealth, is bizarre to our minds; but its difficulty really lies in its simplicity and directness; and there is no sound political philosophy which is not an embodiment of Plato's conception. The central idea is this: that every class of persons in the community – the statesman, the soldier, the workman – has a certain distinctive type of mind which fits its members for their functions, and that the community essentially consists in the working of these types of mind in their connection with one another, which connection constitutes their subordination to the common good. This working or adjustment obviously depends in the last resort on the qualities present in the innermost souls of the members of the community; and thus the outward organisation of society is really as it were a body which at every point and in every movement expresses the characteristics of a mind. We must not pause here to follow up the consequences of such a conception; but it will be seen at once, by those who reflect upon it, to imply that every individual mind must have its qualities drawn out in various ways to answer to – in fact, to constitute – the relations and functions which make up the community; and that in this sense every mind is a mirror or impression of the whole community from its own peculiar point of view. The ethical assumption or principle of Plato's conception is, that a healthy organisation of the commonwealth will involve, by a necessary connection, a healthy balance and adjustment of qualities in the individual soul, and vice versa. An attempt will be made to illustrate this principle further in the latter portion of the present work. The general nature of Plato's conception – the characteristic conception of Greek political philosophy – is all that concerns us here.

It is important to observe that during the very genesis of this philosophical conception of society, an antagonistic view was powerfully represented. The individual could not freely find himself in the community unless he was capable of repudiating it; the possibility of negation, as a logician might express it, is necessary to really significant affirmation. Thus we find in the very age of Plato and Aristotle the most startling anticipations of those modern ideas which seem diametrically opposed to theirs. We find the idea of nature identified not with the mature fullness, but with the empty starting point of life; we meet with the phenomena of vegetarianism, water-drinking, the reduction of dress to its minimum, in short, the familiar symptoms of the longing for the "return to nature," with all that it implies; we find law and political unity treated as a tissue of artifice and convention, and the individual disdaining to identify himself with the citizenship of a single state, but claiming to be a stranger in the city and a citizen of the world. To prove that these ideas were not without their justification, it is enough to point out that in some instances they were accompanied by a polemic against slavery, which, as a form of solidarity, was upheld in a qualified sense at least by Aristotle. The existence of this negative criticism is enough to show how distinctly the Greek intellect set before itself the fundamental problem of the relation between the individual and society, and of how high a quality was the bond of union which maintained this relation in such intimacy among minds of a temper so analytic.

3. Many writers have told the story of the change, which came over the mind of Greece when the independent sovereignty of its City-states became a thing of the past. For our purpose it is enough to draw attention to the fact that with this change the political or social philosophy of the great Greek time not only lost its supremacy, but almost ceased to be understood. From this period forward, till the rise of the modern Nation-states, men's thoughts about life and conduct were cast in the mould of moral theory, of religious mysticism and theology, or of jurisprudence. The individual demanded in the sphere of ethics and religion to be shown a life sufficing to himself apart from any determinate human society – a problem which Plato and Aristotle had assumed to be insoluble. Stoicism and Epicureanism, the earliest non-national creeds of the western world, triumphantly developed the ideas which at first, as we saw, were little more than a rebellion against the central Socratic philosophy. Cosmopolitanism, the conception of humanity, the idea of a "Society of Friends" – the Epicurean league – from which women were not excluded, and the precept of "not expecting from life more than it has to give," take the place of the highly individualised commonwealth, with its strenuous masculine life of war and politics, and its passionate temper which felt that nothing had been accomplished so long as anything remained undone.

With this change of temper in the civilised world there is brought into prominence a great deal of human nature which had not found expression through the immediate successors of Socrates. In the period between Aristotle and Cicero there is more than a whisper of the sound which meets us like a trumpet blast in the New Testament, "neither Jew nor Greek, barbarian nor Scythian, bond nor free." But the unworldliness which took final shape in Christianity was destined to undergo a long transmigration through shapes of other-worldliness before it should return in modern thought to the unity from which it started; and the history of ethics and religion has little bearing upon true political theory between the death of Aristotle and the awakening of the modern consciousness in the Reformation.

In so far as the political ideas of antiquity were preserved to modern times otherwise than in the manuscripts of Plato and Aristotle, the influence which preserved them was that of Roman Jurisprudence. The Roman rule, though it stereotyped the state of things in which genuine political function and the spur of freedom were unknown, had one peculiar gift by which it handed to posterity the germs of a great conception of human life. This is not the place to describe at length the origin of that vast practical induction from the working of the "foreigners' court" at Rome which obtained for itself the name of the Law of Nations, and which, as tinged with ideal theory, was known as the Law of Nature. Whatever fallacies may be near at hand when "natural right" is named, the conception that there is in man, as such, something which must be respected, a law of life which is his "nature," being indeed another name for his reason, and in some sense or other a "freedom" and an "equality" which are his birthright – this conception was not merely a legacy from Stoic ideas, which had almost a religious inspiration, but was solidly founded on the judicial experience of the most practical race that the world has ever seen.

4. In order that the forces which lay hidden in the conception of Natural Right and Freedom, like the powers of vegetation in a seed, might unfold themselves in the modern world, it was necessary that conditions should recur analogous to those which had first elicited them. And these earlier conditions were those of the Greek City-state; for it was here, as we have seen, that the conception of man's nature had flourished, as the idea of a purposive evolution into a full and many-sided social life, while in Stoic philosophy and Roman juristic theory it had become more and more a shibboleth and a formula which lost in depth of meaning what it gained in range of application.

To restore their ancient significance, expanded in conformity with a larger order of things, to the traditional formulae, demanded just the type of experience which was furnished by the modern Nation-state. The growth of Nation-states in modern Europe was in progress, we are told, from the ninth to the fifteenth century. And it is towards and after the close of this period, and especially in the seventeenth century when the national consciousness of the English people, as of others, had become thoroughly awakened, that political speculation in the strict sense begins again, after an interval extending back to the *Politics* of Aristotle. To let one example serve for many; when we read John of Gaunt's praises of England in Shakespeare's *Richard II*, we feel ourselves at once in contact with the mind of a social unity, such as necessarily to raise in any inquiring intelligence all those problems which were raised for Plato and Aristotle by the individuality of Athens and Sparta. And so we see the earliest political speculation of the modern world groping, as it were, for ideas by help of which to explain the experience of an individual self-governing sovereign society. And for the most part the ideas that offer themselves are those of Roman Jurisprudence, but distorted by political applications and by the rhetoric of Protestant fanaticism. As Mr Ritchie[1] points out, the conception of natural right and a law of nature makes a strange but effective coalition with the temper of the Wycliffite cry[2]

> When Adam dalf and Eve span,
> Who was then the gentleman?

The notions of contract, of force, of representation in a single legal "person," are now applied separately or together to the phenomenon of the self-governing individual community. But the solution remains imperfect, and the fundamental fact of self-government refuses to be construed either as the association of individuals, originally free and equal, for

---

[1] [David G. Ritchie,] *Natural Rights* [: *A Criticism of Some Political and Ethical Conceptions* (London: George Allen, 1891)], p. 8. [D.G. Ritchie was Professor of Logic and Metaphysics at the University of St. Andrews; his book on natural rights presented an Idealist interpretation.]

[2] [Jon Wycliffe (1330–1384), was an English theologian and philosopher. He provided the first complete translation of the Bible into English.]

certain limited purposes, or as the absolute absorption of their wills in the "person" of a despotic sovereign.

The revival of a true philosophical meaning within the abstract terms of juristic tradition was the work of the eighteenth century as a whole. For the sake of clearness, and with as much historical justice as ever attaches to an attribution of the kind, we may connect it with the name of a single man – Jean Jacques Rousseau. For it is Rousseau who stands midway between Hobbes and Locke on the one hand, and Kant and Hegel on the other, and in whose writings the actual revival of the full idea of human nature may be watched from paragraph to paragraph as it struggles to throw off the husk of an effete tradition. Between Locke and Rousseau the genius of Vico and of Montesquieu had given a new meaning to the dry formulae of law by showing the sap of society circulating within them.[3] Moreover the revived experience of the Greeks came in the nick of time. It was influential with Rousseau himself, and little as he grasped the political possibilities of a modern society, in matters of sheer principle this influence led him on the whole in the right direction. His insight was just, when it showed him that every political whole presented the same problem which had been presented by the Greek City-state, and involved the same principles. And he bequeathed to his successors the task of substituting for the mere words and fictions of contract, nature, and original freedom, the idea of the common life of an essentially social being, expressing and sustaining the human will at its best.

According to the view here indicated, the resurrection of true political philosophy out of the dead body of juristic abstractions was inaugurated by Vico and Montesquieu, and decisively declared itself in Jean Jacques Rousseau. The idea which most of us have formed of "the new Evangel of a *Contrat Social*" is not in harmony with this representation of the matter. Was it, we may be asked, a genuine political philosophy which inspired the leaders of the French Revolution? And the question cannot

---

[3][Giambattista Vico (1688–1744) was an Italian philosopher and jurist; Vico stresses that nations are characterised by shared traits that change over time, and that the nature of a nation's government must conform to its character. Charles-Louis de Secondat Montesquieu (1689–1755) was a French philosopher who also argued that the laws of a state reflect the nature and circumstances of its people.]

be evaded by denying all connection between the theory and the practice of that age. The phraseology of the revolutionary declarations[4] – which will strike the reader accustomed to nineteenth century socialism as exceedingly moderate and even conservative in tone – is undoubtedly to a great extent borrowed from Rousseau's writings.

Perhaps the truth of the matter may be approached as follows. The popular rendering of a great man's views is singularly liable to run straight into the pit-falls against which he more particularly warned the world. This could be proved true in an extraordinary degree of such men as Plato and Spinoza,[5] and still more astonishingly, perhaps, of the founder of the Christian religion. The reason is obvious. A great man works with the ideas of his age, and regenerates them. But in as far as he regenerates them, he gets beyond the ordinary mind; while in as far as he operates with them, he remains accessible to it. And his own mind has its ordinary side; the regeneration of ideas which he is able to effect is not complete, and the notions of the day not only limit his entire range of achievement – where the strongest runner will get to must depend on where he starts – but float about unassimilated within his living stream of thought. Now all this ordinary side of his mind will partake of the strength and splendour of his whole nature. And thus he will seem to have preached the very superstitions which he combated. For in part he has done so, being himself infected; in part the overwhelming bias of his interpreters has reversed the meaning of his very warnings, by transferring the importance, due to his central thought, to some detail or metaphor which belongs to the lower level of his mind. It is an old story how Spinoza, "the God-intoxicated man," was held to be an "atheist," when in truth he was rather an "acosmist"; and in the same way, on a lower

---

[4]See the very interesting collection of documents in the Appendix to Professor David Ritchie's *Natural Rights,* [loc. cit., note 1]. The reference to "representatives" as taking part in the formation of the general will, in two of the revolutionary declarations of right, is interesting as an improvement on Rousseau's theory which must have been introduced by the politicians. See my article "Les idées politiques de Rousseau," *Revue de métaphysique et de morale*, [Vol. XX] May, 1912, p. 335, note 2.

[5][Baruch Spinoza (1632–1677) was a moral and political philosopher. Spinoza's views are, as Bosanquet indicates, subject to dispute and misunderstanding; he has been associated with Machiavellianism, Hobbesianism and democracy.]

plane, the writer who struggled through to the idea that true sovereignty lay in the dominion of a common social good as expressed through law and institutions, is held to have ascribed absolute supremacy to that chance combination of individual voices in a majority, which he expressly pointed out to have, in itself, no authority at all.

But there is something more to be said of cases, like that under discussion, where a great man's ideas touch the practical world. If the complete and positive idea becomes narrow and negative as it impinges upon everyday life, this may be not only a consequence of its transmission through every-day minds, but a qualification for the work it has to do. The narrower truth may be, so to speak, the cutting edge of the more complete, as the negation is of the affirmation. And the vulgar notion of popular sovereignty and of natural right may have been necessary to do a work which a more organic social theory would have been too delicate to achieve. Like the faith in a speedy second coming of Christ among the early Christians, the gospel according to Jean Jacques may have taken for the minds of Revolutionary France a form which was serviceable as well as inevitable at the moment. If, as we said above, the great man is always misunderstood, it seems to follow that when his germinal ideas have been sown they must assert themselves first in lower phases if they are ever to bear fruit at all. And therefore, while not denying the influence of Rousseau on the Revolution, we shall attempt to show that he had another and a later influence, more adequate to the true reach of his genius.

CHAPTER II

SOCIOLOGICAL COMPARED WITH PHILOSOPHICAL THEORY

1. There is no doubt that Sociology and Social Philosophy have started, historically speaking, from different points of view. The object of the present chapter is to ascertain the nature and estimate the importance and probable permanence of the difference between them. I propose first to explain the difference in general; then to review the sources of social experience, which in other words are facets or aspects of social life, by which social theory has been influenced, and with which it has to deal; and, finally, to form some idea of the distinctive services which may be rendered by sociology and social philosophy respectively in view of the range of experience which it is the function of social theory to organise.

Beginning with Vico's[1] *New Science*, there has been more than one attempt in modern Europe to inaugurate the Science of Society as a new departure. But the distinctive and modern spirit of what is known as Sociology, and under that name has had a continuous growth of half a century at least, first found unmistakable expression in Auguste Comte.[2] The conception which he impressed upon the science to which he first gave the name of sociology, or social physics, was a characteristically modern conception. Its essence was the inclusion of human society among the objects of natural science; its watchwords were law and cause – in the sense in which alone Positivism allowed causes to be thought of – and scientific prediction.[3] It is true that the large conception of unity which Comte embodied in his philosophy had very much in common with the principles insisted on by the Greek social philosophers. The close interdependence of all social phenomena among each other, the

---

[1]J.D. Rogers, "Social Science" in *Dictionary of Political Economy*, ed., [Robert Harry Inglis] Palgrave [(London: Macmillan, 1894–99).]

[2][Auguste Comte (1798–1875) is often viewed as one of the founders of sociology – he is credited with giving the field its name.]

[3]See [Franklin Henry] Giddings, [*Principles of*] *Sociology* [*An Analysis of the Phenomena of Association and of Social Organization* (London: Macmillan, 1898), "Comte believed that by following the positive method sociology could become in good measure a science of previsions, forecasting the course of progress," pp. 6–7.]

unity of man with nature, and the consequent correlation of moral and political theory with the organised hierarchy of mathematical and physical sciences, are ideas which Comte might have borrowed directly from Plato and Aristotle. Nevertheless the modern starting-point is wholly different from that of antiquity. The modern enquirer – the sociologist as such – was to ask himself, according to Comte, in the language of physical science, what are the laws and causes operative among aggregations of human beings, and what are their predictable effects? The ancient philosopher – the ethical and metaphysical theorist – had before him primarily the problem, "what is the completest and most real life of the human soul?" The work of the latter has been revived by modern idealist philosophy dating from Rousseau and Hegel, and finding a second home in Great Britain, as that of the former has developed itself within the peculiar limits and traditions of sociological research, flourishing more especially upon French and American soil. The continuance of these two streams of thought in independent courses, though not without signs of convergence, is a remarkable phenomenon of nineteenth century culture; and it will be one of the problems which the present chapter, and in a larger sense the whole of the present work, must deal with, to consider how far it is necessary or desirable that they should blend.

2. Every science, no doubt, is to some extent the playground of analogies; but the complexity and the unmateriality of human relations has forced this character upon social theory in an extraordinary degree. It is impossible to account for the tendencies of sociological as well as of philosophical thought without making some attempt to pursue the line of investigation suggested by Mr Bagehot in his *Physics and Politics*.[4] Predominant modes and types of experience necessarily colour the whole activity of the mind, and, as indicated above, this influence more especially affects a province of research which is not prima facie accessible to direct experiment or sensuous observation. I must, therefore, endeavour to review, in a brief outline, the principal branches of experience which have furnished ideas for application to social theory, and to indi-

---

[4][Walter Bagehot, *Physics and Politics*, or *Thoughts on the Application of the Principles of Natural Selection and Inheritance to Political Society*, 5th edn (London: Paul, 1879).]

cate the leanings in speculation upon society, which have been due to preoccupation with one or another special analogy.

(i) The Newtonian theory of gravitation is the entrance gate to the modern world of science. "When the Newton of this subject shall be seated in his place"[5] is the aspiration of the modern investigator in every matter capable of being known. It is not surprising, therefore, that the inclusion of human society within the range of matters capable of being definitely understood, should have been symbolised by demanding for social science a completeness of explanation and a power of prediction analogous to those displayed by astronomy or by mathematical physics. Representative of this conception is the title, Social Physics – for Comte the alternative and the equivalent to the name Sociology. It is easy to see both the merits and the dangers of such an ideal, which, as the embodiment of perfection in a natural science, is presupposed by the attitude of sociology down to the present day. Is a science necessarily a natural science, and is a natural science necessarily an exact science? – these are the fundamental questions involved in the adoption of a mathematical ideal for the study of society. No fault can be found with it on the ground of its implying the highest degree of harmony and precision; the only question is whether an adequate type of comparison is afforded for, let us say, the growth of an institution, by the law of a curve. The general conception, indeed, of a continuity between human relations and the laws of the cosmic order is thoroughly in the spirit of Plato, and betokens a scientific enthusiasm worthy to be the parent of great things. And especially in the sphere of economic science, where certain relatively simple hypotheses have proved on the whole to be effective instruments of explanation, an analysis of intricate phenomena has been effected, which in some degree justifies the aspiration after the ideal of an exact science.

(ii) But it has been recognised from the earliest days of political speculation that, within the general ideal of a perfect natural science, the more special analogy of the living organism had a peculiar bearing upon social phenomena. Beginning in the ancient world with the comparison

---

[5][August] De Morgan, [*A*] *Budget of Paradoxes* [(London: Longmans, Green, 1872)], p. 355.

between individuals as "members" of a social whole, and the parts or organs of a living body, or even the constituent elements of a mind, this analogy has been extended and reinforced in modern times by what amounts to the new creation of the biological and anthropological sciences. The sense of continuity thus intensified and implying all that is understood by the modern term "evolution," has brought an immense material of suggestions to sociological research, but has imposed upon it at the same time a characteristic bias from which it is just, perhaps, beginning to shake itself free. This characteristic may be roughly stated as the explanation of the higher, by which I mean the more distinctly human phenomena, by the lower, or those more readily observed, or inferred, among savage nations, or in the animal world. Any one familiar with logic will be aware that there is a subtle and natural prejudice which tends to strengthen such a bias by claiming a higher degree of reality for that which, as coming earlier in temporal succession, presents itself in the light of what is called a "cause." So strong has been this bias among sociologists, that the student, primarily interested in the features and achievements of civilised society, is tempted to say in his haste that the sociologist[6] as such seldom deals seriously with true social phenomena at all; but devotes his main attention to primitive man and to the lower animals, occasionally illustrating his studies in these regions by allusions, showing no great insight or mastery, to the facts of civilised society. Such a complaint becomes less and less justified as the years go by, and sociology recovers its balance as against the overwhelming influence of the sciences of lower life. How far the approach from this "lower" or more purely natural side will remain in the end characteristic of sociological science, is an integral part of the main problem concerning its nature and destiny with which we have to deal in the present work. But it remains true to say and very important to observe, that no such serious successes have as yet been won in the name and by the special methods of sociology as have been achieved by many investigators

---

[6]By a "sociologist as such" I mean a writer who is professedly dealing with sociology as such. Any independent researches, such as Mr and Mrs [Sidney and Beatrice] Webb's *Industrial Democracy* [London: Longman's Green, 1897], may of course be ranked under the heading "Sociology." But works of this kind do not, as a rule, attach themselves to the peculiar method and language of sociological writers.

approaching their problems directly and with an immediate interest; whether in the sphere of political economy proper, or in dealing with various questions of social and ethical importance, such as pauperism, charity, sanitation, education, the condition of the people, the comparative study of politics, or the analysis of material and geographical conditions in their reaction upon social and artistic development.

On the other hand, there is no doubt that the epoch and influence of which we speak has bequeathed a legacy of imperishable value to the theory of society. In a word, it has made us sensitive to the continuity of things, and therefore also to their unity. It has shown us the crowning achievements of the human race, their States, their Religion, their Fine Art, and their Science, as the high-water mark of tendencies that have their beginnings far back in the primitive organic world, and in their original sources have also a connection with each other – as in the practical aspects of religion – which too easily escapes notice in their highest individual development. The "return to nature" and the "noble savage" have been invested with a significance which can never be forgotten, and which criticism can never set aside. This is the sum and substance of the general contribution which the latter half of the eighteenth century and the greater part of the nineteenth have made to sociology through the science of life and of man.

More particularly, it is necessary to notice the double operation of biological influence on sociology, according to the unit from which the analogy is drawn.

(α) The idea which still bulks most largely in the popular mind, as contributed by biology to social theory, is unquestionably that of the struggle for life, or the survival of the fittest. It should be noticed that the social application of this analogy rests entirely on the comparison of a human society, not to the individual animal organism, and still less to the individual mind; but to a whole animal species, or even to the aggregate of all animal species, so far as they or their members are in competition with one another. One whole side of the sociological doctrine, which Mr Spencer[7] has advocated with unwearied persistence, is

---

[7][Herbert Spencer (1820–1903), was a social philosopher and sociologist; he is famous for applying Darwin's evolutionary theory to the study of society.]

founded upon this application of the biological analogy, and the paradox which he has made his principle professes to be borrowed directly from the dealings of nature with the individuals of the animal species. This paradox, that benefits should be assigned inversely as services in infancy but directly as services among adults, is his ultimate sociological basis; the modification of which, to suit human society, by the introduction of benevolence or altruism, so to speak, on the top of it, only serves to display its inadequacy. But we may take it that the analogy of the struggle for life has made it clear that, in any given position, life can be maintained only in virtue of definite qualities adapted to that position. And formal as this principle is when taken by itself, its application in human society can never be unnecessary.

(β) A more recent school has insisted on the complementary analogy, which might be taken as resting upon the comparison of a society with an individual organism. Here, it must be remembered, lay the resemblance which, in this region of ideas, first caught the eye of social philosophers in antiquity. But it is alleged that the aspect of co-operation can be traced as between individual members of the animal world no less than between the parts of a single organism, and it is affirmed that the view which sees nothing but internecine competition in the animal kingdom has been too rough and too superficial in its reading of the facts. And therefore it is suggested that the phenomena of social fellowship, no less than those of individual competition, have their source and root in the world of lower nature; and perhaps sociology is now not far from the recognition that competition and co-operation are simply the negative and positive aspect of the same general fact – the fact of the division of labour, of essentiality of function, and of uniqueness of true individual service. If it is suggested by the one organic analogy that life depends upon qualities adequate to the position which is to be filled, it is made obvious by the other that the qualities which satisfy the claims of a certain position are those, in general and in principle, by which a function is discharged in the service of the whole.

In Mr Spencer's doctrine the two sides above indicated have been brought into very marked relation by a suggestive criticism,[8] which he

---

[8] [Herbert Spencer, *The Principles of*] *Sociology*, [3rd edn (London: Williams and Nor-

has taken special pains to answer. If human society corresponds to an individual organism – as is, in many ways, Mr Spencer's well-known doctrine – how is it that the absolute central control in which the perfection of an organism consists is, for Mr Spencer, a note of imperfection when it appears in a human society? And the answer is in effect that human society corresponds in many of its features rather to a local variety of a species than to an individual organism. It is essentially discrete, not individual, and at this point, therefore, the analogy of the individual organism gives way to that of the group or species.

But Mr Spencer does not really mean that a human society has no more intrinsic bond between its members than the local group of an animal species. To indicate its true nature he gives us a good word – but a word only – the word "super-organic."[9] It is a significant term, and brings us perhaps to the limit of what biological sociology is able to suggest with regard to the unity of a human commonwealth, and points us to something beyond. It is remarkable that when the facts of true human society are more thoroughly realised than by Mr Spencer, but the clue of the individual organism and the co-operative side of animal life is not followed up, there is a tendency to sever the links which unite man to "lower" nature, and to represent the ethical and cosmic processes as absolutely opposed. We see this point of view decidedly adopted by Mr Huxley,[10] and its adoption perhaps indicates the inception of an epoch in which sociology will cut itself free from a good deal of pseudo-scientific lumber. Nevertheless, a patient and careful study will continue to recognise the elements both of competition and of co-operation as ineradicable and inseparable moments in human society as in the animal world; the essential meaning of competition in its higher forms being the rejection and suppression of members who are unable to meet the ever advancing demand for co-operative character and capacity; and the study of parasitism[11] and of regressive selection will continue to be a warning

---

gate, 1893–1898), vol.] 1, p. 586.

[9]Ibid., vol. 1, ch. i.

[10][Thomas Henry Huxley,] *Evolution and Ethics* [(London: Macmillan, 1893)], p. 82.

[11][Patrick] Geddes, in *Encyclopedia Britannica*, [9th edn,] vol. XVIII, p. 253a: "Further details of the process of retrograde metamorphosis and of the enormously important phenomena of degeneration cannot here be attempted; it must suffice if the general depend-

against the attempt to emancipate mankind from the sterner general conditions of the cosmic order. It will be recognised that there is an adaptation to conditions which consists in degradation; but the failure will be understood by comparison with the only true "survival of the fittest,"[12] being that which reveals the full unity and significance of organism and environment. It is important to observe that, at least in the two eminent biologists just alluded to, the doctrine of the individual self – of the relation between self-assertion and self restraint – is altogether of an uncivilised and anti-social type. Biological categories do not, in their case at least, appear to have afforded any suggestion for the treatment of the social self as more and greater, in a positive sense, than the self which is less bound up with social obligations. As for the denying spirits in Plato's *Republic*, so for both Mr Spencer and Mr Huxley, "nature" is essentially self-assertion, and "society" self-restraint.[13] Here again we touch the same limitation which met us in Mr Spencer's term "superoganic," and we feel that a different point of view must be brought to bear.

(iii) Political Economy existed before modern Sociology was born, and is still the only part of it which is obviously and indisputably successful as a science of explanation. The triumphant development of this theory reacted even upon Hegel's political philosophy, by suggesting to him the distinction between "Bourgeois Society" and "The State." *A fortiori*,[14] it could not but have a serious influence on the growing science of sociology itself, the ideal of which might not unfairly be regarded as the extension to society as a whole of that type of investigation which had proved so successful in economic matter. From this influence has arisen the tendency in sociological research which has been called by the name of the economic or materialist view of history, and conse-

---

ence of such changes upon simplification of environment – freedom from danger, abundant alimentation and complete repose, etc. (in short, the conditions commonly considered those of complete material well-being) – has been rendered clearer."

[12]Cf. [Alexander] Sutherland, *The Origin and Growth of the Moral Instinct* [(London: Longmans, Green, 1898)], vol. 1, pp. 28, 29.

[13]Huxley, *Evolution and Ethics*, [loc. cit., note 10] p. 31; Herbert Spencer, *[The] Man Versus [the] State* [(London: Williams & Norgate, 1884)], p. 98.

[14][*a fortiori*: with stronger reason]

quently of society. Primarily connected with the name of Marx, it may also be illustrated by many contentions of Buckle and Le Play,[15] and has become, indeed, the formula of a school. In sum, the point of view amounts to this: that the fundamental structure of civilisation, the type of the family, for example, and the order relations and development of classes in society, have been and must be determined by the primary necessities of human existence, and the conditions of climate and nutrition under which these necessities are met. Economic facts alone, it is suggested, are real and causal; everything else is an appearance and an effect.

Before saying a word as to the true importance of this point of view, we may profitably correct the commonplace idea of its nature. Materialism, in a strict philosophical sense, means the conviction that nothing is real but that which is solid, or, perhaps, which gravitates. By a not very convincing analogy from this idea, all those passions and necessities which we speak of in a quite loose and popular way as connected with the body, may be and often are regarded as "material" in opposition to energies which it seems pleasanter to ascribe to incorporeal mind. But it should be noted that this secondary usage, especially in a time when no one denies the physical correlation of all psychical activity, has no important ethical implication. Like the "flesh" or the "body" of St. Paul's religious language, the "bodily" or "material" needs and appetites of man are an element of mind, the rank and value of which must be determined on other grounds than the notion that they are connected in some peculiar degree with "physical" conditions. The economic view of history has been called and has called itself materialist partly because of the commonplace usage, which I have just described, by which certain passions and necessities, which it takes to be fundamental, are apt to be called material as opposed to ethical or ideal – a wholly unjustified opposition – and partly from the notion, which I referred to at the beginning of this chapter, that the success of political economy was in some way analogous to that of the mathematical science of abstract matter.

---

[15][Henry Thomas Buckle (1821–1862) was an historian, noted for his *History of Civilization in England*; Frederic Le Play (1806–1882) is regarded as the founder of modern French political economy.]

Stripping off, then, the unjustified suggestion of philosophical materialism,[16] what we have in the economic view of history amounts pretty much to what is expressed in the saying that while statesmen are arguing, love and hunger are governing mankind. Climate and natural resources make a difference to history; occupations determine the type of the family; an agricultural and an industrial society will never exhibit the same relations between classes, and very vast commercial operations cannot be carried on by the same methods or by the same minds which sufficed for the retail trade of a petty shop. But when it is clearly seen that economic needs and devices are no detached, nor, so to speak, absolutely antecedent department of human life[17] – a fact which the epithet "materialist" has done something to obscure, for, in truth, in economics there is no question of genuine material causation – then it becomes obvious that we have not here any prior determining framework of social existence, but simply certain important aspects of the operations of the human mind, rather narrowly regarded in their isolation from all others. If we seriously consider the import of such an economic conception as the "standard of life," it becomes plain that the contrast too commonly accepted[18] between the mechanical pressure of economic facts and the influence of ideas[19] stands in need of a completely fresh criticism and of entire restatement. Discounting, however, the exaggerations which have

---

[16]Quite probably there may be in the Marxian view an echo of true materialism – the idea that will and consciousness are "epiphenomena" – i.e. are effects which are not causes – generated by molecular movements. Such a view cannot be criticised here, only it may be pointed out that, on such a basis, the "bodily" passions, etc., are in no way more "material" than, e.g., the moral "categorical imperative," and therefore no more causal.

"Material" desires may be taken to mean selfish desires, on the analogy of the possession of physical objects, which cannot be shared (p. 46 above). But in this sense the term would be quite a false characterisation of economic motive, as the facts of the family or of clan loyalty clearly demonstrate ([Note added] 1919).

[17]See note 19.

[18]Cf. e.g., [Émile] Durkheim [1865–1917], *Année Sociologique*, 1897, 159. [Émile Durkheim, *Contributions to L'Année Sociologique*, ed., Yash Nandan, trans., John French et al. (New York: Free Press, 1980).]

[19]I.e. as if economic conditions were a sort of iron girders put up to begin with and civilisation was the embellishment of them. It is the old story of forgetting that the skeleton is later than the body and is deposited and moulded by it.

arisen from confused notions of materialism, and from the genuine achievements of economic science, we have remaining, in the point of view under consideration, a thoroughly just assertion of man's continuity with the world around him. Undoubtedly man lives the life of his planet, his climate, and his locality, and is the utterance, so to speak, of the conditions under which his race and his nation have evolved. The only difficulty arises if, by some arbitrary line between man and his environment, the conditions which are the very material of his life come to be treated as alien influences upon it, with the result of representing him as being the slave of his surroundings rather than their concentrated idea and articulate expression. Do we think that Homer, Dante, and Shakespeare would have been greater or more free in their genius if one had not been the voice of Greece, another that of Italy, and the third that of England? The world in which man lives *is* himself, but is constituted, of course, by presentation to a mind and not by strictly physical causation; and even where strictly physical causation plays a part, as in the bodily effects of a hot climate or of a certain kind of nutrition, still it cannot determine a type of human life except by passing into the world which a human being presents to himself.

The exclusive importance which has been attached to considerations of this kind in recent social theory is partly due to an unfounded opinion of their novelty. It is somewhat striking, though following naturally enough from the sort of schism in the world of letters which modern sociology and ancient social philosophy represent, that the firm and well-balanced handling of these problems which we owe to Plato and Aristotle is for the most part ignored by modern sociologists.

The entire social conception of those writers is a continued application of the principle, fundamental in their whole philosophy, that "form" is the inherent organising life of "matter," so that the better life of a commonwealth can be nothing but the flower and crown of the possibilities inherent in its material conditions and industrial and economic organisation. The law, which is ultimately to reveal itself as the spring of all righteousness in the State, has its most obvious and external symbol – so Plato tells us – in the economic exchange of services; and every circumstance of site, and industry, and trade, and the racial type of the citizen, helps to constitute, both for him and for Aristotle, the living organic possibility from which, in some appropriate individual form, the higher life is to spring. If we ask ourselves what then is the difference between the ancient view of economic causation, and that of the "materialist" historical school, we shall find the answer in the absence, from the former, of that unreal isolation upon which we observed above. The relation of "matter" or "conditions" to "form" or "purpose" is not, for the Greek thinker, the pressure of an alien necessity, of a hostile environment, but the upspringing of a life, continuous in principle through all its phases. The thought of the legislator fixes in the shape of distinct consciousness and will, what the assemblage of conditions embodies as a physical or instinctive tendency, as the artist, to use an ancient simile, finds the statue in the marble. Working with this idea, the connection is far more thoroughly, because more sympathetically, traced than it can be when we think that our science is but laying bare the fetters of humanity. And following in the spirit of the Greek thinkers themselves, modern students of antiquity have devoted themselves to eliciting the positive connection of conditions with history, up to a point of success of which the common run of modern sociologists appear to have no conception. When we reflect how typical and, comparatively speaking, how readily isolated and exhausted is the history of Ancient Greece in the greatest age, it seems extraordinary that the considerable and minute researches which have been bestowed upon its geographical, commercial, and economic conditions should not be commonly drawn into account with a view to the illustration of the relations between natural resources, commercial and economic development, and historical greatness.[20]

---

[20]I have never, for example, seen the great work of Ernst Curtius, on the geography of the Peloponnese in connection with its historical development, referred to in any sociological treatise; [*Peloponnesos; eine historisch-geographische Beschreibung der Halbinsel* (Gotha: J. Perthes, 1851–52.) See also Curtius' *The History of Greece* (New York: Scribner & Company, 1871), p. 740] nor, again, [Maximilian Wolfgang] Duncker [see his *History of Greece, From the Earliest Times to the End of the Persian War* (London: R. Bentley & Son, 1883–86)], nor Büchsenschütz, [see his *Hellenica* (Boston: Ginn & Company, 1892, 1888)]; nor Mr [W.L.] Newman's edition of Aristotle's *Politics* [(Oxford, Clarendon Press, 1887–1902)]. [Augustus] Boeckh's *Treatise on the Public Economy of Athens*, [trans., G.C. Lewis (London: J.W. Parker, 1842)] receives only a word of contemptuous notice in [J.R.] McCulloch's *Literature of Political Economy* [: *A Classified Catalogue of Select Publications in the Different Departments of that Science, with Historical, Critical*

However this may be, here at any rate, in the analysis of economic and quasi-economic conditions in their bearing upon the life of peoples, we get a real subject-matter which is perhaps, so far as can yet be seen, the territory least disputably belonging to the pure sociologist. It is not really a sphere of natural causation, but it is a sphere of certain simple and general conditions in psychical life, corresponding to external facts which admit of more or less precise statement, and, we may hope, of reduction to fairly trustworthy uniformities. Such, for instance, are M. Durkheim's[21] investigations on the effect of density of population upon the division of labour,[22] or Professor Giddings' observations upon the causes and limiting conditions of the aggregation of populations.[23] We now proceed to a branch of experience which seriously strains the working conceptions of the sociologist.

(iv) A completely new vista reveals itself to the student of social theory when he turns from biological analogies and economic conditions to consider the wealth of experience and of ideas which is furnished to him by Jurisprudence and the Science of Right. He knows, indeed, by this time, that the obvious aspect of a province of fact will not be the only one, and that a unity will certainly be traceable between all the facets of

---

and Biographical Notices (London: Longman, Brown, Green & Longmans, 1845)]. (On the great mass of current technical Sociology, the above criticism appears to me still to hold good. But I recognize – how gladly – that a new spirit is abroad in the study of Greek antiquity, in which Sociology joins hands with Archaeology, and both with an enlightened estimate of the meaning of civilisation. Professor Gilbert Murray's *Rise of the Greek Epic* [(Oxford: Clarendon Press, 1907)] is a brilliant example of the combination of methods to which I refer, 1909.)

[21] [Bosanquet uses M. for monsieur when referring to the Gallic philosophers.]

[22] *De la Division du Travail Social* ([Paris:] Alcan, 1893) [For an English translation, see *The Division of Labor in Society*, trans., W.D. Halls (New York: Free Press, 1984).]

[23] [Franklin Henry Giddings,] *Principles of Sociology: [An Analysis of the Phenomena of Association and of Social Organization* (London: Macmillan, 1896)], Bk. II, ch. i, [e.g. "Aggregation is itself a condition favourable to further aggregation; because it affords protection to individuals, and because it normally is followed by social evolution." p. 87.] Few things are more interesting in this respect than Mr [George Vivian] Poore's [*Essays on] Rural Hygiene* [London: Longmans, Green, 1893], on the mechanical conditions of modern city life, as regards drainage and water supply, with their results in encouraging an overcrowded and insanitary mode of living.

social existence. But none the less, he will be able to restrain the itch to explain things away, and he will fairly and candidly give weight to the significance and suggestiveness of the mass of history and of reflection which is now brought before him.

(α) For here, as the plainest and most unmistakable data of experience, we are confronted with *ideal facts*. The vast mass of documents which form the basis of the Science of Right – a more complete and comprehensive set of records, perhaps, than any other branch of social science can boast – bears witness in every case to one social phenomenon at least, to a formal act of mind and will, aimed at maintaining some relative right or hindering some relative wrong, and stamped with what in some sense and in some degree amounts to a social recognition. Theorists have said too hastily, though with a sound meaning, that right is independent of fact. It would be as true to say that reason is independent of civilisation, or the soul independent of culture. Right is not exhausted in the facts of past history; but it is every moment embodied in facts; and to comprehend that the social phenomena which are among the most solid and unyielding of our experiences, are nevertheless ideal in their nature, and consist of conscious recognitions, by intelligent beings, of the relations in which they stand, is to make a great step towards grasping the essential task of science in dealing with society. From the beginning of social theory the facts of law have been set in opposition to the idea of a natural growth. It has been observed that, as a definite institution maintained by formal acts of will, society is artificial, conventional, contractual. We all know to-day that there is much more than this to be said about the nature and principles of social growth. Nevertheless, it remains true that social whole has an artificial aspect, an aspect of will and of design, of the agreement and mutual recognition of free conscious beings. And in so far as the history of law has resulted in the conception of natural right, this in no way derogates from the artificial or ideal character of society as above understood. For "natural" right belongs to a "nature" which includes and does not exclude that action of intelligence in virtue of which society may be termed artificial; and is merely the revelation of the principle towards which the social will is working, and which in some degree it has always embodied.

Therefore the facts of Jurisprudence and the Science of Right, or of "Natural Right," as the issue and outcome of Jurisprudence, necessarily counterbalance the extreme ideas of continuous growth and natural causation which social science derives from other analogies. We are reminded that, after all, we are dealing with a self-conscious purposive organism, which is aware of a better and a worse, and has members bound together by conscious intelligence, though, it may be, not by conscious intelligence alone. At one time the ideas of Jurisprudence, such as Sovereignty or Contract, were considered sufficient by themselves to equip a social theory. And if they are now seen to need completion from both sides – from the side of lower nature, and from the side of the national spirit and culture – this should not make us neglectful of the important truths which the facts of law and recognised obligation, more than any others, establish on solid ground.

(β) It is of course the case that Law has been treated from the standpoint of economic history in the same way as the other phenomena of civilised life. It may be taken simply as the form into which substantive relations crystallise, under the influence of economic conditions or of other elementary social forces. And obviously such a view has its truth. The social will, like the will of any one of us from day to day, is formed not *in vacuo*, but as the focus of all the influences which penetrate our being. It is a fair object of research to ascertain the economic or other social meaning of the statutes which we find on the statute book; and it is because they have so much meaning that they are excellent object-lessons in the play of the social consciousness and sense of right. But this focussing of social influences makes the laws not less acts of social will, but more. To suppose the contrary would be like supposing that nothing is a true act of will which embodies an individual's distinctive purposes in life.

I will explain by an illustration the relative value of sociological analysis in dealing with the facts of positive law. I am indebted for it to M. Durkheim, whose writings appear to me among the most original and suggestive works of modern sociology. I regret that my immediate purpose does not justify me in stating and appreciating the whole very interesting theory of repressive and contractual law from which the point in question is selected.

An act is a crime,[24] we are told, for the pure sociologist, when it offends the strong and definite collective sentiments of society. This is the strictly causal view of the matter. The act is a crime because it offends; it does not offend because it is a crime. And the corollaries are valuable. It is idle to distinguish, on such a basis, between the reformatory, the retributive, and the deterrent views of reaction which is punishment.[25] An offensive act is in itself at once an exhibition of character, an injury, and a menace. If a man assaults me in the street, and I knock him down, how futile to ask if my action is meant to cure him of his insolence, to punish him for having hit me, or to prevent him from hitting me again! The real fact is that I am offended, and I react by way of injury and negation against that which offends me. Now, this view, I think, illuminates the subject. By going back to the simple operative cause, as it may be supposed to exist especially in the minds of a tribe in an early stage of development (M. Durkheim is chiefly referring to religious offences) we have got a plain type of mental reaction, easy to imagine and to understand. In this type we see at once the unity of aspects which the forms of law, and legal or philosophical theory, tend later to dissociate in a fictitious degree. And moreover we are reminded that a law must have something behind it, some positive sentiment or conviction, without which it would be unaccountable and unmeaning.

But when all this is said, it must not be supposed that penal law has been reduced to the level of a strong and definite collective sentiment, or a crime to the level of an annoyance. The simplest penal law of a self-existent social group is different from the anger of a crowd or mob. There is in it some sense of permanence, and permanence means responsibility and generality – a distinction of right and wrong. The fact of formally constituting a crime, i.e., of announcing a law, implies that mere distaste is no ground of punishment. The law means that there is something worth maintaining, and that this is recognised, and that to violate this recognition is not merely to be unpopular, but to sin against the common good, and to break an obligation. With less than this there is no true crime.

---

[24]Durkheim, loc. cit., [note 22] livre 1, ch. ii.
[25]See below, ch. viii.

Thus, if I am right, the relation of pure "sociological" causation to juristic facts is the well-known relation of the more abstract to the more concrete sciences, usually illustrated in logic by the relation of the physical and the musical account of musical sound. For the pure physicist, a harmony and a discord are only two different combinations of shakings. For the musician they are not only opposite effects, but are causes of divergent consequences. So with the relation between a strong collective sentiment and a true law. A strong sentiment, as such, is a mere fact, a mere force; and as such the sociologist regards it. A law involves the pretension to will what is just, and is therefore a sentiment and something more, viz., the point of view of social good. It aims at a right and implies a wrong, and demands to be apprehended and judged on this ground. A mere force cannot by its reaction constitute a crime; for that a law is necessary. The ideal aspect of law as recognition of right is no less actual, no less solid and verifiable, than the facts of sentiment or necessity which may have suggested and sustained it. In this way the relation of sociological causation to the facts of Jurisprudence is typical of the whole relation of Sociology conceived as a natural science, to the larger facts with which social theory has to deal.

(v) But the ideas involved in mere legality, though they bear emphatic testimony to the conscious and artificial aspect of the social whole, have always been regarded with some justice as the type of what is empty and formal. To treat a law as a command with a penalty annexed, or to enunciate the tendency of social progress as being from status to contract,[26] may convey important meanings, but is obviously very far short of the whole truth. And, indeed, generalisations of this kind, though characteristic of a certain class of reflective Jurisprudence, do not at all represent the highest level which has been reached within the science of right it-

---

[26][The claim that "progressive" societies (i.e., Western Europe) evolved from a reliance on status to determine a person's obligations and property holdings to modern society, focussed on contractual rights, is associated with Sir Henry Maine (1822–1888); see his *Ancient Law: its Connection with the Early History of Society and its Relation to Modern Society* (London: Murray, 1885), ch. v. The idea is repeated by F.W. Maitland: "The march of the progressive state is, as we all know, from status to contract." *Selected Essays*, eds., H.D. Hazeltine, G. Lapsley and P.H. Winfield (Cambridge: Cambridge University Press, 1936), p. 233.]

self. But yet, as we pass beyond these everyday working conceptions, we are beginning to leave the central ground of Jurisprudence, and to move towards a point of view which deals more completely with life and culture. The need and occasion for such a point of view may be measured by that revival of national individuality which was referred to in the last chapter as constituting the true ground and occasion for the rebirth of genuine political philosophy in modern times. Montesquieu's investigation into the "spirit of laws," and his treatment of a law as something deeper than a command, following upon the similar endeavours of Vico, was in fact a recognition of the fundamental unity of a national civilisation, which, on its political side, even Hobbes and Locke had already attempted to explain by help of the inadequate instruments furnished to them by legal theory. Montesquieu's and Vico's conceptions were only the forerunners of the many-sided study of civilisation which characterised the latter part of the eighteenth century, following up the problem which was enunciated in Rousseau's paradox, that "law itself must be created by the social spirit which it aims at creating."[27] To recognise the social spirit of a people, as the central unity behind its law and culture and politics, was the principle of the various researches dealing with formative art, poetry, language, religion and the state, which marked the close of the eighteenth century (compare Wolf's theory of Homer as the utterance of a racial mind),[28] and laid the foundation of nineteenth century idealism.

The true Greek renaissance, initiated in the age of Winckelmann,[29] forcing modern minds into contact with Hellenic ideas in their original

---

[27][See Jean-Jacques Rousseau, *The Social Contract*, trans., G.D.H. Cole (London: Dent, 1913), Book II, ch. vii.]

[28][Friedrich August Wolf (1759–1824) is known for his texts of the *Iliad* and the *Odyssey* and, most famously, his *Prolegomena ad Homerum*. The "theory of Homer" to which Bosanquet refers is Wolf's claim that the *Iliad* and the *Odyssey* were not written by a single man, but were composed orally by more than one author; Wolf claims that their coherence was the result of later work. See the *English Prolegomena to Homer*, 1795, trans., Anthony Grafton, Glenn W. Most and James E.G. Zetzel (Princeton: Princeton University Press, 1985).]

[29][Johann Joachim Winckelmann (1717–1768) is known for his 1764 work, *Geschichte der Kunst des Altertums* (*The History of Ancient Art*) trans., Giles Henry Lodge (Boston: J.R. Osgood and Company, 1880). It is often said that the study of art history as a distinct

form, and no longer through Latin intermediaries, furnished a type and focus for these researches by bringing before the thoughts of students the brilliant individuality of the ancient City-state, the crude traditions of which had already exercised the most powerful influence on Rousseau, and through him on the Revolution. At the same time the organic sciences were full of activity. The life-work of Goethe marks the parallelism of the two movements. It is plain that the doctrines of Comte were no more than a very one-sided attempt to formulate the significance of the fermentation around him, and that deeply as he felt the unity of the social being, his expression of it ignored half the lesson of the times. Thus the generalities of Jurisprudence are vitalised and completed by the work of the sciences of culture; and the conception of a national mind and character takes its unquestioned place in modern social theory. It may be well at this point also to call attention to the researches which later historians have directed to what may be called "Comparative Politics"; the relations, that is, of communities under government with respect to the mode in which they are governed.[30] For this branch of inquiry once more, though narrow and empty by itself, yet does aid in bringing to light the purposive and conscious character of society, and in correcting the tendency to treat it altogether as a "natural" phenomenon.

(vi) "And so the whirligig of Time brings about his revenges."[31] French Sociology to-day is a psychological science, though its founder banished psychology from his sociological method. Nothing is more instructive than to watch the gradual pressure of the various points of view which are emphasised by the various departments of social experience, as they reveal, under criticism, their tendency to complete themselves and one another by suggesting the only category which is adequate to them as a whole. As every serious student of social matters knows by his own experience, it is impossible to touch a physical fact, or a statistical datum, or a legal enactment, in reference to its social bearing, without its at once, so to speak, coming alive in his hands, and attaching itself to an

---

discipline dates from Winckelmann's work.]

[30][Edward Augustus] Freeman's *Comparative Politics* [(London: Macmillan, 1871, 1896)], and [Sir John Robert] Seeley's *Introduction to Political Science* [(London: Macmillan, 1896)].

[31][William Shakespeare, *Twelfth Night* V, i.]

underlying relation of mind as the only unity which will make it intelligible, and correlate it with other experiences, by themselves no less fragmentary. In statistics, for example, you touch a moving creature, as if through the holes in a wall, at this point and the other, and write down where you have touched him.[32]   But to see the creature as he is, and combine your information of all kinds in a just and complete idea, you must get him into the open. And that, when the question is of a life, you can only do by reconstructing his mind, for even to see a social unit with your eyes gives you a fragment only, and not a whole. On Fridays, we are told, the passenger traffic returns of French railways, omnibuses, and steamers show a decline.[33] What dumb fact is this? People do not like to travel on Fridays, or prefer to travel upon other days. What is this preference? The only unity that can really afford an explanation, that can correlate this irregular fragment of fact with the whole to which it belongs, is the living mind and will of the society in which the phenomenon occurs. Explanation aims at referring things to a whole; and there is no true whole but mind. Necessarily, therefore, with widening experience and deepening criticism, mind has become the centre of the experiences focussed by sociology.

We may note some significant points in this development, although, indeed, the whole course of modern sociology is one single illustration of what has just been said. Discussions of the problem in what the differentia of society consists, no longer deal with organic or economic conceptions, but with such ideas as the "Consciousness of kind,"[34] the "Mind of a Crowd,"[35] "Imitation" and "Invention,"[36] similarities and dif-

---

[32]Cf. C.S. Loch on "Returns in Social Science," in *Aspects of the Social Problem* [ed., Bernard Bosanquet] (London: Macmillan, 1895), p. 287.

[33][Gabriel de] Tarde, *Les Lois de l'Imitation* [Paris: F. Alcan, 1895], p. 115.

[34]["The original and elementary subjective fact in society is the consciousness of kind. By this term I mean a state of consciousness in which any being, whether low or high in the scale of life, recognizes another conscious being as of like kind with itself."] Giddings, [*Principles of Sociology*, loc. cit.,] p. 17.

[35][Gustave] Le Bon, *Psychologie des Foules* [(Paris: F. Alcan, 1899). See the English translation, *The Crowd: A Study of the Popular Mind* (Marietta, Ga.: Larlin, 1982)]. Cf. above, pp. 41–43. [This cross-reference was added in 1919.]

[36]Tarde, *Les Lois de l'Imitation*.

ferences in the social consciousness,[37] "Social logic" and society considered as a syllogism,[38] and the imitative and inventive person.[39] The work of M. Tarde in particular is typical of the whole movement, and his phrases have largely been adopted whether in agreement or in controversy. For him the one fact coextensive with the social character is "Imitation" – the means by which ideas and practices spread throughout groups and masses of intelligent beings. For the characteristic of knowable phenomena, in his view, is Repetition,[40] and Imitation is the means and vehicle of Repetition in social matters. Here, however, we have accounted only for generalisation, and differentiation needs a separate origin. This will be supplied by the idea of "Invention"; Invention and Imitation, therefore, are the general form of all social process, the matter on the other hand being analysable as Belief and Desire. Every institution is a belief,[41] every activity is a want or desire. In the *Logique Sociale* these conceptions of the general medium and process of social life are pushed home into the actual formative operation of the social mind and will. Society, we are told, may be compared not indeed to an organism, but rather to a brain; it is a co-operative mind, a syllogism, in which the principles held by one part are modified and applied by another. M. Tarde's extreme illustrative hypothesis corresponds strangely with one thrown out by Mr Sidgwick. Mr Sidgwick[42] has simplified an ethical question by supposing only a single sentient conscious being in the universe; for M. Tarde there is, we might say, no single being at all; the typical social man is a hypnotical creature, a somnambulist acting under suggestions from others, though he does not know it, and is under the

---

[37]Durkheim, *La Division du Travail Social*, [loc. cit., note 22].

[38][Gabriel de] Tarde, *La Logique Sociale* [(Paris: F. Alcan, 1895)].

[39][James] Baldwin, *Social and Ethical Interpretations in Mental Development* [:*A Study in Social Psychology* (London: Macmillan, 1897)].

[40]For a logical criticism of this idea see my *Logic* [, *or the Morphology of Knowledge*], 2[nd edn, (Oxford: Clarendon Press, 1911), vol.] II, p. 174. [Note added in] (1919).

[41]Perhaps this expression originates with Fustel de Coulanges in *La Cité Antique*, [(Paris: Hachette, et cie, 1872)].

[42]*Methods of Ethics*, 1st edn, [London: Macmillan, 1874)], p. 374. In 6th edn, [(London: Macmillan, 1901)], p. 405, the passage is greatly modified.

illusion that he is himself.[43] Nothing could be of higher interest than to see the necessities of social science thus working themselves out, on slippery and unfamiliar ground, by the sheer force of facts and experience. That a science of man must be a science of mind seems no longer disputable.

On the substance of this development there is one observation which inevitably suggests itself to any critic who approaches the problem from the philosophical side.

Necessarily, as the relation of the individual to society is the root of every social problem, psychological sociology consists to a great extent in exercises upon the theme of identity and difference. These exercises have hitherto been for the most part unconscious and involuntary. And the high degree of substantial truth which is attained by inquirers who have not thought the logic of identity worthy of a single glance, is the strongest possible confirmation of the common experience that it is safer to neglect theory than to be careless of facts. Nevertheless, it has now become apparent that a point has been attained at which logical criticism is absolutely essential, or if not logical criticism, at least some reference to the familiar and well-established results of ancient or modern social philosophy.

For it is a universal characteristic of the sociological movement before us, that identity and difference are referred to different spheres, and the "one" and the "other" are regarded as reciprocally exclusive atoms.[44] The difficulties and fallacies which thus arise are innumerable. Thus we have the contagious common feeling of a crowd[45] taken as the true type of a collective mind, obviously because it is not understood how an identical structure can include the differences, the rational distinctions and relations, which really constitute the working mind of any society. So again we have one type of law marked off as corresponding to social

---

[43] *Les Lois de l'Imitation,* [loc. cit., note 33], p. 83.

[44] M. Tarde's view just mentioned might seem to conflict with this. But note that he regards the man influenced by others as under an illusion in thinking that he is himself; i.e., with Spencer and Huxley, he regards the "self" and the "other" as irreconcilable factors.

[45] Le Bon, op. cit, [note 35].

similitude,[46] while a different type corresponds to the social division of labour; simply because the category of resemblance has been substituted for that of identity, and is treated as exclusive of differentiation; with the result of a really terrible distortion of facts in the attempt to separate the whole sphere of penal enactment from that which deals with industrial organisation. So with the entire set of notions of "Imitation," "Repetition" and "Invention."[47] The separation of Imitation and Invention is simply the popular exclusion of Difference from Identity; while the treatment of Repetition as the characteristic of knowable phenomena and the mode of utterance of social Imitation means the restriction of rational Identity to its barest form, and the exclusion from social theory of absolutely every case of true co-operative structure. For true co-operative structure is never characterised by repetition, but always by identity in difference; it is the relation not of a screw to an exactly similar screw, but of the screw to the nut into which it fastens.[48]

In the discussions of Egoism and Altruism[49] the difficulty comes to a head. Some writers think Egoism prior to Altruism; others – the more wary and enlightened – incline to treat Altruism as a phase earlier than Egoism; M. Durkheim, whose eye for a fact is very keen, seeing the absurdity of both these suppositions, is determined to include the two characters in question from the very beginning in the human consciousness,[50] but, of course, as contents belonging to different spheres and consisting of contrasted elements. The conception of a whole held together by its

---

[46]Durkheim, op. cit, [note 22].

[47]Tarde and Baldwin, op. cit. [notes 33 and 39].

[48][It is crucial to keep in mind here Bosanquet's insistence that "it takes all sorts to make a world [or organism]." *The Principle of Individuality and Value* (London: Macmillan, 1912), p. 29; *Social and International Ideals* (London: Macmillan, 1917), p. 133. As he stresses here a "true co-operative structure is never characterised by repetition, but always by identity in difference; it is the relation not of a screw to an exactly similar screw, but of the screw to the nut into which it fastens," a point he repeats elsewhere: "The Relation of Sociology to Philosophy" in his *Science and Philosophy* (London: Allen And Unwin, 1927), p. 243; *The Value and Destiny of the Individual* (London: Macmillan, 1913), pp. 49–50). See below, ch.. vii, e.g. p. 171.]

[49]Compare Professor A.E. Taylor, *The Problem of Conduct* [: *A Study in the Phenomenology of Ethics.* (London: Macmillan, 1901)] p. 123.

[50]*Division du Travail*, [loc. cit., note 22, (London: Macmillan, 1901)] , p. 216.

differences, its identity consisting in and being measured by their very profoundness and individuality, is not at the command of any of these writers, although the greater part of M. Durkheim's theory seems imperatively to demand such a conception.

(vii) Before considering, in conclusion, the relation of Sociology as influenced by the above-mentioned sources and points of view, to social philosophy proper, it will be well to devote a few words to emphasising the way in which these "sources" ought to be regarded.

Every "source" of sociological science is at once a category, or point of view, and also a certain group of actual social conditions. This relation is effectively illustrated by the study of any social unity which is such as to invite a thorough conspectus of its life from top to bottom of the social growth and underlying conditions. I repeat that the history and life of ancient Greece, a singularly complete working model of society on a very small scale, analysed with remarkable thoroughness, and individual throughout, is the prerogative example of such a treatment; but next to this, or in addition to it, a thoroughly careful study of local history, life, and conditions, in a limited region,[51] with which we are familiar from top to toe, is an essential propaedeutic to true social theory. To focus a number of groups of fact, and co-ordinate the points of view which they substantiate, into the conception of a living being, with its individual character and spiritual utterance, needs more than a merely literary or statistical study. But by making this effort we shall learn, as no economic charts or general scientific works can teach us, what a social life is, and in what sense it is true that all partial facts and experiences within it demand ultimate co-ordination in the category of mind. It is not meant that consciousness can make the weather hold up, but it is meant that no fact has a true social bearing except in as far as, sooner or later, it comes to form part of the world which a being capable of sociality and therefore intelligent, presents to himself as his theatre of action.

3. Thus it may seem that by mere force of facts a necessary solution has been arrived at, and that psychological sociology must be one and the same science with social philosophy.

---

[51] Cf. Professor Geddes' idea of a "Regional Survey" with which visitors to his delightful "Summer School" become acquainted, [loc. cit., note 11].

But this is not quite the case. Up to the present time these two sciences continue to approach their object-matter, as it were, from different ends, and whether the two views will ultimately amalgamate is perhaps mainly a problem of the personal division of labour. But a question of principle, with reference to the true nature of psychology, is indirectly involved. Only there seems no reason why two kinds of psychology should not exist.

Psychology, as at present conceived by its best working representatives, is a positive, though not a physical science. "For (the psychologist) the crude superstitions of Australian Aborigines have as much interest and value as the developed and accurate knowledge of a Newton or a Faraday."[52] Its aim is "the establishment of continuity among observed facts, by interpolating among them intermediate links which elude observation."[53] If not a "physical" science, then, it is, in a common sense of the term, a "natural" science. It has the impartiality, and uses the watchwords – law, process, genesis – which belong to a natural science. And like every impartial science, to which process and genesis are watchwords, it tends to explain the higher by the lower. This springs from no malice aforethought, but from the conditions of the case. The lower is simpler, and usually comes first in time. It is naturally dwelt upon, as that into which it is hoped to resolve the more complex, and the explanation which is more adequate for the simple is less adequate for the complex. No difference of higher and lower is recognised by the impartial science, and its ideal, as a science, is inevitably the expression of the complex in terms of the simple; while, as far as genesis in time is insisted on, the bias towards temporal causation is pretty sure to operate by attaching a quasi-causal significance to the earlier phases.

In all these characteristics psychology is at one with sociology. And, therefore, though it is a gain that other points of view should be resolved into the point of view of mind, yet the positive bias of sociology is not transcended simply by this resolution.

---

[52][George Frederick] Stout, *Analytic Psychology* [(London: S. Sonnenschein, 1896)], Introduction [p. 12].

[53]Ibid., [p. 8.] From a logical point of view this idea of explanation seems seriously defective. See F.H. Bradley's *Principles of Logic* [(Oxford: Clarendon Press, 1883)], p. 491.

Philosophy starts, we have said, as it were, from the other end. It is critical throughout; it desires to establish degrees of value, degrees of reality, degrees of completeness and coherence. Its purpose might be termed "Ethical," but for the extreme narrowness of the meaning of that term. Society, for it, is an achievement or utterance of human nature – of course not divorced from nature in general – having a certain degree of solidity, so to speak; that is to say, being able, up to a certain point, to endure the tests and answer the questionings which are suggested by the scrutiny of human life from the point of view of value and completeness. Is the social life the best, or the only life for a human soul? In what way through society, and in what characteristics of society, does the soul lay hold upon its truest self, or become, in short, the most that it has in it to be? How does the social life at its best compare with the life of art, of knowledge, or of religion, and can the same principle be shown to be active in all of them? And what have they in common, or peculiar to each, which has an imperative claim on the mind of man?

Now it was hinted above that there might be two kinds of psychology, or two tendencies within it. And if psychology were to be impelled, as it has been more than once in the past, by the recognition that where there is more of its object – of mind – its interest is greater and the rank of its object-matter is higher, then there would not be much to choose between the temper of psychology and that of philosophy. And as sociology has found itself driven forward into the territory of social "logic," a name which at once suggests a critical and philosophical science, it may well be that sociological psychology will not remain wholly "positive" and impartial, but will assume, as in the hands of Professor Giddings, for example, it seems inclined to, at least a teleological attitude, testing social phenomena by the quantity and quality of life which they display.

But, at any rate, the points of view of sociology, and of social philosophy as above described, will continue to supplement each other. Philosophy gives a significance to sociology; sociology vitalises philosophy. The idea of mind is deepened and extended by the unity and continuity which sociological analysis, throughout all its many-sided sources, vindicates for the principle of growth and order down to the roots and in all the fibres of the world. Every natural resource and condition must be thought of as drawing forth or constituting some new element in the mind which is the universal focus; just as every shape and colour of the trees in the landscape or every note of a melody finds its definite and individual response in the contemplative consciousness. The error lies, not in identifying the mind and the environment, but in first uncritically separating them, and then substituting not merely the one for the other, but wretched fragments of the one for the whole in which alone either can be complete.

Philosophy, on the other hand, in treating of society, has to deal with the problems which arise out of the nature of a whole and its parts, the relation of the individual to the universal, and the transformation by which the particular self is lost, to be found again in a more individual, and yet more universal form. In all these respects its view is what might be called teleological; that is to say, it recognises a difference of level or of degree in the completeness and reality of life, and endeavours to point out when and how, and how far by social aid, the human soul attains the most and best that it has in it to become. As long as these two points of view are clearly recognised, it is a matter of the mere personal division of labour whether they are brought to bear by the same thinkers and within the same treatises.

CHAPTER III

1. To every-day common sense there is something paradoxical in the phenomena of political obligation; however it may acquiesce in what, although not satisfactorily explicable, is plainly seen to be necessary. Where, indeed, we meet with any form of absolutely despotic government, we have not so much a paradox as a defect; for, although government may exist in such a shape, it is open to question how far true political obligation can be said to arise under such a system. In as far as it does so, we shall find that the fact is due to unacknowledged conditions and relations, which we shall more easily analyse as they appear in free or constitutional states. It would then be easy to show, if we were interested in doing so, that the principles which will have been recognised as operative in the freest states known to history, are and have been, in various degrees, at the root of the common life of every state or community which has held together effectively enough to be treated as in any sense a political whole. But this would be a historical investigation, unnecessary for the purpose of pure social theory. In this we may fairly start from the highest form of political experience, in which, as we shall see, the mere defects of political immaturity being outgrown, the paradox of political obligation emerges with intensified emphasis.

Let us take as our starting point, then, the conception of "self-government," to which, it will be admitted on all hands, the thought and feeling of mature communities has clung both in ancient and modern times, as in some way containing the true root and ground of political obligation. We shall find in it a striking illustration of the strength and weakness of widespread popular notions. A universal popular notion cannot but have a hold of some essential truth, otherwise it could not survive and spread, and form a working theory for an immense area of experience. On the other hand, a popular notion, as such, cannot be critical of itself and aware of its own foundations; and so in defending and applying itself it is pretty sure to plunge deep into fallacy. "Self-government" is an idea which will be found, as has been said, to contain the true ground and nature of political obligation. But the rough-and-ready application of it which, for example, represents the individual as simply one with the community, and the community therefore as infallible in its action affecting him, is a pure example of fallacy, and may be justly characterised as a confusion pretending to be a synthesis. Of this idea as of so many we must say that those who have pronounced it to be self-contradictory have understood it much better than most of those who accept it as self-evident.

In the conception of self-government then we have the paradox of obligation in its purest form. As applied to the individual himself, it gives the paradox of Ethical Obligation. As applied to the individuals who compose a society, it gives the paradox of Political Obligation. This must be the preliminary distinction by which we approach the subject; but we shall find that the two problems and the two cases cannot be ultimately separated, although they are to be distinguished in a certain respect. The paradox of Ethical Obligation starts from what is accepted as a "self," and asks how it can exercise authority or coercion over itself; how, in short, a metaphor drawn from the relations of some persons to others can find application within what we take to be the limits of an individual mind.[1]

The paradox of Political Obligation starts from what is accepted as authority or social coercion, and asks in what way the term "self," derived from the "individual" mind, can be applicable at once to the agent and patient in such coercion, exercised prima facie by some persons over others. Both relations and their connection have been pointed out by Plato.[2]

Our object in the present chapter is to enforce the reality of the difficulties which attach to the idea of political self-government, so long as current assumptions as to the union of individuals in society are maintained. And for this purpose we are to examine the views of some very distinguished philosophers to whom the paradox has appeared irreconcilable, and law or government has seemed essentially antagonistic to the self or true individuality of man; while the term "self," if applied to the collective group by or within which government is undoubtedly ex-

---

[1] On this problem, see below, p. 148.

[2] *Republic*, 430, 431. [See the complete and unabridged Jowett translation of Plato's *Republic* (New York: Vintage Books, [1894] 1991)].

ercised, appears to them an empty and misleading expression. The curious and significant point to which we shall call attention is, in brief, that while maintaining law and government to be in their nature antagonistic to the self of man – whether as pain to pleasure or as fetters to individuality – they nevertheless admit with one voice that a certain minimum of this antagonistic element is necessary to the development of the sentient or rational self. We have here a dualism which challenges examination.

2. The attitude towards law and government which Bentham adopted (1748–1832) was in a great degree that of the philanthropic reformer. His principle of the greatest happiness of the greatest number is said[3] to have been derived from Beccaria,[4] whose work on "Crimes and Penalties" had great influence throughout Europe. And Howard, "the philanthropist," who was just twenty-two years Bentham's senior (1726–1790),[5] represented a revolt against the abuses of the treatment of criminals at that time, by which Bentham, who eulogised him as "a martyr and apostle," was strongly affected. The movement which Bentham led was, in short, markedly hostile to the existing system of law, and to the reasonings of its advocates. And substantial as his knowledge and constructive genius proved to be, it never lost the character which the direction of his approach to the subject had marked upon it, a character of suspicion and antagonism, which is expressed in his description of law as a necessary evil, and government as a choice of evils.[6]

---

[3]Professor Holland's article on "Bentham" in the *Encyclopaedia Britannica*, 9th edn.

[4][Cesare Beccaria (1738–1794), the eldest son of an Italian aristocratic family, published *Dei delitti e delle pene* (*On* [or *Of*] *Crimes and Punishments*) a critical study of criminal law, in 1764, at the age of 26. His work was soon after translated into English and French and in 1771 he was appointed to the Supreme Economic Council of Milan. Beccaria argued against the death penalty because it had a bad effect on society by reducing its sensitivity to human suffering, and he held that Governments should seek the greatest good for the greatest number. He also denied Locke's suggestion that people forfeit their right to life when they initiate a state of war, and claimed that we negotiate away only the minimal number of rights necessary to bring about peace.]

[5][John Howard was a reformer and philanthropist; like Bentham, he was noted for his penal and legal reforms.]

[6]Bentham, *Principles of Legislation*, p. 48. [The reference is actually to *Theory of Legislation*, 2nd edn, trans., (from the French of Etienne Dumont,) Richard Hildreth (London: Trubner, 1871. Compare *An Introduction to the Principles of Morals and Legislation*,

Pain being the ultimate evil, it is clear why, on Bentham's principles, every law is an evil. For every law, for him, is contrary to liberty; and every infraction of liberty is followed by a natural sentiment of pain.[7] Against those who would deny the proposition that every law is contrary to liberty he brings a charge of perversion of language, in that they restrict liberty to the right of doing what is not injurious to others. They give the term, that is to say, a partly positive implication. For him then liberty has the simplest and apparently widest meaning,[8] which includes liberty to do evil, and is defined, we must suppose, purely as the absence of restraint. And he therefore has no doubt whatever that the citizen can acquire rights only by sacrificing part of his liberty. And in this there is an appearance of truth, if we forget that in saying that a part of one's liberty is sacrificed it is implied that one had, to begin with, a certain area of liberty, of which a portion is abandoned to save the rest. But the idea of any such antecedent liberty is just such a fiction as Bentham himself delighted to expose. It is true, however, that some degree of restraint on what we can *now* easily imagine ourselves free to do, is involved in political society. The point on which we have to fix our attention, for the purposes of social theory, is the remarkable representation of this state of things under the figure, as it were, of an amount of general liberty, which is increased by subtraction, or which can only attain its maximum by the conversion of a certain edge or border of it, so to speak, into constraint. This border of constraint is implied to be capable of a minimum, such as to condition a maximum of liberty, or possible individual initiative; a relation which, being at first sight contradictory, demands further analysis. For it would appear that if the sacrifice of some liberty is to be instrumental to the increase of the whole amount, that whole can hardly be a homogeneous given quantity, like, for instance, a piece of land; for such a one must surely be diminished by the subtraction of any part of it.

---

eds., J.H. Burns and H.L.A. Hart (Oxford: Clarendon Press, 1996), ch. xiii, sect. I and II].

[7]Bentham, *Principles [Theory] of Legislation,* p. 94. [See *An Introduction to the Principles of Legislation*, ch. viii, sect. 4, xiv; see also ch. xvii, sect. 1, xii. It is important here to note that Bentham is not simply claiming that, since the law punishes, the infliction of publishment constitutes an evil; he claims that simply being prevented from doing what you want constitutes a pain. Thus even the law-abiding incur this pain.]

[8]It is not really the widest, as will appear in the sequel.

It must, one would infer, be something which has a complex nature like that of a living plant, such that certain restrictions or negations which are essential to its prosperity are dictated by its individual characteristics (which must be positive), and express the same principle with them, and therefore are wholly relative to the positive type and phase of the plant to be cultivated. Only in some such sense can it be intelligible how constraint is instrumental to effective self-assertion.

But if this is so, the restrictive influences of law and government, which are the measure of the constraint imposed, cannot be alien to the human nature which they restrict, and ought not to be set down as in their own nature antagonistic to liberty or to the making the most of the human self. The root of the difficulty obviously lies in assuming that the pressure of the claims of "others" in society is a mere general curtailment of the liberty of the "one," while acknowledging, not contrary to fact, but contrary to the hypothesis of that curtailment, that the one, so far from surrendering some of his capacity for life through his fellowship with others, acquires and extends that capacity wholly in and through such fellowship. On the above assumption the terms of the paradox of self-government become irreconcilable, and government is made an evil of which it is impossible to explain how it ministers to the self which stands for the good. So long as to every individual, taken as the true self, the restraint enforced by the impact of others is alien and a diminution of the self, this result is inevitable.

It is instructive, therefore, to note Bentham's uncompromising hostility to all the theories of philosophical jurists. The common point of all their theories, from Hobbes and Grotius[9] to Montesquieu and Rousseau, not to mention Kant and his successors, has lain in the fact that their authors divined under the forms of power and command, exercised by some over others, a substantive and general element of positive human nature, which they attempted to drag to light by one analogy after another. But neither Montesquieu's "eternal relations," nor the "Social Contract," nor "General Will," nor "Natural Rights" of other thinkers

---

[9][Hugo Grotius (1583–1646), was a Dutch philosopher and legal theorist; he was a crucial figure in the development of modern natural law thinking, and is best known for his *De juri belli ac pacis* (*The Law of War and Peace*).]

finds favour in Bentham's eyes. One and all they are to him fiction and fallacy. He can understand nothing in law but the character of a command; he can see no positive relation of it to human nature beyond the degree in which it dispenses with the pain of restraint while increasing the pleasure of liberty.

To describe the magnificent success which attended the use of this rule of thumb in the practical work of reform does not fall within our immediate subject. Our purpose was merely to illustrate the paradox implied in the conception of self-government, by pointing out how fundamentally hostile to one another Bentham took its constituent elements to be.

3. The same point may be further insisted on by examining the main ideas of Mill's *[On] Liberty*, without by any means professing to give a full account of Mill's opinions on the relation of individuals to society. What indeed is instructive in his position, for our immediate purpose, is that, having so deep a sense, as he has, of social solidarity, he nevertheless treats the central life of the individual as something to be carefully fenced round against the impact of social forces.

(i) Mill's idea of Individuality is plainly biased by the Benthamite tradition that law is an evil. It is to be remembered that Anarchism of a speculative kind, the inevitable complement of a hide-bound Conservatism, was current in the beginning of this century, as in Godwin and Shelley.[10] Thus we find concentrated in a few pages of the *Liberty*[11] all those ideas on the nature of Individuality, Originality, and Eccentricity which are most opposed to the teaching derived by later generations in England from the revival of philosophy and criticism. It is worth while, after reading Mill's observations upon the relation of individuality to the Calvinistic theory of life,[12] to turn to the estimate expressed by

---

[10][William Godwin (1756–1836) is best known for his book, *Political Justice* which defends an anarchistic utopia; Percy Bysshe Shelley (1792–1822) was an English romantic poet. His *Laon and Cythna*, later reissued as *The Revolt of Islam*, was a utopian take on peaceful revolution.]

[11][John Stuart Mill, *On Liberty*,] ch. iii, paras. 8–13. [The editors have replaced Bosanquet's page references with the chapters and paragraphs of *On Liberty* to enable readers to consult different editions of Mill's work.]

[12]Ibid., ch. iii, para. 7.

Mark Pattison[13] of the force of the individual character generated by the rule of Calvin at Geneva. That the individuality, or genius, the fullness of life and completeness of development which Mill so justly appreciates, is not nourished and evoked by the varied play of relations and obligations in society, but lies in a sort of inner self, to be cherished by enclosing it, as it were, in an impervious globe, is a notion which neither modern logic[14] nor modern art criticism will admit. In the same way, the connection of originality and eccentricity, on which Mill insists, appears to us to-day to be a fallacious track of thought; and in general, in all these matters, we tend to accept the principle that, in order to go beyond a point of progress, it is necessary to have reached it; and in order to destroy a law, it is necessary to have fulfilled it. Here, however, is the heart of the point on which we are insisting. If individuality and originality mean or depend upon the absence of law and of obligation; if eccentricity is the type of the fully developed self, and if the community, penetrated by a sense of universal relations, is therefore a prey to monotony and uniformity, then it needs no further words to show that law is a curtailment of human nature, the necessity of which remains inexplicable, so that self-government is a contradiction in terms.

(ii) How then does Mill bring the two terms into relation? How does he represent the phenomenon that, in the life of every society, the factors of self and of government have to be reconciled, or at any rate to coexist?

To find the answer to this question, the whole of the chapter, "Of the limits of the authority of society over the individual,"[15] should be carefully studied. A few characteristic sentences may be quoted here.

> What, then, is the rightful limit to the sovereignty of the individual over himself? Where does the authority of society begin? How much of human life should be assigned to individuality, and how much to society?
>
> Each will receive its proper share, if each has that which more particularly concerns it. To individuality should belong the part of life in which it is chiefly the individual that is interested; to society, the part which chiefly

---

[13] *Essays* [by the late Mark Pattison (Oxford, Clarendon Press, 1889)], vol. I, "Calvin."

[14] See below, p. 104.

[15] *On Liberty*, ch. iv.

interests society.

Every one who lives in society, he continues in effect, is bound not to interfere with certain interests of others (explicitly or implicitly constituted as "rights"), and is bound to take his fair share of the sacrifices incurred for the defence of society and its members. These conditions society may enforce, at all costs to recalcitrants. Further, it may punish by opinion, though not by law, acts hurtful to others, but not going so far as to violate their rights. But acts which affect only the agent, or need not affect others unless they like, may be punished, we are given to understand, neither by law nor by opinion. Mill expects his conclusion to be disputed, and the following is the conclusion of the passage in which he explains and reaffirms it:

> ...when a person disables himself, by conduct purely self-regarding, from the performance of some definite duty incumbent on him to the public, he is guilty of a social offence. No person ought to be punished simply for being drunk; but a soldier or policeman should be punished for being drunk on duty. Wherever, in short, there is a definite damage, or a definite risk of damage either to an individual or to the public, *the case is taken out of the province of liberty, and placed in that of morality or law.*[16]

It will probably occur at once to the reader that, considered as a practical rule, the view here maintained would by no means curtail unduly the province of social interference. We should rather anticipate that it would leave an easy opening for a transition from administrative nihilism to administrative absolutism;[17] and some such transition seems to have taken place in Mill's later views. This tendency to a complete *bouleversement*[18] is the characteristic of all conceptions which proceed by assigning different areas to the several factors of an inseparable whole, which then reasserts itself in its wholeness within the area of either factor to which we may happen to attend. Indeed, even in the passage before us, the defence of individuality has already well-nigh turned round

---

[16]Italics are mine. [Ibid., ch. iv, para. 10.]

[17][By "administrative nihilism" Bosanquet means something akin to what is usually called laissez-faire; Bosanquet was a critic of both state socialism and unregulated capitalism. See this volume, pp. 324ff.]

[18][*bouleversement*: violent inversion]

into its annihilation. Every act that carries a definite damage to any other person belongs to the sphere of law, and every act that can be supposed likely to cause such a damage, to that of morality; and individuality has what is left. The extraordinary demarcation between the sphere of morality and that of liberty is to be accounted for, no doubt, by the Benthamite tradition which identified the moral and social sanctions; so that in this usage the sphere of morality means much the same as what, in the first passage referred to, was indicated as the sphere of opinion.

Now, it is obvious that the distinction which Mill is attempting to describe and explain is one practically recognised by every society. The question is whether it can be rightly described and explained by a demarcation which, if strictly pressed, excludes individuality from every act of life that has an important social bearing; while, owing to the two-sided nature of all action, it becomes perfectly arbitrary in its practical working as a criterion. For every act of mine affects both myself and others; and it is a matter of mood and momentary urgency which aspect may be pronounced characteristic and essential. It may safely be said that no demarcation between self-regarding and other-regarding action can possibly hold good. What may hold good, and what Mill's examples show to be present to his mind, is a distinction between the moral and the "external" aspects of action on the ground of their respective accessibility to the means of coercion which are at the disposal of society. The peculiar sense in which the term "external" is here employed will explain itself below.[19]

For our present purpose, however, what we have to observe is merely that the demarcation between individuality and society, contrived in defence of the former, has pretty nearly annihilated it. And thus we see once more how overwhelming is the prima facie appearance that, in the idea of self-government, the factors of self and government are alien and opposed; and yet how hopeless it remains to explain the part played by these factors in actual society, so long as we aim at a demarcation between them as opposites, rather than at a relative distinction between them as manifestations of the same principle in different media.

---

[19]See below, ch. viii.

(iii) A few words may here be said on the applications by which Mill illustrates his doctrine, in order to point out what confusion results from relying on a demarcation which cannot strictly be made.

It will be noted in the first place that he objects altogether to the attempt to prevent by punishment either immorality or irreligion as such.[20] This objection a sound social theory must uphold. But if we look at Mill's reason for it, we find it simply to be that such an attempt infringes liberty, by interfering with action which is purely self-regarding. Without entering further upon the endless argument whether this or any action is indeed purely self-regarding, we may observe that by taking such ground, Mill causes the above objection, which is substantially sound, to appear as on all fours with others which are at any rate very much more doubtful. Such is the objection on principle to all restrictions imposed upon trade with a distinct view to protecting the consumer, not from fraud, but from opportunities of consumption injurious to himself. The regulation or prohibition of the traffic in alcoholic liquors is of course the main question here at issue; and it may be admitted that Mill's discussion, with the many distinctions which he lays down, is full of shrewdness and suggestiveness. But the ultimate ground which he takes, as above stated, is quite different from the genuine reasons which exist against attempting to enforce morality by law and penalty, and introduces confusion into the whole question of State interference by ranking the two objections together. Closely analogous are his objections to the statutes respecting unlawful games,[21] which, whether wise or unwise, are quite a different thing from an attempt to punish personal immorality as such. And lastly, the same principle is illustrated by his whole attitude to the strong feeling and the various legal obligations which determine and support the monogamous family. In maintaining the general indissolubility of marriage, and supporting the parental power, the State is interfering, for him, with the freedom of parties to a contract, and conferring power over individuals, the children, who have a right to be separately considered. Such interference is for him *ipso facto*[22] of a suspected na-

---

[20] Mill, *On Liberty*, ch. iv, paras. 14ff.

[21] Ibid., ch. v, para. 8.

[22] [*ipso facto*: by the fact itself]

ture. It is an interference hostile to liberty; and whether it is or is not an external condition of good life, which the State is able effectively to maintain, is a question which he does not discuss. Throughout all these objections to authoritative interference we trace the peculiar prejudice that the criterion of its justifiability lies in the boundary line between self and others, rather than in the nature of what coercive authority is and is not able to do towards the promotion of good life. On many points indeed, when the simple protection of "others" is concerned, Mill's doctrine leads to sound conclusions. Such, for example, is the problem of legislation after the pattern of the Factory Acts.

But yet a strange nemesis attaches to grounds alleged with insufficient discrimination. Just as, by ranking inner morality and outer action alike under the name of freedom, Mill is led to object to interference which may be perfectly justified and effectual; so by the same confusion he is led to advocate coercive treatment in impossibly stringent forms, and in cases where it runs extreme risk of thwarting a true moral development. We are amazed when he strongly implies, in respect to the education of children and the prospect of supporting a family, that the existence of a moral obligation[23] to an act is a sufficient ground for enforcing the act by law. The proposal of universal State-enacted examinations by way of enforcing the parental duty of educating children, to the exclusion of the task of providing education by public authority, in which Mill sees danger to individuality, opens a prospect of a Chinese type of society, from which, happily, the good sense of Englishmen has recoiled. And just the reverse of his proposal has come to pass under the influence of the logic of experience. The State has taken care that the external conditions of an elementary education are provided, and, while doing this, has no doubt exercised compulsion, in order that these conditions may be a reality. But the individual inquisition by examination is tending to drop out of the system; and the practical working of the public education is more and more coming to be that the State sees to it that certain conditions are maintained, of which the parents' interest and public spirit leads them to take advantage. Sheer compulsion is not the way to enforce a moral obligation.

---

[23]Ibid., ch. v, para. 12.

Still more startling is the suggestion that it might be just to interdict marriage to those unable to show the means of supporting a family, on the ground of possible evil both to the children themselves through poverty, and to others through over-population. This is a case in which authoritative interference (except on account of very definite physical or mental defects) must inevitably defeat its object. No foresight of others can gauge the latent powers to meet and deal with a future indefinite responsibility; and the result of scrupulous timidity, in view of such responsibilities, is seen in the tendency to depopulation which affects that very country from which Mill probably drew his argument. To leave the responsibility as fully as possible where it has been assumed is the best that law can do, and appeals to a spring of energy deeper than compulsion can reach.

Thus we have seen that by discriminating the spheres of non-interference and interference, according to a supposed demarcation between the sphere of "self" and of "others," a hopelessly confused classification has been introduced. Sometimes the maintenance of external conditions of good life, well within the power of the State, is forbidden on the same grounds as the direct promotion of morality, which is impossible to it. In other cases the enforcement of moral obligations is taken to lie within the functions of the State, although not only is the enforcement of moral obligations *per se*[24] a contradiction in terms, but almost always, as in the cases in question, the attempt to effect it is sure to frustrate itself, by destroying the springs on which moral action depends.

It is worth noticing, in conclusion, that in two examples,[25] the one trivial, the other that of slavery, both theoretically and practically very important, Mill recognises a principle wholly at variance with his own. Here he is aware that it may be right, according to the principle of liberty, to restrain a man, for reasons affecting himself alone, from doing what at the moment he proposes to do. For we are entitled to argue from the essential nature of freedom to what freedom really demands, as opposed to what the man momentarily seems to wish. "It is not freedom to be allowed to alienate his freedom," as it is not freedom to be allowed to

---

[24][*per se*: by themselves]

[25]Mill, *On Liberty*, ch. v, paras. 5, 11.

walk over a bridge which is certain to break down and cause his death. Here we have in germ the doctrine of the "real" will, and a conception analogous to that of Rousseau when he speaks of a man "being forced to be free."

4. Before referring to Mill's explicit utterances on the problem of self-government, which are of the same general character as those of Mr Herbert Spencer, it will be well to note some instructive points in the views of the latter thinker. The study of Mr Spencer's writings, and more especially of those which appear most directly opposed to the popular conceptions of the day, cannot be too strongly urged upon the sociological student. And this for two reasons. In the first place, no other writer has exhibited with equal vividness the fatal possibilities of a collective governmental stupidity. That in practice these possibilities are continually tending to become facts, just as in theory they are represented by recurrent fallacies,[26] is a proof of the extreme arduousness of the demands made by the task of self-government upon the people which undertakes it. And no theorist is fitted to discuss the problem of social unity who has not realised the arduousness of these demands in all its intensity. And, in the second place, the student will observe an instructive meeting of extremes between elements of Mr Spencer's ideas and popular social theories of an opposite cast. The revival of doctrines of the natural rights of man on a biological foundation[27] is a case in point. An uncriticised individualism is always in danger of transformation into an uncritical collectivism. The basis of the two is in fact the same.

---

[26]As, for example, in Rousseau's attempts to explain the action of a collective mind, in which he constantly falls into the advocacy of a soulless *régime* of mass-meetings. [See Jean-Jacques Rousseau, *The Social Contract*, trans., G.D.H. Cole (London: Dent, 1913), Bk. III, chs. xii-xv.]

[27][Herbert Spencer,] [*The*] *Man Versus* [*the*] *State* [(London: Williams & Norgate, 1884). "Animal life involves waste; waste must be met by repair; repair implies nutrition. Again, nutrition presupposes obtainment of food; food cannot be got without powers of prehension, and, usually, of locomotion; and that these powers may achieve their ends, there must be freedom to move about. If you shut up a mammal in a small space, or tie its limbs together, or take from it the food it has procured, you eventually, by persistence in one or other of these courses, cause its death. Passing a certain point, hindrance to the fulfilment of these requirements is fatal. And all this which holds of the higher animals as large, of course holds of man."], pp. 95–6.

(i) A comparison of the conception of "right" as entertained by Bentham and by Herbert Spencer forms a striking commentary on ideas in which "government" is antagonistic to "self." Bentham, seeing clearly that the claims of the actual individual, taken as he happens to be, are casual and unregulated, fulminates against the idea of natural right as representing those claims. Right is for him a creation of the State, and there can be no right which is not constituted by law. And the truth of the contention seems obvious. How, in fact, could individual claims or wishes constitute a right, except as in some way ratified by a more general recognition?

But to Mr Herbert Spencer the contrary proposition is absolutely convincing, and, indeed, on their common premises, with equal reason.[28] It is ridiculous, he points out, to think of a people as creating rights, which it had not before, by the process of creating a government in order to create them. It is absurd to treat an individual as having a share of rights qua member of the people, while in his private capacity he has no rights at all.

We need not labour this point further. It is obvious that Mr Herbert Spencer is simply preferring the opposite extreme, in the antithesis of "self" and "government," to that which commended itself to Bentham. If it is a plain fact that "a right" can only be recognised by a society, it is no less plain that it can only be real in an individual. If individual claims, apart from social adjustment, are arbitrary, yet social recognitions, apart from individual qualities and relations, are meaningless. As long as the self and the law are alien and hostile, it is hopeless to do more than choose at random in which of the two we are to locate the essence of right.

(ii) And how alien and hostile the self and the law may seem we see even more crudely enunciated in Herbert Spencer than in Bentham or Mill, as the fundamental principle of the tradition has worked itself more definitely to the front. "The liberty[29] which a citizen enjoys is to be

---

[28]Ibid., p. 88.

[29]Ibid., pp. 15–16. Cf. [Sir John Robert] Seeley, *Introduction to Political Science*, [(London: Macmillan, 1896)], p. 119: "Perfect liberty is equivalent to total absence of Government." I have attempted to point out the fallacy of this in a way applying to its practical and everyday meaning in my essay on "Liberty and Legislation," in the volume of essays

measured, not by the nature of the governmental machinery he lives under, whether representative or other, but by the relative paucity of the restraints it imposes on him." And so we are astounded to find it maintained that the positive and active element in the right to carry on self-sustaining activities is of a non-social character, depending only on the laws of life,[30] and if the matter were pushed home, would have to be identified, one must suppose with the more strictly animal element of the mind; while only the negative element arises from social aggregation, and it is this negative element alone which gives ethical character to the right to live. Though these distinctions apply primarily to the ground of the *right to live*, yet it appears inevitable that they represent the point of view from which the active self or individuality must be regarded on the principle we are pursuing. The ground of the right to live, as here stated, is simply the recognition that life is a good; and if the positive element of this good is non-social and only the negative is of social origin, and this alone is ethical, it seems clearly to follow that the making the most of life – its positive expansion and intensification – is excluded from the ethical aspects of individuality, and, indeed that individuality has no ethical aspect at all. Here is the ultimate result of accepting as irreducible the distinction between the self and government, or the negative relation of individuality and law. Liberty and self are divorced from the moral end, a tendency which we noted even in Mill. Selves in society are regarded as if they were bees building their cells, and their ethical character becomes comparable to the absence of encroachment by which the workers maintain the hexagonal outline due to their equal impact on each other as they progress evenly from equidistant centres. The self, which has ranked throughout these views as the end, to whose liberty all is to be sacrificed, turns out to be the non-ethical element of life.

Thus, when Professor Huxley speaks of "self-restraint as the essence of the ethical process,"[31] while "natural liberty" consists in "the free play of self-assertion," we see how the whole method of approaching social

---

called *The Civilisation of Christendom* [ed., Bernard Bosanquet (London: Swan Sonnenschein, 1899), pp. 358–83.]

[30] *Man v. State*, p. 98. [See above note 27.]

[31] [Thomas Henry Huxley,] *Evolution and Ethics* [(London: Macmillan, 1893)], pp. 27 and 31.

and ethical phenomena is turned upside down unless the paradox of self-government is conquered once for all. The idea that assertion and maximisation of the self and of the individuality first become possible and real in and through society, and that affirmation and not negation is its main characteristic; these fundamental conceptions of genuine social philosophy[32] can only be reached through a destructive criticism of the assumptions which erect that paradox into an insoluble contradiction.

5. We may now restate the essence of the problem of self-government as it presents itself to the thinkers whom we have been reviewing. On the assumptions which they accept, the annihilating criticism of self-government in the first chapter of Mill's *Liberty* is indeed irresistible. He begins by pointing out that in times of political immaturity, the conception of political liberty consisted in setting limits to the power which the ruler, considered as an independent force opposed in interest[33] to his subjects, should be suffered to exercise over the community. But as it was found possible, in a greater and greater degree, to make the ruling power emanate from the periodical choice of the ruled,

> some persons began to think that too much importance had been attached to the limitation of the power itself. *That*, it might seem, was a resource against rulers whose interests were habitually opposed to those of the people. What was now wanted was, that the rulers should be identified with the people; that their interest and will should be the interest and will of the nation. The nation did not need to be protected against its own will. There was no fear of its tyrannising over itself.[34]

Rousseau in some moods was the victim of this fallacy, and it is widely triumphant to-day.

But with the success of the democratic principle,

> elective and responsible government became subject to the observations

---

[32]For the Greek, it is society which is natural, positive, and promotive of man's individuality. See ch. ii, above.

[33]So early an analysis of government as that made by Plato in the *Republic* shows indeed that this was never the sole theory, as it is not the truest, of the cohesive forces of any community whatever. But it has a certain validity, proportioned to the degree of political imperfection.

[34][Mill, *On Liberty*, ch. i, para. 3.]

and criticisms which wait upon a great existing fact. It was now observed that such phrases as "self-government," and "the power of the people over themselves," do not express the true state of the case. The "people" who exercise the power are not always the same people with those over whom it is exercised; and the "self-government" spoken of is not the government of each by himself, but of each by all the rest. The will of the people, moreover, practically means the will of the most numerous or the most active *part* of the people; the majority, or those who succeed in making themselves accepted as the majority...and precautions are as much needed against this as against any other abuse of power. The limitation, therefore, of the power of government loses none of its importance when the holders of power are regularly accountable to the community, that is, to the strongest party therein.... In political speculations, "the tyranny of the majority" is now generally included among the evils against which society requires to be on its guard.[35]

The paradox of self-government then, so far from being theoretically solved by the development of political institutions to their highest known maturity, is simply intensified by this development. When the arbitrary and irrational powers of classes or of individuals have been swept away, we are left face to face, it would seem, with the coercion of some by others as a necessity in the nature of things. And, indeed, however perfectly "self-government" has been substituted for despotism, it is flying in the face of experience to suggest that the average individual self, as he exists in you or me, is *ipso facto* satisfied, and at home, in all the acts of the public power which is supposed to represent him. If he were so, the paradox of self-government would be resolved by the annihilation of one of its factors. The self would remain, but "government" would be superfluous; or else "government" would be everything, and the self annihilated. If, on the other hand, we understand the "self" in "self-government" to stand for the whole sovereign group or community, which is usually called a "self-governing," as opposed to a subject, state, then we have before us the task of showing that this self is a reality in any sense which justifies the acceptance of what is done by the public power as an act of the whole community. But on the ground where we stand in the theories reviewed in the present chapter, no such self can be

---

[35][Ibid., ch. i, para. 4.]

shown. Government, in fact and in principle, reveals itself as coercion exercised by "the others" over "the one." And so long as this is the case, and as the government is alien to the self, not only do the rights of majorities remain without explanation, but no less is it impossible to say on what rational ground an entire community can apply coercion to a single recalcitrant member. We have seen that Mill would solve the problem by a demarcation, according to which the aim and ground of government is to protect the self from the impact of others, and leave it in its isolated purity. Herbert Spencer, it may be noted,[36] has recourse to one of those hypotheses of tacit consent which would reduce a community to the level of a joint-stock company,[37] *minus* a written instrument of association; which in the case of the State has to be replaced by Mr Spencer's estimate of purposes, which would *probably* be accepted with unanimity *if* the question were asked! Bentham alone, founding himself on the actual nature of social life, genially overrides the whole question of individual right, and while maintaining law to be a necessary evil, and pouring scorn on all attempts to exhibit a positive unity throughout the selves which compose a society, makes the promotion of a free and happy life the sole criterion of governmental interference.

On the basis of every-day reflection, then, we are brought to an absolute deadlock in the theory of political obligation. If, as popular instinct maintains, and as common sense seems somehow to insist, there is a theory and a justification of social coercion latent in the term "self-government," we cannot find a clue to it in the reasoning of our most recent and popular political thinkers. Nor should we find a comprehensive theory, though we might find suggestions towards one, if we recurred to our more philosophical teachers, such as Hobbes and Locke, who are further from popular modes of thought. If there is anything satisfactory in the conception of self-government, every interpretation of it is at once condemned which does not give the fullest force to both terms of the

---

[36] *Man v. State*, p. 83 sq.

[37] It is a remarkable testimony to the inherent vitality of associations of human beings that even a joint-stock company often finds its works and aims so developing on its hands that it has to obtain additional powers from Parliament. It transcends, therefore, the limits of the shareholders' original contract, and Herbert Spencer's loud complaints of this procedure show how little he recognises the nature of social necessity.

paradox, at the same time that it exhibits their reconciliation. What this fullest force is, and the antagonism which it involves, we have seen in the present chapter. We must start from an actual self, which is capable of rebelling against law and government; and from an actual "government," which is capable of tyrannising over the individual self. We must not treat the self as *ipso facto* annihilated by government; nor must we treat government as a pale reflection, pliable to all the vagaries of the actual self. Nor, again, must we divide the inseparable content of life, and endeavour to assign part to the assertion of the individual as belonging to self, and part to his impact on others, as belonging to government. We must take the two factors of the working idea of self-government in their full antagonism, and exhibit, through and because of this, the fundamental unity at their root, and the necessity and conditions of their coherence. We must show, in short, how man, the actual man of flesh and blood, demands to be governed; and how government, which puts real force upon him, is essential, as he is aware, to his becoming what he has it in him to be. And if we fail to destroy the assumptions which hinder us from doing this, we shall have to admit that the maturity of democratic institutions has only liberated us from arbitrary despotism to subject us to necessary tyranny; and though, in spite of such a failure, we might still acquiesce in "counting heads to save breaking them," we should have to agree that this may indeed be the shrewdest device of political expediency, but that the difference between the two processes corresponds to no real capacity of the human individual for partaking, by the exercise of will and intelligence, in a peacefully organised and yet effectually governed whole. We shall then, in short, be compelled to agree with Bentham and Mill and Spencer that "self-government" and "the general will" are meaningless phantoms, combinations of hostile factors, incapable of being united in a real experience.

CHAPTER IV

THE PROBLEM OF POLITICAL OBLIGATION MORE RADICALLY TREATED

1. The reader will no doubt have observed that the theory dealt with in the last chapter belongs to the general type of what is currently known as Individualism. For several reasons I have preferred not to make use of this hackneyed word. In the first place, it is very hackneyed; and the employment of such terms takes all life and expressiveness out of philosophy. And, in the next place, Individualism may mean many things, and in its fullest, which is surely, for the student of philosophy, its truest meaning, is far too good for the theories under discussion. An "Individual" may be "individual" or indivisible because he has so little in him that you cannot imagine it possible to break him up into lesser parts; or because, however full and great his nature, it is so thoroughly one, so vital and so true to itself, that, like a work of art, the whole of his being cannot be separated into parts without ceasing to be what it essentially is. In the former case the "individual" is an "atom"; in the latter he is "a great individuality."[1] The sense in which we shall make use of the notion of the individual, so far as we use it at all, will be the latter and not the former. And, therefore, we shall as far as possible discard the hackneyed term "Individualism," which embodies the former meaning only.[2]

If then we are to coin an expression which will indicate the common features of the theories outlined in the previous chapter, we may venture upon some such phrase as "prima facie theories," or "theories of the first look." By this I do not mean that they stand in the same rank with the views of the Greek thinkers, who, undisturbed by previous speculation, saw the great facts of social experience with a freshness and wholeness of vision with which they can never be seen again. The "first look" of our own day is of a different kind. It is the first look of the man in the

---

[1]See [*Philosophical Lectures and*] *Remains* [of Richard Lewis Nettleship, eds. A.C. Bradley and G.R. Benson (London: Macmillan, 1897), vol.] i, [p.] 160.

[2][Bosanquet develops his understanding of individuality as completeness and self-sufficiency in his Gifford Lectures for 1911 and 1912, *The Principle of Individuality and Value* and *The Value and Destiny of the Individual* (London: Macmillan, 1912 and 1913).]

street or of the traveller, struggling at a railway station, to whom the compact self-containedness and self-direction of the swarming human beings before him seems an obvious fact, while the social logic and spiritual history which lie behind the scene fail to impress themselves on his perceptive imagination.

We see then that these theories of the first appearance are mainly guided by this impression of the natural separateness of the human unit. For this reason, as we noted, the experience of self-government is to them an enigma, with which they have to compromise in various ways. And because their explanations of it are not true explanations but only compromises, they rest on no principle, and dictate no consistent attitude. For Bentham all solid right is actually in the State, though conceived by himself as a means to individual ends; for Mill it is divided between the State and the individual, by a boundary which cannot be traced and therefore cannot be respected; for Herbert Spencer all right is in the individual, and the State has become little more than a record office of his contracts and consents.

The assumption common to the theories in question is dictated by their very nature. It is not precisely, as is often supposed to be the case, that the individual is the end to which Society is a means. Such a definition fails to assign a character which is distinctive for any social theories whatever. For since Society is, at the lowest rate, a plurality of individuals, whatever we say of "the individual" may be construed as true of Society and vice versa, so long as all individuals are understood as differing only in number from one. Thus the "means" and the "ends" are liable to change places, as, for practical purposes, we saw that they did in Bentham.[3] The ethical term "altruism" illustrates this principle. It shows that by taking "the individual" as the "end," nothing is determined as to the relation between each individual and all, and it remains a matter of chance how far it is required of "each" individual in the name of the welfare of "the individual," to sacrifice himself to "all."

---

[3]See above, pp. 101–102. Thus, if we say what Bentham implies, that all the individuals (= "the individual") are the end, then there is no theoretical limit to the sacrifice which may be demanded from every individual on behalf of all the individuals. And thus the Society becomes the imperative end.

The fact is that the decisive issue is not whether we call the "individual" or "society" the "end," but what we take to be the nature at once of individuals and of society. This is the question of principle; and views which are at one in this have nothing which can in principle keep them apart, although they may diverge to the seemingly opposite poles of the liberty of each and the welfare of all. We have observed this sliding from one narrowness to its opposite, as between Bentham, Mill, and Herbert Spencer.

The root idea, then, of the views which we have been discussing, is simply that the individual or society – it makes no difference which we take – is what it prima facie appears to be. This is why we have called them "prima facie" theories or "theories of the first look." It would be a long story to explain how a first look can be possible in the eighteenth or nineteenth century A.D. But in brief, the history of thought shows certain leaps or breaks in culture; when the human mind seems to open its eyes afresh or to emerge on a new platform, from which new point of view all its adjustments have to be re-made and its perceptions re-analysed. In these new stages a great advance is involved; but the advance is potential, and the possible insight has to be paid for by an initial blindness.

Such an occasion it was on which the legislator or economist or natural philosopher of the modern world turned his gaze upon man in society. He saw him as "one of millions enjoying the protection of the law,"[4] and society as the millions of which he is one. Such an onlooker inevitably proceeds to treat the social whole as composed of units A, B, C, etc., who, *as they stand, and just as they seem to us when we rub against them in daily intercourse,* are taken to be the organs and centres of human life. From this assumption all the rest follows. Each of us, A, B, C, and all the others, seems to be, and to a great extent in the routine of life actually is, self-complete, self-satisfied, and self-willed. To each of us, A, B, or C, all the rest are "others." They are "like" him; they are "repetitions" of him, but they are not himself. He knows that they are something to himself; but this "something" is still "something else," and even

---

[4]B. Jowett, in conversation, to author. [Benjamin Jowett (1817–1893) was Master of Balliol College, Oxford, best known for his translations of Plato; he exercised immense influence on generations of English scholars.]

in ethical reflection he is apt to call his recognition of it "altruism" – an indefinite claim and feeling, touching his being at its margin of contact with neighbouring circles, the centres of which are isolated.

To the individual and society thus conceived – A, B, C, and the rest – it is plain that government can be nothing but self-protection. It is, in fact, a form of the impact of "others," scientifically minimised, and accepted because it is minimised. For this reason it is, as we saw throughout, alien to the self, and incapable of being recognised as springing from a common root with the spontaneous life which we pretend to be aware of only within our private magic circle. Then the forcible impact of B and C upon the circle of A is a necessary evil, a diminution, *pro tanto*,[5] of A. And the more altruistic A is the more he will recognise this, as affecting not himself only, but B and C also.

It is for this reason that, on the views in question, all law and government necessarily remain formal and negative as compared with the substantive and positive ends of the self. The maintenance of "liberty," of the circular or hexagonal[6] fences round A, B, C, and the rest is conceived as involving no determinate type of life, no relation to the ends which the units pursue within their hexagons. If in any way the self went beyond itself, and A recognised a positive end and nature which peremptorily bound him to B and the others, it would be impossible to keep this nature and end from reflecting themselves in the determinate content of the conditions of association between them. The assumption would be destroyed which keeps "government" alien to "self," and it would be possible to consider in what sense and for what reason the nature of a spiritual animal turns against itself with the dualism which the paradox of self-government embodies, and that in pursuit of its true unity.

2. We will now discuss Rousseau's treatment of the paradox of "self government." And we discuss it, not because it is complete or self-consistent, but rather because, while breaking through to the root of the whole matter, it is as incomplete and as inconsistent as are the efforts of our own minds to lay hold of any profound truth. It displays, in fact, on the great stage of the history of philosophy, precisely the struggle which

---

[5][See above, p. 18.]
[6]See p. 99.

each of us has to go through if he tries to pierce the surface of common-place fiction and tradition which persistently weaves itself about social facts. On almost every page there is relapse and vacillation. The fictions which are being cast aside continually reassert themselves; the embodi-ment of the principle which the author's genius has discerned is sought for in expedients essentially opposite to its nature, while the instruments which it has developed for itself are contemptuously rejected.

We are going to examine the main thesis of Rousseau's *Contrat So-cial*. The reader who is surprised to find in our account little or nothing of the "return to nature," "natural equality," and the "natural rights of the individual," may refer for these to Rousseau's earlier essays on theses propounded by the Academy of Dijon.[7] The first of the theses (1750) ran, "Whether the re-establishment of the sciences and the arts contrib-uted to purify morals"; and Rousseau's discourse, which won the prize, followed the lead of the thesis, started from the later Renaissance, and dealt in general with the phenomena of decadence – a very real problem. The notable feature of this brief essay is its constant vacillation between the attack on science, art, and education as such, and the criticism, by no means an undiscerning criticism, of their abuses. Rousseau's head is full, not of a primitive man, but of Socrates and Cato, of Sparta and republi-can Rome. A writer who speaks of Newton and Verulam[8] as preceptors of the human race can hardly be hostile to true intellectual achievement.[9] It is noteworthy that his zeal for educational reform is already apparent in this first published work.

---

[7][For translations of both discourses, see Jean-Jacques Rousseau, *The First and Second Discourses Together with Replies to Critics*, ed., trans., Victor Gourevitch (New York: Harper and Row, 1986).]

[8][In 1618, Francis Bacon was made Baron Verulam.]

[9]The whole piece breathes a spirit of prize essay paradox, and though, if sympathetically read, it is seen to be most characteristic of the author, no serious conclusion should be drawn from it as to his hostility to civilisation. A comic instance of his vacillation is pro-duced by the necessity he felt himself under, of excepting, from his general dispraise of modern letters, such Academies as that of Dijon, which was to judge his essay. For an ex-cellent appreciation of these earlier works, and of Rousseau in general, see the essay on "Our Natural Rights," in the *Lectures and Essays* of the late Professor W. Wallace, [(Ox-ford:] Clarendon Press, 1898.)

The second essay (1754), a much longer and more serious piece, is on the thesis, "What is the origin of Inequality among mankind, and is it justified by natural law?" It was dedicated, with expressions of extravagant laudation, to Rousseau's native state, the Republic of Geneva. His enthusiasm for this community, as for the ancient City-states, is a far truer guide to his genuine social ideas than any of his paradoxes about the state of nature and the bondage of social man. His genius, in fact, is very much under-rated by those who suppose him at any time to have believed the primitive state of nature, or earliest imaginable condition of the human race, to be capable of furnishing an ideal of life. He is perfectly aware that a state of nature, which is to furnish an ideal, must be selected at least from among the higher phases of man's evolution, after morality and the family have begun to form themselves, and language and property have made some advance. Here, again, vacillation is strikingly observable, and we can see that it arises from his profound insight. The vices of civilisation tend to force the desirable state of man down the scale of evolution, but the value of morality and respect for human nature tend to force it up, and Rousseau's argument embodies the struggle. For Rousseau is far too critical and clear-sighted to ascribe true morality or strictly human nature to a state of animal innocence, and he knows that virtue involves potential vice;[10] and therefore it is with hesitation and regret that he selects a middle state as representing his ideal, fully aware that it has forfeited animal innocence, without having attained human morality. Even the famous declamation against the first founder of property in land[11] seems to pass away in an admission that this was an inevitable stage in the growth of human capacities, which the author would not seriously desire to remain undeveloped. Two further points may be noted: first, the fundamental contention that men are by nature not equal but unequal, the evil of civilisation lying just in the replacement of natural by political inequality. If this political inequality

---

[10] He seems to regard the beginnings of industrial co-operation as the end of the "state of nature" in the widest sense. The remark that "iron and corn civilised man and ruined the human race," anticipates much in later speculations.

[11] ["The first man who, having enclosed a piece of ground, to whom it occurred to say this is mine and found people sufficiently simple to believe him was the true founder of civil society." Rousseau, *The Second Discourse*, loc. cit., note 7, p. 170 (Part II, para. 1).]

were considered as modifiable, it is plain that the view would point to an advantage in the way of equality[12] possessed by society over nature. Secondly, the view taken of natural liberty in relation to the social pact should be compared with that of the *Contrat Social*. In the essay, "natural liberty" is on the whole preferred; in the *Contrat*, another kind of liberty is held a truer good, although much of the tone and language associated with the preference of natural liberty continues by the side of the latter view. It is plain that we are dealing, not with an unconsidering fanatical enthusiasm for one or another state of man, but with the struggling insight, which sees evil but also good in all, and, with hesitation and reluctance, depresses the scale first in favour of the one, and then in favour of the other condition of human beings.

3. The famous opening words of chap. i of the *Contrat Social* (published 1762) sound like the beginning of a tirade against civilisation and the State. "Man is born free, and everywhere he is in chains. One thinks himself the master of others, who does not fail to be more of a slave than they." Here we might well suppose ourselves to be reading the preface to a demonstration that all social constraint is slavery, and that man, in a state of nature, possessed a liberty which he has now lost. We expect such an opening to be followed by a denunciation of the fetters of society, and a panegyric on the pre-social life. And there can hardly be a doubt that these sentences, along with a few similar phrases which stick in the memory, are the ground of the popular idea of Rousseau, shared by too many scholars.[13] But how does Rousseau go on? Here are the succeeding sentences. "How did this change take place? I do not know.

---

[12]We find Rousseau actually drawing attention to this in the *Contrat Social*. See *Cont. Soc.*, [Bk.] I, [ch.] ix, fin., where observe (1) that he half believes himself to have spoken of natural equality, and not of natural inequality, in the "Essay"; and (2) the "hedging" footnote on the illusoriness of social equality.

[13]Professor Henry Sidgwick and Professor Ritchie are notable exceptions. See also, and pre-eminently, the essay of the late Professor Wallace referred to above. [Sidgwick briefly but seriously discusses Rousseau in *The Methods of Ethics*, 7th edn (Chicago: University of Chicago Press, [1907] 1962), pp, 298–99 (Book III, ch. vi, sect. 2). However, in his *Outlines of the History of Ethics* (5th edn, (London: Macmillan, 1902), p. 267) Rousseau enters in as providing a "bold and fervid exaltation of nature at the expense of civilisation" – the sort of reading Bosanquet is criticising. For Ritchie's view, see his *Natural Rights: A Criticism of Some Political and Ethical Conceptions* (London: George Allen, 1891).]

What can render it legitimate? I think I can tell." Here, as previously in the *Discourse on Equality*, he (1) cuts himself loose in principle from the historical fiction of a social act succeeding a state of nature; and (2) he promises to furnish a justification for the change (or, striking out the quasi-historical term "change," for the condition of man), which is expressed by the words, "is everywhere in chains."

This then is the task which he has set himself. The sentences last cited show that his answer will, in some degree, turn its back on his question, and that really man had little natural freedom to lose, and is not everywhere in chains. But the fact that the problem first struck Rousseau's mind through a feeling of rebellion against social slavery, and a loathing for the civilisation of his day, sets him at the very beginning of the path which social theory has to traverse, and ensures that the difficulties which we all feel at times will be met in their sharpest form. He knows, in short, that something, which can look like utter bondage, is a fact; and he knows that this fact has to be justified.

After some chapters devoted to clearing away inadequate solutions of the problem, he re-states it as follows, in terms of that form of the supposed social contract in which it was regarded as a compact of all with all for the constitution of a community:

> To find[14] a form of association which shall defend and protect, with the entire common force, the person and the goods of each associate, and by which, each, uniting himself to all, may nevertheless obey only himself, and remain as free as before.

4. Before proceeding to examine the true meaning of this formula and its answer, we will briefly notice the conflict of ideas suggested by it. Man's freedom, it is implied, remains at the same level. Even his power is not increased; it is only that individuals combine their forces, previously isolated. These implications suit neither the view he starts from, nor the view he arrives at. If man had a natural freedom, and then submitted to society, though merely to increase his force of action, some of his freedom must be lost, and he cannot remain as free as he was before. But if man in society has a nature, which he could not have out of society, such that his individuality is maximised by the organisation of a so-

---

[14]*Contrat Social*, Book I, ch. vi.

cial whole, then it is plain that he is not merely as free "as he was before," but very much more free; free, indeed, strictly speaking, under social conditions alone. The notion which Rousseau started from, that man
has surrendered some part of a previous freedom in order to make the
most of the remainder, appears, as here, in the language of compromise,
frequently through the *Contrat Social*. But it is not effectively relied on,
for Rousseau is too acute to attempt a demarcation theory, and while he
assumes, for example, according to the literal notion of a compact, that
man only surrenders as much of his liberty as is necessary to the community, he sees that the sovereign is sole judge of this proportion and
consequently is absolute.[15] In the same way he first deduces the sovereign's right of inflicting capital punishment from the individual's pre-
existing right to risk his life in order to save it, in virtue of which he has
transferred to the sovereign a right to demand his life when necessary to
the public safety, which includes his own. And then, feeling this to be a
fiction, he ekes it out by the precisely contrary suggestion that a criminal
has broken the social treaty, has ceased to be a member of the community, and is dealt with as an enemy on terms of war.[16] This supplementation shows that Rousseau is aware of the weakness of his other account
of the matter, based on a right transferred to society. His constant failure,
entire or partial, to free himself from the language of "first appearance
theories," as we have ventured to call them, is just what makes him so
instructive, in view of the similar inclination which besets us all.

5. We will now examine the real nature of his solution. For the historical
fiction of a social contract, he substitutes, in answer to the problem formulated above (see section 3, end), the conditions which constitute a
"people" or commonwealth. He speaks, indeed, of the "act" or "contract" which constitutes it – a survival of the language which belongs to
the fiction.[17] But it is plain, even if he had not said so distinctly in the
first chapter, that he is dealing not with an act in historical time, but with
the essential nature of a social body. The "clauses of the contract," he
explains, are dependent on "the nature of the act"; they are implicit and

---

[15]Ibid., Book II, ch. v.

[16]Ibid.

[17]Ibid.

universal – that is to say, not capable of being affected by any actual or supposed agreement in contravention of what the essence of a body politic requires. He is, as he has clearly said in the previous chapter, analysing the "act" "by which a people is a people," i.e. the conditions of political unity.

The "clauses of the contract" then reduce themselves to a single one, "the total alienation of each associated member, with all his rights, [the language is moulded by the fiction of an actual contract and pre-social rights,] to the community as a whole." The community as a whole is therefore absolute. The subsequent passage, referred to above,[18] in which he speaks as if individual rights were retained, is a case of the vacillation on which we have remarked.

The essence of this "social pact" is further reducible to the following formula: "Each of us puts into the common stock his person and his entire powers under the supreme direction of the general will: and we further receive each individual as an indivisible member of the whole."

Instantaneously, in place of the particular person of each contracting party, this act of association produces a moral and collective body, composed of as many members as the assembly has voices, which receives from this same act its unity, its common self (*son moi commun*), its life, and its will. This public person which thus forms itself, by the union of all the others, used to take the name of city,[19] and now takes that of republic or body politic, which is called by its members State when it is passive, Sovereign when it is active, Power when comparing it with others.[20]

In this passage the formula of association, and much of the commentary upon it, imply the "contract" to have been an event in history. Such is the bearing of the words "act of association," "produces," "receives," "forms itself." It is admitted that Rousseau's thoughts are always more or less struggling with this conception, which, it must however be re-

---

[18]P. 112.

[19]From Rousseau's footnote in loc: "The true sense of this word is almost entirely effaced among the moderns; most of them take a town for a city, and a townsman for a citizen. They are not aware that the houses make the town, but the citizens make the city." Cf. Thucydides, *Histories* (*The Peloponnesian War*) 7.77.7, ἄνδρες γὰρ πόλις.

[20][Rousseau, *Contrat Social*, Book I, ch.vi.]

membered, he explicitly refuses to rely on; and henceforward, having sufficiently called attention to it, we shall not encumber ourselves with observing upon it in every instance.

Putting aside then the defective terminology, and bearing in mind that Rousseau considers himself to be analysing the essence of that act or character "by which a people is a people," we find in this passage very far-reaching ideas. We find that the essence of human society consists in a common self, a life and a will, which belong to and are exercised by the society as such, or by the individuals in society as such; it makes no difference which expression we choose. The reality of this common self, in the action of the political whole, receives the name of the "general will," and we shall examine its nature and attributes in the following chapter.

The primary point which it is necessary to make clear, however, is whether the whole set of ideas is to be seriously pressed, or whether the unity which they indicate is merely formal and superficial. For phrases of the kind here employed may be found in many earlier writers. The term "person," for example, comes through Hobbes from the Roman law. "*Persona*," in Roman law, we are told,[21] means either a complex of rights or the possessor of those rights, whether an individual or a corporate body. "*Unus homo sustinet plures personas.*" Thus a man may devolve his "persona" on another man. A corporation has a single "*persona.*" It is in this sense that for Hobbes, the State is a "real unity in one person," which person has been devolved by all the individuals of a multitude upon one man or a definite assembly of men, whose acts therefore are, politically speaking, the acts of the whole multitude so united in one "person."

This use of the term "person" is one of the cases alluded to in chapter i, where an abstraction of law has preserved the seed of a philosophical idea of unity. How far the unity thus indicated is an empty fiction, or how far it is grasped as something vital, into which the individual mind goes out and in which it finds what its nature demands, is what we now have to consider further.

---

[21] See e.g., [Thomas Hill] Green's, *Lectures on the Principles of Political Obligation*, [with preface by Bernard Bosanquet (London: Longmans, Green, 1895), sect. 44,] p. 61.

6. Chapters vii and viii of Book I of the *Contrat Social* show the out-come of Rousseau's conflicting ideas in a very few remarkable proposi-tions.

The question is whether the unity of a body politic is an arbitrary ab-straction or a fundamental force and reality.

Rousseau is discussing in chapter vii the guarantees which exist for a fulfilment of obligations by the sovereign (or whole) to its members and by the members to the sovereign respectively. As regards the obligation of the sovereign to its members, he runs straight into the fallacy referred to in chapter i [above]. He contends, that is to say, that the whole is nec-essarily, by its constitution, that which it ought to be, and being com-posed of all the individuals can have no interest opposite to theirs as a whole, while, qua sovereign, it is debarred from any such special[22] ac-tion as might be hurtful to any single individual. This presupposes that the whole always acts according to its idea as a whole, and neither is "captured" by individual interests nor transgresses the limits set to its action by restriction to true public concerns. But if this were so, the State would be perfectly wise and good; and we do not need to be told that a State, qua wise and good, could do no injustice to its members. The whole is of course liable to vices correlative to those which Rousseau is about to guard against when they arise in the individual.

And his view of individual disloyalty is decisive as to the vitality of his conception of political unity.

"Indeed," he says;

each individual may, as a man, have a particular will contrary to or unlike the general will which he has as citizen; his particular interest may speak to him quite differently from the common interest; his absolute and natu-rally independent existence may make him regard what he owes to the common cause as a gratuitous contribution, the loss of which would be less injurious to others than its payment is burdensome to himself; and considering the moral person which constitutes the State as an abstraction (*être de raison*), because it is not a man, he would enjoy the rights of the citizen without consenting to fulfil the duties of the subject – an injustice the progress of which would cause the ruin of the body politic.

---

[22]See below, p. 128.

In order, then, that the social pact may not be a vain formula, it tacitly includes the covenant, which alone can confer binding force on the others, that whoever shall refuse to obey the general will shall be constrained to do so by the whole body, which means nothing else than that he will be forced to be free.

In this passage Rousseau lays bare the very heart of what some would call political faith, and others political superstition. This lies in the conviction that the "moral person[23] which constitutes the state" is a reality, as opposed to the natural idea that it is an abstraction or fiction of the reflective mind (an *"ens rationis," être de raison*) because it is not an actual individual human being. The theories of the first appearance, as we have called them, are characterised by accepting as ultimate "the absolute and naturally independent existence" of the physical individual, and therefore regarding government as an encroachment on the self and force as oppression. Whereas, if the social person is taken as the reality, it follows, as Rousseau points out, that force against the physical individual may become a condition of freedom. We saw even in Mill how extreme cases bring out the necessity for assuming a "real" will at variance with the individual's immediate desire.[24] There is more to be said, of course, as to the limits within which force can be so applied.[25]

---

[23]For the meaning of "person," see account above, p. 114. Note on the meaning of "moral" as here used that it is determined by a general opposition to physical, as in "moral certainty." Nonetheless, this use of "moral person" forms an interesting stage in the advance from the physical individual through the legal "person" towards the notion of a higher or greater self.

[24]The trivial case which he takes, of its being no curtailment to freedom to keep a man off an untrustworthy bridge, as he certainly does not want to be drowned, has received terrible illustration of late ([21st] June, 1898) by the disaster at the launch of the "Albion." The disaster occurred because not enough force was used against the passionate momentary eagerness of individuals, and in favour of what it is fair to presume their real will would be. [Bosanquet is referring to the tragic deaths of 39 people due to the collapse of a wooden bridge at the launch of a new battleship at the Thames Iron Works in Blackwall. Those who died were mostly women and children who crowded onto the bridge in the hope of sighting the Duke and Duchess of York who were christening the vessel. According to *The Times* (June 22, 1898): "[T]he wood was old and boards had been erected as a warning to people not to venture upon the staging. The police and other officials also

It is worth while to cite here the whole of the short chapter viii, which draws out the consequences of the above conception of a social pact and of sovereignty.

Of the Civil Condition. – This passage from the state of nature to the civil state produces in man a very remarkable change by replacing, in his conduct, instinct by justice, and giving to his actions the morality which they lacked before. It is then alone that, the voice of duty succeeding to physical impulse, and right to appetite, man, who till then had only considered himself, sees himself compelled to act on other principles, and to consult his reason before listening to his inclinations. Although he deprives himself in this state of several advantages which he holds from nature, he gains such great ones in their place, his faculties exercise and develop themselves, his ideas expand, his sentiments are ennobled, his whole soul is exalted to such a degree that, if the abuses of his new condition did not often degrade him below that from which he has emerged,[26] it would be his duty to bless without ceasing the happy instant which tore him from it for ever, and from a stupid and narrow animal, made him an intelligent being and human.

---

endeavoured to keep the place free. Notwithstanding these warnings, however, a number of people succeeded in getting upon the bridge and very soon from 100 to 150 men, women, and children...were congregated there....[T]he launch took place...[and]...the plunge of the vessel produced a huge back-wash, and this, rising high above the bridge swept the people off into the river, which became a struggling mass of drowning people....Asked why the people were allowed on, a policeman replied, 'You know, people about here are not like a West-end crowd. Tell a West-end crowd to stand back and they do so, but these people, why, you would have to chuck them off before they would move.'"]

[25] See below, ch. viii.

[26] Cf. the well-known lines of Faust:

"Ein wenig besser würd' er leben,

Hätt'st Du ihm nicht den Schein des Himmelslichts gegeben;

Er nennt's Vernunft, und braucht's allein

Nur thierischer als jedes Thier zu seyn."

[A little better would he live, poor wight,

Had you not given him that gleam of heavenly light.

He calls it Reason, only to pollute

Its use by being brutaler than any brute.

Goethe, *Faust*, trans., George Madison Priest (Chicago: Encyclopaedia Britannica, 1955), "Prologue in Heaven."]

Let us reduce these *pros* and *cons* to terms easy to compare. What man loses by the social contract is his natural liberty and unlimited right to all which attracts him and which he can obtain; what he gains is civil liberty and the property of what he possesses. To avoid error in these reckonings we must carefully distinguish natural liberty, which has no bounds but the powers of the individual, from the civil liberty which is limited by the general will; and possession, which is only the effect of force or the right of the first occupant, from property, which can only be founded on a positive title.

We might, in view of the preceding, add to the gains of the civil state the moral freedom which alone makes man master of himself; for the impulsion of appetite alone is slavery, and obedience to the law which we have prescribed to ourselves is liberty. But I have already said too much on this head, and the philosophical sense of the word liberty is not my subject here.

Besides the terminology of the historical fiction this curious passage shows in the strongest light the struggle by which Rousseau passed from the position of the *Discourse on the Origin of Inequality* to that of the *Contrat Social*. The "hedging" of the sentence, "Although he deprives himself," etc., represents a loathing of the decadent society of his day, which was deep seated in Rousseau's mind, and which his life enables us thoroughly to understand. The son of a Genevese artisan, with a touch of vagabond impulses, and more than a touch of Wordsworthian genius, he was the first, perhaps, of great modern writers to feel the true democratic passion,[27] and to see his artificial age as Plato or as Ruskin[28] might have seen it. It was no small feat of insight to subdue his just repugnance so far as to estimate, in the language of the chapter before us, the use, as distinct from the abuse, of law and society.

---

[27] Note the sentence in *Émile*, "C'est le peuple qui compose le genre humain; ce qui n'est pas peuple est si peu de chose que ce n'est pas la peine de le compter." (Bk. IV, 3rd maxim.) ["The people are mankind; those who do not belong to the people are so few in number that they are not worth counting." *Émile*, trans., Barbara Foxlet (London: Dent, 1911), p. 186.]

[28] [John Ruskin (1819–1900) was an English art critic; he is best known for his role in the Gothic Revival movement in architecture and his *Modern Painters* (Kent: George Allen, 1883, 1888).]

As a feature of this conflict of ideas, we may observe more especially the notion of original individual right, ascribed to a condition of man in which, according to the previous paragraph, right could not exist. The phrase is merely taken up from previous writers, as is also the so-called "right of the first occupant." And the antithesis with true right and property, recognised by the social mind, in which this chapter presents them, has the effect of a destructive analysis of these uncritical conceptions.[29]

True right, then, begins with that social unity "by which a people is a people," figured by Rousseau under the image of the social compact. This unity is one aspect of the rule of reason, the sense of duty, and the essence of humanity. The quality of man is liberty,[30] and we here see that this fundamental principle which Rousseau has above laid down in an undetermined sense, must, in the course of his reasoning, take on the higher meaning demanded by the conceptions of this chapter.

And the import of the term "liberty" in this chapter is a measure of the modification of ideas which has been brought about in the process of "justifying" the "bondage" of man.[31] The famous sentence, "Man is born free, and everywhere he is in chains," now turns out to mean, "Man is born in natural liberty (which, if it refers to any actual condition at all, implies, 'in animal isolation'), and by subservience to social law, he attains the civil liberty through which alone he becomes truly man." Of course, however, the phrase "born free" has the undercurrent of meaning, "is born *for* the truest freedom," but in order that this import may be elicited the rhetorical antithesis, "and everywhere is in chains," must be abandoned.

The final paragraph of chapter viii makes it clear that Rousseau considers the civil state as an embodiment of moral liberty, while he is rightly anxious not to seem to cut the knot of his problem by appealing to the merely ethical or philosophical sense of the term "freedom." For this latter conception, taken by itself, is apt to be understood as the establishment of unity in the self by the path of renunciation. Now, the

---

[29]Rousseau's brilliant criticism, Book. I, ch. iii [of *Contrat Social*], has finally destroyed the conception of a right, whether natural or social, founded merely on force.

[30][*Contrat Social*] Book I, ch. iv.

[31]See [ibid.,] Book I, ch. i.

freedom of the true civil state is, on the one hand, only a stage in the ascent towards perfect ethical freedom or unity, for it involves rather the recognition of such freedom as the imperative end of social law, than the actual attainment of it; and, on the other hand, it is something broader and more substantial than ethical freedom is apt to be conceived as implying, because of that outgrowth of the self into an organised social content which the civil condition involves. The distinction between the civil state and ethical freedom is therefore a sound one, but yet does not prevent their juxtaposition in this passage from throwing important light on Rousseau's conception of the former.

The expansion of old conceptions in Rousseau's hands, and the direction in which his views are advancing, are well illustrated by the paragraph before us in comparison with Locke's idea of consent. A recent editor of the *Contrat*[32] cites in illustration of the words, "Obedience to the law which we have prescribed to ourselves is liberty," Locke's sentence, "The liberty of man in society is to be under no other legislative power but that established by consent in the commonwealth."[33] But Locke is speaking, according to his theory, of the actual or tacit consent of individuals to the establishment of a governing power; a consent which, for him, is conditional and revocable, and therefore fails to meet the full difficulty of self-government. Rousseau, borrowing very likely his actual phrases from Locke, is speaking of something quite different, viz., the recognition of a law and a will, with which one's everyday self may be at odds, as nevertheless one's truer and fuller self, and imperative as against the commonplace trivial moods which constitute one's inferior existence.

Thus far, then, we have seen how the problem of self-government is transformed by a deeper insight. (a) The negative relation of the self to other selves begins to dissolve away before the conception of the common self; and (b) the negative relation of the self to law and government begins to disappear in the idea of a law which expresses our real will, as

---

[32]M. Dreyfus-Brisac [See Jean-Jacques Rousseau, *Du Contrat Social*, ed., Dreyfus-Brisac, (Paris: F. Alcan, 1896).]

[33][John Locke], *Civil Government* [*The Second Treatise of Government* in *Two Treatises of Government*, ed., Peter Laslett (Cambridge: Cambridge University Press, [1690] 1960), p. 301 (sect. 22).]

opposed to our trivial and rebellious moods. The whole notion of man as one among others tends to break down; and we begin to see something in the one which actually identifies him with the others, and at the same time tends to make him what he admits that he ought to be. We have now to follow these ideas to their application.

CHAPTER V

THE CONCEPTION OF A "REAL" WILL

1. We saw in the course of the last chapter that for Rousseau's political theory everything turns on the reality of the "moral person" which constitutes the State. When active, this "moral" or "public person," or common self, is called sovereign;[1] and sovereignty for Rousseau consists in the exercise of the General Will;[2] and it is in this characteristic of political society that he finds that justification for the use of force upon individuals[3] which he set out to seek. At the close of the last chapter we noted the transformation in the problem of "self-government" which such a conception tends to produce. In face of it, the opposition between self and others, and between self and law or government, will have to be interpreted altogether afresh. The present chapter will be devoted to explaining the idea of a General Will with reference to Rousseau's presentation of it, and the rest of the work will develop and apply it more freely.

A few words may be said upon Rousseau's relation to Hobbes[4] and Locke, simply to illustrate the process by which deepening political experience awakened the ancient meaning within abstractions which had preserved it in a latent form.

Both Hobbes and Locke use expressions, in treating of the government and unity of a commonwealth, which closely resemble Rousseau's phrases respecting the General Will, the moral person, and the real unity.

Hobbes, for example, insisted that sovereignty must lie in a will and that this will must be real and must be taken as representing or standing for the will of the community. "This is *more than consent or concord, it is a real unity of them all* in one and the same person."[5] Only, interpreting "real" as implying inherence in tangible determinate individuals, he in fact *substituted* the will (taking the word in its ordinary sense) of a

---

[1] [*Contrat Social*], Book I, ch. vi.

[2] [Ibid.,] Book II, ch. i.

[3] [Ibid.,] Book I, ch. vii: cf. Book I. ch. i.

[4] See also p. 114 above.

[5] *Leviathan*, Part II, ch. xvii. Italics mine.

certain individual or certain individuals *for* the will of the community or moral person as such. His temperament was emphatically one of those described by Rousseau as treating the "*moral* person" as a fiction. But so far from abandoning for that reason all idea of actual effective unity, he replaces the fictitious or abstract unity of the "person" by the "real unity" of an actual human being or a determinate group of human beings, to be *taken as* the unity of the Commonwealth as such. Thus, for instance, with a logic which is irresistible on the basis which he adopts, he denies all possibility of other representation of the people where there is already a sovereign power. For the one and only representative of the people is for him the sovereign, on whom the "person" of the community is, by the very fact of his sovereignty, assumed to be conferred. We may say then, in short, that Hobbes places the unity of political society in a will, and that, in his sense, a real or actual will, but emphatically not in a general will. He inherits the language which enables him to predicate unity and personality of the state, but in his mouth the terms have not recovered a true political meaning, and the social right, which they are intended to account for, remains a mere name.

Locke brings to bear a truer political experience, but a far less coherent logic. He feels that actual government is a trust, and that the ultimate supreme power remains in the community as a whole. The difficulty in his case is to understand how the will or interest of the community as such obtains determinate expression. Generally, and apart from particular causes of dissent, it is to be taken as one with the will of the governing body to which, according to the constitution, the work of government is given in trust. But the trust is conditional, and theoretically revocable; the ultimate supreme power is in the community at large, which may withdraw the trust if its conditions are violated. Of course, no determinate means of doing this in a lawful manner is, or can be, suggested,[6] and therefore the will of the people is not expressed by Locke as a real or actual will. And so the right, which was to be displayed as social, re-

---

[6]The referendum is not really such a means. It can only work within a well organised constitution, and could not be used to re-make the whole constitution – the forms and conditions of sovereignty – at a blow.

mains a latent right in individuals to assent or to dissent, and society is not represented as a genuine unity.

For Hobbes, then, we might venture to say, political unity lies in a will which is actual, but not general; while for Locke it lies in a will which is general, but not actual. If the two are pressed to extremes, the former theory annihilates "self," and the latter annihilates "government." For the former there is no true right, because the will of the state is related as mere force to the actual individual will; for the latter there is no true right, because the individual's will remains a mere natural claim, which is never thoroughly transformed by social recognition and adjustment.

But if it were possible to inspire a logic as coherent as that of Hobbes, with a political content as large as that which animates Locke, a new ground would be won. And this is what Rousseau has attempted in his conception of a will at once actual and general; on the one hand, an absolute and determinate adjustment and recognition of rights; on the other hand, embodying in its recognitions all individual claims which represent a true individuality. Here, if such a theory were workable, we should have a genuine account of self-government, political obligation, and social right. It may be admitted that the theory is not workable in the form which Rousseau gave it. As Bentham contemptuously said, his doctrine would make all laws invalid, excepting, perhaps, those of the Republic of San Marino.[7] But we shall see that these difficulties arise just where Rousseau failed to be true to his own best insight; and we shall find indications in his writings which suggest a different conclusion.

2. What Rousseau means to indicate by his expression, "the General Will," may seem to many persons, as he clearly saw, to have no actual existence. It is of the nature of a principle operating among and underneath a great variety of confusing and disguising factors, and can only be defined by the help of an "as such" or "in so far as." It is, we might say, the will of the whole society "as such" or the wills of all individuals "in so far as" they aim at the common good. It is expressed in law, "in so far

---

[7][Jeremy Bentham, *The Theory of Legislation*, edited with an Introduction and Notes by C.K. Ogden, trans. (from the French of Etienne Dumont) Richard Hildreth (London: Kegan Paul, Trench, Trubner, 1864), p. 69.]

as" law is what it ought to be; and sovereignty, "as such," i.e. when truly itself because rightly acting for the common interest, is the exercise of the General Will. In its idea, as the key to the whole problem of self-government and freedom under law, it is that identity between my particular will and the wills of all my associates in the body politic which makes it possible to say that in all social co-operation, and in submitting even to forcible constraint, when imposed by society in the true common interest, I am obeying only myself, and am actually attaining my freedom. It embodies indeed the same factors as the conception of self-government, but in a shape which is a stage nearer to reconciliation. It postulates a will which in some sense transcends the individual whose will it is, and is directed upon an object of wider concern. And in one way or other, we know that this may be, and indeed always is the case, for our will is always directed to something which we are not.

We may, perhaps, approach Rousseau's thought more successfully by starting from the idea of what is implied in the nature of will, as a characteristic of an intelligent being. We may then find ground for conceiving that my will or yours, as we exercise it in the trivial routine of daily life, does not fulfil all that it implies or suggests. It is narrow, arbitrary, self-contradictory. It implies a "true" or "real" or "rational" will, which would be completely, or more completely, what ours attempts to be, and fails. Thus, it has been said that what Rousseau really aimed at, with his conception of the General Will, was the will "in itself," or the will as it would be if it carried out what its nature implies and demands.

We can see that some notion of this kind floats before Rousseau's mind from the predicates which he assigns to Sovereignty and the General Will, which are for him nearly convertible terms.

Sovereignty, for example, is inalienable and indivisible;[8] that is to say, it is a simple consequence of the nature of a body politic, "that by which a people is a people." You can no more alienate or break it into parts than you can alienate or break into parts the use of your own judgment. To be capable of sovereignty means to be a people "as such" or "as a whole," that is a living and choosing people. The people may of course give general orders to subordinates to hold good till revoked, as I may

---

[8][*Contrat Social*], Book II, chs. i and ii. Here Rousseau is following Hobbes very closely.

give a power of attorney for more or less specified purposes to another man. But that is the delegation "of power, not of will."

We see the author's intention still more clearly when he maintains that the General Will is always right,[9] and is indestructible.[10] Though it is always right, as Will, yet the people may be misled in their knowledge and judgment of details; though it is indestructible in the human breast, yet a man may vote at the polling booth on another issue than that which he would have before him if he consulted the General Will. He may answer by his vote not the question, "Is this for the public good?" but the question, "Is this for my private good?" If so, he does not indeed extinguish the General Will in himself, but he evades it. Or, as we might say, the man does not altogether cease, however ignorant or interested, to possess a man's leaning towards making the real best of himself, though his private interest may at times so master his mind as to throw the higher or common good into the second place. Thus, the relation of the general will to a community is plainly apprehended by Rousseau much in the spirit of the doctrine that man always aims at something which he takes to be good. And so the General Will is as much implied in the life

---

[9][ibid.,] Book II, ch. iii. In an article in the *New Statesman*, Mr Belloc had criticised the translation of "droite" by "right," and the author in reply (*New Statesman*, May 22, 1920) wrote "to urge that Mr Belloc or some other first-rate French scholar should, after carefully examining *Contrat Social*, livre II, chs. i-vi inclusive, express a considered opinion as to the exact nuance of Rousseau's meaning in calling the general will *toujours droite*. Mr Belloc says 'direct' is the word. I take it a translator must harmonise normal usage and context, and here context demands, I think, a rendering rather less neutral morally. It occurs to me, after considering Mr Belloc's suggestion, that 'straight,' with the moral connotation we give it in slang, pretty nearly says what is wanted, though we could not use it in literature. I believe that what Rousseau wanted to insist on *was* a sort of directness, viz., that the general will by definition aims at the public welfare, and so far ceases to be itself if any sinister interest diverts its path. But to an English ear the word 'direct' hardly connotes all this. 'Pure' as opposed to 'corrupt' – a feature Rousseau strongly emphasises – though it loses the metaphor, would perhaps represent what he wished to say." [Hilaire Belloc (1870–1953), author, essayist, journalist and, twice, Member of Parliament, was born in France, educated at the Oratory School Birmingham, under Cardinal Newman, and at Balliol College, Oxford. A brilliant debater and a devout Catholic, he engaged in lengthy controversies with such authors as the Fabian socialist H.G. Wells, and generally was contemptuous of the political, literary and social establishment.]

[10][*Contrat Social*], Book IV, ch. i.

of a society as some sort of will for good in the life of an individual. The two, in fact, are not merely analogous but to a great extent identical. The General Will seems to be, in the last resort, the ineradicable impulse of an intelligent being to a good extending beyond itself, in as far as that good takes the form of a common good. Though this impulse may be mastered or cheated in a degree, yet, if it were extinct, human life would have ceased.

We need not enter at length upon the question whether the good which extends beyond oneself is adequately described as the good which is general or common to oneself and others. It is plain that the unity of myself with others in a common good is the same in principle as the unity of myself with myself which I aim at in aiming at my own good. Thought and language, we should bear in mind, unite me to myself just as they unite me to others, and they expand my being by binding my own life into a whole no less than by making intercourse possible between my fellow men and myself. Just so, the good at which I aim extends beyond my trivial or momentary self − that is to say, is universal as against myself as particular − in ways which are not prima facie exhausted by saying that they include the good of others. But again, just like thought and language, the good which enables me to enter deeper into communion with myself or with the world must always have an aspect of extending that communion to others; and therefore, for the purposes of social philosophy, we may treat the universal good or self as also in its nature a general or common good or self. It is that at least, though it may be more, in accordance with the logical relation between the rational universal and the numerical generality.

This indestructible impulse towards the Good, which is necessarily a common good, the substantial unity and filling of life by the interests through which man is human, is what Rousseau plainly has before him in his account of the General Will. But it has rightly been observed[11] that he did not really distinguish this conception, analogous as it is to what Plato or Aristotle might have said of the "divine reason which is the source of the laws and discipline of the ideal polity," from the legal idea

---

[11] [Thomas Hill] Green, *Lectures on the Principles of Political Obligation* [with preface by Bernard Bosanquet, (London: Longmans, Green, 1895), sect. 68], p. 82.

of the sovereign "in the sense of some power of which it could reasonably be asked how it was established in the part where it resides, when and by whom and in what way it is exercised." We will point out, however, the negative and positive indications which he furnishes as to where it is not and where it is to be looked for. That he fails to emancipate himself from the fallacies which he acutely indicates is a phenomenon for which the reader is, I trust, sufficiently prepared.

3. Rousseau develops his idea of a General Will by the contrast which he draws between the General Will and the Will of All.[12] The General Will aims at a common interest; and it is this community of interest, and not the number of votes in which it may find expression, which in truth "generalises the will."[13] The Will of All aims at private interest as such ("*l'intérêt privé*"), and is only a sum of particular wills. Only, Rousseau fancies, if you let the particular wills fight it out freely, their differences are likely to cancel each other, and the General Will to make itself felt, like any pervading factor through a chaos of indefinite variations.

The important point in the idea of the "Will of All" lies in its being "a sum" of "particulars," as opposed to something common or general in its nature. Thus, in the limiting case, you may have a unanimous vote in favour of a certain course of action, and yet the voters may severally have been determined by aims and considerations which Rousseau would not admit to be capable of entering at all into a determination of the General Will. For a private affair *as such* is incapable in Rousseau's view of being made the subject of law, that is of an act of the General Will. Such an act must be general, not only in the number of votes (which, as we have seen, is the less important factor), but in the nature of its subject-matter, which must be, as we should say, a question of genuine public interest.[14] Now, when men's minds leave out of sight the public or truly general aspect of a question, and are determined, each of them severally, by the expected consequences to himself as a private individual; then, though all may practically agree on the decision which is arrived at, yet such a decision is founded on no view of truly public interest, but is

---

[12]*Contrat Social*, Book II, ch. iii.

[13]Ibid., Book II, ch. iv, cf. above.

[14][Ibid.,], Book II, ch. iv.

what Rousseau calls "a sum of particular wills." The distinction between such a sum of wills, and a will that aims at a truly common interest or good, rests upon that fundamental contrast between a mere aggregate and an organic unity, which is embodied in the opposing views of society which we have been discussing. Pushed to extremes, it might raise a difficulty for those who are not familiar with the logical distinction between a Judgment of Allness and a true Universal Judgment.[15] What harm can there be, it may be asked, in my voting according to the effect a measure will have upon my affairs, if everyone else is allowed to vote according to the effect it will have upon his affairs, especially as in the extreme case suggested, the result is that we are all agreed? What can be more for the general interest than a decision in which every particular interest is satisfied? On the mere basis of comparative generality, as estimated by number, there is plainly no answer to this objection. We meet here with another instance of the difficulties which arise from working with the notion of society as "self and others," and of the good as an altruistic aim. For in the case supposed, the others are all satisfied as much as myself; and so I should give weight to no higher aim by considering their interest than by considering my own, unless I considered it on different grounds from those which I admitted in judging of my own advantage. But any different, higher, or deeper grounds might just as well present themselves to me with reference to my own advantage as with reference to theirs; and would differ from motives of private interest, not by bringing about a more unanimous adhesion, but by belonging to a deeper appreciation of the common good, and therefore producing a less superficial unity of resolve. The real difference between Allness and true Universality is that a "universal" characteristic goes more deeply into the nature of that which it characterises than does a mark or attribute which, like the owner's name in the books of a library, simply happens to be attached *ab extra*[16] to all the objects in question. So here, the supposed accordant decisions of all the voters, as guided each by his strictly private interest, are not really or completely accordant. They happen to come together in one point which has to be settled at the moment; but

---

[15]See p. 127 above.

[16][*ab extra*: from outside]

beyond that they express no oneness of life or principle; still less can they give voice to any demand of the greater or rational self in which the real common good resides. This is what Rousseau means by saying that it is the community of the interest or the nature of the object, and not the number of voices, which distinguishes the General Will from the Will of All. It follows, therefore, that the private interest as such, which in the case supposed determines the individual voter, is not ultimately his true interest; and it may be said, "But if each followed his own true interest, the Will of All would be right." But a true interest, as opposed to an apparent interest, necessarily has just the characters which the true Universal has as against the collection of particulars, or the General Will against the Will of all. So that to say, "If everyone pursued his own *true* private interest the Will of all would be right," is merely to say, "If everyone pursued his *true* private interest he would pursue the common interest"; or "The Will of All, if directed to the common good, would be one with the General Will." The reason why it is necessary to insist upon the distinction between true and apparent interest, universal and aggregate of particulars, General Will and Will of All, is just that a true interest generally requires some degree of energy or effort, perhaps of self-sacrifice; while the purely private or apparent interest, the interest of each of us in his routine frame of mind, is that by which many are always determined, and a whole community is only too likely to be guided. That is why it is worth while to distinguish the Will of All from the General Will. Let us suppose that Themistocles had been beaten in the Athenian Assembly when he proposed that, instead of dividing the revenue from the silver mines among all the citizens, they should devote this revenue annually to building a fleet – the fleet which fought at Salamis.[17] It is easy to see that in such a case a relatively ideal end, demanding a certain self-denial, might appear less attractive to all the individuals – each keeping before himself his own separate share of profit – than the accustomed distribution of money. And if such a view had

---

[17][The battle of Salamis took place in 480 BC. The Persian fleet sought to destroy the Greeks ship anchored near the Salamis coast, and to defeat the Greek army stationed there. In the ensuing battle approximately two hundred Persian ships were destroyed, while the Greek losses were estimated to be around forty.]

gained the day, history would never have told, and no free Europe would have existed to understand, by what decision the true general will and common interest of Athens might have transcended the aggregate private interests of all her citizens. No doubt, it may be added, a true universal end is usually more powerful than a limited interest even in the mere idea of its operation; and we may ultimately find, in the benefits conferred by Athens on the world, a justification of her courage and self-denial, even by the rough and unreliable standard of the number of individuals beneficially affected.

If such a theory as that just stated were to be literally pressed, it would lead to the conclusion that a law which was not *really* for the general interest was not binding on the subjects of a state. For, by the definition, such a law could not be a true act of sovereignty. No political theorist, however visionary, could accept such a conclusion as this, and Rousseau, seeing that the decision of the recognised sovereign must be final, attempts to show how and when it comes nearest to a true General Will.

The decisive point of his doctrine on this subject is his hostility to representative government,[18] and his consequent demand of a primary assembly and a small community as the only guarantees for the genuine expression of a will for the common good. "The English people," according to his well-known saying, "is only free during a general election." Further, it is a sign that the Will of All is, on the whole, coinciding with the General Will, when unanimity prevails in the assembly. But long discussions and the organisation of minor "interests" and associations within the state, in short, all the phenomena of mature political life, are signs and conditions of failure to express the General Will, which is most likely to make itself felt when particular wills neutralise one another in the way explained above.[19]

Now all this makes it clear that in endeavouring to point out the signs of the General Will, Rousseau is really enthroning the Will of All. He aims at eliciting a direct opinion, uncontaminated by external influence or interest, from each and every member of the citizen body. In this aim, what is present to his mind is of course the popular idea of the ancient

---

[18][*Contrat Social,*] Book III, ch. xv; cf. Book IV, ch. ii.
[19]See p. 128 above.

City-state. But the actual working even of Athenian or of Roman institutions was far more subtle and complex than this. And more especially, the very core of the common good represented by the life of a modern Nation-state is its profound and complex organisation, which makes it greater than the conscious momentary will of any individual. By reducing the machinery for the expression of the common good to the isolated and unassisted judgment of the members of the whole body of citizens, Rousseau is ensuring the exact reverse of what he professes to aim at. He is appealing from the organised life, institutions, and selected capacity of a nation to that nation regarded as an aggregate of isolated individuals. And, therefore, he is enthroning as sovereign, not the national mind, but that aggregate of private interests and ideas which he has himself described as the Will of All. He is so far aware of this that, as we have seen, he refuses to contemplate a great modern nation as a political whole, because he fails to conceive how, for such a community, the General Will can satisfactorily find expression. But in as far as he commits himself to the view that the sovereign, constituted as he would have it, "necessarily is what it ought to be," or "is incapable of injustice to any of its members," so far he has forgotten the dangers of the Will of All, and has affirmed the absolute supremacy of the popular will in the very sense against which his conception of the Will of All is a protest. The notion of primary assemblies and of direct participation in citizen life has no doubt a real lesson for the political theorist; but it does not point to reducing the whole political system of a great state to a model which never, perhaps, thoroughly fulfilled its idea except under very special conditions.

4. The other and more fruitful direction of Rousseau's speculations upon the General Will is to be found in his remarks on the function of the Legislator. We will approach them by help of a short restatement of the problem as it now stands.

It was observed above that what Rousseau had before him in his notion of the General Will might be described as the "Will in itself," or the Real Will. Any such conception involves a contrast between the Real Will and the Actual Will, which may seem to be meaningless. How can there be a Will which is no one's Will? and how can anything be my Will which I am not fully aware of, or which I am even averse to?

This question will be treated more fully on psychological grounds in a later chapter. For the present, it is enough to call attention to the plain fact that often when people do not know what they mean, they yet mean something of very great importance; or that, as has commonly been said, "What people demand is seldom what would satisfy them if they got it." We may recall the instances[20] in which even Mill admitted that it is legitimate to infer, from the inherent nature of will, that people do not really "will" something which they desire to do at a given moment. The example of slavery is a striking one. A man may contract to become a slave, but no civilised government will enforce his contract at law, and the ultimate reason for the refusal is, as Mill in effect points out, that man's nature is to exercise will – to have liberty – and a resolution to divest himself of this capacity must be taken as *ipso facto* void, by contradicting the very essence of humanity.[21]

Now the contradiction, which here appears in an ultimate form, pervades the "actual" will, which we exert from moment to moment as conscious individuals, through and through. A comparison of our acts of will through a month or a year is enough to show that no one object of action, as we conceive it when acting, exhausts all that our will demands. Even the life which we wish to live, and which on the average we do live, is never before us as a whole in the motive of any particular volition. In order to obtain a full statement of what we will, what we want at any moment must at least be corrected and amended by what we want at all other moments; and this cannot be done without also correcting and amending it so as to harmonise it with what others want, which involves an application of the same process to them. But when any considerable degree of such correction and amendment had been gone through, our own will would return to us in a shape in which we should not know it again, although every detail would be a necessary inference from the whole of wishes and resolutions which we actually cherish. And if it were to be supplemented and readjusted so as to stand not merely for the life which on the whole we manage to live, but for a

---

[20]See pp. 96–97 and 116[n24] above.

[21]"Renoncer à sa liberté, c'est renoncer à sa qualité d'homme." *Contrat Social*, Book I, ch. iv. ["To renounce liberty is to renounce being a man."]

life ideally without contradiction, it would appear to us quite remote from anything which we know. Such a process of harmonising and re-adjusting a mass of data to bring them into a rational shape is what is meant by criticism. And criticism, when applied to our actual will, shows that it is not our real will; or, in the plainest language, that what we really want is something more and other than at any given moment we are aware that we will, although the wants which we are aware of lead up to it at every point.

To obtain something which approximates to a real will, then, involves a process of criticism and interpretation, which may be either natural or intellectual; that is to say, it may proceed by "natural selection," through the method of trial and error, or it may be rapidly advanced at favourable moments by the insight of a great mind. But some forwardness in this criticism and interpretation, bringing with it some deposit, so to speak, of objects of volition in which the private will, so far as it is distinguished at all, finds harmony and expansion, must be coeval with social life, and, in short, with humanity.

It is such a process of interpretation that Rousseau ascribes to the legislator. He fathers on him the whole labour of history and social logic in moulding the customs and institutions of mankind. And in agreement with our general attitude to Rousseau's historical imagination, we may take what he says of legislation and the legislator as an expression of his views on the function of customs and ordinances in the constitution of will. It is very remarkable, considering the other aspects of his views, that he should have conceived so distinctly, as the following passage shows that he did, the immense contrast between a real will and anything which could be presented as a whole in the momentary consciousness of human beings.

Here is his statement of the problem:[22]

> Laws are, strictly speaking, only the conditions of civil association. The people which submits to the laws ought to be their author. Only the associates can have the right to regulate the conditions of the society. But how are they to regulate them? Can it be done by a common agreement, by a sudden inspiration? Has the body politic an organ for pronouncing its acts

---

[22]*Contrat Social*, Book II, ch. vi.

of will? Who will give it the necessary foresight to form such acts and to publish them before they are needed? Or how is it to pronounce them at the moment when they are required? How is a blind multitude, which often does not know what it wills, because it rarely knows what is good for it, to execute for itself so great and difficult an enterprise as a system of legislation? Of itself, the people always wills the good, but it does not always see it. The general will is always right, but the judgment which guides it is not always enlightened. It must be made to see objects such as they are, and, sometimes, such as they ought to appear to it; it must be shown the right road which it seeks, must be protected from the allurements of private will; places and times must be brought close to its eyes, and the attractions of present and visible advantages counter-balanced by the danger of remote and latent evils. Private persons see the good which they reject; the public wills the good which it does not see. All alike need guidance. The former must be obliged to conform their will to their reason; the latter must be taught to know what it wills.[23] Then, from the public enlightenment there results the union of understanding and of will in the social body; and hence the precise co-operation of the parts and the greatest power of the whole. Hence springs the necessity of a legislator.

In the following chapter[24] Rousseau touches the essence of laws and institutions in a few words, which only embody a contradiction or a miracle because he is thinking of the legislator's work as a creation accomplished at one blow.

In order that a people at its birth should have the capacity to appreciate the sound maxims of policy and follow the fundamental rules of political reason, it would be necessary for the effect to become the cause; for the so-

---

[23]There is a prima facie contradiction in this rhetorical antithesis; if all private individuals were enlightened, but selfishly interested, there could be no public goodwill. Compare, to illustrate Rousseau's meaning here, *Considérations sur le gouvernement de Pologne*, ch. vii. "Le législateur en corps est impossible à corrompre, mais facile à tromper. Les représentants sont difficiles à tromper, mais aisément corrompus, et il arrive rarement qu'ils ne le soient pas." [Edmond] Dreyfus-Brisac, *Contrat Social* [Paris: F. Alcan, 1896)], p. 169, n. ["The legislator as a body is impossible to corrupt but easy to put upon. Its representatives are difficult to put upon but easy to corrupt; and it rarely happens that they are not corrupted." Rousseau, *The Government of Poland*, trans., Wilmore Kendall (Indianapolis: Bobbs-Merrill, 1972), p. 35.]

[24]*Contrat Social*, Book II, ch. vii.

cial spirit, which is meant to be the work of the legislation, to preside over the legislation itself, and for men to be, before laws are made, what they are meant to become by their means.

The legislator then, in face of this contradiction, must have recourse to supernatural sanctions.

But the paradox precisely expresses the fact. Laws and institutions are only possible because man *is* already, what they gradually make more and more explicit; because he has a general will, that is, because the good which he presents to himself as his own is necessarily in some degree a good which extends beyond himself, or a common good. The criticism or interpretation which elicits the general will or actual social spirit, by removal of contradictions, and embodiment in permanent form, is essentially one with the work which Rousseau ascribes to the legislator. And his paradox is removed when we understand that the legislator is merely one of the organs of the social spirit itself, as it carries out its self-criticism and self-interpretation, in part by trial and error and in part by conscious insight and adjustment. The habits and institutions of any community are, so to speak, the standing interpretation of all the private wills which compose it, and it is thus possible to assign to the General Will an actual and concrete meaning as something different at once from every private will, and from the vote of any given assembly, and yet as standing on the whole, for what both the one and the other necessarily aim at sustaining as the framework of their life. It is needless to observe that such a representation of the Real Will is imperfect, since every set of institutions is an incomplete embodiment of life; and any given system of life is itself also incomplete. It is more important to remember that, though always incomplete, just as the system of sciences is an incomplete expression of truth, the complex of social institutions is, as we have seen, very much more complete than the explicit ideas which at any given instant move any individual mind in volition.

CHAPTER VI

THE CONCEPTION OF LIBERTY,
AS ILLUSTRATED BY THE FOREGOING SUGGESTIONS

1. We have now seen that the problem of Self-Government may be regarded from a point of view other than that which presented it as a contradiction in terms. The contradiction depended on the absolute opposition between self and others which was embodied in the prima facie idea of society; the result of which was that all increase of individuality and all assertion of self were at the first view hostile as regarded others, and liberty, the condition of individuality, became a negative idea, prescribing as it were a maximum of empty space to be preserved against all trespassers, round every unit of the social whole. We saw that notions of this kind were pushed so far as to endanger the fundamental principle, according to which self-affirmation is the root of morality, and it was maintained that the ethical attitude essentially lay in the negation and limitation imposed by social life upon the natural tendency to self-assertion.[1] According to these ideas, the self in society is something less than, if it could so exist, it would be out of society, and liberty is the arrangement by which, at a sacrifice of some of its activities, it is enabled to disport itself *in vacuo*[2] with the remainder.

But if we may give weight to the suggestions of the two previous chapters, the assumptions which we work with are transformed. The difference of principle is that the average individual, such as each of us takes himself to be in his ordinary[3] trivial moods, when he sees, or thinks he sees, nothing in life but his own private interest and amusement – this average individual is no longer accepted as the real self or individuality. The centre of gravity of existence is thrown outside him. Even his personality, his unique and personal being, the innermost

---

[1] See above, pp. 98–99.

[2] [*in vacuo*: in a vacuum.]

[3] There is a difficulty in stating this point without confusion, just because the "ordinary" individual, being at the bottom different from what he seems, is actually determined in all sorts of ways consciously and unconsciously, by demands and ideas which go far beyond what he would admit to determine him.

shrine of what he is and likes to be, is not admitted to lie where a careless scrutiny, backed by theoretical prejudice, is apt to locate it. It is not in the nooks and recesses of the sensitive self, when the man is most withdrawn from things and persons and wrapped up in the intimacies of his feeling, that he enjoys and asserts his individual self to the full. This idea is a caricature of the genuine experience of individuality. It is true that to feel your individuality is to feel something distinctive, which gives you a hold and substance in yourself and a definite position among others, and, it may be, against them. But on a careful consideration, it will be found that this substance and position are always sustained by some kind of determinate achievement or expansion on the part of the self. It always comes from taking hold of the world in some definite way; which, just because it is definite and affirmative, is at once a distinct assertion of the self, and a transition from the private self into the great communion of reality. The simplest machine will show us that it is the difference of the parts which enables them to make a whole. And so, we are now suggesting, it is in the difference which contributes to the whole that the self feels itself at home and possesses its individuality.

Following up such thoughts as these, we see that there is a meaning in the suggestion that our real self or individuality may be something which in one sense we are not, but which we recognise as imperative upon us. As Rousseau has said of the social self, we say more generally of the self or life which extends beyond our average private existence, that it is more real than we are, and we only feel ourselves real in proportion as we identify ourselves with it.

With such suggestions in our minds, we see the problem of liberty in a new light. Liberty, no doubt, is as Rousseau has told us, so far agreeing with Mill, the essential quality of human life. It is so, we understood, because it is the condition of our being ourselves. But now that it has occurred to us that in order to be ourselves we must be always becoming something which we are not, or in other words, we must always recognise that we are something more than we have become, liberty, as the condition of our being ourselves, cannot simply be something which we have, still less something which we have always had – a *status quo* to be maintained. It must be a condition relevant to our continued struggle to assert the control of something in us, which we recognise as imperative upon us or as our real self, but which we only obey in a very imperfect degree. Thus it is that we can speak, without a contradiction, of being forced to be free.[4] It is possible for us to acquiesce, as rational beings, in a law and order which on the whole makes for the possibility of asserting our true or universal selves, at the very moment when this law and order is constraining our particular private wills in a way which we resent, or even condemn. Such a law and order, maintained by force, which we recognise as on the whole the instrument of our greatest self-affirmation, is a system of rights; and our liberty, or to use a good old expression, our liberties, may be identified with such a system considered as the condition and guarantee of our becoming the best that we have it in us to be, that is, of becoming ourselves. And because such an order is the embodiment up to a certain point of a self or system of will which we recognise as what ought to be, as against the indolence, ignorance, or rebellion of our casual private selves, we may rightly call it a system of self-government or free government; a system, that is to say, in which ourselves, in one sense, govern ourselves in another sense; not as Mill has said, by each one of us being subject to all the "others" (taking "others" in the same sense in which each of us is "one"), but by all of us, as casual private units, being subject to an order which expresses, up to a certain point, the rational self or will which, as rational beings, we may be assumed[5] to recognise as imperative.

2. Before proceeding to develop the idea of liberty, we may consider for a moment the closely analogous idea of "nature" and what is "natural."

Like the notion of "liberty," which is that of "being able to be yourself," the notion of nature, which is that of "coming to be *of* yourself, or *of* itself," has always, however imperfectly apprehended, exercised immense power over the mind. It is felt that you have touch with reality when you have found something which can grow of itself. But again, like the notion of liberty, the notion of nature is apt to be apprehended in a form so partial as to be practically negative, and in this form, to be

---

[4]For limitations see below ch. viii below.

[5]In principle, actual individual assent is not needed. The question when the assumption breaks down belongs to the subject of the duty of rebellion and the significance of punishment. [On punishment, see Bosanquet, *Some Suggestions in Ethics* (London: Macmillan, 1918; 2nd edn 1919). See below, ch.viii, pp. 203ff.]

given a hostile bearing against what are, in fact, completer phases of the same idea.

That which is natural, or by nature, in the most obvious sense – what most plainly appears to have "come of itself" – is what comes first in time, and what comes with the least putting together – the primitive and the simple as against the late and the complex. And so in the theoretical inquiry after what is solid and can be relied upon, there constantly recurs in all ages the tendency to story-telling; to the narration of what is supposed to have come first, as the simple spontaneous beginning out of which the world as we know it has emerged with greatly altered attributes. The note of story-telling is unmistakable in this naive theory, whether we find it in poets who portray the Golden Age, from Hesiod downwards,[6] or represented as a fallacy of social compact by Plato in the second book of the *Republic*,[7] or adopted as a juristic theory by Tacitus[8] and the writers who relied on the idea of a "state of nature," down to Rousseau.

---

[6]The resemblance between Hesiod's dream of the Golden Age and modern doctrines of intensive culture is startling, and there is probably a true historical continuity between them. This does not involve the assertion that there can be no truth in the latter, but it does suggest that the disproportionate emphasis laid upon it (e.g. by Fourier and in *Merrie England*) indicates an element of the old "Nature" fallacy. [Hesoid (8th century BC) is known as providing one of the earliest expressions of utopianism, describing a golden age in which the earth spontaneously bore fruit and all lived in peace. See Hesoid, *Works and Days*, ed., M.L. West (Oxford: Clarendon Press, 1978). Charles Fourier (1772–1837) was a French socialist and utopian writer; in his socialist utopian community – the "phalanstery" – everyone's passions would be fully satisfied. See his *Passions of the Human Soul and Their Influence on Society and Civilization*, trans. Hugh Doherty, (London: Hippolyte Balliere, 1851); Robert Blatchford (1851–1943) was a socialist who wrote for the *Clarion* newspaper; in his *Merrie England* (London: Clarion Office, 1894), Blatchford presented an English centralized socialist utopia, where industrialisation was countered by planning and agriculture.]

[7]*Republic*, 358 E.

[8]*Annals*, [ch.] iii, [p.] 26: cf. *Germania*, ch. xix, 20, "Neque corrumpere et corrumpi 'seculum' vocatur...." ["Nor is corrupting or yielding to corruption called the custom of the age."] Note the identification of "our age" with corruption; cp. use of *fin de siècle*. [Tacitus (approx. 55–117 AD) was a Roman jurist who studied the law of the Germans. See *Annals of Tacitus* (London, Macmillan, 1877); *The Agricola and Germania of Tacitus* (London, Macmillan, 1879).]

It may be observed at this point that the conception of a "law of nature" made a very valuable middle term between the conception of a purely primitive condition of the world and the ideal of a complete society. The logical reason is plain. The instinct of getting at something solid and permanent, which first reveals itself by going back to the supposed original or simple, soon attaches itself also to what is *generally* found to exist, understanding generality as a mark of that tendency to come of itself which it feels to attach to what is real and able to stand in its own right. But generality is a clue which leads a long way; and the mind passes from saying "Fire burns[9] by nature, for it burns everywhere; but law is variable"[10] to observing that there are features of law which have their own generality, and there thus appears to be a "natural" element in law, which may mean the right of the strongest,[11] but may again amount to a tendency to come out of the "state of nature." Just in the same way, the conception of Liberty has always drawn from experience a certain positive tendency to progress, and has never perhaps, even in the most fanatical theory, maintained the full demand for isolation which its negative bearing might seem to imply.

---

[9]Argument cited by Aristotle, *Ethics*, v. 10 [Sir David Ross translates thus: "Of political justice part is natural, part legal; natural, that which everywhere has the same force and does not exist by people's thinking this or that; legal, that which is originally indifferent, but when it has been laid down is not indifferent, e.g. that a prisoner's ransom shall be a mina, or that a goat and not two sheep shall be sacrificed, and again all the laws that are passed for particular cases, e.g. that sacrifice shall be made in honour of Brasidas, and the provisions of decrees. Now some think that all justice is of this sort, because that which is by nature is unchangeable and has everywhere the same force (as fire burns both here and in Persia), while they see change in the thing recognized as just." *Nicomachean Ethics*, trans., W.D. Ross (Oxford: Oxford University Press, 1955), Book V, sect. 7 (1134b18–1134a5).]

[10]Just so, in strict science, from the Atomists downwards, the primary qualities (spatial) are real, the secondary (e.g. colours) conventional (or, as we say, "subjective"); the former hold good more generally than the latter. [By the "atomists" here Bosanquet may be referring to Greek atomists such as Democritus (5th century BC), who sought to reconcile the unchangability of matter with variable sense data.]

[11]Plato, *Gorgias*, [Stephanus reference] p. 484. [See Plato, *Gorgias*, trans., W. Hamilton (Harmondsworth: Penguin Classics, 1963), p. 79.]

But again, the instinct which, in looking for what has power to grow or come of itself, lays hold of what is merely primitive or merely general, has in all great epochs of thought been met by a deeper insight.

It is not merely what we are born *as*, or what the world begins with, that comes of itself. The most ordinary conception of growth involves maturity, and the term "nature" in Greek and Latin, as in English, can indicate not only what we are born *as*, but what we are born *for*, our true, or real, or complete nature. Thus the great thinkers of every age have been led to something like Aristotle's conception, "what a thing is when its growth is completed, that is what we call its nature[12] (growth or evolution)"; and so, if we are to think of "nature" as a whole, it will not be, as when we speak of "natural" science, an outward world, whether of atoms or of organisms, contrasted both with God and with Man, "for nature in Aristotle is not the outward world of created things; it is the creative force, the productive principle of the universe."[13] To us, inclined to contrast the natural at once with the human and the divine, there is something startling in the vivid reality with which the Greek thinkers hold the three ideas together. The creative activity of the divine principle seems for Plato to be actually one with growth, or nature, or evolution.[14] It may be of interest to cite the great passage in which Plato lays his finger on the common fallacy.[15]

Many learned men say that the elements and inorganic and organic world below man came by nature and chance, but that law and justice and man's works and social institutions and religion are merely conventional, variable, and untrue. But we must maintain that law and religion and man's works exist by nature, or are not lower than nature, being the products of mind according to right reason....For they give the name of nature to the

---

[12]Aristotle, *Politics*, i. I. [1252b-1253a. See *The Politics of Aristotle*, trans., Ernest Barker (London: Oxford University Press, 1958), p. 5.]

[13][S.H.] Butcher, *Aristotle's Theory of Poetry and Fine Art* [London: Macmillan, 1898], p. 116.

[14]*Republic*, X, 597 [See the complete and unabridged Jowett translation of Plato's *Republic* (New York: Vintage Books, [1894] 1991)].

[15]*Laws*, 889ff, abridged. [See the *Laws of Plato*, trans., Thomas L. Pangle (New York: Basic Books, 1980), pp. 285ff.]

origin of the earliest things;[16] but if really mind is earliest of all things, then *it* may rightly be said to be superlatively natural.

And so, as the universe is for the great thinkers at once natural and divine, the same applies to human society. Not only in Aristotle's trenchant expressions to the effect that the City-State is a natural growth, but in the whole of Plato's careful analysis of moral and social life, we find society depicted as a living and growing creature, in which man's nature expands itself from more to more, having its own essence progressively communicated to it. And so we find that the peculiar naturalness of the primitive and the simple is only an illusion, caused by the greater difficulty of recognising the larger individuality which comes both of and to itself in the later and more complex phases of life. But whatever it was that was real and that came of itself in the primitive and simple is there to a greater degree – with more reality and as the same self, only more complete – in the later and complex. The idea of a diminution of being as we pass from the simpler to the more developed self is a fallacy of non-recognition.

Rousseau, as we saw, maintains in words the traditional opposition between the natural and the civil or moral condition of man. From the tendency of his views, however, we might have expected that in his philosophy the wheel would come full circle, and the term "nature" would revert to its Greek meaning. But this is not the case, though in *Émile* there is a compromise which points in some such direction. Yet a remarkable passage[17] from Burlamaqui, a Genevese jurist, the earlier contemporary of Rousseau, shows the reversion to the Greek view of social nature completed in principle.

La liberté civile l'emporte de beaucoup sur la liberté naturelle, et, par con-

---

[16]We are not dealing here with Platonic interpretation, but it seems necessary to point out that, literally taken, this passage accepts the principle that nature = primary genesis, and sets out to prove mind to be natural in this sense. We might rather reject the appeal to succession in Time altogether, as at bottom Plato means to. But we see how emphatically mind is for Plato the superlatively natural.

[17][Jean-Jacques Burlamaqui, *Principles du Droit Politique* (Amsterdam: Zacharie Chatelain, 1751), two vols.] cited in Dreyfus-Brisac's edition of the *Contrat Social*, [(Paris: F. Alcan, 1896)] p. 39. [Burlamaqui (1694–1748) was a Swiss political theorist. His main work was *Principles of Natural and Politic Law*.]

séquent, l'état civil qui l'a produit est de tous les états de l'homme le plus parfait, et, à parler exactement, le véritable état naturel de l'homme. L'établissement d'un gouvernement et d'une puissance souveraine, ramenant les hommes à l'observation des lois naturelles,[18] et par conséquent dans la route de bonheur, les fait rentrer dans leur état naturel, duquel ils etaient sortis par le mauvais usage qu'ils faisaient de leur liberté.[19]

Upon this reversion to ancient usage there followed the movement of the age of romantic genius and of organic science, and with Goethe's *Erdgeist*[20] and Wordsworth's religion of Nature the restriction of the natural to the primitive and simple was destroyed. Nature still remains a point of view under which we regard what relatively speaking "comes of itself," but it has ceased to exist as a question-begging predicate, attached to pre-social or extra-social conditions of man.

3. Liberty, as understood by the writers who were discussed in chapter iii of the present work, is related to the State much as Nature, in the mouth of story-telling theory, is related to civilised society. We saw that Seeley in his *Introduction to Political Science*[21] lays it down that "perfect liberty is equivalent to total absence of government." And this no doubt fairly represents our first notion of the matter, when cleared of the limitations imposed upon it by practical life, which limitations – really a first hint of the truth – we are apt to mistake for mere sophistications and imperfections. We noted in Rousseau the surviving contrast between

---

[18]Note the value of "natural law" as a middle term equivalent to the general and rational features of positive law, and forming a step by which the "natural" is carried beyond the supposed "state of nature."

[19]["Civil liberty prevails by far over natural liberty and, consequently, the civil state that produces it is, of all the conditions of man, the most perfect and, to be precise, the true natural state of man. The establishment of a government and of a sovereign power, bringing men back to the observance of natural laws and, consequently, [putting them] on the road to happiness, makes them return into their natural state, from which – through the bad use that they had made of their liberty – they had come out." (Editors' translation.)]

[20]["Earth-spirit." Goethe viewed nature as forming an organic unity, a view that he derived from neo-Platonism. Wordsworth is sometimes also described as a sort of Platonist, though it seems doubtful he read much Plato. He is known, however, for his paeans to nature: "One impulse from a venal wood may teach more of man/ of moral evil and good, than all the sages can."]

[21]Seeley, [See ch. ii, note 30 and ch. iii, note 29] quoted p. 98 [n] above.

natural liberty on the one hand and civil or moral liberty on the other, and we observed that the expanding idea of what was natural could not be prevented from covering the ground of the civil or moral life. The thread of connection, or rather the ferment of expansion, we found to be, in the case of nature, the idea of self-origination. That was natural which came of itself.

(α) In the simple ideal of liberty, as equivalent to the absence of all government – for we must not forget that it is an ideal, obtained by neglecting the facts of life which run counter to it – there is clearly embodied a claim which commands our respect. The claim is so self-evident and so convincing to average human feeling – Mr Spencer would indeed say, with some truth, to animal feeling in general – that its precise nature is seldom stated in distinct language. We have assumed above that the root of it lies in the claim to be ourselves. But it is safer to take it in the shape which it actually has for the average consciousness, and this is the negative shape, as a claim to be free from constraint.[22] If we ask, "What is constraint?" the answer is founded on the current distinction between myself and others as different minds attached to different bodies. It is constraint when my mind is interfered with in its control of my body either by actual or by threatening physical violence under the direction of another mind. A permanent and settled condition of such constraint, by which I become in effect the instrument of another mind, is slavery. And it will not lead us far wrong if we assume that the value put upon liberty and its erection into something like an ideal comes from the contrast with slavery. The ideal of positive political freedom presupposes more complex experiences. But Homer already knows that "Zeus deprives a man of half his manhood when he becomes a slave."[23]

This, then, we may take as the practical starting-point in the notion of freedom. It is what, with reference to a formed society, we may call a status; the position of a freeman as opposed to a slave; that is, of one who, whatever oppression he may meet with de facto from time to time,

---

[22]We must assume, I suppose, that in Seeley's sentence "Government" = "Constraint," or its *vraisemblance* is lost.

[23][Homer, *The Odyssey*, Book XVII. See Samuel Butler's translation (Chicago: Encyclopaedia Britannica, 1955).]

or whatever specified services he may be bound to render, normally regards himself and is regarded by others as, on the whole, at his own disposal, and not the mere instrument of another mind.

Thus the juristic meaning of the term "liberty," based on the normal distinction between one self-determining person and another, we may set down as its literal meaning, and so far the English writers, of whom Seeley is the latest type, are on solid ground when they define liberty as the absence of restraint, or perfect liberty as the absence of all government (in the sense of habitual constraint by others).

(β) It is obvious that the above definition would be wholly inadequate to the simplest facts respecting the demands which have through all history been asserted and achieved under the name of political liberty. A man may be a long way more than a slave and yet a long way less than a citizen. If, as Seeley says, the English writer of the verses, "Ah, Freedom is a noble thing,"[24] only meant by Freedom, being out of prison, it is certain that he meant much less than the Greek historian who two thousand years before used almost the same words. "The right of equal speech," he wrote, "demonstrates itself in every way as a noble thing."[25] By this, as his words and their occasion make plain, he meant a certain determinate security for the positive exercise of activities affecting the welfare of the social whole, and some such security is always understood to be involved in the notion of political liberty. But we will content ourselves at this point with noting the distinction and connection between the negative or juristic, and the varyingly positive or political conception of liberty. For the latter is, in its degree, a case of that fuller

---

[24][John Barbour (approx. 1316–1395), *The Bruce: an epic poem written around the year AD 1375* (Glasgow: W. MacLellan, 1964), Bk I, 1, 225).]

[25]Hdt. [Herodotus (484 BC–425 BC), *History*, Bk] V, 78. [Greek historian and author of *The History*, Herodotus traveled extensively in Greece, Egypt, and Asia Minor. He is referred to both as "the Father of History" and, because of the many (unintended) inaccuracies in his work, "the father of lies." Bosanquet may be referring to the following passage: [5.78.1] "So the Athenians grew in power and proved, not in one respect only but in all, that equality is a good thing...while they were oppressed, they were, as men working for a master, cowardly, but when they were freed, each one was eager to achieve for himself." Trans., A.D. Godley (London: William Heinemann, 1926) (Text modernized by Lynn Sawlivich, to remove archaisms, as part of the Perseus project. See ch. xi, note 12.)]

freedom which we are about to trace to its embodiment in the state; and the phenomena of political liberty are covered, of course, by the point of view which we shall take in indicating the state as the main organ and condition of the fuller liberty.

(γ) The connection, we said, between juristic and political liberty should be observed at this point. It is merely an example of what we shall find throughout, that the apparently negative has its roots and its meaning in the positive, and, in proportion as its true nature becomes evident, its positive aspects become explicit. There is no true security for juristic liberty apart from political liberty; and it has constantly been the infraction of juristic liberty that has been the origin of the demand for a share in highly positive political duties and functions. Mere protection for person and property may seem an easy thing to define and maintain with just a little goodwill; but the questions when, how, and in what sense it is to be maintained involve the positive character of the political system, and there is no ultimate security unless that system is moulded by the whole compass of individuality which society contains.

(δ) Recurring then to the literal or elementary sense of liberty, as the absence of constraint exercised by one upon others, we may admit that, in going beyond it, we are more or less making use of a metaphor.[26] We are passing from the idea of non-constraint pure and simple to the idea of more or less moulding and selection within the powers and activities of the self. It is true, indeed, and must be maintained as a fundamental principle, that the "higher" liberty is also in fact the "larger" liberty, presenting the greater area to activity and the more extensive choice to self-determination.[27] But this larger development remains within a positive general character, and if more alternatives are open, there are also, by that very fact, more which are closed. We cannot wholly exhaust the new meaning of liberty as applied to the law-abiding and moral life of a conscientious citizen even by changing the negative into the positive, and saying that, whereas mere juristic freedom was only freedom *from*

---

[26]In this and the following section I have made great use of Green's discussion in the first chapter of the *Principles of Political Obligation*. [With preface by Bernard Bosanquet. (London: Longmans, Green, 1895).]

[27]Perhaps I may refer on this head to "Liberty and Legislation" in my *Civilisation of Christendom* ([London: Swan] Sonnenschein, [1893]).

constraint, political freedom means freedom *to* act. The higher sense of liberty, like the lower, involves freedom *from* some things as well as freedom *to* others. And that which we are freed from is, in this case, not the constraint of those whom we commonly regard as others, but the constraint of what we commonly regard as a part of ourself. Here is the reason for saying that, when we speak of liberty in the higher sense, we must be admitted to be speaking metaphorically.[28]

In the straightforward sense of the word, we saw, I am free when I am not made the instrument of another person's will through physical violence or the threat of it. The subtle questions which may arise with regard to due or undue degrees of influence, by which I may become the instrument of another's mind, with more or less willingness on the part of my own, are here disregarded. I am assumed to be acting freely so long as I follow the inclination of my mind, apart from any painful conflict forced upon it by the prospect of physical interference with its belongings.

But from the earliest ages of ethical reflection, a further sense has been ascribed to the term "liberty." It has been pointed out by moralists and philosophers – first, perhaps by Socrates and Plato – that the condition of man as to being himself is fundamentally affected not only by the power to do what he likes without constraint, but by the nature of that which he likes to do. The human mind, it is explained, is never wholly at one with itself, and the common phrases "self-mastery" or "self-control" are adduced by way of presenting what we spoke of above as the ethical paradox of self-government.[29] The mind, then, is treated by a metaphor as if it were two or more persons; and the term "liberty," which applies prima facie to the non-constraint of one person by another, is applied to the non-constraint of something within an individual mind by something else within it. Now, apart from further scrutiny, it does not appear why the term "liberty," when thus applied, should mean anything of ethical value. As Plato observed,[30] in a passage from which the current use of all these phrases is probably derived, it seems absurd at first sight to

---

[28]But see below, p. 150–53.

[29][See above,] p. 86.

[30]*Republic*, 430 E. [loc. cit., note 14].

speak of self-control as a distinctive predicate of certain states of mind. For surely, within the mind, that which is controlled must be of the nature of self no less than that which controls it, so that, in saying that I have self-control, I am saying that I am self-indulgent; in saying that my mind is free, I am at the same time saying that it is a slave. Within certain limits this paradox represents a truth, and the ethical rank of the elements which coerce and are coerced may be quite oppositely estimated. We may think fit to call ourselves free either when love conquers reason or when reason triumphs over love. Still, as Plato proceeds to point out, the general adoption of the metaphor, the fact that we think and call ourselves "free" or "self-controlled" or "fully ourselves" in some cases and not in others; and that we do not in each of these cases regard the opposite attribution "slave," "self-indulgent," "not ourselves" as equally true with the former, indicates that some substantial fact is forcing itself upon us through the metaphor in question. It is the same problem as that which Professor James has wittily stated when he points out that "the sluggard, the drunkard, the coward never talk of their conduct in that way (i.e. as 'conquering' their impulses and temptations) or say they resist their energy, overcome their sobriety, conquer their courage, and so forth."[31]

It is most important, we may venture to observe in passing, not to understand the substantive fact, or Plato's presentation of it, as if it lay in an alternative between two psychological factors, say intelligence and desire, the one of which was to be preferred and the other to be repudiated, through some quasi-ethical conception of rank, such as the supposed affinity of the one factor with divine or of the other with animal life. We are speaking of the sense in which it can be asserted that the human self is, comparatively speaking, free in one kind of life and unfree in another, both being assumed to be chosen, in the absence of constraint by an external will. It is plain that the only ground on which such an assertion can really be sustained is that the one life more than the other gives effect to the self as a whole, or removes its contradictions and so makes it most fully what it is able to be, or what, by the implied

---

[31][William James,] *Principles of Psychology* [(London: Macmillan, 1890), vol.] ii, [p.] 548.

nature of each and all of its wants, it may be said really to want to be. The claims of intelligence and desire in their various phases must be criticised according to this principle, and not advocated upon presuppositions drawn from external comparisons.

But our question at the present moment is not as to the deeper nature of that which we call the self *par excellence*, but as to the bearing of the metaphor by which the assertion of such a self is identified with liberty or absence of constraint. And the point is plainly this:[32] that in the conflict between that which stands for the self *par excellence* and that which, at any time, stands opposed to it, we have the clear experience that we are capable of being determined by a will within our minds which nevertheless we repudiate and disown,[33] and therefore we feel ourselves to be like a slave as compared with a freeman if we yield, but like a freeman compared with a slave if we conquer. We may be determined by something which not only is not ourself – for in the greatest moments of life, when our being touches its maximum, we, in a sense, feel an impulse which is not ourself – but it is not ourself as something which has got hold of us by force, and operates upon us by conflict and violence, without having the kind of power needed to carry us away and sweep our whole self harmoniously into its current. That we can be determined by a will in us which neither is ourself nor represents it at a higher level, and which we loathe and disown, is the experience on which the metaphor of freedom and slavery is based, when applied to the life of man considered apart from external constraint.[34]

(ε) The metaphorical application of the term "liberty" to a state of the individual mind has both its danger and its justification. The state of mind in question, we repeat, is that in which the impulse towards self-

---

[32]See Green's *Principles of Political Obligation*, [loc. cit., note 26] p. 1.

[33]This remains substantially true, even if we agree with Socrates that it is impossible to know the better and prefer the worse at a given moment. Our normal self will repudiate the view we took at some moment.

[34]There is something worthy of Dante in Rousseau's observation (*Contrat Social*, Book IV, ch. ii, n.) that the convicts in the galleys at Genoa had "liberty" stamped on their chains. The fetters of the bad self are the symbol of freedom. Rousseau turns his remark to commonplace, after his fashion, by referring it to the mere liberation of society from malefactors.

satisfaction sets itself upon an object which represents the nature of the self as a whole, as free from contradiction or as at its maximum of being, and triumphs over the alien and partial will, the tendency to narrower tracks of indulgence, when entangled in which it feels itself oppressed and constrained by a foreign influence. When the mind does what, as a whole, it wills, as Plato implies,[35] it feels free. When it cannot be said to will anything as a whole, but is distracted among aims which cannot satisfy it, then there is no sense in which it can be said to do what *it* wills, and it feels itself under constraint and a slave.

The metaphor has this danger. The contrast between whole and part is too readily transformed, in popular theory, into the contrast between an empty generality and everything in particular. The claim to be free then involves the separation between mind as a general faculty of volition, and every particular object. Mind is then said to be free as an undetermined faculty, but as filled and moulded by any object or idea, (the passive participles "filled" and "moulded" imply a relation which is not real, but, as assumed, is the ground of the fallacy in question), it has lost its freedom and become a slave. But if we retain the conception that mind has reality only as a whole of determinate character, self-determined through its power of being a self, but not through any power of creating particulars out of nothing, we shall avoid this caricature of the higher freedom.

But it is far more important to note the justification of the metaphor. We saw that, from Homer downwards, the conviction has been ineradicable that liberty is the true nature of man. And we now observe that the metaphor, through which the deepest sense of this quality has expressed itself, depends upon the same principle as the literal usage from which it is drawn. In the case of Liberty, conceived as a condition of the mind, just as in the case of Liberty, conceived as the absence of physical menace or coercion on the part of other persons, the root of the matter is the claim to be determined only by ourself. But, in the literal case, what we mean by ourself is the given self, the group of will and wishes, of feelings and ideas, associated from time to time with my particular body; in short, the actual uncriticised "mind," as we experience it all day and

---

[35] *Republic*, IX, 577 E, [loc. cit., note 14].

every day. In the metaphorical case, we have made so much progress in self-criticism as to know at least that our "self" is something of a problem. We know that the given self, the mind from day to day[36] is not satisfactory; and we throw the centre of gravity outside it, and place the true self in something which we rather want to be than actually are; although, at the same time, it is clear that to some extent we are this something or we should not want to be it. We realise, indeed, that to be ourselves is a principle at once of distinction or position among others, and of thorough transition into and unity with the life which is at the root of theirs. And it is for this reason that we feel so confident, in proportion as we at all lay hold upon a life which can thus distinguish and identify us, that we have here the grasp of what is in its nature our true self. Here then, as in the literal case of liberty from personal constraint, we are putting in act the principle of "being determined only by ourself."

And thus Liberty as understood by "theorists of the first look," or by those who in all ages have resisted arbitrary tyranny, belongs after all to the same principle with the civil or moral liberty of the philosopher. The claim to obey only yourself is a claim essential to humanity; and the further significance of it rests upon what you mean by "yourself." Now if it is true that resistance to arbitrary aggression is a condition of obeying only ourselves, it is more deeply true, when man is in any degree civilised, that, in order to obey yourself as you want to be, you must obey something very different from yourself as you are. And it has been well pointed out[37] that the consciousness of civilised peoples is deeply alive to this significance of liberty, so that any work of self-improvement may be most effectively presented to a popular audience as an effort to attain freedom by breaking the bondage of drink, for example, or of ignorance, or of pauperism. In spite of the objection that Freedom as thus represented is a mere metaphor, "the feeling[38] of oppression, which always goes with the consciousness of unfulfilled possibilities, will always give meaning to the representation of the effort after any kind of self-improvement as a demand for 'freedom.'"

---

[36]See, however, note 3 on p. 137 above.

[37]Green's *Principles,* [loc. cit. note 26], p. 18.

[38]Ibid.

We have followed the usual course of English thought, and the example of a writer whose caution equalled his enthusiasm, in admitting that the lower sense of the term "liberty" is the literal sense, and that the deeper meaning may be treated as metaphorical.[39] It is worth while to observe that the justice of this way of looking at the matter is very doubtful. It is because we know, however indefinitely, that our self has a reach beyond its daily needs, that arbitrary oppression becomes a thing to be resisted at the price of life itself. Herbert Spencer draws attention to the struggles of an animal which we try to confine, as a proof of the innate feeling of liberty. But the domesticated animal is the highest animal, or at any rate not the lowest; while the man domesticated on similar terms is what we call a slave, because he has sold his liberty for his life. It is therefore in truth the sense of the higher liberty – the greatness and unity of life – that has communicated uncontrollable force to the claim for the lower; and if the fuller meaning is the reality and the lesser the symbol, it would be nearer the truth to say that the reality is the liberty of a moral being whose will finds adequate expression in its life, of which liberty the absence of external constraint is only an elementary type or symbol. The claim of the dictionary-maker that the earliest or the average meaning is also the truest or the "proper" meaning of words has no foundation.[40]

4. Liberty, then, throughout, is the being ourselves, and the fullest condition of liberty is that in which we are ourselves most completely. The ideal thus implied may be further explained by help of the philosophical expression, "The free will is the will that wills itself." We have already seen, by implication, the meaning of this. If we are asked, "But does not our will always will itself?" we have the answer ready, that in one sense it does, but in another it does not. We always want what we will, but what we will is not always what would satisfy our want. A will that willed itself would be a will that in willing had before it an object that would satisfy its whole want, and nothing but its want. Its desires would not be narrow and partial desires, in the fulfilment of which a man feels

---

[39][The writer referred to is T.H. Green.]

[40]Nettleship's [*Philosophical Lectures and*] *Remains*, [eds., A.C. Bradley and G.R. Benson (London: Macmillan, 1897), vol.] I, [pp.] 27 and 30.

choked and oppressed like one lost in a blind alley which grows narrower and narrower. They would not be artificial desires stimulated and elaborated into a tyranny of the machinery of life by the self which gropes for more and cannot find the "more" which it needs. That is to say, the volitions of the self would have undergone a process just such as is undergone by a casual sensuous observation as it passes into a great scientific theory. As the observation stands it is inadequate to itself; for it poses as a truth, and is manifestly a false connection. So it is supplemented on the one hand and purged away on the other; conditions and qualifications are inserted into it to harmonise it with other knowledge, until it makes some approach to being an expression of experience fit to occupy a permanent place in man's conception of the world. This, the adjustment of a partial element to unity with the whole, is the essence of criticism. And it is just such another process by which the experience of life fills up and purifies the objects presented to the casual volition. That is to say, the nature of the process may be represented by considering it as having an effect of this kind on an unharmonised will; and relatively at any given moment such a process is in some degree going on. But we must bear in mind that we are not to think of the sensuous individual as totally prior in time to the social consciousness, and as a pre-existing matter, upon which such an effect is to be thought of as super-induced. That would be precisely the fallacy with which Rousseau struggles so hard, and the escape from which we are attempting to illustrate; none the worse, perhaps, if our own language betrays how very difficult it is to throw it off altogether. We really know the sensuous individual as such, the will in its impure and uncriticised form, only in our experience, constant as that is, of failure, error, and forgetfulness, in adhering to the rational life, which, on the whole, is inherent in the very nature of our rational being, and which we only desert in the same way and to the same extent as we make mistakes in intellectual matters. We go wrong by narrowness and confusion, by erroneous abstractions out of the whole, in a way only possible for a social and intellectual being, and not prior to our entire social and intellectual character.

Understanding then that we are dealing with narrowness and confusion and their opposites within a social intelligence already existing and predominant on the whole, we may note the sort of relation in which the more adequate will is analogous to the more adequate piece of knowledge.

Take, as we said above, the actual casual will of any individual at any given moment, especially if it is of a nature which, within the context of civilised life, we commonly pronounce to be wrong. Let it be, for example, an impulse of sensual passion. It is a commonplace that in such impulses the self can find no abiding satisfaction. They pass and leave him empty. They bring with them no opening out of fresh possibilities, no greater stability to the mind. Yet they have their meaning, and belong to human nature. They imply a need for union, and an attraction outside the immediate self. If we compare them with the objects and affections of a happy and devoted family, we see the difference between a less adequate and a more adequate will. The impulse, in passing into family affection, has become both less and more. It is both disciplined and expanded. The object presented to the will is transformed in character. Lawlessness is excluded; but, in place of a passing pleasure, a whole world of affections and interests, extending beyond the individual life, is offered as a purpose and a stimulus to the self. In short – for it is idle to expatiate upon what everybody recognises at once – you can make a life out of the one, and you cannot out of the other. In the family at its best the will has an object which is real and stable, and which corresponds to a great part of its own possibilities and capacities. In willing this object, it is, relatively speaking, willing itself. We might compare in the same way the mere will to earn our daily bread with the horizon of a great intellectual profession; or the routine of an industry or profession vacantly and formally pursued with the very same routine conscientiously followed in a spirit of enlightenment. In every case we are led up to the contrast of the actual indolent or selfish will, and the will, in as far as it comes to be what its nature implies, namely that which we have spoken of as the real or rational will embodied in objects which have power to make a life worth living for the self that wills them.

Now, our nature as rational beings implies the imperative claim upon us of a will which is thus real or rational. Recognised or unrecognised, it is rooted in our own wills, as the claim to be true is rooted in our assertions. Any system of institutions which represents to us, on the whole, the conditions essential to affirming such a will, in objects of action such as to constitute a tolerably complete life, has an imperative claim upon our loyalty and obedience as the embodiment of our liberty. The only question that can arise is whether the system is that which it pretends to be. But even if rebellion is a duty, it can only be so because the imperative obligation, as we recognise it, is irreconcilable with the particular system which claims our obedience in its name. The imperative claim of the will that wills itself is our own inmost nature, and we cannot throw it off. This is the ultimate root of political obligation.

5. It is such a "real" or rational will that thinkers after Rousseau have identified with the State. In this theory they are following the principles of Plato and Aristotle, no less than the indications which Rousseau furnished by his theory of the general will in connection with the work of the legislator. The State, when thus regarded, is to the general life of the individual much as we saw the family to be with regard to certain of his impulses. The idea is that in it, or by its help, we find at once discipline and expansion, the transfiguration of partial impulses, and something to do and to care for such as the nature of a human self demands. If, that is to say, you start with a human being as he is in fact and try to devise what will furnish him with an outlet and a stable purpose capable of doing justice to his capacities – a satisfying object of life – you will be driven on by the necessity of the facts at least as far as the State, and perhaps further. Two points may be insisted on to make this conception less paradoxical to the English mind.

(α) The State, as thus conceived, is not merely the political fabric. The term "State" accents indeed the political aspect of the whole, and is opposed to the notion of an anarchical society. But it includes the entire hierarchy of institutions by which life is determined, from the family to the trade, and from the trade to the Church and the University. It includes all of them, not as the mere collection of the growths of the country, but as the structure which gives life and meaning to the political whole, while receiving from it mutual adjustment, and therefore expansion and a more liberal air. The State, it might be said, is thus conceived as the operative criticism of all institutions – the modification and adjustment by which they are capable of playing a rational part in the object of human will. And criticism, in this sense, is the life of institutions. As exclusive objects, they are a prey to stagnation and disease – think of the temper which lives solely for the family or solely for the Church; it is only as taken up into the movement and circulation of the State that they are living spiritual beings. It follows that the State, in this sense, is, above all things, not a number of persons, but a working conception of life. It is, as Plato has taught us, the conception by the guidance of which every living member of the commonwealth is enabled to perform his function. If we ask whether this means that a complete conception of the aims and possibilities of the common life exists even in the minds of statesmen, not to speak of ordinary citizens, the question answers itself in the negative. And yet the State can only live and work in as far as such a conception, in however fragmentary, one-sided shapes, pervades the general mind. It is not there mostly in reflective shape; and in so far as it is in reflective shape it is according to ultimate standards contradictory and incomplete. But everyone who has a fair judgment of what his own place demands from him, has, at his own angle, so to speak, a working insight into the end of the State; and, of course, practical contradictions would be fewer if such conceptions were completer and more covered by each other. But a complete reflective conception of the end of the State, comprehensive and free from contradiction, would mean a complete idea of the realisation of all human capacity, without waste or failure. Such a conception is impossible owing to the gradual character of the process by which the end of life, the nature of the good, is determined for man. The Real Will, as represented by the State, is only a partial embodiment of it.

(β) The State, as the operative criticism of all institutions, is necessarily force; and in the last resort, it is the only recognised and justified force. It seems important to observe that force is inherent in the State, and no true ideal points in the direction of destroying it. For the force of the State proceeds essentially from its character of being our own mind extended, so to speak, beyond our immediate consciousness. Not only is the conduct of life as a whole beyond the powers of the average individual at its average level, but it is beyond the powers of all the average individuals in a society taken together at their average level. We make a great mistake in thinking of the force exercised by the State as limited to the restraint of disorderly persons by the police and the punishment of intentional law-breakers. The State is the fly-wheel of our life. Its system is constantly reminding us of duties, from sanitation to the incidents of trusteeship, which we have not the least desire to neglect, but which we are either too ignorant or too indolent to carry out apart from instruction and authoritative suggestion. We profit at every turn by institutions, rules, traditions, researches, made by minds at their best, which, through State action are now in a form to operate as extensions of our own minds. It is not merely the contrast between the limited activity of one individual and the greater achievement of millions put together. It is the contrast between individuals working in the order and armed with the laws, customs, writings, and institutions devised by ages, and the same individuals considered as their daily average selves, with a varying but always limited range of immediate consciousness. For at any given moment, no judge knows all the law; no author knows all his own books, not to mention those of others; no official of an institution has the whole logic and meaning of the institution before his mind. All individuals are continually reinforced and carried on, beyond their average immediate consciousness, by the knowledge, resources, and energy which surround them in the social order, with its inheritance, of which the order itself is the greater part. And the return of this greater self, forming a system adjusted to unity, upon their isolated minds, as an expansion and stimulus to them, necessarily takes the shape of force, in as far as their minds are inert. And this must always be the case, not merely so long as wills are straightforwardly rebellious against the common good, but so long as the knowledge and energy of the average mind are unequal to dealing, on its own initiative and out of its own resources, with all possible conjunctions in which necessary conditions of the common good are to be maintained. In other words, there must be inertia to overcome, as long as the limitations of our animal nature[41] exist at all. The State is, as Plato told us, the individual mind writ large, or, as we have said, our mind reinforced by capacities which are of its own nature, but which supplement its defects. And this being so, the less complete must clearly submit to find itself in the more complete, and be carried along with it so far as the latter is able to advance. It is very important to note, however, that

---

[41] Not "of our individuality." Individuality is not, in principle, a limitation which makes us unequal to our part in the whole.

our mind at its best is very different from our mind at its average; and it has understood and approved, when at its best, a great deal which in its average moments comes upon it as force or custom from the outside. Thus, there is no abrupt division between our conscious mind and the social system of suggestion, custom, and force, which supports and extends and amends it. The two are related much as the focus of consciousness is related to the sub-conscious and automatic habits by which daily life is rendered possible. It is no more conceivable that social life should go on without force and authoritative custom, because the end of social life is reflected in the varying intelligence of individuals, than that individual life should go on without sub-consciousness and automatism, because it is ultimately relative to the ends which appear as ideas in the shifting focus of the mind. The inherent limitations of State action will be dealt with in a later chapter. We have thus far been attempting to make clear what is meant by the identification of the State with the Real Will of the Individual in which he wills his own nature as a rational being; in which identification we find the only true account of political obligation.

CHAPTER VII

PSYCHOLOGICAL ILLUSTRATION OF THE IDEA OF
A REAL OR GENERAL WILL[1]

1. The object of the present chapter is to assist the reader in bringing together the conception of the State or the Community on the one hand,
and that of an actual personal will, existing in an individual mind, on the
other.[2] We have seen that Self-Government can only be explained if the
centre of gravity of the self is thrown outside what we are continually
tempted to reckon as our individuality, and if we recognise as our real
being, and therefore as imperative upon us, a self and a good which are
but slightly represented in our explicit consciousness, at its ordinary
level. We have seen that all sound theory and all good practice are
founded on the insight or on the faith[3] that the common self or moral
person of society is more real than the apparent individual; and we have
followed Rousseau's clue in criticising as defective and contradictory
the actual will of given persons, and in looking for its interpretation and
completion in law and institutions as the embodiment of the social spirit.

But Society and the State present themselves at first sight as indefinite
multitudes of persons. Institutions are many-sided facts; and an un-
reflective citizen could hardly say of what he takes them to be composed. And though law and custom approach more nearly to what we
commonly understand by a "will," yet they again are apt to be regarded
as a sort of dead external weight with which the living volition of the ordinary man has little or nothing to do.

Our purpose, therefore, is to explain what is meant by saying that "a
will" can be embodied in the State, in society, in law and institutions;
and how it is possible for the individual, as we know him, to be in an
identity with this will, such as continually to vary, but never wholly to

---

[1] [For more on Bosanquet's psychology, see the "The Organisation of Intelligence," from
Psychology of the Moral Self, below, p. 294–304.]

[2] Cf. ch. ii, p. 77 [above].

[3] The faith may of course exist in minds which would absolutely repudiate the theoretical
form here propounded for it. No one could have had a more ardent actual faith in the reality of the greater self than Bentham and Mill.

disappear. How can a man's real self lie in a great degree outside his normal self, and be something which he only now and then gets hold of distinctly, and never completely?

2. We will begin (α) by pointing out the analogy between the groups or systems of which our intelligence is composed, and the groups or systems which make up the fabric of society, and we will then go on (β) to exhibit them as up to a certain point aspects of the same fact.

(α) We may note two degrees of connection between the members of a whole, which we may call "Association" and "Organisation."

(i) When two individuals are so connected that where you find the one you expect to find the other, they may be called associates. And any kind of habitual grouping, from a gang of thieves to a scientific or philanthropic institution, may be called an Association. Owing probably to the verbal force which it borrows from the verb "to associate," the term "association" implies the intentional coming together of units which have been separate, and which may become separate again. The word "Society," on the other hand, has not this verbal force, and although an "association" may call itself "a society," yet "Society" as such is not spoken of as an "Association." When we speak of "Society" we do not emphasise the aspect of being put together out of elements which exist apart, and therefore we habitually apply the word to that natural grouping which, at any rate, we do not normally think of as purposely put together and liable to be dissolved again. When the State is treated as an Association, a definite theory of its nature is implied, such as is involved in Herbert Spencer's comparison between it and a joint stock company.

Now this same term "Association" is the most familiar expression for a connection between elements of mind, analogous to that between persons who are called associates. If two elements of mind are so connected that, where we find the one we expect to find the other, they are said to be "associated." If the engine's whistle makes me think the train is going to start, then it would be said that the idea "train starting" is associated in my mind with the idea "engine whistling." They have before entered into the same mental group or whole, and so, where we find the one, we expect to find the other, just as, where my friend X is, his comrade Y is probably not far off.

We may here note the analogy between these two modes of association – that of persons and that of mental elements. In both cases, according to the plain man's view of the matter, we are dealing with wholly casual conjunctions of units naturally independent. The associates in either case need no better reason for now being together than that they had been together before. Their connection expresses nothing intimate or essential in their natures, and, if they fall apart again, they will not be seriously affected by the separation.

Now, of course, this idea of mere conjunction is not strictly true even of the connections between the most casual associates. Every association, whether of comrades or of ideas, is a connection between qualities, and therefore a general connection between the natures of the related terms. People are not really companions for no reason at all; and ideas are not really units or atoms which stick together by mere juxtaposition, so that when one is pulled up out of the Hades of oblivion it drags the other with it. Both the association of companions and the association of ideas are tendencies in which some general connection of qualities is at work and expresses itself through the detail of the actual surroundings, so far as an opening is left to it. When the association is made explicit by both members being present together, there is an outlet or utterance of the nature of the associates which there is not when they are separated.

But though all this is true, and can be detected in cases of association by careful analysis, it is, relatively speaking, the fact that commonplace association depends upon qualities which are so superficial that they may set up a tendency to connection between any units which are members of the same world. And, therefore, as compared with any more thorough-going kind of connection, such association may be set down as casual, and as determined by the mere chance of juxtaposition.

(ii) Let us compare the kind of connection just described as association with that which we have agreed to call organisation.

Associates,[4] we saw, were together, as might roughly be said, simply because they found themselves together. That is to say they were, after

---

[4] An "association," it may be urged, generally has a definite purpose, and so far, as indeed we said above, the associates come together, and do not merely find themselves together. But this is only an apparent difficulty. In comparison with the whole compass of their na-

their association, what they were before it, and would not be seriously affected if they were to be separated. Connections of this kind are essentially between unit and unit. They fall short of the nature of a plan which determines a great range of elements, variously but with reference to an identical operation.

Beginning, as before, with the connection between persons, we may illustrate the difference by the comparison between a crowd and an army. The mind of a crowd has indeed been taken as the type of a true social mind. But it is really something quite different. It is merely the superficial connection between unit and unit on an extended and intensified scale. As unit joins unit in the street, each determines his immediate neighbours, and is determined by them through the contagion of excitement, and with reference to the most passing ideas and emotions. What acts upon them in common is necessarily what there is in common between persons meeting, as it were, for no reason, and not knowing what they share beyond what they immediately see and feel. The crowd may indeed "act as one man"; but if it does so, its level of intelligence and responsibility will, as a rule, be extraordinarily low. It has nothing in common beyond what unit can infect unit with in a moment. Concerted action, much more reasoning and criticism, are out of the question. The doing or thinking of a different thing by each unit with reference to a single end is impossible. The crowd moves as a mere mass, because its parts are connected merely as unit with unit. Any form of connection which could effect an organisation in the whole would make a demand on the nature of every unit, which, where their conjunction is merely casual, could not possibly be met.

An army,[5] no less than a crowd, consists of a multitude of men, who are associated, unit to unit. Influences must pass and repass between

---

ture, associates who come together for some limited purpose – Bimetallism, Philanthropy, a political cause – do merely find themselves together. They form, as the cynic will say, an extraordinary menagerie, and their association may break up without any apparent effect upon their nature. Obviously, however, there are some purposes which go deeper into men's characters, and others which are shallower; and this merely illustrates our point that the most casual association is a universal connection of qualities in disguise.

[5]The illustration was suggested to me by a passage in Mr [George Frederick] Stout's *Analytic Psychology* [(London: Swan Sonnenschein, 1896) vol. II, pp. 116–18.]

every one of the men and those men with whom he is standing in the ranks, or with whom he passes his leisure time. We may note by the way, that these influences are themselves of a more permanent nature than those which pass between members of a crowd, and that they must necessarily be modified by that other connection of which we are about to speak. For the links of "association" between man and man are not the determining force in the operations of the army as such. The army is a machine, or an organisation, which is bound together by operative ideas embodied on the one hand in the officers, and on the other hand in the habit of obedience and the trained capacity which make every unit will- ing and able to be determined not by the impulse of his neighbours, but by the orders of his officers. What the army does is determined by the General's plan, and not by influences communicating themselves from man to man, as in a crowd. In other words, every unit moves with refer- ence to the movements of a great whole, with most parts of which he is not in direct touch at all. He is not determined by simple reference to the movements of his immediate neighbours. The army, that is, is a system or organised group, the nature of which, or the predominant idea em- bodied in its structure, determines the movements and relations of its parts or members. The difference of the two modes of determination is plainly visible on a review day, if we first watch the compact regiments marching off the ground, and then the crowd streaming away irregularly in search of rest or refreshment. By organisation then, as opposed to as- sociation, we mean determination of particulars by the scheme or gen- eral nature of a systematic group to which they belong, as opposed to their determination by immediate links uniting them with what, rela- tively speaking, are other particulars in casual juxtaposition with them.[6]

In the working and composition of mind the same difference is ob- servable between association and organisation. Mere association means that any perception or idea may suggest absolutely any mental element whatever with which it has developed a connection by entering into the same mental whole. A study of the purely associative mind is sometimes

---

[6]Ultimately, of course, the distinction is one of degree. What operates is always a general connection between members of a whole; the only question is what kind of whole, and, therefore, what kind of connection.

said to be found in the character of Miss Bates in *Emma*.[7] Perhaps, as really uncontrolled association can hardly be found in a sane intellect, we may say that the character in question is something more subtle and more true to nature; and that is, a study of the tendency to pure association continually breaking out, and as continually repressed, or "herded back" to the main subject, to use the expression which Walter Scott applies to the way in which just such an associative talker[8] is brought back to his point by his hearer.

In mind, as in the external world, the higher stage of association is organisation. The characteristic of organisation is control by a general scheme[9] as opposed to influence by juxtaposition of units. The zigzag course of thought which is represented in such a character as Miss Bates is due to the absence of control by any general scheme. Every idea – every significant word – has practically innumerable connections in the mind. If the course of thought has no general direction impressed upon it, no selective control operative within it, it may change its line altogether at every principal word.[10] The possibilities of the ideas at our command make them like a complex of railways, wholly consisting of turn-tables, so that, on any one of these component parts, the train may swing round and go off in a wholly new direction. This is notably illustrated by the sense of context in interpretation. For anyone who has no such sense, possible errors are endless, beyond the hope of correction.

The opposite of such a zigzag course is a train of thought such as an argument. In a train of thought, one general idea prescribes the direction, or forms the "subject," or limits what has been called the universe of discourse. Attention is wholly guided by the general idea, and refuses to be distracted by any interest or suggestion which does not bear upon it. Let the general idea be, for example, the relation of wealth to the best life. Experience shows that it is most difficult to resist the varied inter-

---

[7][Jane Austen (1775–1817), *Emma*, ed., James Kinsley (Oxford: Oxford University Press, 1990).]

[8]Claude Halcro in [Sir Walter Scott (1771–1832)] *The Pirate* [(London: Black, 1898).]

[9]For the psychological theory of such control see Stout, *Analytic Psychology*, [loc. cit., note 5] vol. II, p. 3.

[10]If it has not enough control to complete a significant sentence, of course there is insanity or idiocy.

ests and distractions which present themselves in the attempt to keep this relation in view. Easy and attractive modes of acquisition, easy and attractive modes of expenditure, force themselves upon the mind as isolated suggestions, and divert it from the question: "Shall I, or will any one else, be the better for it, as I understand 'better'?" The effort of control, needed to keep in view the general nature of our conception of what is best in life, and to attend to suggestions which offer themselves as to acquisition and expenditure, only in so far as they seem likely to promote that conception, means the predominance of a scheme or general idea through all the varied circumstances of economic possibility. It makes no difference whether we are speaking of reasoning or of practice. The nature of the control which insists on relevancy, and of the intellectual system in which it exhibits itself, is the same in both cases. Every mind, in fact, is more or less organised under the control of dominant ideas, which belong to its habitual preoccupations and determine the constant bias of its thoughts. There is a well-known story how a traveller in a railway carriage undertook to detect the vocation of each of his fellow travellers from their respective answers to a single question. The question was: "What is that which destroys what it has itself produced?" and a naturalist, so the story runs, revealed himself by the answer, "vital force," a soldier replied "war," a scholar "Kronos," a journalist "revolution," and a farmer "a boar."[11] Each answer was determined by the dominant bias or idea which selected out of the possible answers to the riddle that which would harmonise with the general mental system under its control. Selection, it must be remembered, is at the same time creation. In every situation, theoretical or practical, the surroundings as a whole are new, and the rule or scheme has to assert itself in conditions which are not precisely repeated from any former case. In so asserting itself it does not simply *reproduce* something old, any more than a batsman recalls a former movement when he plays a ball, but it *produces* that thought or deed which expresses its nature with reference to the new surroundings in which it has to act.[12] For it is a univer-

---

[11]Steinthal in [William] James', [*Principles of*] *Psychology* [(London: Macmillan, 1890), vol.] II, [p.] 108.

[12]See Mr Stout on "Proportional Systems," *Analytic Psychology*, [loc. cit., note 5, vol.] II,

sal tendency, a scheme partly defined, and in process of further defining itself by moulding the material presented to it.

There is one more essential point. A mind has its dominant nature, but is no single system equally organised throughout. It is rather a construction of such systems, which may be in all degrees of alliance indifference, and opposition to one another. Each of such systems, or groups of ideas and experiences, has its own dominant scheme, and its own tendency in controlling thought or action. And, as a general rule, in proportion as one system is active, all the others are quiescent; in proportion as we are intent or engaged upon one train of thought or one pursuit, we are not alive to suggestions belonging to any other. Every system, or group of this kind, is called in psychology an "appercipient mass," because it is a set of ideas, bound together by a common rule or scheme, which dictates the point of view from which perception will take place, so far as the system in question is active. And without some "apperception," some point of view in the mind which enables the new-comer to be classed, there cannot be perception at all. The eye only sees what it brings with it the power of seeing. Hence some of the most striking instances of apperception are drawn from elementary cases in which a really remote system is active in default of a better, just because the action of some system is necessary and the nearest responds. A child calls an orange "a ball"; a Polynesian calls a horse "a pig." These are the nearest "heads" or rules of apperception under which the new perception can be brought. Every scientific idea we apply, every set of relations in which we stand, and every pursuit with which the mind is familiar, is a case of such an appercipient mass, or rule or scheme of attention. And we know by common experience how entirely quiescent is one such factor of the mind while we are absorbed in the activity of another; how utterly, for example, we disregard the botanical character of wild flowers when we are clearing them out of the garden as weeds, and how wholly we neglect the question whether they are "flowers" or "weeds" when we are occupied in studying their botanical character. And in the action of every appercipient mass, in as far as it determines thought by the general nature of a systematic whole, rather than through the isolated attraction

---

[p.] 167.

exercised by unit upon unit, we have an example of organisation as opposed to association; or, if we like, of systematic connection or association between whole and part, as opposed to the same principle operating casually and superficially between unit and unit.

The scheme or systematic connection, it must be added, may work unconsciously. Not all ideas which control our thought and action are explicit ideas in abstract form; and perhaps the general nature and limits of a man's mind are something of which he can never be reflectively conscious, though he is aware of what he takes to be his leading ideas. It is well known that principles which are not presented to reflection may be intellectually operative, and embodied in a train of results. Thus our appercipient masses may have very different degrees of explicit system. But their action is always systematic – the nature of the whole modifying what it comes in contact with, and being modified by it.

With this conception of psychical systems before us let us cast one more glance at the organisation of society and the State. We refused to take a crowd as a true type of society, and we looked to the example of an army for the leading features of organisation as opposed to casual "association." The characteristic of an army on which we insisted was the determination of every unit in it, not by the movements and impulses of his immediate neighbours, but by the scheme or idea of the whole. Now, on looking closer, we see that society as such is a vast tissue of systems of this type, each of them a relatively, though not absolutely, closed and self-complete organisation. There are wheels within wheels systems within systems, groups within groups. But, speaking generally, the business and pleasure of society are carried on by persons arranged in groups, which exhibit the characteristic of organisation that the capacity of every person is determined by the general nature and principle of the group considered as a whole, and not by his relations to the units who happen to be next him. Such groups, for example, are the trades and professions. Their structure may be very different. In some the workshop is again a subordinate self-organised group. In others the professional man works alone, and to all appearances goes his own way. It is common to all of them, however, that they form groupings of members, within each of which groupings all members are determined in a certain way by the common nature of the group. Within his trade or profession, a man acts, as it is said, in a definite "capacity." He regards himself and is regarded from a definite point of view, and all other points of view tend to be neglected while and in so far as he is acting in the capacity corresponding to his membership of a certain group.[13]

Prima facie, there may be, as with systems which compose the mind, all degrees of alliance, indifference, or opposition between these groupings of persons; and the same person, belonging to many different groups, may find his diverse "capacities" apparently at variance with one another. A conscientious Trade Unionist may find his capacity as a member of the Union, interpreted as binding him to do his utmost for the amelioration of working class conditions in general, apparently at variance with his capacity as the head of a family bound to provide immediately for those whom he has brought into the world. Or a judge or magistrate, obliged to enforce what he conceives to be a bad law, may find his official capacity apparently at variance with his duty as a conscientious citizen. It is plain that unless, on the whole, a working harmony were maintained between the different groups which form society, life could not go on. And it is for this reason that the State as the widest grouping whose members are effectively united by a common experience, is necessarily the one community which has absolute power to ensure, by force if need be, at least sufficient adjustment of the claims of all other groupings to make life possible. Assuming, indeed, that all the groupings are organs of a single pervading life, we find it incredible that there should ultimately be irreconcilable opposition between them. That they should contradict one another is not more nor less possible than that human nature should be at variance with itself.

Thus, we have seen that the mind, and society or the State, are identical in the characteristic of being organisations, each composed of a system of organisations every superior and subordinate grouping having its own nature and principle which determines its members as such, and every one, consequently, tending to impose upon its members a peculiar capacity or point of view which, in so far as a given system is active,

---

[13]The group to which he belongs, as bound together by differences, is often rather that of his clients or customers than of his colleagues in his vocation. But there is generally a differentiation within the vocation-group also.

tends to put all other systems out of sight. The connection between these systems is of very different kinds, and very unequal in degree; but in as far as the mind and the community are actual working wholes, it is to be presumed that in each there is an ultimate or pervading adjustment which hinders contradiction from proceeding to destructive extremes. And neither the mind nor the community, as working organisations, can be accounted for on the principle of mere association.

(β) After pointing out the analogy between the organised structure of minds and the organised structure of society, we now go on to show that minds and society are really the same fabric regarded from different points of view. The explanation may be divided into three parts.

i) Every social group is the external aspect of a set of corresponding mental systems in individual minds.

ii) Every individual mind is a system of such systems corresponding to the totality of social groups as seen from a particular position.

iii) The social whole, though implied in every mind, only has reality in the totality of minds in a given community considered as an identical working system.

(i) Society and the State and every institution present themselves to us at first sight as a number of persons, together, perhaps, with certain buildings and other external apparatus, and certain kinds of work carried on and tangible results produced – so many children "educated," so many workmen "employed," so many ships built or fields tilled.

But if we could bring before ourselves the complete reality of any social group or institution, we should find ourselves considering a very different order of facts. Let us think for a moment of a rate-supported elementary school. We imagine it as a heap of buildings and a mass of children with a percentage of teachers scattered among them. But in what does its actual working really consist, and on what does it depend?

The actual reality of the school lies in the fact that certain living minds are connected in a certain way. Teachers, pupils, managers, parents, and the public must all of them have certain operative ideas, and must be guided according to these ideas in certain portions of their lives, if the school is to be a school. Now, the being guided by certain operative ideas is, in other words, the activity of certain appercipient masses dictating a certain point of view, in so far as those particular masses are awake. And it must be noted that the connection or identity in which the school exists presupposes a different activity, that is, a different apper-cipient system, in every mind, and more especially in every class of mind concerned. It is the same as in our old example of the screw and the nut.[14] No school could be made of teachers alone or of pupils alone; nor, again, could a school be made with teachers who were all the same, or with pupils who were all the same.

So, if we could visualise the reality of the school – the institution – what we should see would be an identical connection running through a number of minds, various and variously conditioned. But within each mind the connection would take a particular shape such as to play into the connections with all other minds as a cogwheel plays into the other cogwheels of a machine. The pupil must be prepared to learn in his par-ticular way and the teacher to teach in his particular way. The parents and the public also have their own relations to the work of teaching, and whether for good or for evil they take up some attitude to it, and their attitude modifies it. Thus the connection, as it is within any one mind, is useless and meaningless if you take it wholly apart from what corre-sponds to it in the others. It is like a wheel without an axle or a pump handle without a pump. And it is because of this nature of the elements which make up the institution that it is possible for the institution itself to be an identity, or connection, or meeting point, by which many minds are bound together in a single system.

It may seem as if this way of analysing an institution was reducing a solid fact into mere thoughts. But it is not really so. Taking the ideas of all concerned as they really are, we have the facts in space and time – buildings, appliances, hours of work and attendance, and so on – in-cluded in them. It is impossible to state the idea fully and correctly with-out including the environment on which it rests, and the activities in which it is realised. We are not to omit the facts in space and time from what we mean by an institution; the only thing is that we have not known them as they really are till we have known them as bound into unity by the mental systems of which they are the context or the expres-

---

[14][See above, ch. ii, note 48.]

sion. The child and the teacher alike must think of their work with reference to particular times and places, or they would not do it at those times and places; and it is only in actually doing it at those times and places that the idea, or point of view, which stands for the school in each of their minds is able to assert itself without frustration.

Thus we may fairly say that every social group or institution is the aspect in space and time of a set of corresponding mental systems in individual minds. We may draw corollaries from this conception, both as to the nature of the individual will, or active mind, and as to the nature of the social and political whole.

(ii) Every individual mind, in so far as it thinks and acts in definite schemes or contexts, is a structure of appercipient systems or organised dispositions. Now, we do not suggest at present that all appercipient systems can be represented as social groups, though there are few, if any, such systems which do not involve some relations with persons connected in time and space. But it is clear, from the explanations of the last section, that every social group or institution involves a system of appercipient systems, by which the minds that take part in it are kept in correspondence. Every individual mind, then, so far as it takes part in social groupings or institutions, is a structure of appercipient systems, answering, each to each, to the different capacities in which it enters into each grouping respectively. We have already remarked on the way in which the distinction between different "capacities" answers to the psychological tendency for the activity of one appercipient system to obstruct the activity of all others. It is hardly necessary to point out that, partly for this reason, though the mind must be an actual structure of systems, it is very far from being a rational system of systems. The fact that, when one system is active, all others, as a rule, are inert, conceals the contradictions which underlie the entire fabric, and protects them from criticism and correction.

But though the mind is thus implicitly self-contradictory in various degrees, this does not alter the fact that its general nature is to be a unity of organised ideas answering to the actual set of parts which the individual plays in this world of space and time. Thus each individual mind, if we consider it as a whole, is an expression or reflection of society as a whole from a point of view which is distinctive and unique. Every social factor or relation, to which it in any way corresponds, or in which it in any way plays its part, is represented in some feature of its appercipient organism. And probably, just as, in any man's idea of London, there is hardly any factor of London life which does not at least colour the background, so, in every individual impression of the social whole, there is no social feature that does not, in one way or another, contribute to the total effect. In the dispositions of every mind the entire social structure is reflected in a unique form, and it is on this reflection in every mind, and on the uniqueness of the form in which it is reflected, that the working of the social whole, by means of differences which play into one another, depends. If, so to speak, we lay a mind on the dissecting table, we find it to consist for the most part of a fabric of organised dispositions, each disposition corresponding to a unique point of view or special angle[15] from which it plays a part in some human function. About the precise relation of a human function to the fact that, as a rule, it connects together a plurality of human beings, we shall have more to say in the following chapter. It is enough for the present that whatever does connect a plurality of human beings depends on the operation of appercipient systems in their minds, and therefore every individual mind is, as Plato has told us, so far as it goes, for good or evil, the true effective reality of the social whole. And it is easy to see when we consider the working of organised apperception, how it is possible actually to will more or less of our own volitional system. There is first the contrast between appercipient systems which are at any time active and those which are not active, and then there is the contrast between our actual volitional nature at its actual fullest, and the demands implied by the nature of the whole, from which it is inseparable. These demands are always appearing more or less in every act of willing our own will.

(iii) The social whole, regarded from a corresponding point of view, would be a whole consisting of psychical dispositions and their activities, answering to one another in determinate ways. It would therefore be

---

[15]I owe this comparison to a lecture by Prof. S. Alexander. [Samuel Alexander (1859–1938) was a British philosopher, and Professor of Philosophy at Victoria University, Manchester, from 1883 to 1924. His work was influenced by F.H. Bradley and Bosanquet, though during his career he moved from his earlier neo-Hegelianism to metaphysical realism.]

of the nature of a continuous or self-identical being, pervading a system of differences and realised only in them. It differs from a machine, or from what is called an "organism" pure and simple, by the presence of the whole in every part, not merely for the inference of the observer, but, in some degree, for the part itself, through the action of consciousness. But it would be a mistake, we should observe at this point, to identify the presence of the whole for the part by means of consciousness, with the consciousness of the part that the whole is present to it. The latter is a speculative idea, the former is a fact which embodies this idea for the observing theorist, but not necessarily or usually for the working consciousness itself. In the shape of our minds and their adjustment to our work, of which we are unconscious, there is an irreducible analogy between human society and the lower organisms. The consciousness which guides our lives is a consciousness of something, but not as a rule a consciousness of the place of that something in the whole of life. We live in our objects, but we do not know how or how far our objects identify us with the whole to which we ultimately belong.

It is plain that the social whole can, in practice, only be complete in a plurality of individuals. We know that in the development of human nature, which we take as the ultimate standard of life, no one individual can cover the whole ground. As in the natural world in space and time, so, in the world of human beings which on one side belongs to it, differentiation implies dispersion into a plurality of centres. The same man, according to what seems to be the limit of physical and psychical possibility, could not be both Plato and Aristotle, nor both Greek and Jew, not even both Spartan and Athenian, not to say both man and woman. We are on less secure ground when we say that he could not, effectively and as a rule, be both statesman and shoemaker, or soldier and clergyman. It is plain that in some cases capacities may be united which in other cases are found apart. The same man may be a good architect and a good workman, or again, the architect and the workman may be different persons, though suited to work together. We may reply, of course, that whatever abilities lie within one personality, effective work demands the division of labour. This is true, but is obviously a matter of degree. The man who does only one thing does not always do it best, and it is not easy to say what "one thing" means.

The point of these suggestions is to make it clear that, while plurality of human beings is necessary to enable society to cover the ground, as it were, which human nature is capable of covering, yet actual individuals are not ultimate or equal embodiments of the true particulars of the social universal. We thus see once more that the given individual is only in making, and that his reality may lie largely outside him. His will is not a whole, but implies and rests upon a whole, which is therefore the true nature of his will. We also gain some light on the unity of the social mind. For it seems plain that one actual human being may cover the ground which, in other instances, it takes many men to occupy. And in some such examples – not, or not obviously, in those where a high intensity of genius is the essential quality – there seems little reason to distinguish the correlation of dispositions within the one person from the correlation of the same dispositions if dispersed among different persons. If I am my own gardener, or my own critic, or my own doctor, does the relation of the answering dispositions within my being differ absolutely and altogether from what takes place when gardener and master, critic and author, patient and doctor, are different persons? My instructions to my gardener are conveyed in language, it will be said, while I know my own wishes directly. And this is not the place to press the problem home either psychologically or metaphysically. But, just to induce reflection, it may be asked whether my instructions to myself are not as a rule conveyed and remembered in language. If we consider my unity with myself at different times as the limiting case,[16] we shall find it very hard to establish a difference of principle between the unity of what we call one mind and that of all the "minds" which enter into a single social experience.[17]

In any case, we have said enough to suggest that Society prima facie exists in the correlated dispositions by which a plurality of individual minds meets the need for covering the ground open to human nature, by division of labour in the fullest sense. But we have further pointed out

---

[16]Cp. above, p. 127.

[17][Cf. L.T. Hobhouse's remark: "Common sense confronted by these statements has a feeling of outrage which makes it disinclined to argue." *The Metaphysical Theory of the State* (London: Allen and Unwin, 1918), p. 51.]

that the true particularisation of the human universal does not necessarily coincide with the distinction between different persons, and that the correlation of differences and the identity which they constitute remain much the same whether they chance to fall within a single human being or to be dispersed over several. The stress seems, therefore, to lie on the attainment of the true particularisation, which does justice to the maximum of human capacity, rather than on the mere relations which arise between the members of a de facto plurality. Not that the presence of human nature in any individual does not constitute a claim that it shall be perfected in him, but that its perfecting must be judged by a criticism addressed to determining real capacities, and not by the accidental standard of a given plurality. We shall pursue these ideas further in the following chapter.

CHAPTER VIII

NATURE OF THE END OF THE STATE
AND CONSEQUENT LIMIT OF STATE ACTION

1. According to the course of thought which we have been pursuing, the distinction between the individual on the one hand, and the social or political whole on the other, is not relevant to the question where the "end" of man in Society is to be sought. For the conceptions of Society and the individual are correlative conceptions through and through; at whatever level, therefore, we take the one, we are bound to construe the other as at the same level; so that, to distinguish the one element from the other as superior from inferior, or as means from end, becomes a contradiction in terms. If we begin by drawing boundaries round the individual, the boundaries which we draw reproduce themselves in society conceived as a total of such individuals, and the question of means and end, as we saw in Bentham's case,[1] takes the form whether "each" is the means to the welfare of "all," or "all" to the welfare of "each"; the distinction thus becoming purely verbal. While, if we set no limit to individuality, accepting it as an end which may involve any degree of self-completeness and therefore of comprehensiveness, we find it to be actually one with, to consist in, a realisation of the stuff and content of which social unity is made. Such apparent exceptions as art and religion, which may be taken to be independent of the social medium, are really, as we shall see, its quintessence,[2] though at a stage where plurality of persons becomes unimportant. They are therefore not truly to be considered as ends pertaining to the individual, in any sense in which the individual is held to have an essence separable from that of society. This antithesis is really, however, absurd. There are not two opposable sets of contents concerned in the matter at all; but a single web of content which in its totality is society and in its differentiations the individuals. To make the totality the means to the differentiations or vice versa is like making a

---

[1] Chapter iii.

[2] This is well put, if slightly exaggerated, by Mr [R.R.] Marett, *Threshold of Religion*, [London: Methuen, 1909, 1914, pp.] 159–60: "Primarily and directly the subject, the owner, as it were, of religious experience, is the religious society not the individual."

drama the means to the characters, or the characters to the drama. But the poet or the religious genius may be like a character that concentrates in itself the significance of the entire drama, and so in some degree transcends the dramatic form. Only, this is done by including the essence of the whole plurality, not by being independent of it.[3]

The only way, then, in which the idea of means and end can be applied to the social whole and its parts, is to take Society when at its lower level, being dealt with under the aspect of mere plurality, as a means to what it is at its higher level, when realised as a communion of individualities at their best. But from this point of view we get no distinction of means and end as between Individuals and Society. What we get is Individuals and Society alike, as understood and partly existing at one level (that of commonplace Individualism and Collectivism), taken as a means to both Individuals and Society at a higher level. As we have seen, the only true explanation of self-government is to throw the reality of the self outside what passes for its average nature, and in this sense the average nature may be treated as a means to the truer or fuller self – as something, that is to say, which is instrumental to the latter, and has no rights against it.[4]

2. For us, then, the ultimate end of Society and the State as of the individual is the realisation of the best life. The difficulty of defining the best life does not trouble us, because we rely throughout on the fundamental logic of human nature qua rational. We think ourselves no more called upon to specify in advance what will be the details of the life which satisfies an intelligent being as such, than we are called upon to specify in advance what will be the details of the knowledge which satisfies an intelligent being as such. Wherever a human being touches practice, as wherever he touches theory, we find him driven on by his intolerance of contradictions towards shaping his life as a whole. What we mean by "good" and "truth" is practical and theoretical experience in so far as the logic which underlies man's whole nature permits him to re-

---

[3]See Introd. to 2nd edn, p. 23 [above].

[4][Compare here T.H. Green's remark that "a right against society, as such, is an impossibility." *Lectures on the Principles of Political Obligation*, with preface by Bernard Bosanquet (London: Longmans, Green, 1895), p. 145 (sect. 141).]

pose in it. And the best life is the life which has most of this general character – the character which, so far as realised, satisfies the fundamental logic of man's capacities.

Now, it is plain that this best life can only be realised in consciousness, that being the medium of all satisfaction and the only true type of a whole in experience. And all consciousness, as experienced by man, is on one side particular, attached to bodies, and exclusive of consciousnesses attached to other bodies. In a sense, it is true that no one consciousness can partake of or actually enter into another. Thus, it is apt to be held, as we have amply seen, that the essential danger of State interference lies in the intrusion of something originated by "others" upon a distinct particular consciousness, whose distinction and particularity – its freedom – are thus impaired. It is all-important to our point of view that this prejudice should be dispelled. Force or automatic custom or authoritative tradition or "suggestion" are not hostile to one individuality because they come from "others," but because their nature is contradictory to the nature of the highest self-assertion of mind, because they are, so to speak, in a medium incompatible with its medium. They are just as hostile to this self-assertion, just as alien, if they emanate, as they constantly do, from conflicting elements in our complex private experience, as if they come to us, as we say, "from without." The question is of their "nature" and tendency, not of their centre of origin. Individuals are limited and isolated in many ways. But their true individuality does not lie in their isolation but in that distinctive act or service by which they pass into unique contributions to the universal. True individuality, as we have said, is not in the minimisation which forbids further subdivision, but in the maximisation which includes the greatest possible being in an inviolable unity. It is not, therefore, the intrusion upon isolation, as such, that interferes with individuality, it is the intrusion, upon a growing unity of consciousness, of a medium hostile to its growth.

But we have seen that force, automatism, and suggestion are in some ways necessary to the support and maintenance of the human consciousness, owing to its animal limitations. They are, indeed, as is well known, the condition of its progress. Therefore, in promoting the best life, these aids must be employed by society as exercising absolute power – viz., by the State. And the problem presented by their employment is *not* a question of the "interference of the State with the Individual" – an antithesis which is meaningless so far as it implies that society can be interfering with the individual, and not interfering with itself; but it is a question how far and in what way the use of force and the like by the State is a hindrance to the end for which the State, the social power, itself exists. In other words, it is to be ascertained how far the fullest self-assertion of the social universal in its differences – the best life – can be promoted or is likely to be endangered by means which are of a different order, and so in some circumstances opposed to it. The point is not that I and some thousands more break in by force upon *you* in particular and violate *your* isolation; but that such breaking in by force, whoever does it and whoever suffers by it, and even if through passion or obsession *you* do it to *yourself* and *I* to *my* self, is hostile prima facie to the living logic of the will, which alone can create a unity and realise a best. How then, and under what reservations, in the complicated conflict of the fuller and narrower self, can this dangerous drug of violence be administered, so to speak, as a counter-poison to tendencies which would otherwise give no chance to the logical will? With this difficulty in our minds, we will endeavour to determine the general principle on which force and menace should be used by the State, and a routine be mechanically maintained by it.

3. We have hitherto spoken of the State and Society as almost convertible terms.[5] And in fact it is part of our argument that the influences of Society differ only in degree from the powers of the State, and that the explanation of both is ultimately the same. But on the other hand, it is also part of our argument that the State as such is a necessary factor in civilised life; and that no true ideal lies in the direction of minimising its individuality or restricting its absolute power. By the State, then, we mean Society as a unit, recognised as rightly exercising control over its members through absolute physical power. The limits of the unit are, of course, determined by what looks like historical accident; but there is logic underneath the apparent accident, and the most tremendous political questions turn upon the delimitation of political units. A principle, so

---

[5]See, however, pp. 156ff, and Introd. to 2nd edn, p. 22. [On the distinction between state and society, see "Letters on 'Society and State,'" below, pp. 312–23.]

to speak, of political parsimony – *entia non sunt multiplicanda praeter necessitatem*, "two organisations will not survive when one can do the work" – is always tending to expand the political unit. The limits of the common experience necessary for effective self-government are always operating to control this expansion. We might therefore suggest, as a principle determining the area of states, "the widest territorial area compatible with the unity of experience which is demanded by effective self-government." But the State de facto (which is also *de jure*) is the Society which is recognised as exercising compulsory power over its members, and as presenting itself qua a single independent corporation among other independent corporations. Without such power, or where, if anywhere, it does not exist, there can be no ultimate and effective adjustment of the claims of individuals, and of the various social groups in which individuals are involved. It is the need for this ultimate effective adjustment which constitutes the need that every individual in civilised life should belong to one state, and to one only. Otherwise conflicting adjustments might be imposed upon him by diverse authorities having equal power and right to enforce his obedience. That Society, then, is a State, which is habitually recognised as a unit lawfully exercising force. We saw that the characteristics of Society pass gradually into those of the State. It would not be true that Society is a State only as actually exercising force; but it would perhaps be true to say that State action as such, though far from being limited to the downright exercise of force, yet consists of all that side of social action which depends on the character of ultimate arbiter and regulator, maintainer of mechanical routine, and source of authoritative suggestion, a character which is one with the right to exercise force in the last resort.

The end of the State, then, is the end of Society and of the Individual – the best life, as determined by the fundamental logic of the will. The means at its disposal, qua State, always partake of the nature of force, though this does not exclude their having other aspects as well. Taxation may have the most reasonable and even the most popular purpose, yet the generality and justice of its incidence, and the certainty of its productiveness, can only be secured by compulsion. No State could undertake its work on the basis of voluntary contributions. A universal end, we might say, is indeed not a mere general rule; but you cannot carry out a universal end in a plurality of units – and a set of human individuals is always in one aspect a plurality of units – without enforcing general rules.

4. Here, then, we have our problem more closely determined than in previous chapters. There we saw, in general, that self-government can have no meaning unless we can "really" will something which we do not always "actually" will. And we were led to look for a clue to our real or implied will in the social spirit as incorporated in laws and institutions, that is to say in Society as a working whole reflected in the full system of the consciousness which composed it.

We supposed ourselves prepared, then, it would seem, to do and suffer anything which would promote the best life of the whole – that maximisation of our being which, from the nature of our real will, we saw to be imperative upon us – a demand implied in every volition and from which we could never escape.

But now we are face to face with the question what we *are* called upon to do or to suffer as members of a State, in promotion of the best life. We have here to renew, from another standpoint, the discussions of chapter iii. The governing fact of the situation is that the means of action at our disposal as members of a State are not, on their distinctive side, *in pari materia*[6] with the end. It is true that the State, as an intelligent system, can appeal by reasoning and persuasion to the logical will as such. It constantly does so in various forms, and a State which did nothing of the kind either directly or indirectly would not possess the recognition which is necessary to its very existence. So far its work is *in pari materia* with the end, being a direct element in the expansion of mind and character in their own spiritual medium of thought and will. But this side of its work is not distinctive of the State, and, therefore, is not that for which more particularly it exists. Its distinctive attribute is to be ultimate arbiter and regulator of claims, the guarantor of life as *at least* a workable system in the bodily world. It is in its ultimateness de facto that the differentia lies which separates it from the innumerable other groupings and associations which go to make up our complex life. This is shown in the fact that each of us, as we have said, must belong to a State, and can

---

[6][See Introd. to 2nd edn, note 10.]

belong to one only. It is because the authority is ultimate that it must be single. Now, authority which is to be ultimate in a sphere including the world of bodily action, must be an authority which can use force. And it is for this reason that, as we said, force is involved in the distinctive attributes of the State.

But force is not *in pari materia* with the expansion of mind and character in their spiritual medium. And, thus, there at once appears an inadequacy of means to end as between the distinctive *modus operandi*[7] of the State and the end in virtue of which it claims to represent the "real" will.

What is the bearing of this inadequacy? What is the most that the State, in its distinctive capacity, can do towards promoting a form of life which it recognises as desirable? Its direct power is limited to securing the performance of external[8] actions. This does not mean merely the performance of outward bodily movements, such as might be brought to pass by actual physical force. It is remarkable that actual physical force plays a very small part in the work of any decently ordered State. When we say that the State can do no more than secure the performance of external actions, we do not exclude from the action the intention to act in a certain way. Without such an intention there is no action in the sense of human action at all, but merely a muscular movement. It is necessary for the State to attach importance to intention, which is involved in the idea of human action, and is the only medium through which the muscular movements of human beings can be determined with any degree of certainty. The State, then, through its authority, backed ultimately by physical force, can produce, with a fair degree of certainty, the intention to act in a certain way, and therefore the actions themselves. Why do we call intentional actions, so produced, external actions only?

It is because the State is unable to determine that the action shall be done from the ground or motive which alone would give it immediate value or durable certainty as an element in the best life. On the contrary, in so far as the doing of the action is due to the distinctive mode of operation which belongs to the State, due, that is to say, to the hope of re-

---

[7][*modus operandi*: a plan of working]

[8]Green, *Principles of Political Obligation*, [loc. cit., note 4] pp. 34, 35 [sect. 11].

ward or the fear of punishment, its value as an element in the best life is *ipso facto* destroyed, except in so far as its ulterior effects are concerned. An action performed in this sense under compulsion is not a true part of the will.[9] It is an intention adopted from submissiveness or selfishness, and lacks not only the moral value, but what is partly the same thing, the reliable constancy of principle, displayed in an action which arises out of the permanent purposes of a life.

The State, then, as such, can only secure the performance of external actions. That is to say, it can only enforce as much intention[10] as is necessary to ensure, on the whole, compliance with requirements stated in terms of movements affecting the outer world. So far from promoting the performance of actions which enter into the best life, its operations, where effective, must directly narrow the area of such actions by stimulating lower motives as regards some portion of it.

5. The State, then, in its distinctive capacity, has no agency at its command for influencing conduct, but such as may be used to produce an external course of behaviour by the injunction or prohibition of external acts, in enforcing which acts the State will take note of intentions, so far as it can infer them, because it is only through them that its influence can be exerted.

The relation of such a means to the imperative end, on which we have seen that political obligation depends, must be in a certain sense negative. The means is one which cannot directly promote the end, and

---

[9]The theory of punishment will modify this proposition in some degree.

[10]On this question *vide* [see] Green's very thorough discussion. [*Principles of Political Obligation*, loc. cit., note 4, sects. 11 ff.] It is true, of course, that the law takes account of intention, and does not, e.g., treat accidental homicide as murder, the difference between them being a difference of intention. But it is obvious that, in attempting to influence human action at all, so much account as this must be taken of intention; for intention is necessary to constitute a human action. An unintentional movement of the muscles cannot be guarded against by laws and penalties; it is only through the intention that deterrent or other motives can get at the action, and a constant law-abiding disposition is the best security for law-abiding action. On the importance of intention and disposition as affording a certainty of action, Bentham, who wholly rejects judgment according to moral motive, is as emphatic as possible. [See Jeremy Bentham, *An Introduction to the Principles of Morals and Legislation*, eds. J.H. Burns and H.L.A. Hart (Oxford: Clarendon Press, 1996), chs. viii, x, xi.]

which even tends to narrow its sphere. What it can effect is to remove obstacles, to destroy conditions hostile to the realisation of the end. This brings us back to a principle laid down by Kant,[11] and in its bare statement strongly resembling Mill's contention. When force is opposed to freedom, a force that repels that force is *right*. Here, of course, all depends upon what we mean by freedom, and in what sense we think that force can hinder hindrances to it. If freedom meant for us the empty hexagon[12] round each individual, the principle would take us back to Mill's Liberty. If, on the other hand, we failed to grasp the discrepancy between force of any kind and the positive nature of the common good which we take to be freedom, the principle would lead us straight to a machine-made Utopia. For its negative character cannot restrain it from some degree of positive action. It is only through positive operation that a negation or opposition can find reality in the world. And the limits of its positive action must depend on the precise bearings of the negation which it puts in force.

Now, for us, after the explanations which have been given, the negative nature of our principle is to be seriously pressed, although its action has to take positive form. The State is in its right when it forcibly hinders a hindrance to the best life or common good. In hindering such hin-

---

[11] *W.*, [ch.] ix, [p.] 34. [See *Immanuel Kant's Sämmtliche Werke*, eds., Karl Rosenkranz and Wilhelm Friedrich Schubert (Leipzig: L. Voss, 1838–42), 14 v. Kant argues that "Any opposition that counteracts the hindrance of an effect promotes that effect and is consistent with it. Now, everything that is unjust is a hindrance to freedom according to universal laws. Coercion, however, is a hindrance or opposition to freedom. Consequently, if a certain use of freedom is itself a hindrance to freedom according to universal laws (that is, unjust), then the use of coercion to counteract it, in as much as it is the prevention of a hindrance to freedom, is consistent with freedom according to universal laws; in other words, this use of coercion is just." See Kant, *The Metaphysical Elements of Justice*, trans., John Ladd (Indianapolis: Bobbs-Merrill, 1965), pp. 35–36, (Introduction, sect. E), vol, VI, p. 231 of the Königliche Preussische Akademie der Wissenschaft edn (Berlin, 1902–1938)]. Fichte remarked on the pregnancy of this principle. [Gottlieb Fichte (1762–1814) was a disciple of Kant, and an important idealist philosopher in his own right. See his *The Science of Ethics as Based on the Science of Knowledge*, trans., A.E. Kroger (London: K. Paul, Trench, Trubner, 1897)] See further on this question, Introd. to 2nd edn, pp. 20ff.

[12] See above p. 99.

drances it will indeed do positive acts. It may try to hinder illiteracy and intemperance by compelling education and by municipalising the liquor traffic. Why not, it will be asked, hinder also unemployment by universal employment, overcrowding by universal house building, and immorality by punishing immoral and rewarding moral actions? Here comes the value of remembering that, according to our principle State action is negative in its immediate bearing, though positive both in its actual doings and its ultimate purpose. On every problem the question must recur, "Is the proposed measure *bona fide* confined to hindering a hindrance, or is it attempting direct promotion of the common good by force?" For it is to be borne in mind throughout that whatever acts are enforced are, so far as the force operates, withdrawn from the higher life. The promotion of morality by force, for instance, is an absolute self-contradiction.[13] No general principle will tell us how in particular to solve this subtle question, apart from common sense and special experience. But there is perhaps more to be learned from this principle, if approached with *bona fides*,[14] than from most generalities of philosophy on social or ethical topics. It is well, I think, constantly to apply the idea of removing hindrances, in criticism of our efforts to promote the best life by means involving compulsion. We ought, as a rule, when we propose action involving compulsion, to be able to show a definite tendency to growth, or a definite reserve of capacity, which is frustrated by a known impediment, the removal of which is a small matter compared to the capacities to be set free.[15] For it should be remarked that every act done by the

---

[13]"You will admit," it was once said, "that compulsory religion is better than no religion." "I fail to see the distinction," was the reply.

[14]Among true students *bona fides* [good faith, honest intention] is presupposed. The range opened to sophistry by a principle of this kind, which commends positive action with a negative bearing for a positive end, is, of course, immeasurable. Practically, I believe that *bona fides* is about the first and last necessity for the application of political ideas.

[15]Perhaps I may adduce an instance of real interest. It has been argued that ship-masters should be induced by a premium to ship boys as apprentices to the trade of seamanship, and that training for this trade should be fostered by local authorities like any other form of technical education. The argument which really told in the discussion consisted of statistics which seemed to prove a widespread eagerness on the part of boys and their parents that they should enter a maritime life, and the existence of a hindrance simply in the absence of adequate training for a few years during boyhood.

public power has one aspect of encroachment, however slight, on the sphere of character and intelligence, if only by using funds raised by taxation, or by introducing an automatic arrangement into life. It can, therefore, only be justified if it liberates resources of character and intelligence greater beyond all question than the encroachment which it involves. This relation is altogether perversely presented, as we saw above, if it is treated as an encroachment of society upon individuals. All this is beside the mark. The serious point is, that it is an interference, *so far as compulsion operates in it*, of one type of action with another and higher type of action; of automatism, so to speak, with intelligent volition. The higher type of action, the embodiment of the common good in logical growth, is so far from being merely individual as opposed to social, that it is the whole end and purpose in the name of which allegiance to society can be demanded from any individual. As in the private so in the general life, every encroachment of automatism must be justified by opening new possibilities to self-conscious development, if it is not to mean degeneration and senility.

It is the same principle in other words which Green lays down when he says in effect[16] that only such acts (or omissions) should be enforced by the public power as it is better should take place from any motive whatever than not take place at all. When, that is, we enforce an act (or omission) by law, we should be prepared to say, "Granting that this act, which might conceivably have come to be done from a sense of duty, now may come to be done for the most part from a fear of punishment, or from a mechanical tendency to submit to external rules (attended by the practical inconveniences of insensibility, half-heartedness, and evasion which attach to acts so enforced), still so much depends, for the higher life of the people, upon the external conditions at stake, that we think it worth while to enforce the act (or omission) though our eyes are fully open to the risk of extended automatism."

Here we may have to meet our own arguments against Mill. "You said it was a contradiction," we shall be told, "to admit coercion as a means to liberty. But here you are advocating coercion as a means to something as incompatible with it, in so far as it is operative, as our 'liberty,' viz., a

---

[16] *Principles of Political Obligation*, [loc. cit., note 4] p. 38 [sect. 15].

certain state of mind and will. If the area of coercion is necessarily subtracted from the area of liberty, as you argued above, is not the area of
coercion necessarily subtracted from that to be occupied by the desired
growth of will and character?"

The answer depends, as we indicated in chapter iii, on the difference
between bare liberty and a determinate growth. If your liberty is wholly
indeterminate, then every restraint is a reduction of it. You cannot increase a quantity which is all of one kind by taking away a part of it.
And, in fact, the idea that there was or could have been a previous general liberty, of which a part was given up in exchange for more, is a
mere illusion. Liberty has grown up within the positive determinations
of life, as they have expanded and come to fit mankind better.

But if the quantity to be increased is a determinate growth, of a type
whose general character is known, the problem is transformed. It is the
commonest of experiences that hindrances can be removed and favourable conditions maintained, if this has to be done, not with a view to
every conceivable and inconceivable development, but for a growth the
general line of which is known. In this case, as the whole expands, the
restraints and the liberty, the room for action, may even increase together.[17] This is not only true in universal theory, but much more important than is always remembered in special theory or practice. The
possibility of promoting freedom or well-being by compulsion depends
very greatly indeed on the unity of habit and experience which binds together a single community. The more the life has in common, the more
definite and automatic arrangements you may safely make in promotion
of it. The rules of my household, which inconvenience its members no
more than their clothes do, would produce a rebellion if they were enforced by law even throughout our village.

Thus, then, we may maintain our principle of the limits of distinctive
State action. The peculiarity of it is that it allows of positive acts and interferences motived by an ultimate positive purpose, but with a bearing
on that purpose which is primarily negative or indirect. However positive, as actual facts, are the conditions which it may become advisable to

---

[17]See the author's essay "Liberty and Legislation" in [his] *Civilisation of Christendom*
[(London: Swan Sonnenschein, 1899), pp. 358–83.]

maintain, they may always, on the side which is distinctively due to State compulsion, be regarded as the hindrance of hindrances. And the *bona-fide* application of this principle will really be, when aided by special experience, in some degree a valuable clue to what ought to be done. It is only putting in other words the rule of action followed by all practical men in matters of which they have genuine experience. We may think, for instance, of the problem involved in State maintenance of universities. It is easy to vote money, to build buildings, and to pass statutes. But none of these things will secure the objects of a university. Money and buildings and statutes may throw open an arena, so to speak, for the work of willing minds in learning and education. But the work itself is in a different medium from anything which can be produced by compulsion, and is so far less vital as it is conditioned by the operation of force upon minds which demand no work of the kind.

But here we meet a difficulty of principle.[18] Do we say that no external conditions are more than hindrances of hindrances to the best life? Do we deny that the best life can be positively promoted by external conditions; or if we admit this, do we still deny that it can be positively promoted by the work of the State? The answer has already been implied, but may be explicitly restated. We refused[19] to separate mind from its embodiment in material things, and so to be drawn into a purely inward theory of morality. It would be exaggeration to call such external conditions as, e.g., first-rate educational apparatus,[20] mere negative conditions of the best life. But then, we are now asked, cannot the State supply such external conditions by expenditure compulsorily provided for, and if so, is not our principle destroyed, viz., the limitation of State action to the hindrance of hindrances?

The difficulty springs from the fact, that the State, as using compulsion, is only one side of Society, and its action is only one side of social

---

[18]See further Introd. to 2nd edn, pp. 25ff.

[19]See above, pp. 66ff.

[20]See Thring on the importance of this, in Parkin's Life of him. [Sir George Robert Parkin, *Edward Thring* (London: Macmillan, 1898).] Note, however, also the modification of his view by the adventure of Uppingham-on-the-Sea. [Edward Thring (1821–1887) was a school master and reformer; his reforms at the Uppingham School influenced English public schools.]

action. If first-rate educational apparatus is called into existence by a State endowment, the first-rateness of the apparatus is not due to the compulsion applied to taxpayers, which rather, so far, negatives the action of intelligent will as such. But it must be due, in one way or another, to the fact that first-rate ability in the way of devising apparatus was somewhere pressing for an outlet, which, by a stroke of the pickaxe, so to speak, the public power was able to provide for it. We must not confuse the element of compulsion, which is the side of social action distinctly belonging to State interference, with the whole of the material results which liberated intelligence produces. When we say, then, that the State as such can do nothing for the best life but hinder hindrances to it, the principle applies in the strictest sense only to the compulsory or automatic side of State action, which must, so to speak, be reckoned against it[21] in comparing its products with those which are spontaneous social growths throughout.

But it is further true that material conditions which come close to life, such as houses, wages, educational apparatus, do not wholly escape our principle. They occupy a very interesting middle region between mere hindrances of hindrances and the actual stimulation of mind and will. On the one side they are charged with mind and character, and so far are actual elements in the best life. On the other side they depend on external actions, and therefore seem accessible to State compulsion, which extends to all external doings and omissions. But what we have to observe is, and it is in practice most important, that, *as charged with mind and will*, these material facts may not be accessible to State compulsion while, *as accessible to State compulsion* pure and simple they may forfeit their character of being charged with mind and will. This shows itself in two ways. First, just because they are facts of a kind which come so close to life (in other words depend so greatly upon being charged with mind and will), state compulsion cannot with certainty secure even their apparent existence. They fail bodily, like human beings, if there is no spirit to keep them alive. The relation of wages to the standard of life illustrates this point. Secondly, supposing that for a time, by Herculean efforts of compulsion, which must call active intelligence to its aid, such

---

[21]Subject to what will be said on the theory of rights and punishment.

facts are made to present a satisfactory appearance of existence, none the less, so far as they are characterised by compulsion, they may lose their character as elements in the best life. That is to say, they may fail to benefit those whom they are meant to benefit. The fact may fail to be absorbed in the life.

The principle of the hindrance of hindrances is most valuable and luminous when rightly grasped, just in these middle cases. A pretty and healthy house, which its inhabitant is fond of, is an element in the best life. Who could doubt it who knows what home life is? But in order that putting a family out of a bad house into a good one should give rise to such an element of the best life, it is strictly and precisely necessary that the case or policy should come under our principle. That is to say, unless there was a better life struggling to utter itself, and the deadlift of interference[22] just removed an obstacle which bound it down, the good house will not be an element in a better life, and the encroachment on the ground of volition will have been made without compensation – a fact which may show itself in many fatal ways. If, on the other hand, the struggling tendency to a better life has power[23] to effect the change without the deadlift from outside, then the result is certain and wholly to the good.

Thus we may say that every law and institution, every external fact maintained by the public power, must be judged by the degree in which it sets at liberty a growth of mind and spirit. It is a problem partly of removing obstacles to growth, and partly of the division of labour between consciousness and automatism.

It ought to occur to the reader that the ground here assigned for the limitation of State action – that is, of social action through the public power – is not prima facie in harmony with the account of political obligation, according to which laws and institutions represented a real self or

---

[22]The policy of a deadlift in the housing of the people is justified by the arrears incurred during the war, and by the public demand that has been awakened. But it is quite plain that if a recurrence of the deficit is to be avoided, a quite new and thoroughly popular interest in the work must be sustained. [Note added in] 1919.

[23]Many forms of *social* co-operation, it must be remembered, need no deadlift from the *State* as such. We are not setting self-help against co-operation, but will against automatism.

general will, recognised by individuals as implied in the common good which was imperative upon them. We spoke, for example, of being forced to be free, and of the system of law and order as representing the higher self.[24] And yet we are now saying that in as far as force is operative through compulsion and authoritative suggestion, it is a means which can only reach its end through a negation.

But this prima facie contradiction is really a proof of the vitality of our principle. It follows from the fact that we accept self-government in the full strength of both its factors and can deal with it on this basis. The social system under which we live, taking it as one which does not demand immediate revolution, represents the general will and higher self as a whole to the community as a whole and can only stand by virtue of that representation being recognised. Our loyalty to it makes us men and citizens, and is the main spiritualising force of our lives. But something in all of us, and much in some of us, is recalcitrant through rebellion, indolence, incompetence, or ignorance. And it is only on these elements that the public power operates as power through compulsion or authoritative suggestion. Thus, the general will when it meets us as force, and authority resting on force, and not as a social suggestion which we spontaneously rise to accept, comes to us *ex hypothesi* as something which claims to be ourself, but which, for the moment, we more or less fail to recognise. And, according to the adjustment between it and our complex and largely unintelligent self, it may abandon us to automatism, or stir us in rebellion or recognition, and so may hinder the fuller life in us or remove hindrances to it. It seems worth while to distinguish two main cases of the relation between the ordinary self and the general will. One of these cases covers the whole of our every-day law-abiding life, in its grades of active loyalty, acceptance of suggestion, and automatic acquiescence; and consists of the relation of our ordinary self to the general system of rights maintained by the State as ultimate regulator and arbiter. The other is confined to more exceptional situations, and has to do with collision between the particular and the general will, as treated in the theory of punishment. The subject of reward may be mentioned at the same time, if only to show why it is almost an empty heading in po-

---

[24][See above, pp. 101ff, 116, 153ff].

litical theory. We will end this chapter, therefore, with a general account of the system of rights and of reward and punishment.

6. The idea of individual rights comes down to us from the doctrine of natural right, and has generally been discussed with reference to it. We need not now go back upon the illusions connected with the notion of natural right. It is enough if we bear in mind that we inherit from it the important idea of a positive law which is what it ought to be. A right,[25] then, has both a legal and a moral reference. It is a claim which can be enforced at law, which no moral imperative can be; but it is also recognised to be a claim which ought to be capable of enforcement at law, and thus it has a moral aspect. The case in which positive enactment and the moral "ought" appear to diverge will be considered below. But a typical "right" unites the two sides. It both is, and ought to be, capable of being enforced at law.

Its peculiar position follows from what we have seen to be the end of the State, and the means at its disposal. The end of the State is moral purpose, imperative on its members. But its distinctive action is restricted to removing hindrances to the end, that is, to lending its force to overcome – both in mind and in externals essential to mind – obstacles which otherwise would obstruct the realisation of the end. The whole of the conditions thus enforced is the whole of "rights" attaching to the selves, who, standing in definite relations, constitute the community. For it is in these selves that the end of the State is real, and it is by maintaining and regulating their claims to the removal of obstructions that the State is able to promote the end for which it exists. Rights then are claims recognised by the State, i.e., by Society acting as ultimate authority, to the maintenance of conditions favourable to the best life. And if we ask in general for a definition and limitation of State action as such, the answer is, in a simple phrase, that State action is coincident with the maintenance of rights.

The system of rights which the State maintains may be regarded from different points of view.

---

[25] This is a right in the fullest sense. The nature of a merely legal or merely moral right will be illustrated below.

First, (α) from the point of view of the whole community, that is, as the general result in the promotion of good life obtained by the working of a free Society, as a statesman or outside critic might regard it. Thus looked at, the system of rights may be described as "the organic whole of the outward conditions necessary to the rational life," or "that which is really necessary to the maintenance of material conditions essential to the existence and perfection of human personality."[26] This point of view is essential as a full contradiction of that uncritical conception by which rights are regarded as something with which the individual is invested in his aspect of isolation, and independently of his relation to the end. It forces us away from this false particularisation, and compels us to consider the whole State-maintained order in its connectedness as a single expression of a common good or will, in so far as such a good can find utterance in a system of external acts and habits. And it enables us to weigh the value which belongs to the maintenance of any tolerable social order, simply because it is an order, and so far enables life to be lived, and a determinate, if limited, common good to be realised. From other points of view we are apt to neglect this characteristic, and to forget how great is the effect, for the possibilities of life throughout, of the mere fact that a social order exists. Hegel observes that a man thinks it a matter of course that he goes back to his house after nightfall in security. He does not reflect to what he owes it. Yet this very naturalness, so to speak, of living in a social order is perhaps the most important foundation which the State can furnish to the better life. "*Si monumentum quaeris, circumspice.*"[27] If we ask how it affects our will, the answer is

---

[26]Kraus and Henrici, cited by Green, *Principles of Political Obligation*, [loc. cit., note 4], p. 35 [sect. 11]. Cp, "The system of right is the realm of realised freedom, the world of mind produced by the mind as a second nature." (Hegel, *Philosophie d. Rechts*, sect. 4). [In his note Green actually cites Herman Ulrici's discussion of Kraus' and Henrici's two definitions of "Recht" or "jus naturæ." Ulrici, *Gott und der Mensch*, vol. II, *Grundzüge der Praktischen Philosophie, Naturrecht, Ethik und Aesthetik* (Leipzig: Y. O. Weigel, 1873–74), p. 219. See also Hegel, *The Philosophy of Right*, trans. T.M. Knox (Oxford: Clarendon Press, 1942), p. 30 (sect. 4). Knox translates the passage: "the system of right is the realm of freedom made actual, the world of mind brought out of itself like a second nature."]

[27][*Si monumentum quaeris, circumspice*: If you seek his monument, look around.]

that it forms our world. Speaking broadly, the members of a civilised community have seen nothing but order in their lives, and could not accommodate their action to anything else.

It should be mentioned as a danger of this point of view that, fascinated by the spectacle of the social fabric as a whole, we may fail to distinguish what in it is the mere maintenance of rights, and what is the growth which such maintenance can promote but cannot constitute. Thus we may lose all idea of the true limits of State action.

(β) We may regard this complex of rights from the standpoint of the selves or persons who compose the community. It is in these selves, as we have seen, that the social good is actual, and it is to their differentiated functions,[28] which constitute their life and the end of the community, that the sub-groupings of rights, or conditions of good life, have to be adjusted each to each like suits of clothes. The rights are, from this point of view, primarily the external incidents, so far as maintained by law – the authoritative vesture as it were – of a person's position in the world of his community. And we shall do well to regard the nature of rights, as attaching to selves or persons, from this point of view of a place or position in the order determined by law. It has been argued, I do not know with what justice, that, in considering the relations of particles in space, the proper course would be to regard their positions or distances from each other as the primary fact, and to treat attributions of attractive and repulsive forces as modes of expressing the maintenance of the necessary positions rather than as descriptive of real causes which bring it about. At least, it appears to me, such a conception may well be applied to the relative ideas of right and obligation. What comes first, we may say, is the position, the place or places, function or functions, determined by the nature of the best life as displayed in a certain community, and the capacity of the individual self for a unique contribution to that best life. Such places and functions are imperative; they are the fuller self in the particular person, and make up the particular person as he passes into the fuller self. His hold on this *is* his true will, in other words, his apprehension of the general will. Such a way of speaking may

---

[28] I do not say merely social functions, i.e., functions dealing directly with "others" as such.

seem unreally simplified when we look at the myriad relations of modern life and the sort of abstraction by which the individual is apt to become a rolling stone with no assignable place – indeed "gathering no moss" – and to pass through his positions and relations as if they were stations on a railway journey. But in truth it is only simplified and not falsified. If we look with care we shall see that it, or nothing, is true of all lives.

The Position, then, is the real fact – the vocation, place or function, which is simply one reading of the person's actual self and relations in the world in which he lives. Having thoroughly grasped this primary fact, we can readily deal with the points of view which present the position or its incidents in the partial aspects of rights or obligations.

(i) A right, we said, is a *claim* recognised by society and enforced by the State. My place or position, then, and its incidents, so far as sanctioned by the State, constitute my rights, when thought of as something which I claim, or regard as powers instrumental to my purposes. A right thus regarded is not anything primary. It is a way of looking at certain conditions, which, by reason of their relation to the end of the whole as manifested in me, are imperative alike for me and for others. It is, further, the particular way of looking at these conditions which is in question when I claim them or am presumed to claim them, as powers secured to me with a view to an end which I accept as mine. I *have* the rights no less in virtue of my presumed capacity for the end, if I am in fact indifferent to the end. But, in this case, though attributed *ab extra*[29] as rights, they tend to pass into obligations.

(ii) If rights are an imperative "position" or function, when looked at as a group of State-secured powers claimed by a person for a certain end, obligations are the opposite aspect of such a position or group of powers. That is to say, the conditions of a "position" are regarded as obligations in as far as they are thought of as requiring enforcement, and therefore, primarily, from the point of view of persons not directly identified with the "position" or end to which they are instrumental. Rights are claimed, obligations are owed. And prima facie rights are claimed *by*

---

[29][*ab extra*: from without].

a person, and obligations are owed *to* a person, being his rights as regarded by those against whom they are enforceable.

Thus, the distinction of self and others, which we refused to take as the
basis of society, makes itself prominent in the region of compulsion. The
reason is that compulsion is confined to hindering or producing external
acts, and is excluded from producing an act in its relation to a moral end,
that is, the exercise of a right in its true sense; though it can enforce an
act which in fact favours the possibility of acting towards a moral end –
that is, an obligation. This is the same thing as saying that normally a
right is what *I* claim, and the obligation relative to it is what *you* owe; as
an obligation is that which can be enforced, and that is an act or omission apart from the willing of an end; and a right involves what cannot
be enforced, viz., the relation of an act to an end in a person's will. But
even here the distinction of self and others is hardly ultimate. The obligation on me to maintain my parents becomes almost a right[30] if I claim
the task as a privilege. And many rights of my position may actually be
erected into, or more commonly may give rise to, obligations incumbent
on me for the sake of my position or function. If the exercise of the fran-
chise were made compulsory that would be a right treated also as an obligation; but it might be urged that qua obligation it was held due to the
position of others, and only qua right to my own "position." But if the
law interferes with my poisoning myself[31] either by drains or with alco-

---

[30]I do not know that I can compel my parents to be maintained by me, and therefore it is
not my legal right to maintain them; but at least the obligation, if I claim it, ceases to depend on force. An East-End Londoner will say, "He had a right to maintain his father,"
meaning that he was bound to do so; and Jeanie Deans says, "I have no right to have stories told about my family without my consent," representing her own claim as a negative
obligation on herself as well as on others. She represents the thought, "I have a right that
you should not tell stories," etc., in a form which puts it as a case of the thought, "You
have no right to tell stories," disregarding the distinction between herself and others as accidental. [Jeannie Deans is the heroine of Sir Walter Scott's *The Heart of Midlothian*
(London: J.M. Dent, 1988). Jeannie Deans goes to London to obtain a pardon for her half-
sister, who has been convicted of the murder of her illegitimate child.]

[31]The law used to interfere with bad sanitation only as a "nuisance," i.e. as an annoyance
to "others." It now interferes with any state of things dangerous to life as such, which
probably means that a change of theory has unconsciously set in. Legislation for dangerous trades almost proves the point, though here it is possible to urge that the employer is

hol, that, I presume, is the enforcement of an obligation arising out of my own position and function as a man and a citizen, which makes reasonable care for my life imperative upon me.

(γ) It is commonly said that every right implies a duty. This has two meanings, which should be distinguished.

In the one case, (i) for "duty" should be read "obligation," i.e., a demand enforceable by law. This simply means that every "position" may be regarded as involving either powers secured or conditions enforced, which are one and the same thing differently looked at. Roughly speaking, they are the same thing as differently looked at by one person and by other persons. My right to walk along the high-road involves an obligation upon all other persons not to obstruct me, and in the last resort the State will send horse, foot and artillery rather than let me be causelessly obstructed in walking along the high-road.

It is also true that every position which can be the source of obligations enforceable in favour of my rights is likewise a link with obligations enforceable on me in favour of the rights of others. By claiming a right in virtue of my position I recognise and testify to the general system of law according to which I am reciprocally under obligation to respect the rights, or rather the function and position, of others. My rights then imply obligations both in others, and perhaps in myself, correlative to these rights, and in me correlative to the rights of others. But it cannot strictly be said that the obligations are the source of the rights, or the rights of the obligations. Both are the varied external conditions of "positions" as regarded from different points of view.

But (ii) there is a different sense in which every right implies a duty. And this, the true meaning of the phrase, is involved in what we have said of the nature of a "position." All rights, as claims which both are and ought to be enforceable by law, derive their imperative authority from their relation to an end which enters into the better life. All rights, then, are powers instrumental to making the best of human capacities, and can only be recognised or exercised upon this ground.

---

put under obligation for the sake of his workers, and not the workers for their own sake. But the distinction is hardly real.

In this sense, the duty is the purpose with a view to which the right is secured, and not merely a corresponding obligation equally derived from a common ground; and the right and duty are not distinguished as something claimed by self and something owed to others, but the duty as an imperative purpose, and the right as a power secured because instrumental to it.

(δ) We have treated rights throughout as claims, the enforcement of which by the State is merely the climax of their recognition by society. Why do we thus demand recognition for rights? If we deny that there can be unrecognised rights, do we not surrender human freedom to despotism or to popular caprice?

(i) In dealing with the general question why recognition is demanded as an essential of rights, we must remember what we took to be the nature of society and the source of obligation. We conceived a society to be a structure of intelligences so related as to co-operate with and to imply one another. We took the source of obligation to lie in the fact that the logic of the whole is operative in every part, and consequently that every part has a reality which goes beyond its average self and identifies it with the whole, making demands upon it in doing so.

Now, we are said to "recognise" anything when it comes to us with a consciousness of familiarity, as something in which we feel at home. And this is our general attitude to the demands which the logic of the whole, implied in our every act, is continuously making upon us. It is involved in the interdependence of minds which has been explained to constitute *the mind* of which the visible community is the body. A teacher's behaviour towards his pupils, for example, implies a certain special kind of interdependence between their minds. What he can do for them is conditioned by what they expect of him and are ready to do for him and vice versa. The relation of each to the other is a special form of "recognition." That is to say, the mind of each has a definite and positive attitude towards that of the other, which is based on, or rather, so far as it goes, simply *is*, the relation of their "positions" to each other. Thus, social positions or vocations actually have their being in the medium of recognition. They *are* the attitudes of minds towards one another, through which their several distinct characteristics are instrumental to a common good.

Thus, then, a right, being a power secured in order to fill a position, is simply a part of the fact that such a position is recognised as instrumental to the common good. It is impossible to argue that the position may exist, and not be recognised. For we are speaking of a relation of minds, and, in so far as minds are united into a single system by their attitudes towards each other, their "positions" and the recognition of them are one and the same thing. Their attitude, receptive, co-operative, tolerant, and the like, is so far a recognition, though not necessarily a reflective recognition. Probably this is what is intended by those who speak of imitation or other analogous principles as the ultimate social fact. They do not mean the repetition of another person's conduct, though that may enter in part into the relation of interdependence. They mean the conscious adoption[32] of an attitude towards others, embodying the relations between the "positions" which social logic assigns to each.

(ii) But then the question of page 199 presses upon us – "If we deny that there can be unrecognised rights, do we not surrender human freedom to despotism or to popular caprice?"

The sting of this suggestion is taken out when we thoroughly grasp the idea that recognition is a matter of logic, working on and through experience, and not of choice or fancy. If my mind has *no* attitude to yours, there is no interdependence and I cannot be a party to securing you rights. You are not, for me, a sharer in a capacity for a common good, which each of us inevitably respects. A dog or a tree may be an instrument to the good life, and it may therefore be right to treat it in a certain way, but it cannot be a subject of rights. If my mind *has* an attitude to yours, then there is certainly a recognition between us, and the nature of that recognition and what it involves are matters for reasoning and for the appeal to experience. It is idle for me, for instance, to communicate with you by language or to buy and sell with you, perhaps even idle to go to war with you,[33] and still to say that I recognise no capacity in you for a common good. My behaviour is then inconsistent with itself, and

---

[32] To call this imitation is something like calling fine art imitation. Really, in both cases, we find a re-arrangement and modification of material, incident to a new expression. The process, if we must name it, is "relative suggestion" rather than imitation.

[33] As distinct from hunting. We do not go to war with lions and tigers.

the question takes the form what rights are involved in the recognition of you which experience demonstrates. No person and no society is consistent with itself, and the proof and amendment of their inconsistency is always possible. And, one inconsistency being amended, the path is opened to progress by the emergence of another. If slaves come to be recognised as free but not as citizens, this of itself opens a road by which the new freeman may make good his claim that it is an inconsistency not to recognise him as a citizen.

But no right can be founded on my mere desire to do what I like.[34] The wish for this is the sting of the claim to unrecognised rights, and this wish is to be met, as the fear that our view might lead to despotism was met. The matter is one of fact and logic, not of fancies and wishes. If I desire to assert an unrecognised right, I must show what "position" involves it, and how that position asserts itself in the system of recognitions which is the social mind, and my point can only be established universally with regard to a certain type of position, and not merely for myself as a particular A or B. In other words, I must show that the alleged right is a requirement of the realisation of capacities for good and, further, that it does not demand a sacrifice of capacities now being realised, out of proportion to the capacities which it would enable to assert themselves. I must show, in short, that in so far as the claim in question is not secured by the State, Society is inconsistent with itself, and falls short of being what it professes to be, an organ of good life. And all my showing gives no *right*, till it has modified the law. To maintain a right against the State by force or disobedience is rebellion, and, in considering the duty of rebellion, we have to set the whole value of the existence of social order against the importance of the matter in which we think Society defective. There can hardly be a duty to rebellion in a State in which law can be altered by constitutional process.

The State-maintained system of rights, then, in its relation to the normal self and will of ordinary citizens with their varying moods of enthusiasm and indolence, may be compared to the automatic action of a human body. Automatic actions are such as we perform in walking, eating, dressing, playing the piano or riding the bicycle. They have been formed

---

[34]Green, *Principles of Political Obligation*, [loc. cit., note 4] p. 149 [sect. 144].

by consciousness, and are of a character subservient to its purposes, and obedient to its signals. As a rule, they demand no effort of attention, and in this way attention is economised and enabled to devote itself to problems which demand its intenser efforts. They are relegated to automatism because they are uniform, necessary, and external – "external" in the sense explained above, that the way in which they are required makes it enough if they are done, whatever their motives, or with no motives at all.

By far the greater bulk of the system of rights is related in this way to normal consciousness. We may pay taxes, abstain from fraud and assault, use the roads and the post-office, and enjoy our general security, without knowing that we are doing or enjoying anything that demands special attention. Partly, of course, attention is being given by other consciousnesses to maintaining the securities and facilities of our life. Even so, the arrangement is automatic in so far as there is no reason for arousing the general attention in respect to it; but to a varying extent it is automatic throughout, and engrained in the system and habits of the whole people. We are all supposed to know the whole law. Not even a judge has it all in his knowledge at any one time; but the meaning is that it roughly expresses our habits, and we live according to it without great difficulty, and expect each other to do so. This automatism is not harmful, but absolutely right and necessary, so long as we relegate to it only "external" matters; i.e. such as are necessary to be done, motive or no motive, in some way which can be generally laid down. Thus used, it is an indispensable condition of progress. It represents the ground won and settled by our civilisation, and leaves us free to think and will such matters as have their value in and through being thought and willed rightly. If we try to relegate these to automatism, then moral and intellectual death has set in.

But if the system of rights is automatic, how can it rest on recognition? Automatic actions, we must remember, are still of a texture, so to speak, continuous with consciousness. "Recognition" expresses very fairly our habitual attitude towards them in ourselves and others. We might think, for example, of the system of habits and expectations which forms our household routine. We go through it for the most part automatically, while "recognising" the "position" of those who share it with us, and respecting the life which is its end. At points here and there in which it affects the deeper possibilities of our being, our attention becomes active, and we assert our position with enthusiasm and conscientiousness. Our attitude to the social system of rights is something like this. The whole order has our habitual recognition; we are aware of and respect more or less the imperative end on which it rests – the claim of a common good upon us all. Within the framework of this order there is room for all degrees of laxity and conscientiousness; but, in any case, it is only at certain points, which either concern our special capacity or demand readjustment in the general interest, that intense active attention is possible or desirable.

The view here taken of automatism and attention in the social whole impairs neither the unity of intelligence throughout society nor the individual's recognition of this unity as a self liable to be opposed to his usual self. As to the former point, every individual mind shows exactly the same phenomena, of a *continuum* largely automatic, and thoroughly alive only in certain regions, connected, but not thoroughly coherent. As to the latter point, permeation of the individual by the habits of social automatism does not prevent, but rather gives material for, his tendency to abstract himself from the whole, and to frame an attitude for himself inconsistent with his true "position," against which tendency the imperative recognition of his true self has constantly to be exerted.

7. We have finally to deal with the actual application by the State of its ultimate resource for the maintenance of rights, viz., force. Superior force may be exercised upon human nature both by rewards and by punishments. In both respects its exercise by the State would fall generally within the lines of automatism; that is to say, it would be a case of the promotion of an end by means other than the influence of an idea of that end upon the will. But, owing to the subtle continuity of human nature throughout all its phases, we shall find that there is something more than this to be said, and that the idea of the end is operative in a peculiar way just where the agencies that promote it appear to be most alien and mechanical. In so far as this is the case, the general theory of the negative character of State action has to be modified, as we foresaw,[35] by the

---

[35]See pp. 190ff.

theory of punishment. Prima facie, however, it is true that reward and punishment belong to the automatic element of social life. They arise in no direct relation of the will to the end. They are a reaction of the automatic system, instrumental to the end, against a friction or obstacle which intrudes upon it, or (in the case of rewards) upon the opposite of a friction or obstacle. There is no object in pressing a comparison into every detail; but perhaps, as social and individual automatism do really bear the same kind of relation to consciousness, it may be pointed out that reward and punishment correspond in some degree to the pleasures and pains of a high-class secondary automatism, say of riding or of reading, i.e. of something specially conducive to enhanced life. Such activities bring pleasure when unimpeded, and pain when sharply interrupted by a start or blunder which jars upon us. Putting this latter case in language which carries out the analogy to punishment, we might say that the formed habit of action, unconsciously or semi-consciously relevant to the end or fuller life, is obstructed by some partial state of mind, and their conflict is accompanied with recognition, pain, and vexation. "What a fool I was," we exclaim, "to ride carelessly at that corner," or "to let that plan for a holiday interrupt me in my morning's reading."

It may seem remarkable that reward plays a small and apparently decreasing part in the self-management of society by the public power. To the naive Athenian,[36] it seemed a natural instrument for the encouragement of public spirit, probably rather by a want of discrimination between motives than by a real belief in political selfishness. In European countries honours still appear to play a considerable part, but on analysis it would be found less than it seems. Partly they are recognitions of im-

---

[36]"Speech of Pericles," Thucydides, ii. 46: "Where there are the greatest rewards of merit, there will be the best men to do the work of the State." [Rex Warner translates the passage thus: "Where the rewards of valour are the greatest, there you will find also the best and the bravest spirits among the people." "Pericles' Funeral Oration," in Thucydides, *The Peloponnesian War* (Harmondsworth: Penguin, 1978), p. 151 (Book II, 46).] Contrast Plato's principle that there can be no sound government while public service is done with a view to reward. ["And for this reason, I said, money and honour have no attraction for them; good men do not wish to be openly demanding payment for governing and so to get the name of hirelings, nor by secretly helping themselves out of the public revenues to get the name of thieves. And not being ambitious they do not care about honour." Jowett translation of Plato's *Republic* (New York: Vintage Books, [1894] 1991), Book I, 347.]

portant functions, and thus conditions rather than rewards. To a great extent, again, they recognise existing facts, and are rather consequences of the respect which society feels for certain types of life (with very curious results in regions where the general mind is inexperienced, e.g. in fine art) than means employed to regulate the conduct of citizens. We should think a soldier mean whose aim was a peerage, still more a poet or an artist. I hardly know that rewards adjudged by the State, as distinct from compensations, exist in the United States of America.[37] Rewards then fill no place correlative to that of punishments, and the reason seems plain. Punishment corresponds much better to the negative method which alone is open to the State for the maintenance of rights. For Punishment proclaims its negative character, and no one can suppose it laudable simply to be deterred from wrong-doing by fear of punishment. But though precisely the same principle applies to meritorious actions done with a view to reward, an illusion is almost certain to arise which will hide the principle in this case. For, if reward is largely used as an inducement to actions conducive to the best life, it is almost certain that it will be used as an inducement to actions the value and certainty of which depend on the state of will to which they are due. And then the distinction between getting them done, motive or no motive, which is the true region of State action, and their being done with a certain motive, which is necessary to give them either the highest practical or any moral value, is pretty sure to be obliterated, and the range of the moral will trenched upon in its higher portion and with a constant tendency to self-deception.[38] It is the same truth in other words when we point out that

---

[37]The precise theory of the grants in money made to soldiers or sailors, for distinguished service, is not easy to state. But it seems clear that they are not intended to act as motives. They are essentially a recognition after the act, not an inducement held out before it.

[38]It is perhaps permissible to observe in general, what is very well known to all who have much experience of what is called philanthropy, that the tendency to distinguish it by public honours is exceedingly dangerous to its quality, which depends entirely on that energy and purity of intelligence which can only accompany the deepest and highest motives. Mere vulgar self-seeking is not the danger (though it does occur) so much as obfuscation of intelligence through a mixture of aims and ideas. [Bosanquet was deeply involved in the work of Charity Organisation Society. See the editors' Introduction and the essay on "Idealism in Social Work," (pp. 358ff) in this volume.]

taking reward and punishment, as interferences, only to deal with exceptional cases, reward would deal with the exceptionally good. Therefore, again, reward must either make an impossible attempt to deal with all the normal as good which involves the danger of *de*-moralising the whole of normal life, or must take the line of specially promoting what is exceptionally conducive to good life; in which case confusion is certain to arise from interference with the delicate middle class of external actions analysed above.[39] And thus it is only what we should expect when we find that States having no *damnosa hereditas*[40] of a craving for personal honours are hardly acquainted with the bestowal of rewards by the public power.

It will be sufficient, then, to complete the account of State action in maintenance of rights by some account of the nature and principles of punishment.

And we may profitably begin by recalling M. Durkheim's suggestion, which was mentioned in a former chapter.[41] Punishment, he observes, from the simplest and most actual point of view, includes in itself all those sides which theory has tended to regard as incompatible. It is, in essence, simply the reaction of a strong and determinate collective sentiment against an act which offends it. It is idle to include such a reaction entirely under the head either of reformation, or of retaliation, or of prevention. An aggression is *ipso facto* a sign of character, an injury, and a menace; and the reaction against it is equally *ipso facto* an attempt to affect character, a retaliation against an injury, and a deterrent or preventive against a menace. When we fire up at aggression it is pretty much a chance whether we say "I am going to teach him better manners," or "I am going to serve him out," or "I am going to see that he doesn't do that again." A consideration of each of these aspects is necessary to do justice both to the theories and to the facts.

(i) An obvious point of view, and the first perhaps to appear in philosophy, though strongly opposed to early law, is that the aim of punishment is to make the offender good. As test of the adequacy of this

---

[39]See p. 190.

[40][*damnosa hereditas*: a damaging inheritance, an inheritance that involves a loss.]

[41][Chapter ii.] See p. 73.

doctrine by itself, the question may be put, "If pleasures would cure the offender, ought he to be given pleasures?" The doctrine, however, does not, by any means, altogether incline to leniency. For it carries as a corollary the extirpation of the incurable, which Plato proposes in a passage of singularly modern quality, when he suggests the co-operation of judges and physicians in maintaining the moral and physical health of society.[42]

The first comment that occurs to us is, that by a mere medical treatment of the offender, including or consisting of pleasant conditions, if helpful to his cure, the interest of society seems to be disregarded. What is to become of the maintenance of rights, if aggressors have to anticipate a pleasant or lenient "cure"? It may be true that brutal punishments stimulate a criminal temper in the people rather than check it; but it is a long way from this to laying down that there is no need for terror to be associated with crime. To suppose that pleasures may simply act throughout as pains, is playing with words and throws no light on the question. If we leave words their meaning, we must say that punishment must be deterrent for others as well as reformatory for the offender, and therefore in some degree painful. It is true, however, that the offender, as a human being, and presumably capable of a common good, has, as Green puts it, "reversionary rights" of humanity, and these punishment must so far as possible respect.

But there is a deeper difficulty. If the reformation theory is to be seriously distinguished from the other theories of punishment, it has a meaning which is unjust to the offender himself. It implies that his of-

---

[42] *Republic*, 409, 410. ["Why, I said, you join physicians and judges. Now the most skilful physicians are those who, from their youth upwards, have combined with the knowledge of their art the greatest experience of disease; they had better not be robust in health, and should have had all manner of diseases in their own persons. For the body, as I conceive, is not the instrument with which they cure the body; in that case we could not allow them ever to be or to have been sickly; but they cure the body with the mind, and the mind which has become and is sick can cure nothing....This is the sort of medicine, and this is the sort of law, which you sanction in your State. They will minister to better natures, giving health both of soul and of body; but those who are diseased in their bodies they will leave to die, and the corrupt and incurable souls they will put an end to themselves. That is clearly the best thing both for the patients and for the State." Jowett translation of *The Republic*, loc. cit., note 36, Book III, 408–9.]

fence is a merely natural evil, like disease, and can be cured by thera-
peutic treatment directed to removing its causes. But this is to treat him
not as a human being; to treat him as a "patient," not as an agent; to exclude him from the general recognition that makes us men. (If the thera-
peutic treatment includes a recognition and chastisement of the offender's bad will[43] – the form of which chastisement may, of course, be
very variously modified – then there is no longer anything to distinguish
the reformatory theory from other theories of punishment.) It has been
lately pointed out[44] what a confusion is involved in the claim that beings,
who are irresponsible and so incapable of guilt, are therefore in the strict
sense innocent. Here are the true objects for a pure reformatory theory.
Here that may freely be done, as to creatures incapable of rights, which
is kindest for them and safest for society, from quasi-medical treatment
to extirpation. There is no guilt in them to demand punishment, but there
is no human will in them to have the rights of innocence.

But, applied to responsible human beings, such a theory, if really kept
to its distinctive contention, is an insult. It leads to the notion that the
State may take hold of any man, whose life or ideas are thought capable
of improvement, and set to work to ameliorate them by forcible treatment. There is no true punishment except where one is an offender
against a system of rights which he shares, and therefore against himself.
And such an offender has a right to the recognition of his hostile will; it
is inhuman to treat him as a wild animal or a child, whom we simply
mould to our aims. Without such a recognition, to be punished is not,
according to the old Scotch phrase, to be "justified."

(ii) The idea of retaliation or retribution, though in history the oldest
conception of punishment,[45] may be taken in theory as a protest against

---

[43]Plato's reformatory theory seems to involve this. And the author of *Erewhon*, to the best
of my recollection, only half adheres to his principle that disease is to be punished, and
wickedness medically treated. For his "treatment" of wickedness is plainly punitive, and
thus he altogether abandons the idea of medical cure which his antithesis suggests. [Sam-
uel Butler (1835–1902), was the author of the utopian *Erewhon; or, Over the Range*
(London: Trübner, 1872).]

[44]Mr [F.H.] Bradley, ["Some Remarks on Punishment,"] in the *International Journal of
Ethics*, [vol. 4] April, 1894 [pp. 269–84].

[45]We saw that, even in its earliest forms, it cannot really be taken to exclude the other as-

the conception that punishment is only a means for making a man better. Its strong point is its definite idea of the offender. The offender is a responsible person, belonging to a certain order which he recognises as entering into him and as entered into by him, and he has made actual an intention hostile to this order. He has, as Plato's Socrates insists in the *Crito*, destroyed the order so far as in him lies.[46] In other words, he has violated the system of rights which the State exists to maintain, and by which alone he and others are secured in the exercise of any capacity for good, this security consisting in their reciprocal respect for the system. His hostile will stands up and defies the right, in so far as his personality is asserted through a tangible deed which embodies the wrong. It is necessary, then, that the power which maintains the system of rights should not merely, if possible, undo the external harm which has been done, but should strike down the hostile will which has defied the right by doing that harm. The end or true self is in the medium of mind and will, and is contradicted and nullified so far as a hostile will is permitted to triumph.

It is obvious, however, that the means by which the hostile will can be negatived fall prima facie within the region of automatism. The recalcitrant element of consciousness is not susceptible to the end as an idea or it would not be recalcitrant. The end can here assert itself, agreeably to the general principle of State action, only through external action the mental effects of which cannot be precisely estimated. It might, therefore, seem that the pain produced by the reaction of the automatic system on the aberrant consciousness – the punishment – was simply a natural pain, which might act as a deterrent from aberration, but had no visible connection with the true whole or end for the mind of the offender. We shall speak below of the sense in which punishment is deterrent or preventive. But it is to be noted at this point that a high-class secondary automatism, with which all along we have compared the system

---

pects.

[46][In this Platonic dialogue Crito, while visiting Socrates in prison, is trying to convince him to escape. Socrates imagines himself in a discussion with the Laws (about whether he should escape), and they say to him: "Now Socrates, what are you proposing to do? Can you deny that by this act you are contemplating you intend, so far as you have the power, to destroy us, the Laws, and the whole State as well?" *Crito*, 50b, trans., Hugh Tredennick (Harmondsworth: Penguin, 1954), pp. 89–90.]

of rights as engrained in the habits of a people, retains a very close connection with consciousness. We do not indeed will every step that we walk, but we only walk while we will to walk, and so with the whole system of routine automatism which is the method and organ of our daily life. At any interruption, any hindrance or failure, consciousness starts up, and the end of the whole routine comes sharply back upon us through our aberration.

So it is with punishment. Primarily, no doubt, chastisement by pain, and the appeal to fear and to submissiveness, is effective through our lower nature, and, in as far as operative, substitutes selfish motives for the will that wills the good, and so narrows its sphere. But there is more behind. The automatic system is pulsing with the vitality of the end to which it is instrumental; and when we kick against the pricks, and it reacts upon us in pain, this pain has subtle connections throughout the whole of our being. It brings us to our senses, as we say; that is, it suggests, more or less, a consciousness of what the habitual system means, and of what we have committed in offending against it. When one stumbles and hurts his foot, he may look up and see that he is off the path. If a man is told that the way he works his factory or keeps his tenement houses is rendering him liable to fine or imprisonment, then, if he is an ordinary, careless, but respectable citizen, he will feel something of a shock, and recognise that he was getting too neglectful of the rights of other, and that, in being pulled up, he is brought back to himself. His citizen honour will be touched. He will not like to be below the average which the common conscience had embodied in law.

When we come to the actual criminal consciousness, the form which the recognition may take in fact may vary greatly; and as an extreme there may be a furious hostility against the whole recognised system of law, either involving self-outlawry through a despair of reconciliation, or arising through some sort of habitual conspiracy in which the man finds his chosen law and order as against that recognised by the State.[47] But after all, we are dealing with a question of social logic and not of em-

---

[47]See the account of the Mafia in Marion Crawford's *Corleone* [, *a tale of Sicily* (London: Macmillan, 1896)]. Accepting this as described, it simply is the social will in which the population of a certain region find their substitute for the State.

pirical psychology. And it must be laid down that, in as far as any sane man fails altogether to recognise in any form the assertion of something which he normally respects in the law which punishes him (putting aside what he takes to be miscarriage of justice), he is outlawed by himself and the essentials of citizenship are not in him. Doubtless, if an uneducated man were told, in theoretical language, that in being punished for an assault he was realising his own will, he would think it cruel nonsense. But this is a mere question of language, and has really nothing to do with the essential state of his consciousness. He would understand perfectly well that he was being served as he would say anyone should be served, whom he saw acting as he had done, in a case where his own passions were not engaged. And this recognition, in whatever form it is admitted, carries the consequence which we affirm.

In short, then, compulsion through punishment and the fear of it, though primarily acting on the lower self, does tend, when the conditions of true punishment exist (i.e. the reaction of a system of rights violated by one who shares in it), to a recognition of the end by the person punished, and may so far be regarded as his own will, implied in the maintenance of a system to which he is a party, returning upon himself in the form of pain. And this is the theory of punishment as retributive. The test doctrine of the theory may be found in Kant's saying that, even though a society were about to be dissolved by agreement, the last murderer in prison must be executed before it breaks up.[48] The punishment is, so to speak, his right, of which he must not be defrauded.

There are two natural perversions of this theory.

The first is to confuse the necessary retribution or reaction of the general self, through the State, with personal vengeance.[49] Even in the vulgar form, when a brutal murder evokes a general desire to have the of-

---

[48][Kant, *The Metaphysical Elements of Justice*, loc. cit., note 11, p. 102. Vol. VI, p. 333 of the Preussische Akademie edition.]

[49]It may be noted that Durkheim, relying chiefly on early religious sentiment, denies Maine's view that criminal law arises out of private feud. [Sir Henry Maine (1822–1888) is best known for his *Ancient Law: its Connection with the Early History of Society and its Relation to Modern Society* (London: Murray, 1885). Maine was an exponent of historical legal scholarship, seeking to trace the evolution of human society and its forms of social organisation.]

fender served out,[50] the general or social indignation is not the same as the selfish desire for revenge. It is the offspring of a rough notion of law and humanity, and of the feeling that a striking aggression upon them demands to be strikingly put down. Such a sentiment is a part of the consciousness which maintains the system of rights, and can hardly be absent where that consciousness is strong.

The second perversion consists in the superstition that punishment should be "equivalent" to offence. In a sense, we have seen, it is *identical*; i.e. it is a return of the offender's act upon himself by a connection inevitable in a moral organism. But as for *equivalence* of pain inflicted, either with the pain caused by the offence or with its guilt, the state knows nothing of it and has no means of securing it. It cannot estimate either pain or moral guilt. Punishment cannot be adapted to factors which cannot be known. And further, the attempt to punish for immorality has evils of its own.[51] The graduation of punishments must depend on wholly different principles, which we will consider in speaking of punishment as preventive or deterrent.

(iii) The graduation of punishments must be almost entirely determined by experience of their operation as deterrents. It is to be borne in mind, indeed, (a) that the "reversionary rights" of humanity in the offender are not to be needlessly sacrificed, and (b) that the true essence of punishment, as punishment, the negation of the offender's anti-social will, is in some way to be secured. But these conditions are included in the preventive or deterrent theory of punishment, if completely understood; if, that is to say, it is made clear precisely what it is that is to be prevented.

If we speak of punishment, then, as having for its aim to be deterrent or preventive, we must not understand this to mean that a majority, or any persons in power, may rightly prevent, by the threat of penalties, any acts that seem to them to be inconvenient.

That which is to be prevented by punishment is a violation of the State-maintained system of rights by a person who is a party to that system, and therefore the above-mentioned conditions, implied in a true un-

---

[50]Green, *Principles of Political Obligation*, [loc. cit., note 4] p. 184 [sect. 183].
[51]See above, p. 94.

derstanding of the reformatory and retributive aspects of punishment, are also involved in it as deterrent. But, this being admitted, we may add to them the distinctive principle on which a deterrent theory insists. If a lighter punishment deter as effectively as a heavier, it is wrong to impose the heavier. For the precise aim of State action is the maintenance of rights; and if rights are effectively maintained without the heavier punishment, the aim of the State does not justify its imposition. It is well known that success in the maintenance of rights depends not only on the severity of punishments, but also on the true adjustment of the rights themselves to human ends, and on that certainty of detecting crime which is a result of efficient government. And it must always be considered, in dealing with a relative failure of the deterrent power of punishment in regard to certain offences, whether a better adjustment of rights or a greater certainty of detection will not meet the end more effectively than increased severity of punishment. We have seen that the equivalence of punishment and offence is really a meaningless superstition. And there is no principle on which punishment can be rationally graduated, except its deterrent power as learned by experience. This view corresponds to the true limits of State action as determined by the means at its disposal compared with the end which is its justification, and is therefore, when grasped in its full meaning as not denying the nature of punishment, the true theory of it.

We saw, in speaking of punishment as retributive, in what sense it can and cannot rest upon a judgment imputing moral guilt. Of degrees of moral guilt as manifested in the particular acts of individuals, the State, like all of us, is necessarily ignorant. But this is not to say that punishment is wholly divorced from a just moral sentiment. Undoubtedly it implies and rests upon a disapproval of that hostile attitude to the system of rights which is implied in the realised intention constituting the violation of right. Though in practice the distinction between civil and criminal law in England carries out no thoroughly logical demarcation, yet it is true on the whole to say with Hegel that, in the matter of a civil action, there is no violation of right as such, but only a question in whom a certain right resides; while in a matter of criminal law there is involved an infraction of right as such, which by implication is a denial of the whole sphere of law and order.[52] This infraction the general conscience disapproves, and its disapproval is embodied in a forcible dealing with the offender, however that dealing may be graduated by other considerations.

I may touch here on an interesting point of detail, following Green. If punishment is essentially graduated according to its deterrent power, and not according to moral guilt, how does it come to pass that "extenuating circumstances" are allowed to influence sentences? That they do so really, if not nominally, even in England, there can be no doubt. Is it not that they indicate a less degree of wickedness in the offender than the offence in question would normally presuppose? It would seem that judges themselves are sometimes under this impression. But it may well be that they act under a right instinct and assign a wrong reason. For it is impossible to get over the fact that moral iniquity is something which cannot be really estimated. The true reason for allowing circumstances which change the character of the act to influence the sentence is that in changing its character, they may take it out of the class of offences to which it prima facie belongs, and from which men need to be deterred by a recognised amount of severity. If a man is starving and steals a turnip, his offence, being so exceptionally conditioned, does not threaten the general right of property, and does not need to be associated with any high degree of terror in order to protect that right. A man who steals under no extraordinary pressure of need does what might become a common practice if not associated with as much terror as is found by experience to deter men from theft.

It may be said, in some exceptional emergency, "But many men are now starving; ought not the theft of food, on the principle of prevention, to be now punished with extreme severity, as otherwise it is likely to become common?" Or in general, ought not severity to increase with temptation or provocation, as a greater deterrent is needed to counterbalance this? The case in which the temptation or provocation is exceptional has just been dealt with. But if abnormal temptation or provocation becomes common, as in a famine, or in some excited condition of public feeling, then it must be remembered that not one right only, but the system of rights as such, is what the State has to maintain. If starva-

---

[52][See Hegel, *The Philosophy of Right*, loc. cit., note 26, pp. 64–73 (sects. 82–103).]

tion is common, some readjustment of rights, or at least some temporary protection of the right to live, is the remedy indicated, and not, or not solely, increased severity in dealing with theft.[53] If provocation becomes common, then the rights of those provoked must be remembered, and the provocation itself perhaps made punishable, like the singing of faction songs in Ireland. Punishment is to protect rights, not to encourage wrongs.

Thus, we have seen the true nature and aims of punishment as following from the aim of the State in maintaining the system of rights instrumental to the fullest life. The three main aspects of punishment which we have considered are really inseparable, and each, if properly explained, expands so as to include the others.[54]

We may, in conclusion, sum up the whole theory of State action in the formula which we inherit from Rousseau – that Sovereignty is the exercise of the General Will.

First. All State action is General in its bearing and justification, even if particular, or rather concrete, in its details. It is embodied in a *system* of rights, and there is no element of it which is not determined by a bearing upon a public interest. The verification of this truth, throughout, for example, our English system of public and private Acts of Parliament, would run parallel to the logical theory of the Universal Judgment as it passes into Judgments whose subjects are proper names. But the immediate point is that no rights are absolute, or detached from the whole, but all have their warrant in the aim of the whole, which at the same time implies their adjustment and regulation according to general principles. This generality of law is practically an immense protection to individuals against arbitrary interference. It makes every regulation strike a class and not a single person.

And, secondly. All State action is at bottom the exercise of a Will; the real Will, or the Will as logically implied in intelligences as such, and more or less recognised as imperative upon them. And therefore, though

---

[53]Though for the sake of all parties, and to avoid temptation, a strong policing of threatened districts may be desirable in such circumstances.

[54]See further the essay "On the Growing Repugnance to Punishment" in *Some Suggestions in Ethics* (London: Macmillan, 1918) [ch. viii].

in the form of force it acts through automatism, that is, not directly as conscious Will, but through a system which gives rise to acts by influences apparently alien, yet the root and source of the whole structure is of the nature of Will, and its end, like that of organic automatism, is to clear the road for true volition; it is "forcing men to be free." And in so far as by misdirection of the automatic[55] process it encroaches on the region of living Will – the region where the good realises itself directly by its own force as a motive – it is "sawing off the branch on which it sits," and superseding the aim by the instrument.

---

[55]It must not be forgotten that the State is, by its nature, under a constant temptation to throw its weight on the side of the automatic process. A most striking example is its adoption of the automatic water-carriage system in drainage, with far-reaching economic consequences. See [George Vivian] Poore's [*Essays on*] *Rural Hygiene* [(London: Longmans, Green, 1893)] and *The Dwelling House* [(London: Longmans, Green, 1897)].

CHAPTER IX

ROUSSEAU'S THEORY AS APPLIED TO THE MODERN STATE:
KANT, FICHTE, HEGEL.

1. Probably no other philosophical movement has ever focussed in itself so much human nature as the post-Kantian Idealism. It has fallen to the present writer to show elsewhere[1] how the "finding of Greek art," which it owed to Winckelmann,[2] gave it unrivalled insight into mind as embodied in objects of sense. Here we have to deal with another source of its ideas. As we pointed out in the first chapter, the ethical and political theory of Kant, Fichte, and Hegel springs from the same *Evangel of Jean Jacques* from which the French Revolution drew its formulae. It would not be true to say that it springs from this alone. Great philosophers know how to fuse the materials they work in; and particularly the modern abstraction of "freedom" was blended, for Hegel, with the idea of concrete life through the tradition of the Greek city, with its affinity for autonomy on the one hand and for beauty on the other. Nevertheless, few lines of affiliation are better established in the history of philosophy than that between Rousseau's declaration that liberty is the quality of man and the philosophy of Right as it developed from Kant to Hegel.

It has been suggested that the literary intercourse of France, England, and Germany was far closer in the eighteenth century than it is to-day, in spite of the immense mechanical development of communication in the interval. National self-consciousness and the divergent growth of national minds have, it is urged, raised a barrier between peoples, which existed in the last century to a far smaller degree.[3] This question of literary history lies beyond my subject; but at least it seems probable that Rousseau had a power in Germany which no French writer of to-day could possibly exercise outside his own country. His educational influence[4] alone forms a considerable chapter in the history of *Pädagogik*,[5]

---

[1] [A] *History of Aesthetic* ([London:] Sonnenschein, [1892]).

[2] [See ch. ii, note 29 on Winckelmann.]

[3] See M. Lévy-Bruhl, "De l'Influence de Jean Jacques Rousseau en Allemagne," *Annales de l'Ecole libre des Sciences Politiques*, Juillet, 1897.

[4] Cf. [Paul] Duproix, *Kant et Fichte et le Problème de l'Education* [(Paris:] Alcan, 1897);

217

and touches closely on philosophy. Our psychologists of childhood are his spiritual descendants, and indeed the question of the development of the human being is closely akin to the question of liberty.[6]

His literary influence, as the prophet of nature and feeling, and the champion of sentimental religion against the *Philosophes*,[7] carried everything before it. He struck into the path which had been opened in Germany by the translation of Thomson's *Seasons* before 1750, and followed by the Swiss critics and the idyllic poets, who were opponents of the dominant pseudo-classicism.[8] Jacobi, who passed some years of his youth at Geneva, owed his doctrine of feeling as the faculty of relig-

---

and on Rousseau varied initiative, see [Henri Frédéric] Amiel, *Journal Intime* [English translation, *Amiel's Journal: the Journal Intime of Henri-Frédéric Amiel*, trans., Mrs. Humphry Ward (London: Macmillan, [1897)], vol. I. 202: "J.J. Rousseau is an ancestor in all things. It was he who founded travelling on foot before Töpffer, reverie before Réne, literary botany before George Sand, the worship of nature before Bernardin de St. Pierre, the democratic theory before the Revolution of 1797, political discussion and theological discussion before Mirabeau and Rénan, the science of teaching before Pestalozzi, and Alpine description before De Saussure."

[5][*Pädagogik*: literally, pedagogics, or educational theory. German educational theory owed much to Rousseau's *Émile* and its emphasis on free development of individuality; a German expression of this was the ideal of *Bildung*, or many-sided development of personality. This was important to the thinking of Johann Wolfgang von Goethe (1749–1832), Johann Gottlieb Fichte (1762–1814), Friedrich von Schiller (1759–1805) and Wilhelm von Humboldt (1767–1835). Humboldt was instrumental in reforming the Prussian education system; of particular importance in this regard is the *Gymnasium*, or grammar school, focussed on teaching the classics and not concerned with vocational preparation. German educational theory and practice had great impact on the British Idealists; T.H. Green, for example, was much impressed by the distinction between the *Gymnasium* and the *Real-Schule.*]

[6][This statement is striking in the light on the prominence of Jean Piaget's thinking in the later twentieth century, with its deep debt to Rousseau. See Jean Piaget, *The Moral Judgment of the Child*, trans., Marjorie Gabain (New York: The Free Press, 1965).]

[7][The *philosophes* were a group of philosophers stressing rationality over passion and impulse, and philosophy and science over religion; they were often disparaging of the common person. There is some dispute about the membership of this group. It is widely agreed that it includes François-Marie Arouet Voltaire (1694–1778) and Denis Diderot (1713–1784); it is sometimes extended so far as to include Adam Smith (1723–1790) and David Hume (1711–1776).]

[8]See author's *History of Aesthetic*, [loc. cit., note 1], p. 214.

ious truth in part at least to Rousseau.[9] Klinger, whose drama, *Sturm und Drang*,[10] gave its name to the romantic and naturalist revolution, marked by Goethe's *Götz von Berlichingen* (1773) and Schiller's *Räuber* (1781),[11] was responsible, we are told, in later years, for the surprising judgment, that Rousseau (in *Émile*) is the young man's best guide through life.[12] Even Schiller and Herder passed through a period of enthusiastic admiration for Rousseau. It is exceedingly significant that Schiller's *Letters on the Aesthetic Education of Humanity* are addressed expressly to the problem of reconciling the claims of Nature[13] and of the State upon individual man. For, when Schiller suggests that the clue to the required reconciliation between Nature and the State lies in the union of feeling and intelligence which is found in Beauty, we have before us in a single focus three main types of experience, from the fusion of which a new idealism was to emerge.

2. Returning to our immediate subject, the Philosophy of Right, we will consider for a moment the specific relation of Rousseau's idea of Freedom to Kantian or post-Kantian thought. It is permissible, perhaps, to embody the chief part of what has to be said in extracts from works of

---

[9][Friedrich Heinrich Jacobi (1743–1819), was a German literary figure, known for his romanaticism and irrationalism. See his *Woldemar, Eine Seltenheit aus der Naturgeschichte* (Leipzig, 1779).]

[10][Friedrich Maxmillan Klinger (1752–1831), like Jacobi, is known for his antirationalistic literature. The *Sturm and Drang* (storm and stress) movement in Germany is generally characterised by an emphasis on romantic feeling and a devaluation of reason and science. Schiller and Goethe are prominent figures in this movement.]

[11][See *Götz of Berlingen with the Iron Hand. An Historical Drama of the Fifteenth Century*, translated from the German of Goethe by Rose Lawrence (Liverpool, 1799). Friedrich Schiller, *Räuber*, English translation, *The Robbers*, trans., F.J. Lamport (Harmondsworth: Penguin Books, 1979).]

[12]Levy-Bruhl, loc. cit., [note 3], p. 330. The citation appears to be from a romance, and I have not seen the context.

[13]Letter 3 contains a profound criticism of the supposed actual "state of nature," and it might be said with truth that the whole subject of the letters is the problem "how man is to be free without ceasing to be sensuous." [See Schiller, *Über die Ästhetische Erziehung des Menschen in einer Reihe von Briefen*, English translation, *On the Aesthetic Education of Man, in A Series of Letters*, eds. Elizabeth M. Wilkinson and L.A. Willoughby (Oxford: Clarendon Press, 1992).]

great original value and not very generally accessible. Not only the poets and sentimentalists of Germany, but also the great philosophers, distinctly recognised the debt of the German genius to the ideas of Rousseau. The conception of the "Social Contract" has an importance which surprises the modern reader in the political philosophy of Kant and more especially of Fichte, and it is not till we come to Hegel that the literal interpretation of the "Social Contract" is completely discriminated from the truth conveyed by the doctrine of the General Will. Apart from all questions about the literal meaning of the "Social Contract," it is simple fact that the whole political philosophy of Kant, Hegel, and Fichte is founded on the idea of freedom as the essence of man, first announced – such was Hegel's distinct judgment – by Rousseau. I begin by citing the crucial passage from Hegel's *History of Philosophy*, which gives in a few lines the basis of his own theory of Right, as well as his view of Rousseau's position.[14]

After explaining that Rousseau treated the right of Government as on one side, in its historical aspect, resting[15] on force and compulsion, Hegel continues:

> But the principle of this justification (the "absolute justification of the State") Rousseau makes the free will, and, disregarding the positive right (or "law") of States, he answers to the above question[16] (as to the justification or basis of the State) that man has free will, seeing that "Freedom is the distinctive quality of man.[17] To renounce one's freedom, means to renounce one's humanity. Not to be free is therefore a renunciation of one's human rights, and even of one's duties." The slave has neither rights nor

---

[14]Hegel's *Geschichte der Philosophie*, III, 477; English translation, [*Lectures on the History of Philosophy*, trans., Elizabeth S. Haldane and Frances H. Simpson (London: K. Paul, Trench, Trübner, & Co. 1892–96)] III, 401.

[15]In the place referred to, *Contrat Social*, Book I, chs. iii, iv, Rousseau points out clearly that *force* gives *no right*. So when Hegel describes him as saying that the right of rule rested on force, etc., *in its historical aspect*, this is incorrect, unless it means that, this "historical" aspect giving no explanation of right, the term "right" is a mere name so far as it is concerned.

[16]*Contrat Social*, Book I, ch. iv.

[17]I retain Hegel's paraphrastic rendering of Rousseau's words.

duties. Rousseau says therefore:[18] "The *fundamental problem*[19] is to find a form of association which shall protect and defend at once the person and the property of every member with the whole common force, and in which each individual, inasmuch as he attaches himself to this association, *obeys only himself, and remains as free as before*." The solution is given by the *Social Contract*; it (Rousseau says) is this combination, to which each belongs through his Will.

These principles, thus set up in the abstract, we cannot but take as correct; yet ambiguity begins at once. Man is free; this is no doubt the substantive nature of man; and in the State it is not only not abandoned, but in fact it is therein first established. The freedom of nature, the capacity of freedom, is not the actual freedom; for nothing short of the State is the actualisation of freedom.

But the misunderstanding about the *"General Will"* begins at the following point. The notion of Freedom must not be taken in the sense of the casual free-will of each individual, but in the sense of the reasonable will, the will in and for itself.[20] The general will is not to be regarded as compounded of the expressed individual wills,[21] so that these remain absolute; else the proposition would be true, "where the minority has to obey the majority, there is no freedom." Rather the general will must be the rational will, even though people are not aware of it; the State, therefore, is no such association as is determined upon by individuals.

The false apprehension of these principles does not matter to us. What matters to us is that by their means it comes as a content into consciousness, that man has in his mind Freedom as the downright absolute, that the free will is the notion of man. It is just freedom that is the self of thought; one who repudiates thought and talks of freedom knows not what he is saying. The oneness of thought with itself[22] is freedom, the free will. Thought, only taken in the form of will, is the impulse to break through[23]

---

[18]*Contrat Social*, Book I, ch. iv, cf. above p. 111.

[19]Hegel's italics [throughout this paragraph].

[20]Anything is "in and for itself" when it has become *"for itself,"* i.e. consciously and explicitly, what it is *"in itself,"* i.e. in its latent or potential nature.

[21]Rousseau's *Will of All*.

[22]I.e. Anything is free, in as far as it is able to be itself. Thought, as the embodiment of the return upon oneself or being with oneself, is for Hegel the strongest case of this.

[23]I.e. By going beyond it.

one's mere subjectivity, is relation to definite being, realisation of one's self, inasmuch as I will to make myself as an existent adequate to myself as thinking. The will is free only as that which thinks.

The principle of freedom dawned on the world in Rousseau, and gave infinite strength to man, who thus apprehended himself as infinite. This furnishes the transition to the Kantian philosophy, which, from a theoretical point of view, took this principle as its basis. Knowledge[24] was thus directed upon its own freedom, and upon a concrete content, which it possesses in its consciousness.

Everyone is familiar, in general terms, with the part played by the idea of freedom in Kant's philosophy. It may, however, be of interest to point out how definitely it comes to him in the form given it by Rousseau. Omitting the whole subject of Kant's educational interest,[25] I will refer to two passages from Kant's early notes[26] in connection with the tract on the *Feelings of the Sublime and the Beautiful*, and two from the *Philosophy of Right*, which first appeared in the autumn of 1796.

First, then, to establish the definite impulse communicated to Kant in his earlier years by Rousseau in particular. "I am myself," he writes,[27]

a student by inclination. I feel the whole thirst for knowledge, and the covetous restlessness that demands to advance in it, and again the satisfaction of every step of progress. There was a time when I believed that all this might constitute the honour of humanity, and I despised the crowd that knows nothing. It was Rousseau who set me right. That dazzling privilege disappeared; and I should think myself far less useful than common artisans if I did not believe that my line of study might impart value to all others in the way of establishing the rights of humanity.

---

[24]I.e. Philosophy, by basing itself on the idea of freedom, is led to scrutinise the life in which mind realises itself, before it becomes, and on the way to becoming, reflectively philosophical; and which is therefore "*its own* freedom" – as one texture with knowledge – and also a "concrete content," i.e. an actual system of living, as an object in which mind can find itself expressed – a relation which = freedom.

[25]See Duproix, loc. cit. [note 4.]

[26]Between 1765 and 1775.

[27]Kant's [*Sämmtliche*] *Werke*, [Karl] Rosenkranz [and Wilhelm Friedrich Schubert, eds. (Leipzig: L. Voss, 1838–42), vol.] xi, p. 240. Cf. ibid., p. 218.

Kant seems, from the context, to be foreshadowing the idea of his critical philosophy, as putting man in his place in the order of creation. "If there is any science," he says just below, "which man really needs, it is that which I teach, to fill properly *that* place which is assigned to man in creation; a science from which he can learn what one must be in order to be human."

This throws light on the curious passage in the same set of notes,[28] where, in a discussion of the idea of Providence, Kant first refers to Newton's discovery of order in the multiplicity of the planetary motions, and then proceeds,

> Rousseau first discovered, beneath the multiplicity of the forms assumed by man, the deeply latent nature of humanity, and the hidden law, according to which Providence is justified by his observations. Before that the objection of Alphonsus and of Manes[29] held the field. After Newton and Rousseau, God is justified, and henceforward Pope's doctrine is true.

"Pope's doctrine" is no doubt his Leibnizian optimism, founded on a supposed insight into man's true place in creation.[30] Rousseau's "discovery," which Kant here connects with this doctrine, must be his assertion of man's natural goodness and freedom, which he tends to forfeit by departing in civilisation from the place assigned him by nature. It is clear that Rousseau's impeachment of literature and civilisation had at this time made a considerable impression upon Kant. It is all the more interesting to see Kant retracing, on a very different scale, the development which Rousseau had initiated, from natural to social and ethical freedom.

I subjoin two passages from the *Philosophy of Right* (1796), which exhibit this later development, still in its connection with Rousseau's phraseology:[31]

---

[28]Ibid., p. 248.

[29]The Manichean doctrine. [Manes, or Mani (approx. 216–276 AD), founded a religion in southern Babylonia, which is characterized by a dualism that refuses to account for both good and evil by the appeal to the same source; Saint Alphonsus Liguori (1696–1787) was one of the foremost casuists; he stressed the ambiguity of law, allowing flexibility in its interpretation.]

[30]See passage cited from Kant, just above [note 28].

[31]Kant's *Werke* [op. cit., note 27, vol.] ix, [p.] 42. [See Kant, *The Metaphysical Elements*

> *The innate Right is one only.* – Freedom (independence of the constraining will of another), in as far as it can co-exist with the freedom of every other according to a universal law, is this unique original right, belonging to every human being by reason of his humanity.

An indication of the embodiment of this freedom in the State may be given as follows:[32]

> All those three powers in the State (Sovereignty or the Legislative, the Executive, and the Judicial) are offices; and, as essential, and necessarily proceeding from the idea of a State in general with reference to the establishment (Constitution) of one, are offices *of State*. They contain the relation of a universal supreme Power (which, considered according to laws of freedom, can be no other than the united people), to the crowd of individuals which compose it qua the governed; that is, of the ruler (*imperans*) to the subject (*subditus*). The act whereby the people constitutes itself into a State, *or strictly speaking only the idea of that Act, according to which idea alone the justice of the Act can be conceived,*[33] is *the original contract*[34] according to which all (*omnes et singuli*) of the people surrender their external freedom, in order at once to receive it back again as members of a commonwealth, that is, of the people regarded as a State (*universi*). And one cannot say, The State, or man in the State, has sacrificed a part of its innate outward freedom for a certain end; but rather, he has totally abandoned his wild lawless freedom in order to find his entire freedom again undiminished in a lawful dependence, that is, in a condition of right or law; (undiminished), because this dependence springs from his own legislative will.

It is remarkable, in face of these general views, that both Kant and Fichte follow Rousseau, for reasons which Kant explains from the political conditions of the time, in distrusting representative government.[35]

---

of Justice, trans., John Ladd (Indianapolis: Bobbs-Merrill, 1965), pp. 43–44; vol. VI, p. 237 of the Königliche Preussische Akademie der Wissenschaft edition (Berlin, 1902–1938).]

[32]Ibid., p. 160. [See Kant, *The Metaphysical Elements of Justice*, pp. 80–81; vol. VI, pp. 315–16 of the Preussische Akademie edition.]

[33]The italics are mine.

[34]Kant's italics.

[35]Ibid., [p.] 166. [Kant's *Werke*, loc. cit., note 31, vol. ix. See Kant, *The Metaphysical*

The passage just cited is of course a reproduction of Rousseau's view modified by interpretation very much in the sense in which we interpreted it above.

3. When we pass to Fichte (whose earlier work upon *Natural Right* was published actually before that of Kant), we observe the idea of contract in the act of transmuting itself, though by an imperfect transition, into the idea of an organic whole. For Fichte, the State is a necessary implication of the human self; for a self involves a society of selves, and law or right is the relation between selves in a bodily world. And the "contract" on which citizenship rests, by the fact that it is general,[36] forges an indiscernible unity of the social whole. In this connection, Fichte makes the remarkable claim to be first to apply the simile of an organism to the whole civic relation. I cite an important passage:[37] "As far as I know, the idea of the whole of the State has so far only been established through the ideal combination of individuals, and thereby the true insight into the nature of this relation has been cut off." You must, he urges, not merely have an idea of combination; you must show a bond of union beyond the idea, or making the idea necessary.

In our account this has been achieved. In the notion of that which is to be protected, in accordance with the necessary uncertainty *which* individual will need the visible protection, and still further, *which* it will have advantaged invisibly in the case of a wrongful will suppressed by the law before its outbreak, all individuals are forced into unity.

Elements of Justice, pp. 85–86. Vol, VI, pp. 319–20 of the Preussische Akademie edition.] (The deputies are practically dependent on the Ministry,) cf. above, ch. v, note 18. But further cf. loc. cit., p. 193, [See Kant, *The Metaphysical Elements of Justice*, pp. 112–14. vol, VI, pp. 341–44 of the Preussische Akademie edition] which shows that in a true Republic the representative system might, according to Kant, be a reality, and then would be the ideal form. The whole discussion is full of reference to Rousseau.

[36][Johan Gottlieb] Fichte, [*Nachgelassene*] *Werke*, [(Bonn: A. Margus, 1834–35) vol. III, pp.] 203ff, says, "'Indeterminate'; viz. I undertake to aid in protecting whoever is injured. Now, I can never know (he argues) who in particular is to be benefited by this undertaking; many are invisibly benefited by it through the suppression of the injurious will before it comes to be manifest. Therefore the relation is really organic; every part strives to conserve every part, because injury to any part may concern any part." It is the general as indeterminate; really less of a unity than Rousseau's *"moi commun."*

[37]*Werke*, [vol.] III, [p.] 207. The "ideal combination" = the imaginary contract.

The most fitting simile to elucidate this notion is that of an organised natural product, which has often been employed in modern times to describe the different branches of the public power as a unity, but not, so far as I know, to throw light on the whole civic relation. Just as, in the natural product, every part can be what it is only in *this* combination, and out of this combination simply would not be this (indeed outside all organic combination there would simply be nothing...): just so it is only in the combination of the State that man attains a definite position in the series of things, a point of rest in nature; and each attains *this determinate* position towards others, and towards Nature, only through the fact that he is in *this determinate* combination...In the organic body every part continually maintains the whole, and while it maintains it, is itself maintained thereby; just such is the citizen's relation to the State.

Here we seem to be back with Plato and Aristotle. We are in fact too near to Plato; for the distinction between maintenance of the citizen's determinate activity, and maintenance of the general conditions of such activity, being destroyed by Fichte in his desire to make State action positive and not negative, the conclusion necessarily arises that the citizen must be secured and maintained in his definite activity or occupation, and from this springs the notion of the closed commercial State; "closed" against foreign trade in order that the Government may be able to determine prices and assign occupations. In other words, the basis of the State is still the Ego conceived as the individual self; it is not the social good operating by its own power on intelligent will. And, arising from this individualism, the precautions which seem necessary to protect and sustain the individual in his fixed relation to the whole, make Fichte's "Closed Commercial State"[38] perhaps the earliest document of a rigorous State Socialism. Freedom, as he himself recognises to be prima facie the case, is annihilated by the provisions for its protection.[39] It is curious to see Rousseau's phrase "forced to be free,"[40] which refers in him to the supremacy of law, reappearing as a defence of the enforce-

---

[38][In *Der Geschlossene Handelstaat – The Closed Commercial State –* (Tübingen, 1800), Fichte advocated economic autarchy: a state that was largely economically closed off to the world, with foreign trade be controlled by the government.]

[39]Fichte, *Nachgelassene Werke*, [vol.] II, [p.] 535.

[40]Ibid., [p.] 537.

ment of leisure time,[41] as though freedom were not realised in labour and in loyalty. Here is Hegel's judgment of the transition we have just been considering:

> Kant began to found right on freedom, and Fichte too in his *Natural Right* made freedom his principle; but it is, as in Rousseau, the freedom of the particular individual. This is a great beginning; but in order to get to particular results they were obliged to accept presuppositions. The universal (for them) is not the spirit, the substance of the whole, but the external mechanical negative power against individuals.... The individuals remain always hard and negative against one another; the prison-house, the bonds, become ever more oppressive, instead of the State being apprehended as the realisation of freedom.[42]

4. To apprehend the State as the realisation of freedom was the aim of Hegel's *Philosophy of Right*, which has perhaps been more grossly misrepresented than any work of a great political philosopher, excepting Plato's *Republic*.

Popular criticism will tell us that Hegel found his ideal in the Prussian bureaucracy, and will further hint that his doing so was to his advantage.[43] Such suggestions imply two misapprehensions, for one of which Hegel's tactlessness was responsible, while the other depends on a genuine difficulty attending any philosophical analysis of society. I will try to throw light on each of these misapprehensions.

(α) If Hegel had wished to have a partisan tendency attributed to his book, he could not have timed it better nor written a preface more certain to mislead. In 1820, when the book was published, the minds both of Governments and of peoples were full of irritation. The anticonstitutional reaction had recently declared itself. The demonstration at the Wartburg, celebrating the anniversary of the Reformation, and of the Battle of Leipzig, took place in October, 1817. The unaccountable change in the ideas of the Czar from Liberalism to reaction took place,

---

[41] Of course such enforcement *may* have justification.

[42] Hegel, *Geschichte der Philosophie*, [loc. cit., note 14 vol.] III, [p.] 576. The idea of organism was thus mechanically apprehended. [See Bosanquet's essay on "Hegel's Theory of the Political Organism," *Mind*, vol. VII (1898), pp. 1–14.]

[43] See [C.A.] Fyffe's *A History of Modern Europe* [(London: Cassell, 1886–1889)], vol. II, ch. ii.

we are assured,[44] in June, 1818. The murder of Kotzebue, a Russian agent, reactionary journalist, and decayed dramatist, took place in March, 1819. Kotzebue seems to have been popularly credited with perverting the views of the Czar. His assassination had an effect in no way related to his real importance. Hardenberg, the Prussian minister, exclaimed on hearing of it that a Prussian constitution had now become impossible. Innocent persons were arrested in Prussia at Metternich's[45] instigation, and private papers were seized and published in a garbled form. The publication of Hegel's book with a preface attacking Fries for some expressions used by him at the Wartburg festival,[46] took place, as we said, in 1820, and Hegel had moved from Heidelberg to Berlin, having obtained the honour of a Berlin Professorship, in 1818. Small wonder that "it was pointed out that the new professor was a favourite of the leading minister, that his influence was dominant in scholastic appointments, and that occasional gratuities from the Crown proved his acceptability," or that Fries remarked that Hegel's theory of the State had grown, "not in the garden of science, but on the dunghill of servility."[47] Hegel himself "was aware that he had planted a blow in the face of a shallow and pretentious sect, and that his book had given great offence to the demagogic folk."[48]

And yet, so far as the essence of Hegel's political philosophy is concerned, there is nothing in all this. The first sketch of the *Philosophy of Right* was published in the *Encyclopaedia of the Philosophical Sciences*

---

[44]Ibid.

[45][Prince Clemens von Metternich (1773–1859) was an Austrian statesman, becoming foreign minister in 1809. The conservative Metternich was crucial to the Congress of Vienna (1814–15); the period 1815–48 has been called the Age of Metternich. Under his leadership, nationalist and democratic movements were suppressed.]

[46][J.F. Fries (1773–1843) was a professor at both Heidelberg and Jena, and sympathetic to romantic nationalists who supported German student societies seeking to bring about a unified Germany. At the Wartburg festival in 1817 Fries gave an ultra-liberal speech for German unity that led to his suspension in 1819; he was reinstated to his philosophy chair at Jena in 1825.]

[47][William] Wallace, Hegel's *Philosophy of Mind*, [translated by Wallace from the *Encyclopaedia of the Philosophical Sciences* (Oxford: Clarendon Press, 1894)], p. clxxix.
[48]Ibid.

in 1817, before Hegel left Heidelberg. His political interest, in its gradual development, can be traced back in unpublished writings to 1802.[49]
He started from the conception of the Greek State, on which his early
sketch of the ethical system (1802, unpublished in his lifetime) was
founded. And his subsequent development consisted in enlarging this
conception by drawing out its framework to include the more accented
freedom of modern life, as he divined it from the attentive study both of
English and of German politics. His substantive political theory never
changed, except by development, in accordance with his general attitude
towards the differences between Greek and modern life.

(β) "But," popular criticism will rejoin, "here we have Hegel's ideal
State, depicted by his own hand, and it is pretty much the Prussian State
of his time, tempered by a few references to English politics. Is not this a
narrow horizon and a low ideal?" This criticism is of value, because it
leads up to an important feature of true political theory.

To depict what most people call "an ideal State" is no more the object
of political philosophy than it is the object, say, of Carpenter's *Human
Physiology*[50] to depict an "ideal" man or an angel. The object of political
philosophy is to understand what a State is, and it is not necessary for
this purpose that the State which is analysed should be "ideal," but only
that it should be a State; just as the nature of life is represented pretty
nearly as well by one living man as by another.

"Every State,"[51] Hegel says,

> even if your principles lead you to pronounce it bad, even if you detect
> this or that deficiency in it, always has (especially if it belongs to the more
> developed States of our time) the essential moments of its existence in it.
> But because it is easier to discover defects than to grasp the affirmative,
> people easily fall into the error of allowing particular aspects to lead them
> to forget the inner organism of the State. The State is no work of art, it
> stands in the world, that is, in the sphere of caprice, accident, and error;
> evil behaviour is able to mar it in many respects. But the ugliest human

---

[49]Ibid., [pp.] clxxx and clxxxvii.

[50][William Benjamin Carpenter, *Principles of Human Physiology*, 4th edn (London: J.
Churchill, 1853).]

[51]*Philosophie d. Rechts*, p. 313. [See Hegel, *The Philosophy of Right*, trans., T.M. Knox
(Oxford: Clarendon Press, 1942), p. 279 (addition to paragraph 258).]

being, a criminal, a sick man, or a cripple, is all the same a living human being; the affirmative, his life, persists in spite of the defect, and this affirmative is what we are concerned with here.

Of course, no comparison is quite precise, and it may be urged that the State is more artificial than a human body. However this may be,[52] we shall at least understand Hegel's attitude better, and, as I venture to think, adopt by far the most fruitful standpoint for ourselves, if we look at political philosophy like one who is trying to ascertain what is the nature of human life as he observes it in any or every human body if the life is there, its essentials are there, and his aim is to understand them. No doubt a door is here opened to argument with regard to what logicians call a "pure case." In understanding life "as such," you must, it would seem, purge out its mere defects, in regard to which it is not "life," and the remainder, what you pledge yourself to as essential, must be *ex hypothesi* your "ideal" of life. And perhaps there is no reason to reject this responsibility if confined to the emphasis of elements and interconnection of facts. It cannot apply to more.

We cannot construct an ideal body by reducing life,[53] nor an ideal polity by reducing mind, to its pure case or essentials, since we cannot construct organisms or history at all. And it is because this is always being forgotten that the duty of understanding rather than constructing has to be insisted upon. It is true that in understanding, as in constructing, we imply essential relations, and so incur responsibility, and are liable to betray a bias; but still, life can be understood by help of any creature that is alive, and therefore it is not the example with which the student works, but the insight which he shows, that is the decisive point.

5. We have to begin by realising what is involved in the fact that we are about to treat the analysis of a Modern State as a chapter in the *Philosophy of Mind*. For Hegel's *Philosophy of Right* (or of *Law*), though published by him as an independent work, is essentially an expansion of paragraphs which form one sub-division of his *Philosophy of Mind*, it-

---

[52]The comment will probably betray the type of pessimism indicated by Rousseau. See above, p. 116.

[53]"No human mind has ever conceived a new animal." [John] Ruskin, *Modern Painters*, [(Orpington, Kent: G. Allen, 1888), vol.] II, [p.] 148.

self the third and concluding portion of the *Encyclopaedia of Philosophy*, of which the two earlier portions are the *Logic* and the *Philosophy of Nature*.[54]

We saw in the second chapter of the present work that the mere force of facts has driven modern sociologists to handle their science in a more or less intimate connection with Psychology. The differentia of society, we saw, has been stated in various formulae of a psychological character. But it seems to us that, owing to a neglect of the logic of identity, the nature of mind was broken up by such unreal distinctions as that between invention and imitation, varied by the unreal reduction of the one to the other,[55] and also that an unexplained separation and parallelism survived as between the individual and the social mind, bearing witness to the vitality of the superstition which Rousseau's insight picked out for condemnation.[56] We do not deny that mind may be more than social; but in as far as it is social it is still real mind, and that means that it is not something other than what we know as individual lives,[57] a pale and unreal reflection of them, but it is a characteristic which belongs to their most intimate constitution. This was Plato's analysis of moral autonomy, and his work remains classically valid, needing only expansion and interpretation in applying it to modern free intelligence and social self-government.

The position of the analysis of a State in the *Philosophy of Mind* may be briefly indicated as follows. When we embark on the study of ordinary Psychology, we take the individual human being as we find him to-

---

[54][As Bosanquet says here, Hegel's *Encyklopädie der philosophischen Wissenschaften im Grundrisse* – *Encyclopaedia of the Philosophical Sciences in Outline* – (Leipzig: F. Meiner, 1905) includes the Logic, the Philosophy of Nature and the Philosophy of Spirit (or Mind). For an English translation of the last, see note 47. For English translations of the other parts, see *The Encyclopaedia Logic*, trans., T.F. Geraets, W.A. Suchting, and H.S. Harris (Indianapolis: Hackett, 1991) and *Hegel's Philosophy of Nature*, trans., A.V. Miller (Oxford: Clarendon Press, 1970).]

[55]Prof. [James Mark] Baldwin, *Social and Ethical Interpretation[s in Mental Development; A Study in Social Psychology* (London: Macmillan, 1897)], p. 105, at least suggests this unreal reduction.

[56]See above, pp. 115–16.

[57]"Lives," and not merely "consciousnesses," as objective mind is largely in the form of habit.

day. We accept him as a formed individual, distinguishing himself from external things, and possessing what we call a will – a capacity of seeking his own satisfaction, which he represents to himself in general ideas by the help of language. We analyse the self and will with their aspects of memory, attention, association, impulse, and emotion. But all modern psychologists are aware that this formed self and will has much history behind it, and presupposes a long genesis connecting it with simpler forms of soul-life. Hegel, indeed, was among the first in modern times to see how far back the story of mind must be taken. The human intelligence, as the psychologist assumes it, is for him a middle phase in the romance of which mind is the hero. Before it come the chapters of Anthropology, which treat of the fixation of a soul in the disciplined powers and habits of a human body, and then the account[58] of a consciousness which gradually rises from a struggling perception of objects around it to a moral and scientific certainty of being at home in the world.

The story of mind, then, begins long before the free mind, the object of Psychology to-day, has appeared on the scene. And as to this there would be no great difference of opinion. The peculiarity of Hegel's treatment is that his romance of the intelligence not only begins long before the phase of free mind is reached, but continues long after. Investigation can no more stop at the individual of to-day than it can begin with him. His "mind" is not a separable entity, and throughout the story no such entity has appeared. It has been convenient for Hegel to treat the earlier division of the *Philosophy of Mind*, comprising the Anthropology, Phenomenology,[59] and Psychology, as dealing *par excellence* with Mind Subjective. This is because its main purpose was to trace the growth of "subjectivity," the emergence of the man of full mental stat-

---

[58] For this account, to which he has devoted perhaps the greatest of his works, Hegel has coined the term "Phenomenology of the Mind." It is the history of the emergence of the free or modern Spirit from the undeveloped consciousness of the ancient world, to which, for instance, slavery seemed a natural thing. [*The Phenomenology of Mind* was Hegel's introduction to his system of philosophy. For English translations, see Sir James Balllie, 2nd rev. edn (London: Allen and Unwin, 1949) and A.V. Miller, *Hegel's Phenomenology of Spirit* (Oxford: Clarendon Press, 1977).]

[59] See previous note.

ure, aware of himself, of his ideas and purposes, and confident in his "subjectivity" – his self-hood – against all comers.

But the following division of the work, under the title of Mind Objective, deals with a necessary implication which might have been noted at any point of the entire history of consciousness, though at any earlier point it could have been treated as referring to mind only by anticipation.

Here, however, the problem can no longer be deferred. The "free mind" does not explain itself and cannot stand alone. Its impulses cannot be ordered, or, in other words, its purposes cannot be made determinate, except in an actual system of selves. Except by expressing itself in relation to an ordered life, which implies others, it cannot exist. And, therefore, not something additional and parallel to it, which might or might not exist, but a necessary form of its own action as real and determinate, is the actual fabric in which it utters itself as Society and the State. This is what Hegel treats in the second division of the *Philosophy of Mind* under the name of Mind Objective. It is not for him ultimate. A particular society stands in time, and is open to criticism and to destruction. Beyond it lies the reality, continuous with mind as known in the State, but eternal as the former is perishable, which as Absolute Mind is open to human experience in Art, Religion, and Philosophy.

We will pursue in the following chapter Hegel's analysis of the modern State as Mind Objective, a magnified edition, so to speak, of Plato's *Republic*, bringing before the eye in full detail distinctions and articulations which were there invisible.

CHAPTER X

1. We are about to analyse a modern state into groups of facts which are also ways of thinking. And a question may arise in what sense the connection is to be understood which will be alleged to bind together these groups of facts or points of view. When it is urged that group *b* or view *b* is suggested and made necessary by the shortcomings of group *a* or view *a*, does this imply that group *a* or its idea came into existence first, and group *b* or the notion of it sprang up subsequently or as an effect of the former? And could such a relation be reasonably maintained as between the component parts of a unity like the State?

An answer may be indicated as follows. We are dealing, in society and in the State, with an *ideal fact*. As a fact, a form of life, society has always been a many-sided creature, meeting the varied needs of human nature by functions no less varied. As an ideal fact, however, its advance has partaken of the nature of theoretical progress. In the continuous attempt to deal satisfactorily with the needs of intelligent beings, the mind, the intelligent will, has thrown itself with predominant interest now into one of its functions and now into another. And this has not been a chance order of march. Obviously, what it has emphasised and modified in the second place has depended both positively and negatively on what it had emphasised and modified in the first place. Positively, because when one step is thoroughly secured the next may be definitely attempted. Negatively, because the definite attainment of one step exposes the limitations of what has been achieved, and the need for another. At every stage the will is dissatisfied with the expression of itself which it has created. Till some public order has been established, morality can hardly find expression; but when a legal system is thoroughly in force it becomes apparent how far the letter may fall short of the spirit. We see the same action of intelligence in pure theory. Every conquest of science leads to a new departure. It suggests it by its success, and demands it by its failure.

Now, in science it may or may not be the case that the connection which has led to a discovery enters permanently as a discernible factor into the structure of knowledge. The re-organisation of experience may sweep away the steps which led to it. But in the living fact of society this is not so. Its many sides are actual and persist, and the emphasis laid from time to time on the principle of each – e.g. on positive law, on family ties, on economic bonds – merely serves to accent an element which has its permanent place in the whole. Thus, there must always be family ties and economic bonds. But at one time everything tends to be construed in terms of kinship, at another time in terms of exchange. And the tendency means a difference of actual balance between the functions as well as a different theory. The positive and negative connection of elements like these, the true place and limit of each, is permanently rooted in human nature, but may be elucidated by the explicit logic of their attempt and failure to give the tone to the whole social fabric. It follows that the social whole grows, like a great theory, in adequacy to the needs which are its facts; and the dissatisfaction of the will with its own expression, in other words, the contradictions which practical intelligence is continually attempting to remove, becomes more like suggestion than flat contradiction – or change, as we say, becomes less revolutionary. It may seem to be a difference between the social whole and a scientific theory that the former, as it grows, creates new difficulties, by creating new and freshly contradictory matter, as in the social problems of civilisation; while the latter, as we imagine, deals with an unchanging experience. But this distinction is less true than it appears, and the comparison with the growth of a theory will always throw light on the true nature of the will and its continuous effort to satisfy itself.

2. Right or Law may be taken in the widest sense as including the whole manifestation of Will in an actual world – "the actual body of all the conditions of freedom,"[1] "the realm of realised freedom, the world of mind produced out of itself, as a second nature."[2] It is a merit of the German term "*Recht*"[3] that it maintains the connection between the law

---

[1]Hegel, *Philosophy of Mind* (English Translation [by William Wallace, *Hegel's Philosophy of Mind*, translated from the *Encyclopaedia of the Philosophical Sciences* (Oxford: Clarendon Press, 1894)], p. 104. Cf. definitions quoted from Green, above, p. 191.

[2][Hegel,] *Rechtsphil.*, sect. 4. [See Hegel, *The Philosophy of Right*, trans. T.M. Knox (Oxford: Clarendon Press, 1942), p. 20 (sect. 4).]

[3]Cf. the Greek's idea of "*nomos*." [See above, note 26 to ch. viii on Green's discussion of

and the spirit of law,[4] and almost of itself prohibits the separation be-tween positive law, and will, custom or sentiment, which underlies such a theory as Austin's.[5]

This whole sphere of Right or Law, the mind as actualised in Society and the State, naturally divides itself, on the principle which has just been explained, into three connected groups of ideal facts or points of view. The first, or simplest and most inevitable, of these may be called the "letter of the law" as we come upon it most especially in the law of property – Shylock's law[6] – the sheer fact, as it seems, that the world is appropriated by legal "persons."

The second, obviously conditioned by the first both positively and negatively, may be described as the morality of conscience; the revolt of the will against the letter of the law, though this was its own direct ex-pression of itself (e.g. in taking things as property); and its demand to recognise as right nothing but what springs from itself as the good will.

And thirdly, there is the reality or concrete experience in which the two former sets of facts, or ideas, find their true place and justification – the completed theory, so to speak, which adjusts and explains the nar-rower views founded on one-sided contact with life. This is indicated to consist in "social observance," or "ethical use and wont"; the system of working mind where the true will appears as incarnate in a way of liv-ing. This, like the others, it must be remembered, is a fact, though akin to a theory. Not only does it explain and justify the other factors, but its existence has enabled them to exist, as theirs has also been essential to it. And yet each of the three, as one aspect of society which under cer-tain influences may catch the eye, has at times claimed – is, indeed, con-stantly claiming – predominance, and has thus brought into relief its own defects and the need of the complementary ideas. We will speak of these moods of mind or kinds of experience in their order, expecting a further subdivision when we come to treat of the third.

Recht. Nomos is usually translated as "rule" or "law."]

[4]See ch. ii above on Montesquieu and Rousseau.

[5][See Introd. to 2nd edn, note 58.]

[6][The moneylender from Shakespeare's *Merchant of Venice*, who demands a pound of flesh in default of repayment for a debt. Hegel refers to Shylock in the *Philosophy of Right*, sect. 3.]

3. "Law," then, in the directest possible sense – the minimum sense, so to speak – is the hard literal fact that it is a rule of the world we live in for things to be appropriated by persons. This is the first or minimum change of the world from mere matter into the instruments of mind, and it is a necessary change. Things have no will of their own, and it is by having a will asserted upon them that they become organs of life. In the same way, it is by assertion in external things that the will first becomes a fact in the material world. Property is "the first reality of freedom."[7] It is not the mere provision for wants, but the material counterpart of will. Contract belongs to this sphere, the sphere of property. It is an agreement of persons about an external thing – a "common will," but not one "general" or "universal" in its own nature like that involved in the State.

Thus, it is a confusion of spheres to apply the idea of contract to the State, for the State is an imperative necessity of man's nature as rational, while contract is a mere agreement of certain free persons about certain external things. The idea of the social contract is a confusion of the same type as that by which public rights and functions were treated as private property in the Middle Ages. The attributes of private property are nothing more than the conditions of "personal" existence, and absurdity results if they are transferred to functions of the State.

This phase or view of law as, in its letter, an ultimate and absolute rule, may be illustrated, Hegel says, by the Stoic notion that there is only one virtue and one vice; by the Draconic conception that every offence demands the extreme penalty; and by "the barbarity of the formal code of honour, which found in every injury an unpardonable insult."[8] It might also be illustrated by Austin's theory of law as a command enforced by a penalty; or by the theories which account for property sim-

---

[7] *Rechtsphil.*, sect. 41. [*The Philosophy of Right*, loc. cit., note 2, trans. Knox, p. 40.] Not, in its developed form, the first in time. Hegel lays stress on the fact that true, free, property was hardly realised even in his own day.

[8] [*The Philosophy of Right*, loc. cit., note 2, p. 68 (sect. 96). Knox translates: "the crude formal code of Honour which takes every insult as an offense against the infinity of personality." As Knox points out in his notes to this passage, in Plutarch's life of Solon, it is said that "Draco prescribed 'one penality, death, for almost all offences'." It has been said of the Stoics that the "single virtue is to live in accordance with nature, and vice is the converse."]

ply by the fact of occupancy or of labour mixed with the thing.[9] The common point of all these views is that they treat the law, not as a part of a living system,[10] ultimately resting on the will to maintain a certain type of life, but as something absolute in its separateness, and equally sacred in all its accidents and inequalities.

Now, this emphasis and idea of law, being the exaggeration of a single and direct necessity, the necessity of order and property, may be called "primitive" or barbarous, but it cannot of course be identified with the earliest state of social authority known to history or to anthropology. There we should probably find law undifferentiated from custom and from religious sentiment, and consequently, though rigid enough, not in any such one-sided absoluteness as we have been describing. All we can say is that this is the way in which law must come to be regarded whenever its living spirit is forgotten, and an unreal absoluteness is assigned to it; and this connection of principle verifies itself as a fact in recurrent historical phenomena, and in fallacies which perpetually reappear.

4. Within the whole fabric of right or realised will, the element which naturally asserts itself by antagonism to the letter of the law is the morality of conscience, conscientiousness, or the idea of the Good Will.[11] It is connected with the letter of the law, as Hegel puts it, by the various degrees of wrong. The will, that is to say, finds itself at variance in or with[12] the order of law and property which it has created as its direct and necessary step to freedom. Its realised theory, so to speak, is found to break down at a certain point, by being in contradiction with the needs which it was created to meet. "*Summum jus, summa injuria.*"[13] We may

---

[9][The claim that private property grows out of first possession or occupancy was fundamental to the theory of Hugo Grotius (see note 9, ch. iii above); John Locke (see above, ch. iv, note 33) stresses the mixing of labour with unowned resources.]

[10]See, e.g., above, p. 213, how the idea of a *system* of rights may modify punishment.

[11][See *The Philosophy of Right*, sects. 129–141.]

[12]"In it," when my will does not conflict with right as such, but claims the right in an object A to be mine and not yours – a civil dispute. "With it," when my will rebels, and by its act, so far as in it lies, denies and destroys the whole fabric of right, e.g. takes the object A, without alleging a right to it – theft, a criminal offence, cf. pp. 214–215.

[13][*summum jus, summa injuria*: the strict enforcement of law may be the highest injustice.]

object that the anti-legal will is simply wrong. This may be so, and again it may not be so. What the will has awakened to, whether right or wrong, is that it can acquiesce in nothing which does not come home to it as fulfilling its own principle. What so comes home to it is what it calls "good," and it cannot accept any order or necessity which it cannot will as good, i.e. as satisfying its own idea.

When this phase of reaction is pushed to its logical extreme, we have the modern doctrine of my conscience and my pure will. It is the conflict of the inner self with the outer world, expressed in history through the Stoic and through some forms of the Christian consciousness (especially the Protestant consciousness), and in philosophy through the Kantian doctrine of the good will, uttered in the famous sentence, "Nothing can possibly be conceived in the world or out of it which can be called good without qualification except a good will."[14] Nothing is worth doing but *what* one ought, and *because* one ought.

The criticism to which this principle has been subjected is familiar to students of ethics. Its point is, in brief, that there is no way of connecting any particular action with the mere idea of a pure will. The forms assumed by evasions of this difficulty, which we fall into when we desire wholly to separate the inner from the outer, or the "ought" from the "is," are treated by Hegel with unsurpassable vigour and subtlety, as indeed the annihilating criticism of this conception is primarily due to him. The essence of the matter is that the pure will directed towards good for the sake of good, having no real connection with any detailed conduct, may be alleged by self-deception in support of any behaviour whatever, and out of this may spring the whole sophistry and hypocrisy of "pure intention." He makes the shrewd observation,[15] which is still of interest, that the extreme Protestant doctrine of conscience may take the form of ethical vacuity or instability, and that this had in his time been the cause of many Protestants going over to Rome, to secure some sort of moorings, if not precisely the stability of thought.

---

[14]Kant, *Grundlegung zur Metaphysik d. Sitten*, sect. I. [See Immanuel Kant, *Foundations of the Metaphysics of Morals*, trans., Lewis White Beck (Indianapolis: Bobbs-Merrill, 1959), p. 9.]

[15]*Rechtsphil.*, sect. 141 [The *Philosophy of Right*, trans., Knox, loc. cit., note 2, p. 258 (Addition to sect. 141).]

Still, out of all this one-sidedness, there survives the permanent necessity that an intelligent being can acquiesce only in what enters into the object of his will. It is his will which affirms the aim to which his nature draws him, and he is absolutely debarred from reposing in anything which does not appeal to his will. The subjective will is the only soil on which freedom can be a reality.

So, within the general organism of Right or realised Free-will, we have found two opposite groups of facts – for the aspirations of intelligent beings are facts – tendencies or theories, which are connected by opposition, and yet are necessary to the expression of the same underlying need – the letter of the law, and the freedom of conscience.

5. Hegel's name for the third term, which, as he puts it, expresses the "truth" of these extremes, may be rendered "the Ethical System," or "the Moral Life," or "Social Ethics." It expresses "the truth" of the extremes, as a good theory may express the truth of two one-sided views. Only, as we have said, it is a fact as well as a theory, and therefore is something which actually contains what these two views demand, and does the work which they, and the facts they rely on, exhibit as necessary to be done. This relation is not obscure or unprecedented. Every institution, every life, works as a theory, and either masters its facts or fails to master them; though not every theory is a life or an institution.

The German word which the above-mentioned phrases attempt to render is "*Sittlichkeit.*" The word takes its meaning from "*Sitte,*" which in common usage is equivalent to "custom." Hegel's use of the term, in his later writings, as opposed to "*Moralität,*" and as indicating, in comparison with it, a fuller and truer phase of life, is an intentional declaration of war against the Kantian principle of the pure good will, and is the gist of Hegel's ethico-political view in a nutshell.[16] The word would most naturally apply to the life of a community in which law, custom, and sentiment were not yet very sharply distinguished. According to accepted views, the communities of ancient Greece, before they were stirred by the reflective movement which is associated with the names of

---

[16]The most striking representation of this point of view in English is Mr F.H. Bradley's *Ethical Studies* [(London: Henry S. King and Co.,] 1876) [2nd edn, (Oxford: Clarendon Press, 1927)].

Socrates and the Sophists, would be examples of a disposition and order of life which the word "*Sittlichkeit*" might denote. And it was in the Greek communities, as is shown by the work which he sketched as early as 1802,[17] that Hegel found this suggestion of a whole in which law and custom, duty and disposition, were absolutely at one. He subsequently modified the conception in accordance with the modern idea of freedom, by allowing a greater emphasis and relief to its component parts, and insisting (against Plato's *Republic*, for instance,) on the principle of individual choice, initiative, and property, as necessary to the complete communion of intelligent beings. As we have just seen, indeed, he introduces reflective morality or conscientiousness into the sphere of Right, to represent the full nature of mind, which is only exhibited in a consciousness which pursues its aims of its own choice and for their own sake.

The Ethical System, then, or Social Ethics, is put forward as the ideal fact which includes, and does the work of, both the literal law and the moral will, alike in practice and as a theory. It is the idea of freedom developed (i) into a present world, and (ii) into the nature of self-consciousness.

For (i), in the first place, the ethical system or the ways of acting which make up social ethics, constitute a present and actual world. So far it partakes of the nature of the literal law and order, the system of property-holding, which, as we have seen, is all but a natural fact. Social Ethic, we might say, *is* a physical fact. The bodily habits and external actions of a people incorporate it. It transforms the face of a country, "domesticating the untamed earth."[18] Each individual has his own bodily

---

[17]The *System d. Sittlichkeit. The Rechtsphil.* was not published till 1817 in its earliest form. See Wallace, *Hegel's Philosophy of Mind*, [loc. cit., note 1] p. 187. [See *Hegel, System of Ethical Life* (1802–3) (translation of *System der Sittlichkeit*) and *First Philosophy of Spirit* (part III of *the System of Speculative Philosophy* 1803–4), trans. H.S. Harris and T.M. Knox (New York: State University of New York Press, 1979).]

[18]Aeschylus, *Eumenides*, l, 14. [Aeschylus (approx. 525–456 BC) was the earliest of the great tragic poets of Athens, and is often called the "father of Greek tragedy." The trilogy of plays, *Agamemnon, The Libation Bearers*, and *The Eumenides*, tell the tale of Orestes who, in Greek mythology, was the son of King Agamemnon and Queen Clytemnestra of Mycenae. After Clytemnestra and her lover kill his father, he kills them to avenge his father's death.]

existence in a determinate mode as a part of the ethical life of society. The rules and traditions of ethical living are, as has been said, "the nature of things." They are as hard, as "objective" an order as "sun, moon, mountains, rivers, and all objects of nature."[19] Man lives according to them before he knows that he does so, and always, in a great degree, independently of knowing that he does so. As this group of facts, or considered from this point of view, the ethical system is the body of the moral world.

(ii) But it is also and no less the very nature of self-consciousness. It is as much a demand of man's intelligence or an inner and universal law as the "pure will" itself.[20] The difference between them is that the Ethical System is a system, a world, though from the point of view of will regarded as inner, that is to say, as something which is the motive and fulfils the demand of consciousness. Thus, it bears the character of a thoroughly systematised theory, as contrasted with the idea of a good will, which is a mere general point of view. And it is because of this systematic character that it is enabled to connect the individual or particular will with the universal spirit of the community. It is only in a system that a particular fact can be connected with a universal law, as the planetary motions are with the law of gravitation. The particular will, as we have explained above, is universalised by its relation to a systematic purpose which it partly implies and partly realises. A man wishes for this thing or that thing, but not at any price. The reservations to which his wish is subject, by reason of other purposes and postulates of life, are known to him only in part; but if they could be stated in full, they would constitute the system of his life as realised in the universal life of the community. It is precisely analogous to the process which a common judgment of perception has to go through in becoming a scientific truth – the implications have to be stated in full, and the perception modified in accordance with them. And when this is done, we have no longer a fact, but a science.

---

[19]*Rechtsphil.*, sect. 146. [*The Philosophy of Right*, trans., Knox, loc. cit., note 2, pp. 105–6 (sect. 146).]

[20]On all this portion of the subject, see Mr Bradley's Essay, "My Station and its Duties," inin *Ethical Studies* [loc. cit., note 16].

Regarded from this point of view, as the substance of the individual Will, the Ethical System is the Soul of the moral world.

In analysing the Ethical System, we shall say nothing of "duties" or "virtues." Duty is in each case what the relation requires – the attachment of the universal system of will to the individual life. Virtue is a habit of such action, considered as embodied in the nature of an individual. The idea of virtue and virtuousness is not, in Hegel's view, altogether suitable to the members of an ethical commonwealth. It belongs rather to a time of undeveloped social life, when ethical principles and the realisation of them are ascribed to the nature of peculiarly gifted individuals. Virtue or excellence, to the Greek moralist, for instance, suggested doing something better than the average, or being in some way specially gifted, and it is still apt to indicate the desire to be something exceptional, and not simply to find yourself in genuine service. The meaning of the words to-day tends to narrow itself to certain special relations, and does not indicate that life of the member in the whole, which is the essence of what we really value.

The Ethical System, or the Order of Social Ethics, then – the mind and conduct of the citizen in Christendom – may be regarded as affirming freedom in three principal aspects, necessarily connected, and supplementing one another. Outwardly these aspects are different groups of facts – different institutions; inwardly they are different moods or dispositions of the one and indivisible human mind.

Thus, Hegel's analysis regards the social whole or system of social ethics from three points of view. First, in respect of the Family; secondly, in respect of what he has entitled Bourgeois Society; and thirdly, in respect of the Political Organism, or the State in the strict sense.[21]

It is to be borne in mind that, like the three principal divisions in the sphere of Right, these headings represent explicit theories of society, as well as groups of facts.

6. Beginning once more, within an ordered social sphere, at the ethical factor which stands nearest to the natural world, and has taken, so to speak, the minimum step into the realm of purpose and consciousness, we start from the family. As the family exists in a modern civilised

---

[21][These are the divisions of the third part of *The Philosophy of Right*, on Ethical Life.]

community, it is something necessary to society and the State, but absolutely distinct from both.

It first (α) represents the *fact* of the natural basis of social relations, being the embodiment of natural feeling in the form of love, both as between the parents, and as embodied for them in the children. It is in accordance with Hegel's general views of the meaning of a system that he sees this element of mind primarily represented by the family, as an organ preserved and differentiated *ad hoc*, and not, or not merely, distributed indefinitely throughout the community. Thus, the modern family represents for him a higher stage of civilisation – an organ to a fuller embodiment of mind – than the clan or tribe, or, in short, than any form of community in which the *whole* bond of union rests on merely natural feeling, kindness, generosity, or affection. In the nation, indeed, a tinge of natural affection, a colouring of unity by kinship, survives, just as feeling runs through the experience of the individual mind. But the distinctive character of the State is clear intelligence, explicit law and system, and so the natural basis of feeling, though necessary to be preserved and spiritualised, achieves these needs in the family as a special organ, and not in the State as such.

All those theories, therefore, which tend to assimilate the State to a family by a sort of levelling down of the former or levelling up of the latter (Plato's *Republic*, the phalanstery,[22] paternal government, and the like) involve for Hegel a mere confusion of relations. They recognise an element which is essential to society, and may truly be said to be even its foundation. But they do not see its right place in the whole, and do not understand that in order to attain a stronger and deeper unity (which is, in short, a stronger and deeper mind) the different elements must be allowed a greater emphasis and relief, and their respective characteristics must not be slurred or scamped.

But (β), in the second place, the family is a factor in the rational whole, the State, though its function *par excellence* is that of the natural basis of society. Hence its nature and sanction is ethical – it rests neither

---

[22][The phalanstery was the organisation unit of Charles Fourier's (See ch. vi, note 6) utopian community; it was to consist of 1,610 people; children were to be raised communally.]

on mere feeling on the one hand, nor on mere contract on the other. It has a public side, and the acceptance of a universal obligation by a declaration in explicit language (language being the stamp of the universal), in face of the community, is an essential part of marriage, and not a mere accident or accessory, as the votaries of feeling have urged. This view is aimed against the confusion which finds the sole essence of marriage in feeling. This is a perpetually recurring contention, represented in Hegel's day by Friedrich von Schlegel's *Lucinde*, which argues that the form of marriage destroys the value of passion.[23] Hegel's analyses are everywhere directed against this inability to grasp the distinct sides of a many-sided fact.

(γ) The ethical aspect of the family[24] shows itself in the nature and organisation of the household, as an institution embodying permanent interests and relations of the two persons who are its head, and as an organ of public duties in the bodily and spiritual nurture of the children. The permanent and equal relation of the heads of the household, involved in its nature as the ethical aspect of the family, implies monogamy, and it is the monogamous family alone which can count as a true element of the ethical order.

(δ) The household, being the true and operative ethical organ which makes parentage into family, is the unit which demands to be respected and protected by the State against the less differentiated forms of consanguinity, such as the clan. The true family starts from marriage and the foundation of a household, and in the early development of law we find the State, with a just instinct, protecting the household against the clan, e.g. by conferring the power of bequest. This power, though now it may imply a discretion mainly hostile to the family, presented itself in

---

[23][*Philosophy of Right*, trans., Knox, loc. cit., note 2, p. 262 (Addition to sect. 164). Friedrich von Schlegel (1772–1829) was a German critic and literary figure, who played a leading role in the development of German romanticism. Both Hegel and Bosanquet refer to his 1799 sexual utopian romantic *Lucinde;* for an English translation, see *Lucinde and the Fragments*, trans., Peter Firchow (Minneapolis: University of Minnesota Press, 1971).]

[24]Cf. [T.H.] Green's [*Lectures on the*] *Principles of Political Obligation* [with preface by Bernard Bosanquet (London: Longmans, Green, 1895), sect. 238], p. 235.

early law rather as a means of perpetuating the separate household as against the pretensions of the clan to interfere with its property.

Thus, the monogamous family is naturally and necessarily, to some extent, a unit in respect of property; the children, at least, being inevitably under tutelage and incapable of self-support, even if economic equality asserts itself as between husband and wife. This peculiar relation in respect of property is rooted in the unique nature of the household, as an organ for the guardianship of immature lives, and as a unity of feeling rather than of explicit thought. It is noticeable that progress tends to introduce the distinctions of property within its unity[25] (though for children this can never go very far), and very slightly to introduce the relations of the family into the outside world. In as far as such distinctions come to be made, the nature and functions of the household being undisturbed, a somewhat higher intensity of ethical union is rendered necessary, and will no doubt assert itself.

7. When the man (or woman)[26] arrives at maturity and leaves the safe harbour of the family, he finds himself, prima facie, isolated in a world of conflicting self-interests. He has his living to make, or his property to administer. He is tied to others, in appearance, only by the system of wants and work, with the elementary function which is necessary to it, viz. its police functions and the administration of justice.

It is this phase of Social life, and the temper or disposition corresponding to it, which Hegel indicates by the expression Bourgeois Society.[27] It presents itself to him as the opposite extreme of life and mind to that embodied in the family. It is an aggregate of families – for the units of the Bourgeois Society are heads of households – as seen from the out-

---

[25] Married Women's Property, Protection of Earnings of Children, Property assigned by understanding within household to young children.

[26] Hegel would say only or chiefly the man, who is for him the natural earner and chief of the household. [See *The Philosophy of Right*, trans., Knox, sect. 171.]

[27] *Bürgerliche Gesellschaft.* "Society," Wallace points out, is here opposed to "community," and indicates a looser phase of union. [The distinction between *Gesellschaft* (impersonal civil society founded on rights) and more traditional communities (*Gemeinschaft*) is important in nineteenth-century German thought. The crucial work in this tradition is Frederick Tönnies, *Community and Society* (*Gemeinschaft und Gesellschaft*), (1887) ed., Charles P. Loomis (East Lansing: Michigan State University Press 1957).]

side, in the great system of industry and business, where a man has to find his work and do it. It is, in mind, the presence of definite though limited aims, calculation and self-interest.[28]

Bourgeois Society is the aspect of the social whole insisted on by the classical political economy, by which, as an achievement in the way of reducing complex appearances to principles, Hegel was much impressed. It is, again, the view of society embodied in the conception of the purely legal[29] State, and its principle is confused with that of the State proper by one set of theorists, as that of the family is by another.

It is the peculiarity of Hegel's view – probably the most definitely original, as it is the most famous, of all his political ideas – to contend that this aspect of society, with the form of consciousness belonging to it, is necessary to a modern State. According to his logic, indeed, it is inevitable that every true whole shall have an aspect of "difference," of breaking up into particulars.

The principle of the ancient State, as concentratedly expressed in Plato's *Republic*, was weak and undeveloped, and fell short of the true claims of intelligence,[30] just because it dared not really let the individual go – let him assert himself as himself. "Subjectivity" was a principle fatal to it. Not that there was an iron oppression in the States of antiquity. The individual was, for an onlooker, magnificently developed. His

---

[28]Cf. the merchant in Wilhelm Meister's *Lehrjahre*, viii. 2. "I can assure you that I never reflected on the State in my life. My tolls, charges, and dues I have paid for no other reason than that it was established usage," (cited from Wallace, *Hegel's Philosophy of Mind*, [loc. cit., note 1] p. cci. [This is a play by Goethe; see *Wilhelm Meister's Lehrjahre*, English translation, *Wilhelm Meister's Apprenticeship* by Eric A. Blackall in cooperation with Victor Lange (Princeton: N.J.: Princeton University Press, 1995).]

[29]On the question of terminology, see [Johan Casper] Bluntschli, *The Theory of the State*, [authorised English translation, (Oxford, Clarendon Press, 1885)], p. 69. "Police State," the term used here in 1st edn, means more properly what we call a paternal government. The State here referred to, that which tries to restrict itself to protecting life and property, is rather the "legal" State (*Rechtsstaat*).

[30]"Was not ideal enough" (Hegel, *Geschichte der Philosophie*, II. 254), English Translation, [vol.] II, [loc. cit. ch. ix, note 14, p.] 108. The "notion" for him necessarily involves identity, differentiation, and re-integration; and in this respect the ancient State falls short of a true notion, while the modern realises it.

limitations were in him, and did not oppress him; but for all that, free choice and the career open to talents were not for him.

The modern demand – such is Hegel's conception – is harder and higher. The individual's life is not predetermined by his birth, but he is thrown face to face with economic necessity, which is a form of the universal end. He has to strip off his crudeness and vanity, and, of himself, mould himself into something which fulfils a want. This is a step without which there can be no true freedom – the giving one's self by one's own act a definite place in the region of external necessity, the "becoming *something*," or attaching oneself to a definite class of service renderers. Thus, we are startled to find culture or education treated in general, and in respect of its indispensableness, under the head of the Bourgeois Society. For culture is the liberation from one's own caprices, and the acceptance of a universal task. It is a severe process, and therefore unpopular, but it is a necessary one if we are to have true freedom. The criticism that such a world and temper is the world and temper of self-interest does not appeal strongly to Hegel. We shall have to treat of it more fully below.[31]

It may be noted in passing that the insecurity of life, which may seem to attach to dependence on the vast system of wants and work, is more and more seen, as modern economic relations develop, not to be insecurity at all, except in as far as "culture" in the form of industrial training is absent. There is, indeed, in modern life, nowhere any absolute and oyster-like stability. The highest stability to be anywhere attained is that due to fitness for service in the interdependent system of needs.[32]

Therefore, as Hegel saw, but in more ways than he saw, the system of Bourgeois Society – the economic and industrial world – is not a separate reality, but only an appearance within a larger system. The member of it is not so detached as he may seem, or think. He is within, and sustained by, the general life of the State, as the aims which are his motives in "business" or industry are within and inseparable from the whole structure of his intelligence.

---

[31] See below, p. 260.

[32] I may refer to *The Standard of Life*, by Helen Bosanquet [London: Macmillan, 1898], essay on "*Klassenkampf.*"

Thus, the world of Bourgeois Society – a world, on the whole, of cash nexus and mere protection by the State – has a structure or tendency of its own which brings it back by necessary steps to connection with the State proper or explicit and determinate social unity. It is, we must observe, posterior to the State in time. It is only within the State proper, and resting on its solid power, that such a world as that of Bourgeois Society could arise or be conceivable. Its priority to the State is, like that of the family, the priority of comparative narrowness or simplicity, of dealing with fewer factors, and of representing human nature in a more special, though necessary, aspect. And for this very reason it could not exist by itself. It has not the many-sided vitality indispensable to anything which is to hold its own in the actual world.

The working of the Bourgeois Society, then, exhibits an inevitable connection with the State proper, and, so to speak, leads up to it.

In the first place, the economic world implies the administration of justice. In this, as involving a developed system of civilised law, there is an advance on the "letter of the law" in its crudest and most barbarous acceptation. The system of law of a modern State is, and still more ought to be,[33] a fairly reasonable and intelligible definition of the rights and relations of persons. By this determination the economic system of particular wants and services enters upon a first approximation, as it were, to a unity of principle. The law only professes, indeed, to *protect* property and exchange, but in doing so it unavoidably recognises that the particular want has a general bearing; for the developed system of law only comes into existence to enable wants to be supplied, and takes its definite shape according to the system of wants. We may illustrate this first approximation to universality, which law confers upon the particulars of private interest, by a suggestive view which M. Durkheim has propounded.[34] He has pointed out that the current formula for social change, "from status to contract," has a subtler significance than is apt to be recognised.[35] For contract is not really indeterminate, as if it arose *in*

---

[33]Hegel pleads strongly for codification. [*The Philosophy of Right*, trans., Knox, loc. cit., note 2, pp. 135–36 (sect. 211).]

[34]*De la Division du Travail Social*, [pp.] 225 ff. [See above, ch. ii, note 22.]

[35]"The present progress of law is from contract to community." *The New State*, by M.P.

vacuo[36] without a precedent. It runs in forms determined by social experience through law and custom; and thus the law, which professedly aims at protecting property and exchange, necessarily regulates them by the modes in which it chooses to protect them.

A more intimate relation to the State proper – to a definite principle, as we might say, of common good – grows out of the interests of Bourgeois Society which take the shape of what a German calls "Police and Corporation," i.e. State regulation and Trade Societies.

The basis of State regulation is the emergence of aspects of common interest in the system of particular interests. The region of particular interests (supply and demand) has an accidental side, and the State has a right and a duty to protect the general good against accidental hindrances. On the whole, no doubt, the right relation between producer and consumer arises of itself, but miscarriages may occur which call for interference on behalf of the explicit[37] principle of the general good. The *general* possibility of the individual's obtaining what he wants is a public interest, and the State has a right to intervene with this end in view, both by execution of necessary public works, by sanitary inspection and the like, and by inspection and control of fraud in the case of necessary commodities offered for sale to the general public. For the public offer of goods in daily use is not a purely private concern, but a matter of the general interest. If indeed there was complete official regulation, there would be a risk of getting work like the Pyramids, that represented no private want at all; but yet, in the system of private wants, there is a public interest that demands vigilance.

A similar approximation of Bourgeois Society to the State is constituted by the "Corporation," which rests on the facts of class. Every member of the Bourgeois Society belongs by his vocation to a class, and this breaking up into classes is a consequence of the division of labour which prevails in the economic sphere, disguising the common good as private interest or necessity. But in the formation of classes society be-

---

Follett, p. 125, in a very striking chapter on recent legal theory, especially in the United States. [Note added in] 1919. [See Introd. to 2nd edn, note 43.]

[36][See ch. vi, note 2.]

[37]The *explicit* idea of common good always belongs in Hegel to the State proper.

gins as it were to recover from the dispersion which private interest has occasioned. As a member of his class[38] or "estate," the citizen acquires solidarity with his fellows, and his particular interest becomes *ipso facto* a common one. As a member of the class, again, he is, or ought to be, a member of his "trade society" or "corporation." In this he finds his honour or recognition,[39] a definite standard of life (apart from which he is apt to assert himself by aimless extravagance, for want of a recognised respectability), a standard of work, insurance against misfortune, and (as a candidate for admission) the means of technical education.

If the family is the first basis of the State, the classes or estates are the second. The Corporation or Trade Society is a second family to its members. It is the very root of ethical connection between the private[40] and the general interest, and the State should see to it that this root holds as strongly as possible.[41]

"If," Hegel writes,[42]

in recent days the "Corporation" has been abolished, this has the significance that the individual ought to provide for himself. This may be admitted; but the corporation did not alter the individual's obligation to earn his livelihood. In our modern States the citizens have only a limited share in the universal business of the State; but it is necessary to permit the ethical human being a universal activity over and above his private end. This

---

[38]The term "*Stände*," it must be remembered, has for a German the association of elements of the representative assembly; "*états*," estates of the realm.

[39]Cf. the English workman's phrase, "a good tradesman," i.e. competent member of his trade.

[40]"We can only say that these men, if they leave us, will bitterly regret it....The man who is so unselfish as to care nothing for himself or his fellow-men will soon find himself, as years creep over him, and grey hairs and glasses, completely cut out." – "Branch Trade Report (Birmingham) to National Union of Boot and Shoe Operatives, January, 1896."

[41]Sects. 201 and 255. [*The Philosophy of Right*, trans., Knox, loc. cit., note 2, pp. 130–31, 270; 154, 278.] I omit Hegel's characterisation of the classes, which has a good deal in common with theories which represent occupations as determining character. The contrast between agricultural and industrial or commercial life, between country and town, is of great importance in his view. He almost seems to confine Bourgeois industrialism as such to the life of town-dwellers; though, again, ultimately the whole division into classes is characteristic of Bourgeois Society (cf. sects 256 and 305).

[42]Ibid., sect. 255.

universal, which the modern State does not always provide for him, he finds in the "Corporation." We saw before that the individual providing for himself in the Bourgeois Society also acts for others. But this unconscious necessity is not enough; it needs the Corporation to bring it to a conscious and thoughtful social ethics. Of course the Corporation needs the higher superintendence of the State, or it would ossify, shrink into its shell, and be degraded into a wretched guild. But in and for itself the Corporation is no closed guild; it is rather the bringing of an isolated trade into an ethical connection, and its admission into a sphere in which it wins strength and honour.[43]

8. The State proper, or political constitution, presents itself to Hegel as the system in which the family and the Bourgeois Society find their completion and their security. He was early impressed, as we have seen, with the beautiful unity of the ancient Greek commonwealths. And the first and last idea which governs his representations of the modern State is that of the Greek commonwealth enlarged as it were from a sun to a solar system. The family feeling and the individual interest are in the modern State let go, accented, intensified to their uttermost power; and it is out of and because of this immense orbit of its elements that the modern State has its "enormous strength and depth." It is the typical mind, the very essence of reason, whose completeness is directly as the completeness of each of its terms or sides or factors; and secure in the logical confidence that feeling and self-consciousness, the more they attain their fullness, must return the more certainly to their place in the reasonable system which is their very nature. As ultimate power, the State maintains on one side the attitude of an external necessity towards the spheres of private life, of the family, and of the economic world. It may intervene by force to remove hindrances in the path of the common good, which accident and immaturity may have placed there. But, in its essence, the State is the indwelling and explicit end of these modes of living, and is strong in its union of the universal purpose with the par-

---

[43] It is obvious that this treatment of associations arising among classes in industry and commerce does not apply in principle exclusively to trade or professional societies. It would include, e.g., Friendly Societies and Co-operative Societies, by which members of the economic world bind themselves together for help, recognition, and the assertion of their general interests.

ticular interest of mankind. It is, in short, the incarnation of the general or Real Will. It has the ethical habit and temper of the family as a pervading basis, combined with the explicit consciousness and purpose of the business world. In the organism of the State, i.e. in as far as we feel and think as citizens, feeling becomes affectionate loyalty, and explicit consciousness becomes political insight. As citizens we both feel and see that the State includes and secures the objects of our affections and our interests; not as separate items, thrown together by chance, but as purposes transformed by their relation to the common good, into which, as we are more or less aware, they necessarily pass. This feeling and insight are the true essence of patriotism. It is easier to be magnanimous than to be merely right, and people prefer to think of patriotism as a readiness to make great sacrifices which are never demanded. But true patriotism is the every-day habit of looking on the commonwealth as our substantive purpose and the foundation of our lives.

The division of functions in the State is a necessary condition of its rational organisation. But, as Rousseau had insisted, it is altogether false to regard these separate functions as independent, or as checks on one another. There could be no living unity, if the functions of the State were ultimately independent and negative towards each other. Their differentiation is simply the rational division of labour. The State is an image of a rational conception; it is "a hieroglyph of reason."

Sovereignty, therefore, resides in no one element. It is, essentially, the relation in which each factor of the constitution stands to the whole.[44] That is to say, it resides only in the organised whole acting qua organised whole. If, for example, we speak of the "Sovereignty of the People" in a sense opposed to the Sovereignty of the State – as if there were such a thing as "the people" over and above the organised means of expressing and adjusting the will of the community – we are saying what is, strictly speaking, meaningless. It is just the point of difference between Rousseau's two views. We saw that Rousseau clearly explained the impossibility of expressing the general will except by a determinate system of law.[45] But what he seemed to suggest, and was taken to mean, by

---

[44]Cf. the account of Sovereignty in *The New State*, see above, pp. 40–41. [Added] 1919.

[45][See *The Philosophy of Right*, sects. 301–308.]

popular Sovereignty, was no doubt just the view which Hegel condemns. It is essentially the same question as how a constitution can be made. Strictly, a constitution cannot be made except by modification of an existing constitution. If, to put a case, you have a multitude new to each other in some extra-political colony, they must assume a constitution, so to speak, before they can make one. Law and constitution are utterances of the spirit of a nation.

The form of State which Hegel analyses is a modern constitutional monarchy, with an executive (ministers sitting in the chambers, as he is careful to urge) and Chambers or Estates[46] representing the classes developed in the civic community. Representation, he urges, is of bodies or interests rather than of masses of individuals, and the Corporations or Trade Societies have also an important place directly, by their touch with the departments of the executive government.[47] The general principle is, as indicated above, that the problems of connection between considerable particular interests and the universal interests of the community are, so to speak, prepared on the ground of the Corporation and Bourgeois Society for a solution in the interest of the common good by the Legislative and the Executive Government.

The logical division of power, in his language, is that the Legislature has to establish universal principles, the executive has to apply these principles to particular cases, and the prince has to bring to a point the acts of the State by giving them, "like the dot on the i," the final shape of individual volition.

The distinction of States into Monarchy, Aristocracy, and Democracy, Hegel refuses to regard as applicable to the modern world. At best, it could only apply to the undeveloped communities of antiquity. The modern State is a concrete, and, according to its principle, all the elements of a people's life are represented in it as an indivisible unity.

---

[46][See above, note 38.]

[47]Much as through inspectors and commissions the opinion of Trade Unions, Friendly Societies, and Co-operators is elicited by our Government Departments with a view to legislation, independently of the House of Commons. On the relation of the state to local and vocational groups see "The State and Pluralism" with reference to Miss Follett's *The New State*, see above, p. 37. [Note added in] 1919.

A curious point is Hegel's insistence on the function of the personal Head of the State. By a junction of the extremes, he connects it with the recognition of free individuality, which is usually regarded as the democratic principle of the modern world. There is no act, we may say in illustration, according to the modern idea of an act, if it is not done in the end by an individual, though in a developed political system the monarch's action may only consist in signing his name. It is at least remarkable to compare this view with the tendency to one-man government in the administration of the United States of America.

The State, then, is on one side the external force and automatic machinery implied in the maintenance and adjustment of the rights and purposes of the family and the Bourgeois Society as an actual life. On the other side, and most essentially, it is that connection of feeling and insight, working throughout the consciousnesses of individuals as parts in a connected structure, which unite in willing a certain type of life as a common good in which they find their own. It has the same content as that of Religion; but in an explicit and rationalised form as contrasted with the form of feeling. Only the separation of Church and State, and the division of the Churches against one another, have made it possible for the State to exhibit its own free and ethical character in true fullness, apart from both dogmatic authority and anarchic fanaticism.

9. Publicity of discussion in the assembly of the classes or estates is the great means of civic education. It is not in the least true that every one knows what is for the good of the State, and has only to go down to the House and utter it. It is in the work of expression[48] and discussion that the good takes form by adjustment of private views to facts and needs

---

[48]It is a remarkable point in English politics to-day that legislation is practically in the hands of the Government departments. Bills are rejected or "knocked about in Committee"; but the mass of organised knowledge necessary to initiate legislation in a complex society can hardly be found outside the gathered experience of an office which has continuity in dealing with the same problems. This tendency more than justifies Hegel's point of view. An act of the "General Will" has not only, as he said, to be moulded by running the gauntlet of public and critical discussion, but has even to be first drafted by the help of immense piles of experience, which the general mind does not possess, and could not deal with, but which, nevertheless, enable its typical wish and intention to he embodied in effective form.

brought to bear by criticism. "The views a man plumes himself on when he is at home with his wife and friends are one thing; it is quite another thing what happens in a great assembly, where one shrewd idea devours the other."[49]

The free judgment of individuals based on the publicity of political discussion is "public opinion." In public opinion we have an actual existent contradiction. As public, it is sound and true, and contains the ethical spirit of the State. As expressed by individuals in their particular judgments, on which they plume themselves, it is full of falsehood and vanity. It is the bad which is peculiar, and which people pride themselves on; the rational is universal in its nature, though not necessarily common. Public opinion is a contradictory appearance in which the true exists as false. It is no accident, but inevitable insight, that leads both of these characters to be proverbially expressed, as in "Vox populi, vox Dei,"[50] contrasted with Ariosto's

> Che'l Volgare ignorante ogn'un' riprenda
> E parli piu di qual che meno intenda;[51]

or Goethe's

> Zuschlagen kann die Masse
> Da ist sie respektabel;
> Urtheilen gelingt ihr miserabel;[52]

---

[49]*Rechtsphil.* sect. 315. [See Hegel, *The Philosophy of Right*, trans., Knox, loc. cit., note 2, p. 294.]

[50][*Vox Populi, vox Dei*: "The voice of the people is the voice of God."]

[51]"That the ignorant vulgar reproves everyone, and talks most of what it understands least." [As Knox reports (*The Philosophy of Right*, p. 373), this quote is from *Orlando Furioso*, canto xxviii, stanza 1.]

[52]"The masses are respectable hands at fighting, but miserable hands at judging." [Knox notes that Hegel slightly misquotes Goethe, *Sprichwörtlich*, II, pp. 398–400. Goethe writes:

> Zuschlagen muss die Masse,
> Dann ist sie respektabel;
> Urteilen getlingt ihr miserabel.

Interestingly, Knox uses Bosanquet's translations of this passage and that in the previous note in his edition of the *Philosophy of Right*, p. 373.]

or the "mostly fools" of Carlyle.[53]

Now, as public opinion thus combines truth and falsehood, the public cannot be in earnest with both, i.e. both cannot be its real will. But if we restrict ourselves to its express utterance, we cannot possibly tell what it is in earnest with – *because it does not know*. Therefore the degree of passion with which a given opinion is maintained throws no light on the question, on what points the public is really in earnest, in the sense of the "real will." This can only be known from the substantive reality, which is the "true inwardness" of public opinion. This substantive reality, the true merits of any case, is not to be got by the study of mere public opinion as expressed, but when it is successfully divined and asserted, public opinion will always come round to it. If we ask how it is to be divined or known, we must go back to the analogy of a theory. The solution must be constructed so as to satisfy the real facts or needs, and the real facts or needs only become known in proportion as it is constructed, just as in scientific discovery. The man who can see and do what his age wills and demands is the great man of the age. Public opinion, then, demands to be at once esteemed and contemned; esteemed in its essential basis, contemned in its conscious expression. It is, however, the principle of the modern world that every one is allowed to contribute his opinion. When he has contributed it, and so far satisfied the impulse of self-assertion, he is likely to acquiesce in what is done, to which, he can feel, he has thrown in some element of suggestion or criticism.[54]

10. In concluding this chapter, we will attempt to estimate the nearness of such an analysis of the State to the actual facts of life, admitting certain appearances against it, but rejecting pessimistic views which rest on false abstractions.

---

[53]["A Parliament speaking through reporters to Bunscombe and the twenty-seven millions mostly fools." Thomas Carlyle (1795–1881) *Latter-Day Pamphlets*, No. 6, *Parliaments*.]

[54]The author of *The New State* maintains with a good deal of truth that the "real will" would become a much more genuine fact than it is if we were to make a considerable advance in "the art of living together." See above p. 41. [Note added in] 1919.

I will state the difficulties as they appeared to T.H. Green, a cautious and practical Englishman, well experienced in local politics, and acquainted with different classes of men.

> To an Athenian slave, who might be used to gratify a master's lust, it would have been a mockery to speak of the State as a realisation of freedom; and perhaps it would not be much less to speak of it as such to an untaught and underfed denizen of a London yard with gin shops on the right hand and on the left.[55]

> It is true that the necessity which the State lays on the individual is for the most part one to which he is so accustomed that he no longer kicks against it; but what is it, we may ask, but an external necessity, which he no more lays on himself than he does the weight of the atmosphere or the pressure of summer heat and winter frosts, that compels the ordinary citizen to pay rates and taxes, to serve in the army, to abstain from walking over the Squire's fields, snaring his hares, or fishing his preserved streams, to pay his rent, to respect those artificial rights of property which only the possessors of them have any obvious interest in maintaining, or even (if he is one of the "proletariate") to keep his hands off the superfluous wealth of his neighbour when he has none of his own to lose?...A conception does not float in the air. It must be somebody's conception. Whose conception, then, of general good is it that these institutions represent?...[I]s it not seriously misleading, when the requirements of the State have so largely arisen out of force directed by selfish motives, and when the motive of obedience to these requirements is determined by fear, to speak of them as having a common source with the morality of which it is admitted that the essence is to be disinterested and spontaneous?[56]

I have quoted these passages – the whole section should be carefully read – in order to state plainly a paradox which affects the theory of society from beginning to end. It continually shows itself in the pessimistic criticism of economic motive, political motive, and of every-day social motive.

---

[55][Green, "On the Different Senses of 'Freedom' as Applied to the Will and to the Moral Progress of Man" in *Lectures on the] Principles of Political Obligation*, [loc. cit., note 24] p. 8; cf. pp. 127 ff.

[56][*Principles of Political Obligation*, loc. cit., note 24, pp. 127–28.]

The whole question really depends on our understanding of the relation of abstract and concrete. It is plain, as Green says, that the idea of a common good has never been the sole influence operative in the formation or maintenance of States. And, in as far as it has operated at all, it has only done so in very imperfect forms. Green goes so far as to say that Hegel's account of freedom as realised in the State does not seem to correspond to the facts of society as it is, or even as, under the unalterable conditions of human nature, it ever could be; though, no doubt, there is a work of moral liberation, which society, through its various agencies, is constantly carrying on for the individual.

Now, the truth of these criticisms may be granted in the same sense in which we grant the imperfection of knowledge (as currently conceived) or of morality – imperfections not accidental, but inherent in each particular form of human experience. The conflict of interests, the failure to reconcile rights, and the weight and opaqueness, so to speak, of law and custom to the individual mind, are contradictions of the same type and due to causes of the same kind as those which arise in the world of ethics and of theory. And, though the new relations which spring up in society are perpetually resulting in new contradictions, there is no reason to compare the State unfavourably, in this respect, with Morality or with Science. The contradictions, in fact, are the material of organisation.[57]

Without differing profoundly from Green in theory, therefore, we venture to assign a greatly diminished importance to his criticisms.[58]

---

[57]Take, for instance, the chaos of the medical charities of London. It consists of endeavours to adjust help to needs, which endeavours are themselves unadjusted to each other. Thus, precisely as in the, theoretical progress, the unadjustment of adjustments brings out ever new contradictions which demand readjustment. [See Bosnaquet, "Can Logic Abstract from the Psychological Conditions of Thinking?" *Procceedings of the Aristotelian Society*, n.s. vi (1905–06): 237–247.]

[58][Green and Bosanquet thus disagree about the extent to which the life of actual states expresses the common good. Wrote Green: "Civil society may be, and is, founded on the idea of there being a common good, but that idea in relation to the less favoured members of society is in effect unrealised, and it is unrealised because the good is being sought in objects which admit of being competed for. They are of such a kind that they cannot be equally attained by all. The success of some in attaining them is incompatible with the success of others. Until the object generally sought as good comes to be a state of mind or character of which the attainment, or approach to attainment, by each is itself a contribu-

This is due in part to the growth of a more intimate experience, owing in some measure to his initiative, which seems to show the essentials of life to be far more identical throughout the so-called classes of society than is admitted by such a passage as that cited above about the dweller in a London yard.[59] It is due, further, and in connection with such experience, to the psychological conceptions developed in previous chapters, according to which the place of actual fear of punishment in maintaining the social system is really very small, while the place of a habituation, which is essentially ethical, is comparatively large. These suggestions, which lead us to lay decreasing stress on Green's criticism of Hegel, point wholly in the general direction of his own convictions, and we may finally meet the general difficulty, which expresses itself in pessimism, by considerations such as Green himself alleges in mitigation of his own criticism.

We may approach the matter in this way. The paradox is, that if you scrutinise the acts which have made States, and which carry them on, or which go on under and within them, you will everywhere be able to urge that they spring from self-interest and ambition – not from a desire for the common good. How then can we say that the State exists for a common good? Hegel's large conception of a social fabric and the temper of mind which maintains it should have done something to meet this problem. But we may come a little closer to the precise difficulty.

Nothing is so fallacious as mere psychological analysis applied to the estimation of the purposes which rule a mind. In every act there is necessarily an aspect of the agent's particular self. One way or another he is satisfied in it. So the pessimistic or superficial psychologist can always –

---

tion to its attainment by everyone else, social life must continue to be one of war." T.H. Green, *Prolegomena to Ethics*, ed. A.C. Bradley (Oxford: Clarendon Press, 1890), sect. 245 (p. 263).]

[59]Not much stress should be laid on an isolated expression of this kind, used in making clear the difficulties of a theory which on the whole he supported, and putting these difficulties, as was his custom, as high as possible. But it is worth noting that no one, who really knows the class thus rhetorically alluded to, fails to experience in them the same great relations and recognitions which make life worth living for more fortunate persons, and as they feel very keenly, the experience is often more emphatic there than in the richer class. Probably, in fundamental matters, there is as large a proportion of persons untaught and bred up between temptations among the rich as among the poor.

not in some acts merely, but in all – discover a form of self-seeking. Life is a whole made up of particulars, and the universal is a connection within them, not another particular outside them;[60] it is a mistake of principle to suppose that any act can be outside the tissue of aims, impulses, and emotions which affect the sensitive self. Great purposes work through these affections and transform them, but cannot obliterate them without obliterating life. "There is nothing degrading in being alive."[61] But there is a kind of eye which sees all these particulars apart from the substantive aims which give them their character, and treats them as if they were the sole determining motives of the agent. Hegel calls such a critic – he is thinking especially of historians – "the psychological valet, for whom there are no heroes, not because they are no heroes, but because he is only a valet."[62] On the whole, a man is what he does. If his series of actions has the root of the matter in it, it is wrong either for him to be deterred, or for a critic to carp, because they bring him gain or glory, or gratify him by activity and excitement. To shrink from particular occasions of action because one's self may find satisfaction in them is to fall back into the mere general willing of the abstract good. And "the laurels of mere willing are dry leaves that never have been green."[63]

We may illustrate these ideas from the life of the ordinary members of States, and from the career of a great ruler or conqueror.[64]

The life of an English labourer, for example, may concern itself with no such abstract ideas[65] as are expressed by the words "State" or "common good." But, to begin with, he is a law-abiding citizen. He keeps his hands off others and their belongings by the same rule by which he ex-

---

[60][This points to Bosanquet's notion of a concrete universal. See above, Introd. to 2nd edn, p. 30, note 34.]

[61]*Rechtsphil.*, sect. 123. [See *Philosophy of Right*, trans., Knox, p. 252.]

[62][See *Philosophy of Right*, ibid., (para. 124).]

[63][Ibid., addition to paragraph 124, p. 252.]

[64]Green, [*Lectures on the*] *Principles of Political Obligation*, [loc. cit., note 24], [pp. 128–129, 133–134.], sects. 121 and 128.

[65]Although the literary class are liable very seriously to underrate the significance of forms of thought unfamiliar to them.

pects others to keep their hands off him and his belongings.[66] He recognises fairness of bargaining, and is prepared to treat others fairly, as he expects them to treat him. He is aware of his claims, that is to say, as depending on something in common between himself and others; and if he does not practically admit any such community, "he is one of the 'dangerous classes,' virtually outlawed by himself."[67]

So far he is a loyal subject only. If he is to have a fuller sense of a social good, he must either take part in the work of the State, or at least be familiar with such work, through interest in his fellows' share of it, and in the organisations which connect his class interests with the public good. His mind must not merely work in its place in the social mind, but must be in some degree aware of the connection between its place and the whole – of the appercipient structure to which it belongs.[68] He must, in short, have touch with the connection which Hegel represents as that between the Bourgeois Society and the State proper. And this, in modern States, is in principle open to him.

And, further, he must have the feeling for his State, which is connected with the idea of home and fatherland. In a modern nation the atmosphere of the family is not confined to the actual family. The common dwelling-place, history, and tradition, the common language and common literature, give a colour of affection to the every-day citizen-consciousness, which is to the nation what family affection is in the home circle.

Thus, it is not true that either the feeling or the insight which constitute a consciousness of a common good is wanting to the every-day life of an average citizen in a modern State. It may seem full of selfish care, but this is only a narrow view. If we look at the spirit of the whole life we shall see that it is substantially dependent on the recognition of a good, and feels that dependence in concrete form.

---

[66]Habits, such as our habit of relying on security of life and property, are secondarily automatic, i.e. are very intimately connected with ideas. See ch. viii [above].

[67]Green, [*Lectures on the Principles of Political Obligation*], loc. cit., [note 24], [p. 129 (sect. 121).]

[68][See ch. vii, above, and the "Organisation of Intelligence," p. 294ff.]

And, secondly, to take the paradox in its extreme shape, in which the order of the State appears to arise out of the selfish ambition of the most unscrupulous of men. The contradiction may be stated in the form that the actions of bad men are "over-ruled" for good. But this would mean that the "psychological" critic or historian had first mis-stated the cause, and then had rectified his mis-statement by a meaningless phrase. The great ideas and causes which were advanced, for example, by the career of Napoleon, owed neither their nature nor their existence to his selfish ambition. They did not, however, owe them to any non-human cause; to any operation of ideas otherwise than in the minds of men. They came into existence through the working of innumerable minds towards objective ends by the inherent logic of social growth, with various degrees of moral insight, and they were promoted by Napoleon's career in virtue of the common character which united his aims, in so far as they had a reasonable side, with the movement shaped by the ideal forces of the age. There is no reason to doubt, if we do not wilfully narrow our view of the situation, that a conception of good was as much operative in the cause as it is present in the effect – say, in the unity of Italy. We cannot attempt, on the ground of mere ethical and political philosophy, to deal with the problem of the existence of evil; and we are not concerned to deny or to minimise the presence of greed and selfishness as distorting

---

[69]Aristotle's saying of the State, that it *"comes to be* for the sake of life, but *is* for the sake of good life," expresses in the first instance an apparent contrast between origin and purposes of States. But its real point is that the purpose is implied in the origin, for the State is natural, and in every "natural" genesis its purpose is implied; and the origin is implied in the purpose, for the State, in the processes which maintain it, "originates," i.e. renews its material basis, daily, and must do so in order to "be." [See Aristotle, *Politics*, trans., Benjamin Jowett, (Oxford: Clarendon Press, 1905), Bk I, ii. (1252b9–1253a9).]

[70]It must not be ignored that the duty of the State demands that it should reveal and realise for its members a true satisfaction which is yet relevant to their *natural* impulses and desires. Its stability and authority depend on its coping with this problem. This is the strong point of Spinoza's account of the State. "He lays stress on it just for that reason (man's desires – the *jus naturae* which = *potentia*) that in our haste to get to morals, Civil Society and Religion, we do not properly recognise the 'natural basis' of all of them. If man had not these passions, anti-social as well as social, there would be neither morality, nor religion, nor the State." [Robert A.] Duff, *Spinoza['s Political and Ethical Philosophy* (Glasgow: J. Maclehose and Sons, 1903)], p. 161.

forces in the minds of men, or in the organisation of States. All that we needed to show, was that what makes and maintains[69] States as States is will and not force, the idea of a common good, and not greed or ambition;[70] and that this principle cannot be overthrown by the facts of self-interest in ordinary citizens, or of selfishness in those who mould the destinies of nations.

CHAPTER XI

INSTITUTIONS CONSIDERED AS ETHICAL IDEAS

1. We have been guided throughout our argument by the idea that the relation of a given mind to the mind of society[1] is comparable to the relation between our apprehension of a single object and our view of nature as a whole. The former term, in each case, we cannot but suppose to be an individualised case of the latter. The latter seems inevitably to imply a universal principle corresponding to every feature of the former. We can never see through the connections, and the connections of the connections – e.g. of gravitation and of colour – in every fact. But our ideal as theorists would be to analyse the physical object into features, every one of which should be a case of a natural law, and the whole taken together a case of the whole system of natural law, which would be our scientific view of the world.

In treating of a human mind in its relation to Society and the State, our ideal is comparable to this. We should like to analyse any given mind into features each of which should be an individual case of a universal principle, and the whole of which, taken together, should be a case of the whole system of principles incarnate in the world, and proximately in the social world. Plato, simplifying for the sake of elucidation the City-state, which to our minds was already simple, represented a community, in diagrammatic form, as consisting in a threefold structure of classes, in which were incarnate the three main features which he discriminated in the individual soul – the desires necessary to living, the spirit of action, and the power of seeing things as a whole.

2. The principles which constitute a society are facts as well as ideas, and purposes as well as facts. This threefold character is united in what we describe by the general term "institutions," a term which would ap-

---

[1] I neglect, for the moment, the difference between the mind of society and mind at its best. The difference is practically considerable, but I shall attempt to make it appear, in the course of the present chapter, to be a difference of progress, but not of direction.

265

ply perfectly well to Plato's "classes" in virtue of the definite relations with which he invests them.

It is unnecessary to insist on the external aspect of institutions as facts in the material world; but it will be worth while to gather up the leading conceptions of our analysis by tracing the nature of some prominent "institutions," as ideas, constituent elements of the mind, which are also purposes; that is, as ethical ideas. An institution may have grown up without special ordinance, or may have been called into existence by an act of public will. But it has always the character of being recognised *as if* it had been "instituted" or established to fulfil some public or quasi-public purpose.[2] An old servant is sometimes said to be "quite an institution" – he is characterised by the function of keeping alive certain common traditions of a school, perhaps, or a family – an annual custom may be an institution in virtue of the same kind of recognition; Sunday is an institution; the word is indeed very vaguely applied, for obviously almost every object or event can have a significance of this kind attached to it in jest or earnest. But for all that, we can see pretty plainly what usage is driving at. An institution implies a purpose or sentiment of more minds than one, and a more or less permanent embodiment of it. "Of more minds than one," because it is to fix the meeting point of minds that the external embodiment is necessary.

In institutions, then, we have that meeting point of the individual minds which is the social mind. But "meeting point" is an unhappy term, suggesting objects in space that touch at certain spots. Rather let us say, we have here the ideal substance, which, as a universal structure, is the social, but in its differentiated cases is the individual mind. And it is necessary to observe that the material of this fabric has determinate sources. Mind is not an empty point. It is the world as experienced. The institutions, which as ethical ideas constitute mind, are, like a theory, attempts at unity in face of needs, pressures, facts, and suggestions

---

[2]Why is not a memorial statue or building, which expresses a public idea, an "institution" apart from its uses? Apparently because it has not the notion of bringing persons together or inducing persons to act in some definite way. An "institution" then, belongs to the level of society, as such, conceived as a number of persons. Thus, a work of art is hardly an institution, though it expresses the "universal" of many minds; but a weekly concert is an institution, because many persons act together in going, and attending it.

which arise in what we call our surroundings, and to each of which mind reveals a different quality; as every tone of a landscape elicits its peculiar shade of feeling, which but for it might have remained latent for ever. It takes the whole world to call out the whole mind. But it will be enough if we can trace, in some prominent examples, the nature of an institution as at once a dealing with surroundings,[3] an ethical idea, and a social principle.

3. The family starts from the universal physical fact of parentage, but takes its ethical value mainly from the special phase of parental relation which leads to the formation of a household. The association of parents and children in a household, which is permanent until broken up into other households, is due to economic conditions. Calling to mind the original meaning of words, we see that we are asserting the formation of a household to be due to "household"[4] conditions. And this is something more than a pun. Whatever the surroundings may be which favour the formation of households, whether the difficulty of procuring livelihood, which makes the father's continued care essential,[5] or the chances offered by agriculture to a stable group, they operate as elements in a human world, in a world which is constituted by the focussing of "surroundings" (circumstances) in a whole. Conditions which have become "economic" have ceased to be material. They are motives, interests, means to ends. They bring the world into the mind, but in doing so they become factors in the purposiveness and re-adjustment, which the mind, as unity asserting itself throughout varied suggestions, is busied in bringing to pass. By demanding permanence, for instance, economic conditions elicit in the relation of parent and child the simplest form of universality necessary to an ethical idea.

We will not venture upon the history of phases of the family life, but will attempt at once to sketch its position and value in the typical civili-

---

[3]There are, of course, no absolute surroundings. At every point experience rests on mind. But at any point at which we are observing, we must take some facts as, comparatively speaking, given.

[4]"Economy" = household management.

[5]It is said that the household does not readily form itself in very easy conditions of life.

sation of a modern State. Only it must be insisted on once more,[6] that the family or household as an ethical structure is not anterior to the State, but is rather a growth dependent on the spirit and protection of the State, and intentionally fostered by it as against forms of kinship which do less justice to the ethical possibilities of parentage.

As an ethical idea, then, the monogamous family, which is in the normal case also a household, has a unique place in the structure of the citizen mind.

Its peculiarity is in being a natural union of feeling with ideal purpose. That is to say, the ideal purpose, a permanent interest in a comparatively permanent and external life, attaches itself by imperceptible links to the most universal incident of animal existence. The mere remaining together of the units, a demand of their physical needs, is almost enough of itself to transform their inevitable mutual dependence into a relation of intentional service, rooted in affection, and tinged with some degree of forethought.

And, being thus "natural," the idea of the family has a hold like no other upon the whole man. In this respect it anticipates the powers which have been claimed for the love of beauty. The very animal roots of life, and every detail of man's appetitive being, are made, without conscious effort or moralising interference, factors in a round of social service. The meal of a lonely individual[7] is perhaps, at best, a refined and lawful pleasure. But the family meal, quite apart from over-strained religionism, has in it, as a plain matter of fact, the fundamental elements of a sacrament, none the less effective that they are not thought of by that name. And both through maintaining the fitness of the parents for their life work, and through the training of the children to the same end, the natural ethics of the family have an indispensable logical hold upon the more explicit common good known to the social will.

And, in the last place, it should be noted that a feeling and atmosphere of this kind is not confined to members actually living in households formed by families. There is no race, it has been said, that parts with its

---

[6]Cf. pp. 244–45.

[7]Note, however, what is said below of the secondary or transferred idea of the family. The solitary may partake of the family sacrament, so to speak, "by faith."

children so readily, or retains their affections so permanently, as the Anglo-Saxon race. When the type and spirit are once formed, they are contagious and persistent; they affect all who have seen or known them, and even those who have never formed part of a household bound by kinship.

If we contrast the idea of the household with monasticism as its repudiation, and with the tribal state or phalanstery as its exaggeration, we shall see its uniqueness in the strongest light. The naturalness of its foundation, and the completeness of the reciprocal interest (involving monogamy) on which its idea rests, distinguish it from all other forms of union or disunion in which the sexes are concerned. It may be added that the family, and it alone, has the right adjustment of population in its power. The fully trained and equipped human being can never be superfluous in the world. And the production of the fully trained and equipped human being depends on the capacity of forming a true family and meeting its requirements, and when this capacity and idea regulate the union of the sexes no growth nor apparent decrease of population need cause anxiety.

It seems as idle to discuss whether civilisation is conceivable without the family as whether human nature can change. All that we can attempt, as philosophers, is to ascertain the distinctive part which its idea plays in human life as such. There must be, we can see, some such idea – an ethical idea covering some such sides of life – while man is a spiritual animal. But by what precise "institution" such an idea might come to be represented in circumstances which we do not know, it would be beyond the modesty of philosophy to predict.

The institution of Property may be mentioned as a corollary to the household family. Its natural basis and ethical value are very markedly correlative to those of the latter. The outlook upon life which it essentially implies is co-extensive with that demanded by the household, although in the relations of acquisition and exchange many further rights and duties may attach to it. It depends on the fact that, in order to express a will in an individual life (which is incomplete except as the life of a household), there must be a power of moulding the material world in the service of ideas, which is conditioned by free acquisition and utilisation. The institution of property, then, as an ethical idea, consists in the conception of individual (properly speaking, household) life as a unity in respect to its dealings with the material instruments of living. It is not merely the idea of provision for the future; still less the certainty of satisfying wants as they arise from day to day. It is the idea that all dealings with the material conditions of life form part of a connected system, in which our conceptions and our abilities express themselves. It binds together the necessary care for food and clothing with ideas of making the most of our life and of the lives dependent upon us. A being which has no will has so far no property – a child has in practice, and a slave had by Roman law, property in a secondary sense – and a being which has no property has so far no actual will. The "person," or responsible head (or heads), of a household, is the true unit to whom the idea of property attaches, because he is the unit to which we normally ascribe an individualised will, a single distinctive shape of the social mind. A child has not yet such a will; a group of mature persons has more than one. The change which is passing over the household in consequence of the recognition of married women as individual wills is highly instructive on this point. They can hold and manage their own property, because it is admitted that they can have their own view of life. It is not proposed that young children should hold and manage property, because every one knows that they have no mature individualised view of life. The corporate person of the household is so far dissolved by legal recognition of its more individual components; and it is most important, theoretically, to note that its unity is not diminished by the recognition, but is raised to a higher power.

4. It might seem fanciful to say that our district is to our family as space to time; but it would suggest something of the point of view from which it is well to look at the structure of our ethical ideas. It is desirable to realise how the simplest characters of our surroundings and their necessary connections are ethically important, not because they impose anything upon us, but because they respond to something within us, or rather, to a possibility which is to be realised by the world, as in us its variety strives towards unity. Parentage, we saw, was a universal animal fact, and from it, in an experience capable of unity and permanence, springs the family household and all that it implies for our lives. One's district, as an element of life, implies, of course, some stability – a home, not merely permanent as a home, like the Scythian's waggon, but located on some spot of earth. The nomad, we must suppose, to a great extent carries his neighbourhood – his tribe – along with him, and for that very reason the fact of neighbourhood has not its full effect on him.

But when a permanent home is fixed on some spot of earth, presumably with the beginnings of agriculture, a new condition begins to operate – the "indifference" of space. Perhaps we are surprised that "indifference" should be an ethical stimulus. But nothing is more instructive than to note how qualities of our surroundings, which by themselves seem negative or the barest natural necessities, spring into significance when taken up into the unity of life. Locality means a potential neighbourhood. It may be long before any one comes near you except your own cousinhood, your tribe or clan. But the indifference of space is a standing invitation, and it is pretty certain that some day strangers will become your neighbours, and that you will have to take up some mental attitude towards them. Historians and jurists have described to us the struggle between the principle of kinship and the principle of neighbourhood. When we read that a plebeian, in the eyes of a Roman patrician, simply could not make a real marriage any more than the beasts of the field, this is not, as it may have become by survival, intentional arrogance on the patrician's part. It was rather the state of mind of Mrs. Transome towards Rufus Lyon, "sheer inability to consider him."[8] A proof of what a struggle it involved to reach a new attitude of mind as regarded the resident alien is given by the half-way house at which it was found necessary to pause in the process. The recognition of kinship on the ground of residence was the fiction, we are told, by which the mind assisted itself to a positive attitude towards those whom the indifference of space insisted on bringing within its range. And the positive attitude towards which it was groping its way was of course the recognition of humanity, the equality of man in the truest sense which that ambiguous phrase will bear.

---

[8] ["Mrs. Transome hardly noticed Mr Lyon, not from studied haughtiness, but from sheer mental inability to consider him – as a person ignorant of natural history is unable to consider a fresh-water polyp otherwise than as a sort of animated weed, certainly not fit for table." George Eliot, *Felix Holt, The Radical* (London: J.M. Dent, 1997), ch. 38.]

In modern States, in which this struggle is on the whole behind us, our district or locality asserts its full indifference. Its "negative" here becomes a "positive." That is to say, on the whole,[9] and under some reasonable reservations as to evidence of intention to accept duties, and to renounce incompatible ones, men are full members of the district to which they choose to belong. The challenge thrown down by the indifference of space has resulted in a recognition of universal humanity. Our district is our neighbourhood. We will look a little more closely at the ethical idea implied. We notice at once, at least in English experience, that each of us belongs to a variety of districts which are concentric as regards him. Each of these districts represents a different purpose, and we are told that for practical purposes great confusion results. But it is a useful training to be made aware of the distinct purpose of each organised locality which surrounds us – to have the care of our health, of public order, of education, of the relief of the destitute, and of religion according to our view of it, represented by different, or possibly different, boundary lines on the map. Each of these boundaries indicates some common element of thought and feeling – some common interest – in the mind of the neighbourhood, and the difference of the boundaries, where they differ – the difference, e.g., between the civil and ecclesiastical parish – may have a long growth of ideas behind it. At any rate, all these are moral or physical needs, which, like our household necessities, draw us out of ourselves, and reveal us to ourselves as cases of a larger mind.

Every locality, then, is, however imperfectly and unconsciously, a body which has a mind. It is, as an idea which enters into us, the spiritual reflection of our adjacent surroundings, both human and natural, as the family is of our animal parentage. The neighbourhood is for the mind its immediate picture of the world, the frame into which its further vista of society as a whole must be fitted, or, in other words, its sphere of direct relations. The family is a group of natural relations; but the neigh-

---

[9]Settlement, scholarships, fellowships, and charities generally, "close" to localities, and perhaps domicile, maintain qualifications in contradiction with actual residence, and in case of allegiance even depending in part on birth. But some fixity is, of course convenient; and I believe that intention *plus* residence will cancel almost any opposing qualification.

bourhood consists of relations which are as natural in a different way, not through blood, but through contact. It is not a selection, but rather a specimen of life as a whole, for it must include as a rule *all* the necessary elements of the social fabric. It includes all that comes to us by direct sense-perception from day to day; all our chance meetings and dealings with those outside our household, and probably the nearer and more reliable illustrations of all social and political problems. For it is a context of life which we know and feel in its total working, which is impossible with what we only gather from writings or from hearsay.

As such a reflection of our direct surroundings, it colours our whole basis of feeling. A peculiar tinge of happiness, anxiety, depression, or resolution attaches to the streets or fields which we pass through day by day, and the faces which we meet. How far these feelings are true interpretations of what we see, and how far they spring from superficial or sentimental associations, is one of the greatest tests of the mind and heart. Do we see the body of a soul, the symbols of character and happiness, in the houses, the streets, the tillage, the workshops, or the gardens?

No other element of mind can be the substitute for the neighbourhood. It is the faith in which we live, so far as embodied in our contact with a sensuous world. It is a microcosm of humanity, in which, by the very indifference of space, we are liable to the direct impact of all possible factors. It is particularly the sphere of charity and courtesy, of the right behaviour in immediate human relations of all possible kinds.

The District or Neighbourhood, in short, as an ethical idea, is the unity of the region with which we are in sensuous contact, as the family is that of the world bound to us by blood or daily needs. Local self-government, for example, acquires a peculiar character from the possibilities of intimate knowledge of each other among those who carry it on. A man's whole way of living is in question when he sets up to be locally prominent, and though the result may often be corruption or vulgarity,[10] these are only the failure of what, at its best, is a true type of the relation of fellow-citizens.

---

[10] The recriminations or interested intimacies of a vestry or parish council rest at bottom on the personal knowledge which, rightly used, gives security to local life.

As with the family, we may illustrate the significance of Neighbour-hood by the case in which it fails to be duly recognised, and that in which nothing else is recognised.

To a great extent, in the life of modern cities, especially when supple-mented by suburban residence, the principle is disregarded. In a great city, the actual neighbourhood is more than can be dealt with, and has often no distinctive physical character – at least no attractiveness – and the idea of a special relation to it falls away. The fact, indeed, is less universal than is often asserted, and nearness in space, together with lo-cal government, retain and will retain, a certain predominance over the mind. The total disregard of an ethical purpose connecting us with the surroundings nearest to us in bodily presence, tends to deprive the gen-eral life of its vitality, its sensuous health, strength, and beauty. In many ways, circuitous perhaps, but ultimately effective, it may be that this factor of immediacy will regain a proper place in the national mind. We may observe that in as far as electoral districts are treated as mere cir-cumscriptions of such and such numbers of electors, the life of a neigh-bourhood is disregarded. To make the constituency a mere number (Hare's scheme) would be the climax of this tendency.[11]

---

[11]If, as I understand, it is the ideal of Proportional Representation to make the representa-tive assembly a reproduction in miniature of the electorate, I am convinced that its ideal is false. The electorate and the assembly have functions differing in kind. The function of the electorate is surely to decide on a policy in general, that of the assembly and the gov-ernment to work it out in detail. This distinction is destroyed if the elector is taught that his duty lies *not* in forming a judgment of policy, and deciding in favour of men whom he thinks trustworthy and capable to carry it out, *but* in collecting round him a group of per-sons who shared some special bias of his own, and returning a member like-minded with them. No one, probably, would support Hare's scheme to-day, with its total disregard of neighbourhoods. In large though limited electoral areas a representation of minorities is more plausible. But the whole idea is open to the criticism that it is tinkering the defects of a representation which threatens to become merely numerical, by a device which shares the defect. "Most of the plans for stopping the control of majorities look to all kinds of bolstering up of minorities." The vice in both is *the same. The New State*, [loc. cit., Introd. to 2nd edn, note 43] p. 146. [Thomas Hare (1806–1891) advocated a system of propor-tional representations which, as Bosanquet rightly points out, aims at an electoral outcome in which the strength of the parties in the legislature corresponds to their share of the popular vote. See Hare's *A Treatise on the Election of Representatives, Parliamentary and Municipal* (London: Longmans & Roberts, Brown, Green, 1859). John Stuart Mill

In the ancient City-state, on the other hand, the district was all power-ful. The State was almost a sensuous fact. The members of the State were essentially friends and neighbours, who for business or pleasure were meeting all day long. When the district thus absorbs the State, there is a want of what we call freedom, though there may be enough of sen-suous unconstraint. The State and its ideal purposes are not clearly set above all flesh and blood. A great legal system is not created till the State ceases to be a neighbourhood. Individual intimacy[12] and the "hard case" obscure the idea of universal law. The possibility of representative government, of a political faith which does not work by sight, is not conceived. The district, as a natural fact, was at first only a degree more liberating than the natural fact of kinship.[13] It was not conceived that man, as man, belonged "neither to this place nor to Jerusalem." With the ideal unity of a modern nation such conceptions harmonise much more readily, and the neighbourhood can lend them flesh and blood without hiding them.

5. "Class" is in democratic countries no longer a political institution. A man's vote is secured to him on a minimum qualification, and his practi-cal influence and acceptance depend neither on birth nor on occupation, but on the power which he can exercise by his qualities or his posses-

---

was a strong advocate of Hare's system. For an extended discussion by Mill, see his "Re-cent Writers on Reform" in *The Collected Works of John Stuart Mill*, ed., J.M. Robson (Toronto: University of Toronto Press, 1977), vol. XIX, pp. 341–70.]

[12] Imagine a Roman or English judge being addressed as Demosthenes, in his speech against Pantaenetus, addressed (in his client's name) the Athenian jury: "I know I have a hurried gait and a loud voice, and it annoys people; but I am as I was made, and I have a right to justice all the same." It sounds like a speech to a jury of schoolboys. ["Such as I, Pantaenetus, the fast walker, and such are you, who walk slowly. However, regarding my gait and my manner of speech, I will tell you the whole truth, men of the jury, with all frankness. I am perfectly aware – I am not blind to the fact – that I am not one of those fa-vored by nature in these respects, nor of those who are an advantage to themselves. For if in matters in which I reap no profit, I annoy others, surely I am to this extent unfortunate. But what is to come of it? If I lend money to so-and-so, am I for this reason also to lose my suit? Surely not." *Demosthenes against Pantaenetus* (Dem. 37.55–56) ed., Gregory R. Crane, The Perseus Project (http://www.perseus.tufts.edu), March 1998. Demosthenes (384–322 BC) was one of the great Athenian orators.]

[13] [See] above, p. 270.

sions. This is a consequence of the recognition of humanity as such, and has its bad side and its good side according to the baseness and nobility of the influences which tell de facto upon human nature. It is horrible, we may say, that influence should belong to wealth without any security whatever for a discharge of social function. But this, given human nature as it is to-day, is a result of the same causes which enable us to boast, with some truth, that a man ranks in the general world by his powers, character, and behaviour, and that we do not know or care whether his livelihood comes to him as a miner or as a duke. Wealth has weight because people give it weight; but no one need give weight to wealth in politics or social intercourse unless he likes. It is a consequence, then, of the recognition of free humanity that "class" no longer is an institution in political right as such, while in social intercourse, though it practically exists as an institution, it claims to be an expression of what people are in character and behaviour, and its differences are not annexed by any iron bond to differences of occupation.[14]

But though occupation no longer determines either social or political class, in the sense of graduation by any formal bond, yet it remains and must always remain a determinant of class in a narrower sense, and one of the main ideas which constitute the ethical structure of the mind.

The necessities which we compared roughly to time and space – the proximate permanent group and the adjacent locality – give a value to man's animal routine, and a significance to the area of his every-day perceptions. It is when the division of labour, the requital of one service by a different one, becomes prominent in a community, that a further grasp is laid upon the distinctive capacities of the individual consciousness, in which must be reckoned the surroundings which constitute its horizon of possibilities. We still answer the general question, "What is he?" by naming a man's industry or profession. The family and

---

[14]It may be taken as proved that a "gentleman" can make his living as a labourer or mechanic – at least in the U.S.A., where irrational tradition is weaker than in England – and remain a gentleman in the drawing-room sense of the term as well as in essentials. This being so, there can be no inherent impossibility in men born and bred as labourers or mechanics realising the same qualities. It would be cant, I think, to say that full equality of social class, full pleasantness and freedom of intercourse, could be attained without those qualities.

the neighbourhood sustain and colour the individual life, but the vocation stamps and moulds it. The more definite and articulate summons of the organising world – in which of course intelligence is active, ever discerning new purposes in old routine – elicits a deeper response from, or takes a more concrete shape in, the particular centre of consciousness. The individual has his own nature communicated to him as he is summoned to fit himself for rendering a distinctive service to the common good. He becomes "something"; an incarnation of a factor in the social idea.

The Roman word "class," which the English language has adopted, not for every separate employment, but for the character and position roughly connected with a whole group of employments, has an origin worth recalling. Plato's classes were "*genera*" = clans, extended families. The German classes were "*Stände*" = statuses, positions, estates (compare the French "*état*," which practically = trade). But the Roman "*classis*" was "a summoning" to public service; the first and second classes were the first and second summonings;[15] then indeed to military service in an order based on wealth. But the idea may survive. Our "class" may be thought of as the group or body in which we are called out for distinctive service.

One's class, then, in the sense in which it indicates the type of position and service involved in one's occupation, approaches very near the centre of one's individuality. In principle, as an ethical idea, it takes the man or woman beyond the family and the neighbourhood; and for the same reason takes him deeper into himself. He acquires in it a complex of qualities and capacities which put a special point upon the general need of making a livelihood for the support of his household. In principle, his individual service *is* the social mind, as it takes, in his consciousness, the shape demanded by the logic of the social whole. He is "a public worker,"[16] by doing the service which society demands of him. And just

---

[15][Theodor] Mommsen, *The History of Rome*, [trans., W.P. Dickson (London: R. Bentley & Son, 1894), vol.] I, [p.] 101, The "*classicus*" was the trumpet.

[16]Greek δημιουργός, "artisan." Homer speaks of "those who are public workers – the soothsayer, the doctor, and the carpenter." ["Who is likely to invite a stranger from a foreign country, unless it be one of those who can do public service as a seer, a healer of hurts, a carpenter, or a bard…?" Homer, *The Odyssey*, trans., Samuel Butler (Chicago:

because the service is in principle something particular, unique, and distinctive, he feels himself in it to be a member of a unity held together by differences. And in this sense the bond of social union is not in similarity, but in the highest degree of individuality or specialisation, the ultimate point of which would be to feel that I am rendering to society a service which is necessary, and which no one but me can render – the closest conceivable tie, and yet one which, in a sense, really exists in every case. Your special powers and functions supply my need, and my special powers and functions supply your need, and each of us recognises this and rejoices in it. This ethical idea of unique service, or the service of a unique class, involves of course a more or less conscious identity in difference. That is to say, the individual's mind is not reduced to his special service, or he would be a machine. Rather, the whole social consciousness is present in him, but present in a modified form, according to the point of view from which it is looking. The problem is simply put by Plato's diagrammatic scheme of classes. The statesman's function is to be wise for the community; the carpenter's to carpenter for the community. But plainly the community for which the statesman knows that he has to be wise, must include the carpenter's life and the conditions of his work, and the community for which the carpenter knows that he has to work must include some of the order and organisation which belong to it in the statesman's vision. The individual, in short, is unique, or belongs to a unique class, not as an atom, but as a case of a law, or term of a connection. This is what is meant by individuality in the true sense; the character of a unit which has a great deal that, being his very self, cannot be divided from him; not one which has so little that there is nothing by subtraction of which he can be imagined less. Such individuality is in a sense the whole ethical idea, but more particularly is embodied in the idea of a vocation. Our vocation, like our neighbourhood, and usually of course in connection with it, stamps both mind and body; and what we consider most intimately ourself is really the structure of ethical ideas which we are describing, with the feelings and habits in which they are rooted, but none of which are unmodified by them.

Encyclopedia Britannica, 1955), Book XVII.]

Like the other ideas of which we have spoken, the idea of class or specialised function may be illustrated both by the extreme in which it is nothing, and the extreme in which it is everything. The less a society is differentiated – the less that, considered as a mind, it has developed intense and determinate capacities – the more its structure repeats itself from household to household,[17] and fails to exhibit lines of formation pervading the community as a whole. Dicey's *The Peasant State*[18] gives an idea of a social mind thus undifferentiated, without classes, without ambitions, and without interests. Both in this case and in that of the Boers of the Transvaal it would be rash for an outsider to pronounce dogmatically on the value of the life which is achieved. But as cases of social formation and of social minds, they illustrate our present theme. To say that there is no specialised function, is the same as to say that there is no developed intelligence.

"Class" appears to be everything, an absolute and inflexible rule of precedence and privilege, when it has lost or has not gained the power of accommodating itself to function, and function to social logic. Such denials of free adjustment, of the career open to talents, may take the form of a confusion of the principle of class with that of birth, or even with that of private property. In the former case function and position are inherited, in the latter they are bought and sold. The two confusions may even be combined, as when public functions are inherited like or with a house or an estate.[19] Such a "class" system may be an oppression to its members,[20] or to the community, or to both. But the essence of the evil is that a function of mind is divorced from its characteristic of free logical adaptation within the social system. The institution has become ossified; and instead of moulding itself, like a theory or a living organism, to the facts and needs which it is there to meet, it nails itself to an alien

---

[17]Durkheim's "Segmentary Structure," *De la Division*, p. 190. [For an English translation, see *The Division of Labor in Society*, trans., W.D. Halls (New York: Free Press, 1984).]

[18][Edward Dicey, *The Peasant State. An Account of Bulgaria in 1894* (London: J. Murray, 1894).] See also H. Bosanquet, *Standard of Life*, [loc. cit., ch. x, note 32] p. 8.

[19]As in the judicial privileges of the Baron of Bradwardine and his likes. [The Baron of Bradwardine is a character in Sir Walter Scott's *Chronicles of the Canongate* (Edinburgh: Cadell, 1828).]

[20]The hereditary executioner in Maurus Jökai's novel, *Die schöne Michal*.

principle, and becomes a fallacy in social logic, or a dead organ in the social body.[21]

In both of these extreme cases individuality is minimised, In the former the individual does not pretend to any high capacity. In the latter he pretends to a considerable capacity, but this being cut apart from the principle of the whole, and pretending to be everything in itself – to exist absolutely or for its own sake – has lost the connection which gave it value, and becomes a mere pretension.

There is a strange and sad institution in which, it may be suggested, the two extremes of error are combined. This is the institution of "the poor" as a class, representing, as an ethical idea in the modern mind, a permanent object of compassion and self-sacrifice. "Poverty," it has been said, "has become a status." The "*déclassés*" have become a social class, with the passive social function of stimulating the goodness of others.[22] Let any one consider carefully, from the point of view which regards ethical ideas as an embodiment of human or social purposes, the offertory sentences of the Church of England. It is needless to press the criticism, for no one would be likely to deny that here we have ideas gathered from other soils and climates, and rightly applicable only in the spirit, but not in the letter. "Give alms of thy goods, and never turn thy face from any poor man; and then the face of the Lord shall not be turned away from thee." "He that hath pity upon the poor lendeth unto the Lord, and look, what he layeth out it shall be paid him again." The victims of misfortune in a small community, under strict regulations, as were the Jews, for the promotion of industry, are one thing. The recognition of a class marked by *the function of dependence* – to use a contradictory expression – in a vast community whose industrial organisation rests on the individual will, is another thing. The idea of pity and self-denial, inherited, I presume, largely from the Jewish scriptures as also from the New Testament, has tended, in the modern world, to become mechanical, and combine with a false class-conception. All who know

---

[21] [It should be stressed that for Bosanquet, logic "is merely the same as the impulse to the whole"; hence the reference here to "social logic" is not metaphorical. See his *Logic, or the Morphology of Knowledge* (Oxford: Clarendon Press, 1888; 2nd edn, 1911).]

[22] The incurably sick and helpless in all ranks of society do, no doubt, rightly fulfil such a passive function.

the inner life of evangelical Christians a generation ago[23] will admit that, among earnest persons of this type, the notion of the tithe – the devotion of one tenth or more of the income to purposes of religion or benevolence – had been inherited as a guiding idea, representing an end valuable *per se*, almost according to the letter of the offertory. I am not suggesting any vulgar charge of other-worldliness, but recalling a genuine conviction that the surrender of a portion of income to a less fortunate class of the community was in itself desirable and a religious duty.

It would not be difficult to show that the true and highest idea of Christian charity is remote from this conception of a dependent status as inherent in a certain portion of society. What seems to be needed here, as in so many aspects of morality and religion, is to combine the inspiration and *abandon* of the modern mind with the definiteness of purpose and lucidity of plan that characterised the ancient City-state.

Socialism, at its best,[24] unites with recent political economy and with those who try to "organise" or rationalise charity, in challenging the preconception that poverty must be recognised as a permanent class-function. And this brave denial may remain written to its credit when the controversies of immediate method are forgotten.

We may attempt to indicate in a few words the direction in which the ethical idea incarnate in the institution of the "poor" is tending to supplement and modify itself as clearer notions of a commonwealth arise. It may be observed, by way of introduction, that we cruelly misconceive the Greek mind when we ascribe to it a want of love and compassion, because we miss in its utterances the religious note of devotion to the

---

[23]Or for an earlier example see *Clarissa Harlowe*, [ch.] iii, [p.] 154. [In this reference to "the inner life of evangelical Christians," Bosanquet is alluding to the principal character in Samuel Richardson's (1689–1761) *Clarissa Or, The History of a Young Lady* (7 volumes, 1747–48). In this novel – reputed to be the longest in the English language – Clarissa Harlowe, a virtuous young woman, refuses to marry a man chosen by her family, and runs off with Robert Lovelace, a libertine. She comes to realise Lovelace's motives, and dies of grief and shame. The reference is most likely to a three volume abridgement of the novel, by E.S. Dallas (London: Tinsley Brothers, 1868).]

[24]I cannot think that in detail its advocates are consistent with their principles on this point. But controversy is not my object here. [See Bosanquet's essay on "The Antithesis Between Individualism and Socialism Philosophically Considered," in this volume, pp. 324–46.]

poor. To a great extent the truest idea of charity was presupposed in the very axioms of a Greek commonwealth. The Greek spoke little[25] of "the poor," because he recognised no such status.[26] It would have meant to him a functionless class, a dislocation of the body politic. This, in fact, is what it did mean when pauperism began to press upon the Greeks, and the philosopher[27] at once diagnoses the evil, and uses the term, "people without means," i.e. without ways of supporting themselves, instead of the older word, which rather suggests the "object of 'charity'." To get them back into a function, "a means," is the course which *ipso facto* rises before him; not to create a new ethical idea for their sake qua *déclassés*.

The full modern conception of the "poor" as an institution, if they must be an institution, ought at least to avoid the pitfall of acquiescence. Granting the fire and love of the Christian mind to be a gain, yet its object must be brought into relation with the true meaning of a mind or a commonwealth. Devotion to man at his weakest must not be separated from devotion to the possibilities of man at his strongest – possibilities

---

[25]Not altogether true, of course. In Homer "all strangers and poor men come from Zeus." ["To this you answered, O swineherd Eumaeus, 'Stranger, though a still poorer man should come here, it would not be right for me to insult him, for all strangers and beggars are from Jove'." *The Odyssey*, trans., Samuel Butler, loc. cit., note 16, Book XIV.]

[26]It is a mistake to treat all these problems as automatically solved for the ancients by slavery. The citizen population had enough dependence on industrial life to be liable to disaster from its dislocation, and that this happened so little was a true success while it lasted.

[27]Aristotle, *Politics*, 1320, b. 29. The older word is πτωχός, "one who crouches or cringes, a beggar"; it always had a bad sense till it was ennobled in the *Gospels* (Liddell and Scott). Aristotle's word is ἄπορος, "without ways and means." Different from both is πένης, for which we have no proper word, having spoilt "poor" by the idea of dependence. It means a poor man in the sense of one who is not rich enough to live without working. The speeches in which Poverty (πενία) defends her merits against Wealth, and in distinction from Beggary (πτώχεια), in Aristophanes' *Plutus*, are fine, though mixed with fallacies. [(1) Henry George Liddell (1811–1898) and Robert Scott (1811–1887) were known for their Greek-English lexicon. See, e.g. *A Lexicon abridged from Liddell and Scott's Greek-English Lexicon* (New York, Harper & Brothers, 1878). (2) Aristophanes (448–385 BC) was an Athenian playwright, considered to be one of the greatest writers of comedy. *Plutus* (388 BC) depicted the absurdity of the redistribution of wealth in Athens.]

either existent or at least symbolised in the most unhappy of the functionless poor. Self-sacrifice for the poor should not mean a tribute to the
maintenance of a vicious status, but an abiding and pervading sense of
the claims which the weaker humanity has to be made strong.

6. The Nation-state, we have already suggested, is the widest organisation which has the common experience necessary to found a common
life. This is why it is recognised as absolute in power over the individual, and as his representative and champion in the affairs of the world
outside. It is obvious that there can be but one such absolute power in
relation to any one person; and that, so far as the world is organised,
there must be one; and, in fact, his discharge from one allegiance can
only be effected by his acceptance of another. The analysis of the previous chapter releases us from the task of setting out the elements which
combine in the Nation-state, as the conception of sovercign and ultimate
adjustment between the spheres which realise the elements of our ethical
life. It should be noted, however, that the principles of the family, the
district, and the class, not only enter into the nation in these definite
shapes, but affect the general fabric of the national State through the
sense of race, of country, and of a pervading standard of life and culture.
The reaction of ideal unity on the natural conditions of a State is exem-
plified by the tendency to substitute ideal frontiers – a meridian or a parallel[28] – for frontiers determined by natural boundaries.

The Nation-state as an ethical idea is, then, a faith or a purpose – we
might say a mission, were not the word too narrow and too aggressive. It
seems to be less to its inhabitant than the City-state to its citizens; but
that is greatly because, as happens with the higher achievements of
mind, it includes too much to be readily apprehended. The modern nation is a history and a religion rather than a clear cut idea. Its power as
an idea-force is not known till it is tried. How little the outsider, and
even members of the community concerned, were able to gauge beforehand the strength of the sentiment and conception that pervaded the
United States through the war of secession.[29] The place of the idea of the

---

[28]See, e.g., the map of North America.

[29]The dangers besetting the French Republic to-day (December, 1898) are, in essence,
tests applied to the strength of a national idea. If the idea cannot maintain itself, we must

Nation-state in the whole of ethical ideas may be illustrated by the Greek conception of Happiness, as that organisation of aims, whatever it may be, which permits the fullest harmony to life. The State, as such, we saw, is limited to the office of maintaining the external conditions of a good life; but the conditions cannot be conceived without reference to the life for which they exist, and it is true, therefore, to say that the conception of the Nation-state involves at least an outline of the life to which, as a power, it is instrumental. The State, in short, cannot be understood apart from the nation, nor the conditions from the life, although in exerting political force it is important to distinguish them. As an ethical idea, the idea of a purpose, it is essential to hold the two sides together, if we are not to walk blindly.

7. Our analysis of the Nation-state suggests a point of view which may be applied to the vexed question of whether State action is to be judged by the same moral tests as private action.[30]

The first step is to get a clear idea of the nature of State action. It must be confined, one would think, to what is done in the name of the State, and by something approaching to an act of Will on its part as a State. We only pass moral judgment on individuals in respect of their acts of will, and we ought to extend the same justice to a State. The question is complicated by the fact that a State has, as its accredited agents, individuals whose acts it must normally avow. But it can hardly be saddled with moral responsibility for their personal misdoings, except under circumstances which are barely conceivable.[31] The State, as such, can have no ends but public ends; and in practice it has none but what its organs conceive to be public ends. If an agent, even under the order of his executive superior, commits a breach of morality, *bona fide* in order to what he conceives to be a public end desired by the State, he and his superior are certainly blamable, but the immorality can hardly be laid at the door of the public will.

---

reluctantly suppose that it ought not – that the common life has not the necessary depth. (The question seems to have answered itself. [Parenthetical comment added in] 1919.)

[30]See above, [Introd. to 2nd edn], p. 36. [Note added in] 1919.

[31]I.e., That it should actually order a theft, murder, or the like.

Indeed, a strict definition of State action might raise a difficulty like that of defining the General Will – if the act was immoral, can the State, *as such* really have willed it? And waiving this as a mere refinement, it still seems clear that the selfishness or sensuality, which has at least a good deal to do with the immorality of private actions, can hardly be present in an act of the public will, in the same sense as in a private volition. The State, as such, certainly cannot be guilty of personal immorality, and it is hard to see how it can commit theft or murder in the sense in which these are moral offences. To speak of the question as if it concerned the conduct of statesmen and their agents, instead of the volition of a State as such, seems to introduce confusion. We are discussing the parallel between public and private acts, and we are asked to begin by treating the public acts as private.[32]

It may be said that this distinction between public and private acts leads to the casuistry of pure intention. We are saying, it will be urged, that the State remains pure, because its will is on the whole towards a public interest, whatever crimes its agents may commit. And, no doubt, this line is often taken in practice. A successful agent finds his evil deeds are winked at; an unsuccessful one is disavowed. In either case the State pleads innocence. But this danger cannot alter the conditions of a moral action, and we cannot impute that as an action to the State, of which it knew no particulars, which it never willed, and which can hardly indeed be the object of a public will. It has a duty to see to the character of its agents and punish their excesses; but the conditions under which it is true that *qui facit per alium facit per se*,[33] can seldom apply to a public body with regard to actions of its agent which are not of a nature to embody public ends.

Promises and treaties, however, are acts which embody public ends. And here the State, on its side, is bound to maintain good faith; but still its agent is likely to go wrong if he mixes up the obligations of the State with his private honour. The question for him, if he has to keep or break

---

[32]See note on Sidgwick's essay, p. 37. [Note added in] 1919.

[33][*Qui facit per alium facit per se* – literally, "whatever a man does through another he does himself" – is the formula for the legal doctrine of vicarious liability. Here, Bosanquet is suggesting that the state is *not* necessarily liable in cases where its agents act for private ends.]

a public undertaking, is, to what is the State substantially bound, not to what extent would he be bound if he had made the promise or engagement in question in his private capacity? He, or the power which is to act, must consider the obligations and aims of the State, as a whole, and work for the best fulfilment of them as a whole. The question may be *parallel to* that of a private case of honour, but it is not *his* honour nor *his* promise that is in question. Just so, if he introduces his private conscience about religion or morality into his public acts on behalf of the State, he may cause frightful persecutions or disasters. The religious persecutions, and our position in India, supply examples.

The State, then, exists to promote good life, and what it does cannot be morally indifferent; but its actions cannot be identified with the deeds of its agents, or morally judged as private volitions are judged. Its acts proper are always public acts, and it cannot, as a State, act within the relations of private life in which organised morality exists. It has no determinate function in a larger community, but is itself the supreme community;[34] the guardian of a whole moral world, but not a factor within an organised moral world. Moral relations presuppose an organised life; but such a life is only within the State, not in relations between the State and other communities.

But all this, it may be urged, is beside the question. The question is not, can a State be a moral individual (though this is certainly one question)? but, does an interest of State justify what would otherwise be immorality or wrong-doing on the part of an officer of State?

Again, I think, we must distinguish between acts essentially private and acts essentially public. To steal or murder, to lie, or to commit personal immorality, for instance, as we said, cannot be a public act. Such acts cannot embody a general interest willed by the public will. A State agent who commits them in pursuit of information or to secure a diplomatic result cannot be justified on the ground that they are not his acts but the State's; and they are as immoral in him as in anyone else. Ulti-

---

[34]See pp. 40, 43 above on Sovereignty and the League of Nations. If the League becomes actual, the word "supreme" will become misleading as applied to the Nation-state, because it might indicate that there is nothing beyond. But its Sovereignty will not be diminished but intensified. A whole does not become less by growing, but greater. [Note added in] 1919.

mately, indeed, it may be true that there is no act which is incapable of justification, supposing some extreme alternative; and in this sense, but in this sense only, it might be that, treating the interest of a commonwealth like any other ethically imperative interest, such acts might be relatively capable of justification. But this justification would only mean that some supreme interest was subserved by them, and would have no special relation to the supposed public character of the interest. It is then a case of the conflict of duties. And the commoner occurrence, which results in doubtful acts, probably is that an agent, charged with some public service, finds it easiest to promote it by some act of rascality, and acts on his idea. But over readiness to make capital out of an apparent conflict of duties is neither made worse nor better by the fact that one of the duties is the service of the State.[35]

A public act which inflicts loss, such as war, confiscation, the repudiation of a debt, is wholly different from murder or theft. It is not the act of a private person. It is not a violation of law.[36] It can hardly be motived by private malice or cupidity in the strict sense, and it is not a breach of an established moral order by a being within it and dependent upon it for the organisation and protection of his daily life. It is the act of a supreme power, which has ultimate responsibility for protecting the form of life of which it is the guardian, and which is not itself protected by any scheme of functions or relations, such as prescribes a course for the reconciliation of rights and secures its effectiveness. The means adopted by such a supreme power to discharge its responsibilities as a whole, are of course subject to criticism as respects the conception of good which they imply and their appropriateness to the task of realising it. But it is mere confusion to apply to them names borrowed from

---

[35]Cruelty, it has been said, is a good deal owing to laziness. It is more comfortable to sit in the shade rubbing red pepper into a man's eyes to make him confess than to run about in the sun collecting evidence. I quote from memory, from a lecture, I think, by Mr Leslie Stephen. [Sir Leslie Stephen (1832–1904), brother of the famous conservative Sir James Stephen (1829–1894), was an author, biographer, critic and philosopher. He was noted in philosophy for his *The English Utilitarians* (London: Duckworth, 1900), and his effort to combine ethics and Darwinian theory.]

[36]An act which violates its own law is not an act of the State. And the State is not subject to the law of any other State.

analogous acts of individuals within communities, to impute them, as it were, to individuals under dyslogistic predicates, and to pass moral judgment upon them in the same sense as on private acts. The nearest approach which we can imagine to public immorality would be when the organs which act for the State, as such, exhibit in their public action, on its behalf, a narrow, selfish, or brutal[37] conception of the interests of the State as a whole, in which, so far as can be judged, public opinion at the time agrees. In such a case the State, as such, may really be said to be acting immorally, i.e. in contravention of its main duty to sustain the conditions of as much good life as possible. This case must be distinguished, if I am right, from the case in which the individuals, acting as the public authority, are corrupted in their own private interests[38] not shared with the public. For then the case would rather be that the State, the organ of the public good, had not been given a chance to speak, but had simply been defrauded by those who spoke in its name.

We do not suggest, then, that the action of States is beyond moral criticism, nor that action of individuals in their interest is above or below morality, except in the sense in which one moral claim has constantly to be postponed to another. But we deny that States can be treated as the actors in private immoralities which their agents permit themselves in the alleged interest of the State; or, again, can be bound by the private honour and conscience of such agents; and we deny, moreover, that the avowed public acts of sovereign powers which cause loss or injury, can be imputed to individuals under the names of private offences; that someone is guilty of murder when a country carries on war, or of theft when it adopts the policy of repudiation, confiscation, or annexation.

8. It is obvious that the idea of humanity, of the world of intelligent beings on the surface of our earth, conceived as a unity, must hold such a

---

[37] E.g. If, with the knowledge of Parliament, and without a protest from it, a price were offered for the killing of a hostile statesman or general, or a merciless system of exploitation were pursued in a dependent country. *In such a case the guilty State is judged before the tribunal of humanity and of history.* But it is judged as a State, that is, by the degree of its failure to cope with the duties of a State, all conditions considered. Nothing is gained by treating its action on the analogy of that of a private person. (I have here nothing to alter, except by italicising one sentence. [Parenthetical comment added in] 1919.)

[38] E.g. Bribed by a foreign potentate, or pursuing Stock Exchange interests.

place in any tolerably complete philosophical thinking, as in some way to control the idea of particular States, and to sum up the purposes and possibilities of human life.[39] The idea of humanity is universal, and whatever limits we have tacitly in mind – whatever limits the Greek thinker had in mind while he based his ethics on the distinction between man and beast – yet, when we rely on the idea of man as man, we are committed to treat in some way of the world of mankind.

(α) The first point which forces itself upon our attention is, that the idea which we tacitly entertain when we refer to humanity, is not true of the greater part of mankind. No doubt, we are quite aware of imperfection and inconsistency in the family and the State. But here, in the case of mankind, the problem reaches an acuter form. According to the current ideas of our civilisation, a great part of the lives which are being lived and have been lived by mankind are not lives worth living, in the sense of embodying qualities for which life seems valuable to us.[40] It is true that, in all to whom we give the name of man, we suppose a possibility of such living, in the sense that they have an intelligence distinguishable from that of animals. But it is a possibility which, for the most part, has been very slightly realised, and which involves no conscious connection, so far as we can see, with any realisation. Our idea of man is not formed by simple enumeration, but by framing a law which explains the less perfect and consistent facts with reference to the more perfect and more consistent facts.

(β) This being so, it seems to follow that the object of our ethical idea of humanity is not really mankind as a single community.[41] Putting aside the impossibilities arising from succession in time, we see that no such identical experience can be presupposed in all mankind as is necessary

---

[39] See above, pp. 43–44.

[40] This idea is embodied in the doctrine of Salvation confined to the few, and contains perhaps a similar error. But it has a prima facie truth.

[41] The points which I consider fundamental and to which I adhere in principle, in relation to the problem of a world-community, are two: (a) the necessity of a complete integration of differences, as illustrated by the problem of a universal language, p. 290; and (b) the necessity for a thoroughly coherent general will, as distinct from a superficial agreement based on a temporary coincidence of interests. I hope and trust we are in a way to see these realised. Cf. p. 44 [Note added in] 1919.

to effective membership of a common society and exercise of a general will. It does not follow from this that there can be no general recognition of the rights arising from the capacities for good life which belong to man as man. Though insufficient, as variously and imperfectly realised, to be the basis of an effective community, they may, as far as realised, be a common element or tissue of connection, running through the more concrete experience on which effective communities rest. Such a relation as that of England and India brings the matter home. Englishmen cannot make one effective self-governed community with the Indian populations. It would be misery and inefficiency to both sides. But our State can recognise the primary rights of humanity as determined in the life of its Indian subjects, and enforce or respect these rights, whether India be a dependency or an independent community. The problem is not unlike that raised by the idea of a universal language. As a substitute for national languages, it would mean a dead level of intelligence unsuited to every actual national mind, the destruction of literature and poetry. As an addition to existing languages, or more simply, if it became customary for every people to be acquainted with the tongues of other nations, there would be a common understanding no less firm, and a vast gain of appreciation and enjoyment, a levelling up instead of levelling down. The recognition of human rights through communities founded on organic unity of experience may be compared in just these terms to the idea of a universal society including the entire human race.

(γ) The contrast between humanity and mankind has always uttered itself through a dichotomous mode of expression – Jew and Gentile, Greek[42] and barbarian, Mussulman[43] and infidel, Christian and heathen, white civilisations and the black and yellow races. It will be noted at once that some of these divisions contradict each other, and this fact may suggest the probability that to every people its own life has seemed the crown of things, and the remainder of mankind only the remainder. Such

---

[42]It is remarkable that the limitation of the earth's surface, raising an idea of unity, has always, I believe, been presupposed. For the Greeks, Delphi was the centre of the earth; for us, the earth being a sphere and returning into itself, gives a certainty that it does not stretch away to infinity, so making unity of its inhabitants inconceivable. The remark, I think, is Kant's.

[43][Muslim.]

a suggestion may have a real bearing on our problem, and we will return to it. In the meantime, however, it is plain that humanity[44] as an ethical idea is a type or a problem rather than a fact. It means certain qualities, at once realised in what we take to be the crown of the race, and including a sensibility to the claims of the race as such. Sensibility to the claims of the race as such, is least of all qualities common to the race as such. The respect of States and individuals for humanity is then, after all, in its essence, a duty to maintain a type of life, not general, but the best we know, which we call the most human, and in accordance with it to recognise and deal with the rights of alien individuals and communities. This conception is opposed to the treatment of all individual human beings as members of an identical community having identical capacities and rights. It follows our general conviction that not numbers but qualities determine the value of life. But qualities, of course, become self-contradictory if they fail to meet the demands imposed on them by numbers.

And thus we recur to a suggestion noted above. Every people, as a rule, seems to find contentment in its own type of life. This cannot contradict, for us, the imperativeness of our own sense of the best. But it may make us cautious as to the general theory of progress, and ready to admit that one type of humanity cannot cover the whole ground of the possibilities of human nature. Our action must, no doubt, be guided by what we can understand of human needs, and this must depend ultimately on our own type of life. But it makes a difference whether we start from the hypothesis that our civilisation as such stands for the goal of progress, or admit that there is a necessity for covering the whole ground of human nature. And it may be that, as the ground is covered, our States may go the way which others have gone, without, however, leaving things as they are. If the State, moreover, is not ultimate nor above criticism, no more is any given idea of humanity; and reference to "the interests of mankind" only names the problem, which is to find out what those interests are, in terms of human qualities to be realised.

---

[44]"Humanity" = "humaneness." Scotch "Humanity" = Latin. Oxford "Literae humaniores" = classics and philosophy. Greek φιλάνθρωπον, a sense of what is due to man, e.g. of poetical justice.

(δ) Neither the State, however, nor the idea of humanity, nor the interests of mankind, are the last word of theory. And even political theory must so far point ahead as to show that it knows where to look for its continuation.[45] We have taken Society and the State throughout to have their value in the human capacities which they are the means of realising, in which realisation their social aspect is an inevitable condition (for human nature is not complete in solitude), but is not by itself, in its form of multitudes, the end. There is, therefore, no breach of continuity when the immediate participation of numbers, the direct moulding of life by the claims and relations of selves, falls away, and the human mind, consolidated and sustained by society, goes further on its path in removing contradictions and shaping its world and itself into unity. Art, philosophy, and religion, though in a sense the very life-blood of society, are not and could not be directly fashioned to meet the needs and uses of the multitude, and their aim is not *in that sense* "social." They should rather be regarded as a continuation, within and founded upon the commonwealth, of the work which the commonwealth begins in realising human nature; as fuller utterances of the same universal self which the "general will" reveals in more precarious forms; and as in the same sense implicit in the consciousness of all, being an inheritance which is theirs so far as they can take possession of it.

We have thus attempted to trace in outline the content of the self, implied, but imperfectly and variously reached, in the actual individual consciousness. It is because of this implication, carrying the sense that something more than we are is imperative upon us, that self-government has a meaning, and that freedom – the non-obstruction of capacities – is to be found in a system which lays burdens on the untamed self and "forces us to be free." What we feel as mere force cannot as such be freedom; but in our subtle and complex natures the recognition of a force may, as we have tried to explain, sustain, regularise, and reawaken the operation of a consciousness of good, which we rejoice to see maintained, if our intelligence fails of itself to maintain it, against indolence,

---

[45] See above, pp. 45–46.

incompetence, and rebellion, even if they are our own. This is the root of self-government, and true political government is self-government.

RELATED ESSAYS

THE ORGANISATION OF INTELLIGENCE[1]

Editors' Introduction:

Fundamental to Bosanquet's political philosophy is the idea of the general will; *The Notion of a General Will* and a large part of the *Philosophical Theory of the State* are devoted to articulating this concept. One of the distinctive features of Bosanquet's approach is his attempt to provide psychological grounding for a general will – especially the crucial chapter vii of the *Philosophical Theory of the State*. The foundation of this attempt is the theory of appercipient masses – dominant ideas that organise the mind. When people have "the same or correlative" dominant ideas, he argues in this excerpt, they form a common mind and general will. This lecture from the *Psychology of the Moral Self* represents Bosanquet's most thorough analysis of his notion of an appercipient mass and its relation to similar ideas of other psychologists.

1. The central point of our last lecture was the development of cognition as it takes place in the formation of groups within the psychical continuum. In this lecture we shall consider the names given to different aspects of the processes by which these groups are formed and react upon one another in such a way as to develop thought. We shall find that these processes fall under two main heads, Blending and Reproduction. The aspects known as Assimilation, Discrimination, and Apperception belong chiefly to Blending; while Association belongs to Reproduction. (The subject of *attention* is too wide to be dealt with here. It may be regarded either as a general name for the laws according to which presentation takes place, or in a more special sense for volition.)
2. Assimilation and Discrimination are generally treated as correlative processes, both employed in the "elaboration of mind,"[2] but of an oppo-

---

[1] [This essay is Lecture IV of Bosanquet's *Psychology of the Moral Self* (London: Macmillan, 1897). It has been slightly edited here.]

[2] See [James] Sully, [*The*] *Human Mind* [: *A Text-book of Psychology* (London: Long-

site tendency. The fact is, that apart from the theory of identity,[3] their relation is very hard to state. Generally speaking, they are regarded as alternating, first a little of one and then a little of the other; and according as psychologists have a preference for one or the other, that one is represented as being of primary importance, and preceding the other.[4] We seem to get nearer the truth if we regard them both as different aspects of one and the same process. Certainly we can hardly describe the one without implying the other.

(α) Assimilation is *elementary recognition*,[5] the mere *perceiving* as like; that is to say, it is recognition unaccompanied by any process of localisation, or of conscious comparison. In this sense it is recognition in its earlier stages, or the germ of recognition.[6] The process is something like this: a change in the presentation continuum such as has taken place before, recurs; in recurring, it coalesces with the residuum of its former occurrence, and it thus appears as familiar; i.e. it is recognised as a previous experience, even though the circumstances of its former occurrence cannot be reproduced.

Why does the recurrence of a change make it seem familiar? The mere reinforcement by the residuum of a previous change may make the impression stronger or clearer than it would otherwise have been, but there seems to be no reason why it should give rise to a feeling of familiarity, the *consciousness* that it has been there before. This must probably be due to a *suggestion of difference*. The change itself has occurred before, but under different circumstances, and therefore with different psychical

---

mans, Green, 1892)] ch. vii.

[3]See [*Psychology of the Moral Self,*] Lecture II.

[4]See Sully, *Human Mind*, loc. cit., [note 2].

[5]See Ward, "Psychology," *Encyclopaedia Britannica*, 9th edn, vol. XX (1886): 37–85. [James Ward (1843–1925) was a personalist idealist philosopher, author of *Psychological Principles* and a founder of *the British Journal of Psychology*. Ward's *Encyclopedia Britannica* article was generally regarded as a decisive refutation of Alexander Bain's "associationist psychology."]

[6]I do not feel sure whether the note of familiarity, of "I have seen that before," which marks assimilation *par excellence*, is present in all perception in an appreciable degree, except when there is distinct unfamiliarity. In returning to one's own house or room it is certainly there. But the interest of a positive perception – the "what is it?" – often dwarfs the "seen before."

accompaniments. As the new content blends with the residuum of the old, two different contexts, the present and the past, are brought together, and we are aware – more or less consciously – of the same content in different settings. This is what constitutes familiarity. The process is thus a twofold one; the blending of new and old brings to light, or at any rate suggests, difference, and at the same time the element of identity is reinforced. For instance, I am looking for a street, but have forgotten its name. Suddenly I come upon it, and recognise it; i.e. in the first place I *notice* the name; I pick it out from amongst all the others because it is emphasised by blending with the subconscious residuum. But this by itself is not enough. I might notice it because it was written in larger letters, and so emphasised above the others; and mere noticing is not recognition. But as I notice the name it also faintly suggests the past context in which it was presented, and which differed in some respects from the present; thus a difference, a vague vista of continuity reaching beyond the given context, is suggested, and the feeling of familiarity appears; the feeling of, as it were, comparing the presentation with itself and finding it the same.

Strictly speaking, to assimilate would more naturally mean to *make* like, than to recognise as being like. Wundt[7] brings this out clearly by insisting on the way in which we are apt to transfer the different context of our present perception to the previous one to which it is assimilated, or vice versa, of the previous perception to the present one. This may be done to a degree which actually amounts to illusion; our preconceived idea actually modifies the presentation as we receive it. He gives as an instance the illusion produced by the rough daubs of the scene-painter, which are supplemented by, or assimilated to, our former experience of landscapes, and so endowed with the qualities of reality. It is, no doubt,

---

[7][Wilhelm Wundt (1832–1920), famous as a psychologist, was Professor of Philosophy at Leipzig. As Wundt understood it, psychology concerned the analysis of consciousness into elements, and the laws regulating the connections between these elements. His work was chiefly focussed on the senses, especially vision, touch and the perception of time. He is known as a proponent of the introspection method of psychology, and with the founding of the first psychology laboratory in Leipzig in 1879. He was a prolific author; see e.g., his *Outlines of Psychology* (New York: G. E. Stechert, 1897).]

a question how far there is an illusion by means of the transference of differences, and how far the presentation does actually undergo change.

Why do the groups of presentations within the psychical continuum form as they do? Why, that is, do not colours group with colours, smells with smells, and touches with touches; instead of feel and colour and smell combining, together in one group as one thing? One reason, no doubt, is that Association does not take place – as it has so often been said to do – by similarity.[8]

But the chief reason is, that the groups, in the first place, are *given* in this way, and in the second, *act* (i.e. are interesting for us) in these combinations. Sensations of the same sense, such as two colours or two sounds, tend to exclude each other. It is sensations of different senses that can most naturally be presented together, and when the group has been formed the one sensation becomes a sign of the others. Groups which constantly cohere in this way come to be assimilated (recognised) as wholes which affect us, and are therefore discriminated from the background because of their importance for life, before their elements are *separately* assimilated and recognised as qualities. In science, that is when we begin to reflect upon them, we do arrange our sensations in qualitative series; we disengage them, that is, from the groups in which they are originally given, and re-group them according to their kind.

(β) This leads us to *Discrimination*. Here we may note some points in James's chapter on Discrimination.[9] In the first place the elements to be discriminated must, as he says, *be* different if we are to know them as different. But difference does not of itself make discrimination. Two different elements may be presented without the difference being noticed; this corresponds to an unassimilated presentation. As James points out, impressions, to be discriminated, must be *experienced separately* by the mind. But here we must be careful to define what we mean by *separately;* an isolated impression is never experienced. The point is, that any element, before it can be discriminated, must be presented in different surroundings or in a different *context.* Further, the elements to be discriminated must have a common basis. Take as an instance "good-

---

[8]See Ward, loc. cit., note 5, p. 56.
[9][William James,] *Text-book* [*of Psychology* (London: Macmillan, 1892)], p. 244.

ness" and "two o'clock." Each is itself, the two are, quite different, but there is neither assimilation nor discrimination between them; there is no psychical relation at all. We cannot have discrimination, i.e. felt or perceived difference, without a fight on the basis of identity, without having the *same* content in different contexts,[10] and this begins with assimilation. The very sense of familiarity has the germ of difference in it, of persistence through two contexts.

Using a formula, we may say, A is given in two contexts, AB and AC; when it is presented again it suggests both B and C, which must conflict until they find a *modus vivendi.*[11] This *modus vivendi* is a relation of difference.

> When a red ivory ball, seen for the first time, has been withdrawn, it will leave a mental representation of itself, in which all that it simultaneously gave us will indistinguishably co-exist. Let a white ball succeed to it; now, and not before, will an attribute detach itself, and the *colour,* by force of contrast, be shaken out into the foreground. Let the white ball be replaced by an egg, and this new difference will bring the *forms* into notice from its previous slumber, and thus, that which began by being simply an object cut out from the surrounding scene becomes for us first a red object, then a *red round* object, and so on.[12]

Or we may take as another instance a tree as it appears with its leaves off, and again with its leaves on; here what is needed to make us recognise it as the *same* tree under different conditions is the relation of time-difference, with all that it involves. But quite at first no definite relation is perceived; there is simply a feeling of familiarity, of persistence; a feeling, that is, of a former context accompanying assimilation.

3. *Apperception* – James deals with this term in a short section in his chapter on Perception, and explains that he has not used it because of the very different meanings which have at various times attached to it. It is a word with an eventful history, and played a great part in Kant's system.

---

[10]See last lecture [Lecture III, *Psychology of the Moral Self*].

[11][*modus vivendi*: a temporary working arrangement or compromise.]

[12]Martineau in James, [*Text-book of Psychology*], loc. cit., note 9. [James Martineau (1805–1900) was a Unitarian theologian, philosopher and psychologist. One of his famous psychological writings was the 1860 article on "Cerebral Psychology: Bain" in the *National Review*.]

We may perhaps say that what it meant for Kant was the modification produced in the matter of perception owing to the nature of the perceiving mind. This is an attempt to do what has since been done more fully – to insist, that is, upon the activity of the mind in perception, and to explain the nature of that activity. In this explanation the chief danger to be avoided is that of representing Apperception as some kind of innate faculty, in a sense approaching that of the old faculty-psychology. For its modern or Herbartian[13] meaning we may take Mr Stout's definition of Apperception as "the process by which a mental system appropriates a new element, or otherwise receives a fresh determination."[14] It is one case of blending, sometimes leading to the reproduction of a former context; but the term has special reference to the modifications which are produced in the new element by its incorporation with the old. In this respect it is not unlike Wundt's assimilation. It is important to remark that the old element itself may, or indeed *must,* be modified in the process. We cannot treat the old elements, the "apperceiving mass," as being entirely active, while the new element is entirely passive, and merely allows itself to be appropriated without exercising any influence on its appropriator. On this point James quotes from Steinthal as follows:

> Although the *a priori* moment commonly shows itself to be the more powerful, Apperception-processes can perfectly well occur in which the new observation transforms or enriches the apperceiving group of ideas. A child who hitherto has seen none but four-cornered tables apperceives a round one as a table, but by this the apperceiving mass ("table") is en-

---

[13][Johann Friedrich Herbart (1776–1841) was greatly influenced by Kant; however his most well-known contribution – the notion of "apperception" – can be traced to the influence of Leibniz. Some have traced the idea of apperception all the way back to Alhazen (approx. 965–1039). See Herbart's *A Text-book in Psychology; An Attempt to Found the Science of Psychology on Experience, Metaphysics, and Mathematics*, Margaret K. Smith, trans. (New York: D. Appleton, 1891).]

[14][George Frederick] Stout, *Analytic Psychology* [(London: S. Sonnenschein, 1896): "In extreme enfeeblement of attention, such as we find in typical cases of hysteria, in which continuity of thought is almost abolished, there is a marked inability to acquire new combinations of ideas and new modes of action. Attention considered from this point of view, as a process of mental growth, or, at least, of mental adjustment to conditions not perfectly familiar, is called apperception, and the performed systems which take part in it are called apperceptive systems." Pp. 185–86.]

riched. To his previous knowledge of tables comes this new feature, that they need not be four-cornered, but may be round.[15]

In this way the doctrine connects with that of Connotation and Denotation, illustrating the defectiveness of the view according to which they vary inversely; by adding to the kinds of things *de*noted by a term, the child adds also to the qualities *con*noted by it.

This influence of the mind upon perception, which constitutes what is known as apperception, is capable of infinite illustration. The child who called a fern a "pot of green feathers" interpreted the novel object by an acquired disposition; he saw what he had seen before, not what the country child would see.[16] The different perceptions which different people will have of the same object can only be explained by the contents of their minds, which have interpreted the perception differently in each case.

On a particular occasion during the recent visit of the Empress of Germany to London it became the duty of the reporters of the public journals to describe Her Imperial Majesty's dress. *The Times* stated that the Empress was in "gold brocade," while according to the *Daily News* she wore a "sumptuous white silk dress." *The Standard,* however, took another view – "The Empress wore something which we trust it is not vulgar to call light mauve." On the other hand, the *Daily Chronicle* was hardly in accord with any of the others – "To us it seemed almost a sea-green, and yet there was now a cream and now an ivory sheen to it."[17]

---

[15] [James, *Text-book of Psychology*, loc. cit., note 9. Heymann Steinthal (1823–1899) was known for his *Volkerpsychologie* – the psyche of the people.]

[16] [The reference here is to Thomas Godolphin Rooper (1847–1903), "The pot of green feathers," *School and Home Life. Essays and Lectures on Current Educational Topics* (London: Brown, 1896), pp. 39–80: "I was listening to an object-lesson given to a class of very young children by a pupil-teacher, who chose for her subject a pot of beautiful fresh green ferns. She began by holding up the plant before the class, and asking whether any child could say what it was. At first no child answered, but presently a little girl said, "It is a pot of green feathers.". . . I fell thinking on the matter. Did the child really suppose that the ferns were feathers? Or did she rather use the name of a familiar thing to describe what she knew to be different, and yet noticed to be in some respects like?"]

[17] Quoted from *Globe*, in Rooper on "Object-teaching [:or, Words and Things," in *School and Home Life*, loc. cit., pp. 81–121.]

It is the old truth that "the eye can only see what it brings with it the power of seeing," expanded into a whole theory of mind. It may be illustrated in a wider way from the varying conceptions of history; our "histories" are the offspring of our current interests.

The psychical elements which form the contents of the mind are so grouped and interconnected as to constitute what are technically known as Appercipient masses or systems. M. Paulhan[18] compares this mental grouping to the organisation within a commonwealth. Some of the systems may be very simple, while others are very complex; the simpler ones will be generally subordinate to the complex ones, and throughout there will be more or less interaction. Systems may compete with each other, they may also co-operate. They will compete when, and in so far as, they tend to exclude each other from contact with a given presentation; difficulties in classifying any new object or "specimen" will be due to this rivalry between appercipient systems, or indecision as to which of two interests we will sacrifice. On the other hand they will co-operate in so far as they excite each other by some coherence between them. A system is strengthened in competition by the number of cooperating systems which are excited, so to say, *on its side*. By their adherence it gains in weight and interest, and gradually drives its rival from the field. Appercipient masses are the ideas which are more or less dominant *pro tem*,[19] and they will vary in prominence according to the interest before the mind, whether this interest be internally or externally originated. They "rise to the occasion."

Generic ideas are in this sense appercipient masses. By blending they reinforce that element of the presentation which has a common content, and the other elements which they do not share are thrust out of sight, unless some other appercipient mass is awakened to receive them.

As an instance of the way in which the dominant mass determines *what* content shall hold the field, we may note the effect of *context* in determining the interpretation we put upon words. The word "secular"

---

[18] In Stout, loc cit., note 14. Vol. II, p. 116. [Frédéric Paulhan (1856–1931). For one of his few works translated into English, see *The Laws of Feeling* (*Les phénomènes affectifs et les lois de leur apparition*) trans. C.K. Ogden, (London: Kegan, Paul & Co.: London, 1930).]

[19] [*pro tem* (abbreviation of *pro tempore*): temporarily.]

has two meanings; and if it stands in isolation, there is no way of deciding what meaning is to be attached to it; probably the most common one will be suggested. But in reading the line "Through all the secular to be,"[20] the force of the context is so strong as not only to determine the meaning, but in some cases as to exclude even the suggestion of the alternative. The same is true of all words in so far as they are found in a living context, and not in the isolation of the spelling-book.

Not only may the systems of appercipient masses, be *compared* to organisations of persons; they actually constitute their common mind and will. To say that certain persons have common interests means that in this or that respect their minds are similarly or correlatively organised, that they will react in the same or correlative ways upon given presentations. It is this identity of mental organisation which is the psychological justification for the doctrine of the General Will.

Passing from Apperception we come to Association. In philosophical interest it is subordinate to apperception, which is almost equivalent to the organised working of the mind, and this carries us to the higher stages of conscious life; but as the *machinery* of the mind Association is fundamental. The doctrine really dates from Plato.[21] His point is to bring the whole process of knowledge under the law of reproduction, in order to establish his ἀνάμνησις it is the recovery by Association of mental possessions which we have lost. For him the process of reproduction is the same as that of knowledge. All given presentations act by suggestion, and therefore come under come under the general head of reproduction. In *Phaedo*, 76 [a], he clearly indicates cases of association by contiguity and resemblance.

> For we say that this was possible: that when perceiving something, whether by sight or hearing or any other kind of sense, one may, from this perception get a suggestion of something else which one had forgotten, to

---

[20][From Tennyson, *In Memoriam*, XLI:
  I shall be thy mate no more,
  ..Tho' following with an upward mind
  ..The wonders that have come to thee,
  ..Thro' all the secular to-be.]

[21]*Phaedo*, 73[d-74d].

which the first mentioned was contiguous, though unlike, or to which it was like.

Aristotle, again, suggests as the laws of Association – Resemblance, Contrast, Co-existence, and Succession, or, combining the last two, Contiguity.[22]

Contrast is now admitted to be a case of contiguity, and similarity remains as the great recent crux.[23] It is a difficulty of principle. Similarity only exists when two ideas are before the mind, and therefore it cannot be used to reproduce one of those two. Moreover, it is only needed as an explanation if we regard images as simple; if we admit that they are all complex, it can be reduced to contiguity.[24] The given elements *abc* reproduce their former context by continuity, and that former context persists and is compared with the given object. Take the case of the portrait, which Plato uses;[25] the portrait consists of elements *abcde*, the idea of the actual Person consists of elements *abcfg*. The identical *abc* suggests *fg*, with which it is contiguous in the other context, and then the portrait is compared with the idea of the actual person.

James points out[26] that there is no tendency to this recall by similarity amongst *simple* ideas; it is only where complex ideas have an identical element that we find it. In what he calls "focalised recall," the active element, after awakening its new set of associates, *continues persistently active* along with them; that is, it is an element identical in the two ideas.

Contiguity – It is no doubt an improvement to reduce association to contiguity, as Ward and James have done; but the question of the elements *between which* the contiguity or connection operates still remains. The principle that Association marries only universals has been discussed in dealing with Psychological Atomism.[27] When the identical

---

[22][See Aristotle, *On Memory and Reminsicene* (*De Memoria et Reminiscentia*) J. Beare, trans. and *On the Soul* (*De Anima*) Book III, trans., J.A. Smith, both in *The Basic Works of Aristotle*, ed. Richard McKeon (New York: Random House, 1941).]

[23]See [F.H.] Bradley, [*Principles of*] *Logic* [(Oxford: Oxford University Press, 1883)] and Ward, [loc. cit., note 5].

[24]See Lecture II [*Psychology of the Moral Self*].

[25] [*Phaedo*, 73^d.]

[26]James, *Text-book*, [loc. cit., note 9] p. 270.

[27][See above, ch. vii, *The Philosophical Theory of the State*.]

element in operation has a number of associates, what determines which will be recalled?[28] It resolves itself into a question of apperception; those associates which are in connection with the dominant appercipient system will be introduced, while others will be neglected.

The nature of identity is at the root of the question. We might represent it by a forked line Y; two lines having an identical part. Certainly it is not singularity,[29] for this excludes difference. The way in which the whole question of Atomism is here involved may be brought out by asking ourselves in what our ideal of knowledge consists. Is it "A is A," the mere repetition of the same concept? or is it "man is animal," the connection of two concepts by an element common to both?

The distinction has been drawn between material and individual identity, but perhaps it is not an ultimate one. Individual identity is one of content, in which we may treat a new beginning as constituting an essential difference or not, according to its laws of change. If interruption in time is to be regarded as fatal to individual identity, what becomes of the identity of my mind, with its periodical lapses? or, of the House of Commons as an element in the British Constitution?

To sum up: All cognition is Identity asserting itself.

---

[28]See James, *Text-book*, [loc. cit., note 9], p. 264; Bradley, *Principles of Logic* [loc. cit., note 23].

[29]See Ward, [loc. cit., note 5.], p. 81.

THE NOTION OF A GENERAL WILL[1]

Editors' Introduction:

In this essay, Bosanquet replies to C.D. Broad's criticisms concerning the meaningfulness of the concept of the general will. Broad claimed that nothing could be appropriately called by this name, and that the closest approximation of this concept was, simply, all those propositions which members of a community believed in or believed to be true – e.g., "that everyone who will work should have a certain minimum of comfort." But this, Broad argued, has no explanatory force and would not be sufficient to establish a state. The real "will" in a state, Broad concluded, is "the will of the governing class." Bosanquet uses Broad's examples to reply that one's volitions and one's "standing will" must be supported by other wills and, therefore, by a general will that is reflected in the law and the community. Individuals "share" in, and will, this "general will" in that they take it for granted in acting.[2]

I recognise the courteous tone of Prof. Broad's rejoinder in the October *Mind*, and I will try to meet his criticism by my explanation.[3] But I still maintain that the matter is sufficiently explained in my book, and better than I can explain it in a single paper.

I think that the root of disagreement between us is plain. I hold that my will, and any others which mine implies, or which imply mine, form a

---

[1] [In a review for *Mind* (27 [1918]: 369–70) Broad criticised Bosanquet's notion of the general will as expressed in "The Function of the State in Promoting the Unity of Mankind," *Proceedings of the Aristotelian Society* XVII (1916–17): 28–57; Bosanquet replied in "The State and the Individual," *Mind* 28 (1919): 74–77; Broad then published a rejoinder entitled "The Notion of a General Will," *Mind* 28 (1919): 502–4; this essay is Bosanquet's reply to that rejoinder. It was published in *Mind* 29 (1920): 77–81.]

[2] [For a more recent attempt at articulating this notion in the light of Broad's criticisms, see Bernard Mayo, "Is There a Case for the General Will?" in *Philosophy, Politics and Society*, first series, ed., Peter Laslett (Oxford: Basil Blackwell, 1956), pp. 92–97.]

[3] [C.D. Broad (1887–1971) lectured at St. Andrews, Dundee and Bristol (1920–22), and Cambridge (1922–1953). He was Knightbridge Professor of Moral Philosophy at Cambridge from 1933 to 1953.]

system which is general as against my will taken by itself. Prof. Broad does not admit that several wills can be the same, i.e., can form *a* general will as compared with any one of them, unless they all consciously and explicitly will that the same propositions shall be true. He would not permit the use of such ideas as that I will what is implied in my will, or that my will is a particular within the system formed by other wills which imply it and are implied in it, as conditions *sine quibus non*[4] of the truth of the propositions which it wills to be true. Just in a single reference, where by exception he asserts the reality of a will which is a system willed as a whole, he seems to give me a handle for an argument from his premisses.

For he describes Smith, stockbroker of Brighton, as possessing a system of connected volitions, which has organising principles in it. This is contrasted with Smith's various wants, and his efforts at various times to satisfy them, which are events in his history. I should call the system a standing will. I cannot spend space on Prof. Broad's suggestion of a way in which I might get, out of these facts, a contrast of a private and a general will. My point, so far, is simpler and less ambitious. I do not call Smith's will general as compared with particular in virtue of the contrast between the system of connected volitions and the various sporadic wants. This is not a case of a particular will compared with a unity of many such wills; though it has features analogous to such a relation. But I do draw attention to the point that the various wants are severally "abstract and fragmentary" as compared with the standing will. Imagine Smith's plans and ideas which form his standing will, and then think of such a volition as that of going up to town by train on a given morning. Is it not plain that the latter becomes a meaningless fragment if you strike out what he is planning to do? Certainly it is fragmentary, and I should say abstract as well, but that may be a verbal question.

Yet even here, before I go further, even at the level of Smith's various wants, I must point out that in the instance I happen to have taken, if we argue strictly, a general will, at least relative, is implied. How can Smith will to go to town by train without willing the existence of the railway, the truth, that is, of thousands of propositions, the objects of other wills

---

[4][*sine quibus non*: without which not.]

than his own, which must be true if it is to be possible for him to go to town by train? Obviously his will to go to town, if we are to be pedantically strict, involves the existence of thousands of other particular wills, which are to his as one general will to a particular within it, in the sense that they are directed to objects indispensable to the accomplishment of such volitions as his, while such volitions as his, in turn, are essential to the accomplishment of such objects as theirs. And this though none of the parties concerned may know of each other's individual existence.

But we may waive this argument. It may be said that it is artificial to treat a casual volition as directed to the conditions implied in it. If you take a cab, does your will imply a common element with the will of the cabman? A cab strike perhaps throws light on this question. But I need not insist on it.

I return to the standing will. By introducing this idea Prof. Broad has come a long way to meet me. When the standing will is granted to be real, it is difficult to deny the general will.

For such a system of connected volitions, bound together by organising principles, which, I take it, are considered to be willed more or less explicitly, is *ex hypothesi* comprehensive, and involves the planning of an entire individual life. Now this quite inevitably involves an immense system of implications, consisting in the operations of other private wills, whose objects are implied in those of the standing will first considered, and also imply them. We cannot say in such a case that the agreement between all the particular wills is only in a few abstract propositions, while their main bulk as private wills is unaffected by it. For we have accepted the conception of the whole private will in each case as a will connected throughout, and expressing principles which pervade it, more or less reflectively. It is quite inconceivable that such a system of connected volitions, at every turn implying and implied in other similar systems, should not form together with them a single inclusive system bound together by the nature of the propositions, not all identical, but necessary to one another's truth, which all the particular wills desire to be true. I confess this seems to me too obvious for argument. The man's plans and principles all depend upon the support of other wills, and, apart from such agreement, there is no feature of his life which he could possibly hope to realise. And his organising principles, by which he directs his whole life as a member of a community; they need not, certainly, be word for word the same as those sustained by other wills; but if communal life is to be carried on, they must support and be supported by those willed by others.

It seems to me, then, to be clear, that the standing wills of individuals must enter into a system which forms the standing will of the community. But because of the limitations which make each will a private will, limitations of our personal knowledge, character, and interest, each personal will is related to the whole body of wills as a particular element to a general system which includes it. The whole general will is explicit only in all the wills taken together. Each private will stops at a certain point, and, for what is beyond that, wills the whole by implication, or, so to speak, diagrammatically. I gave as examples of this before my own will for the restitution of certain provinces by Germany to France, and in favour of the League of Nations. My will to each of these objects is diagrammatic; it implies a concrete filling which it cannot supply, but which is present in the whole set of wills bearing on the subject taken together.

The question, then, how far the private will of a member of a community is an element within a general will of that community is ultimately the question how far you must be said to will what is implied in your will. It is a kind of question in which interpretations of fact are very likely to vary, and in which the actual facts are very hard to handle, owing to their enormous complexity and their perpetual movement. The reading which Prof. Broad affirms in his final paragraph seems to me, I confess, like the judgement of a looker-on who is not much interested in the game. But I quite admit that an extremist "evacuating interpretation" is a useful *terminus a quo*[5] to work from in such discussions.

In opposition to this minimising interpretation I will make four suggestions, two in the way of removing hindrances to a more appreciative interpretation, as I consider it, of the common element in wills; and two alleging positive grounds for it.

1. There is no difficulty about willing subject to reservation. Many a man swears daily at the defects of his own house; but he wills to live in

---

[5][*terminus a quo*: starting point.]

it as it is if he cannot cure them or get a better. We must not confuse what we will with what we should like. They are hardly ever the same. The point of this for the present purpose is that you must not reduce the agreement of wills to the residuum in which no distinctions survive. That is the old bad business of excluding from the generic concept all properties which are differently developed in the species. A socialist, and a non-socialist liberal, do not necessarily differ in their will for the immediate treatment of particular forms of property under existing conditions. To represent their relation truly you would have to explain in detail what they respectively wanted to see done, and with what alternatives under different conditions. Each of them wills what he thinks practicable, though he makes reservations for changing circumstances. Of course the whole set of wills is always changing, and is more or less in contradiction with itself. But all their contradictions spring from efforts at adjustment, and this character must be considered in estimating the unity of the will. One man is against proportional representation, and another in favour of it, on one and the same principle, only they differ about the facts. Of course you must allow for this in estimating the unity of their wills.

2. A similar case is the relation of neighbourhood groups to the whole community. Are you to strike out from the general will the intense formulated public feeling in a locality in favour of public drink control, because it is not spread over the whole country? Surely not; as we allow local by-laws to have force of Acts of Parliament, so our own will to self-government implies our approval, under certain safeguards, of the public will of other localities. We will it, as I said, diagrammatically. It is even possible, and obviously usual, to support by our private will different arrangements in different localities, adapted to different conditions; and, in fact, this principle runs throughout our whole social and political life. This is an extension of what is involved when we say that Smith's organising principles pervade and connect his efforts to satisfy his various wants. The principle, though strikingly obvious in the case of neighbourhood groups, applies to occupational groups as well. The standing will of the community is actual in all these phenomena.

3. I attach very great positive importance to the will implied in conduct. Here again Smith's standing will is a parallel. I admit that the principle

may be pressed too far, but I am sure, from its recognition by the practical world, from introspection, and from philosophical theory, that it has very great significance.

Ignorantia juris neminem. excusat[6] = practically "A reasonable man obeys the law without knowing it." His various actions reveal a will which in common with other particular wills throughout the community affirm the law of the land. "On the whole" his will supports the law, that is, the system of life which the law defines and protects. This is the judgement of the practical world in the maxim I have quoted. The fact that "on the whole" has different limits for everybody does not alter the fact that it is false of nobody. This is merely one, of instances, which, if set out, would cover the whole fabric of life. It meets the particular point of the participation of the less educated classes in the general will. But all the other instances would confirm it in this respect.

Introspection and philosophy I take together. I make bold to say, in virtue of both, that it is quite impossible to isolate a volition, as it is impossible to isolate a judgement. Every volition implies and is implied in a supporting system of wills, as every judgement implies and is implied in a systematic real world.[7]

4. It is of fundamental importance to distinguish the true genesis of law and administrative order from the political chances which immediately bring them into application. An important law – an act of sovereignty or expression of the general will, in Rousseau's higher sense – has a growth like a great tree, both in time and in the area from which it draws support. The life-blood of hundreds or thousands of devoted lives is in it, and also the adjusting and readjusting pressures of wills in the whole communal area or over great homogeneous districts of it. The easygoing publicist criticises it, of course, and very likely censures it, from a standpoint which has been won for him by the struggles and experience which moulded and are continually remoulding it. Think of the sincere and laborious lives and the innumerable counter-pressures and adapta-

---

[6][*Ignorantia juris neminem excusat*: literally, "ignorance of the law is no excuse."]

[7][Cf. Brand Blanshard's claim that "Fully coherent knowledge would be knowledge in which every judgment entailed, and was entailed by, the rest of the system." This is the core notion of coherence in idealist theories. *The Nature of Thought* (London: George Allen and Unwin, 1939), vol. II, p. 264.]

tions due to particular wills of every class which have gone to form our education policy, or our poor-law policy, or our policy about alcohol, or our commercial policy, or our local self-government, or our industrial organisation. (It seems an extraordinary thing to say that the "governing classes" have the directing power to-day, unless you make it a tautology by including in them all classes that de facto exercise control.) The Scottish fishwife says, "It's no fish ye're buying; it's men's lives." So we should say, when we think of our laws and institutions; they are not words and phrases, but the quintessence and utterance of men's and women's lives.

I adhere then to the statement that every reasonable private standing will in the community is related to the whole system of such wills as a component particular to a system which includes and defines it. The variations, through the correlation of which this whole is a system, are simply the variations of life, and the State, as a political structure, is an expression in outline, not really separable from the social whole, of the relatively permanent shape which the life of a community existing in all its particular wills, is maintaining and developing. I am sorry to have written at such length, but it is not a subject which it is easy to discuss shortly.

ON "SOCIETY AND STATE":

BOSANQUET–MACIVER LETTERS, 1911–1912[1]

Editors' Introduction:

In a paper sent to Bosanquet (later published as "Society and the State"),[2] R.M. MacIver challenged the importance given by Rousseau, Hegel and Bosanquet to such "Hellenic ideas" as the "general will" and the "state." These accounts, MacIver held, confounded the actual with the ideal and failed to appreciate the distinction between the state and the community – a distinction present, but concealed, by conditions in the ancient Greek world. Based on his reading of the first edition of *The Philosophical Theory of the State*, MacIver argued that there was an ambiguity in Bosanquet's concept of the state, a confusion between society and the state, and an erroneous distinction between the actual and the real will, and that, as a result, Bosanquet had failed to explain one's obligation to obey the law. Society, MacIver insisted, is not only larger than the state, but there are a number of social organisations and institutions which are not (and cannot be) bounded by it.

Through this important exchange of letters – which influenced his later treatment of the state (e.g., in his Gifford Lectures[3] on *The Principle of Individuality and Value* given in the fall of 1911), Bosanquet's reply is that, while social institutions have "a limited aim making for good life" only the state "has for its aim good life as such."

---

[1][From R.M. MacIver, *Politics and Society*, ed., David Spitz (New York: Atherton Press, 1969), pp. 238–247. In reproducing this correspondence abbreviations have been changed to full words – e.g., *wd* to *would*. Spelling and punctuation are unchanged, except where these would have made for clumsy reading. In one or two instances a word has been inserted; this is indicated by brackets.]

[2][*Philosophical Review*, vol. XX (1911): 30–45; reprinted in R.M. MacIver, *Community: A Sociological Study* (London: Macmillan, 1917) Appendix B, "A Criticism of the Neo-Hegelian Identification of Society and the State," pp. 425–433.]

[3][See below, note 12.]

312

BOSANQUET TO MACIVER[4]

Jan. 31, 1911

My dear Sir:

I am very much pressed with work just now, and am unable to write at length about your interesting paper on my book, or rather about the remarks on my book in your paper.

Of course there is a very great deal that might be said, and if I seem curt, it is only that I may not be drawn too far.

Your distinction of Society and the State is, I agree, important. I have recurred to it, and made rather more of it, in the Introduction to the second edition,[5] which I daresay had not reached you when you wrote your paper. But I do not agree that the book fails to put it in the proper light. I don't think you have sufficiently considered the account of the principle of delimitation of states, in connection with the discussion of the relation of state to humanity in the last chapter. And I think that the ultimate expression of the social will must always be the political will. It must finally determine the rank and relations of *all* institutions. I stick to the phrase "operative criticism" which implies, of course, unity with the living principle of the whole, both social and political.

And I think you are plainly wrong about the real and actual will. You would have to say that there is no such thing as a conflict of the good will and bad will, which is in principle the same as that I speak of. You can't make the bad will merely an intention conceived in carrying out the good will – a mere mistake. Of course in ultimate theory something like this comes out; but that the wills are two as well as one seems to me beyond doubt. It is a queer illustration of this but I am sure your interpretation of Balzac's fact is wrong, for most cases at least.[6] When a

---

[4][Robert Morrison MacIver (1882–1970) lectured in political philosophy at the University of Aberdeen, in political science at the University of Toronto (1915–1927), and served as Professor of Social Science at Barnard College (1927–1950). He was also President of the New School for Social Research. Following his move to the United States, he became recognised as one of the founders of American sociology.]

[5][See above, pp. 17–46, esp. 23ff.]

[6][Honoré de Balzac (1799–1850), was a French novelist. Here Bosanquet is referring to

woman hides a red herring in her bonnet to take to her husband in hospital she has not in mind his restoration to health – though that end is implied in her main will – but to take him something tasty which he will like at the moment. It is all but a conflicting end, as her concealment shows. The fact is an everyday fact, and its nature quite familiar to all social workers.

The will of the state is always treated as positive, I think; it is the means that are negative. And one must remember that negation is never bare negation. But I am prepared to defend the indirect nature of political promotion of good life through thick and thin. I have given examples in the book, and indeed every case is an example. But I must not be led further. I hope you will develop the distinction between State and Society fruitfully.

Sincerely,

B. Bosanquet

BOSANQUET TO MACIVER

March 12, 1911

My dear Sir:

Many thanks for your letter and article.[7] I agree with you that one cannot treat these things properly in a letter. One makes it too long for a letter, and too short for complete explanation. If I am able to return to the subject, I will bear your argument in mind. At present I am rather

---

MacIver's example of an incident related in Balzac's *Le Cousin Pons* (1847). Families brought food into hospitals, believing that it would accelerate the recovery of their relatives, whereas it actually led to increased illness. In the paper referred to (later published as "Society and the State," *Philosophical Review*, vol. XX (1911): 30–45), MacIver had argued that Bosanquet's claim that there is a "real" will in persons, distinct from their "actual" (or "private") will, is mistaken. MacIver held that this incident showed that there not were two "wills" present in the actions of the families, but simply that one could distinguish between the actual consequence of the object willed, and the end it was meant to serve.]

[7]"Society and the State." [See previous note.]

pressed, having a new edition of my *Logic* on my hands, as well as a review of Professor Baillie's *Phenomenology*[8] which in any case will be unduly delayed, and other serious work after that.

If I don't mean to start a correspondence, I have no right to raise any points. But it seems pointless with the pen in my hand not to try even to hint at any explanation. And I don't mean that I shouldn't be much interested to hear from you if you cared at any time to write; but only that I couldn't undertake to give a fitting answer.

I will just say then, that I define the state against society mainly by two things: (1) its end, which I take to be that of Ethics – the good for man; and (2) by its means, which I take to be in the main external, in the removal of hindrances to the fulfilment of capacity.

(1) 1 is not, in my view, the end of any (other?) social institution. (Whether you call the state one among other social institutions or not seems to me verbal. If it is an institution, it is the institution of institutions, so to speak.) A church, a dwelling's company, a public house, a temperance association, have each of them a limited aim making for good life; none has for its aim good life as such.

The State (2) differs therefore by being the common adjustment of all these, in virtue of the total idea of good life, and of the universal applicability of its means, viz., external regulation. Left alone, the social institutions are always at loggerheads with each other, and often with themselves. It is, in my view, the State and the State alone, which through its superior idea of good, conjoined with its universal practical controls, forces them to adjust themselves to the order and condition of good life. You may say, "but society as a whole, though no one institution, has this same aim." I reply, society as a whole does not exist, except in and through the state. It alone is conscious of the *whole* social end, surveys it all, and adjusts all details to it.

I don't see your difficulty with "the State." It is merely the subject of a generic judgment is it not? = Every state qua state? Now I have written

---

[8][*Logic, or the Morphology of Knowledge*, 2nd edn, (Oxford: Clarendon Press, 1911). Bosanquet's review of Sir James Black Baillie's (1872–1940) translation of Hegel's *The Phenomenology of Mind*, 2 vols. (London: Sonnenschein, 1910) appeared in the *International Journal of Ethics*, vol. XXII (1911–12): 97–101.]

what would justify you in continuing the argument. But I don't think we can really have it out in letters. I daresay you will write a book about it, and then I shall see your view more fully.

I am assuming you meant me to keep the article.

Sincerely,
B. Bosanquet

MacIver to Bosanquet

April 24, 1911

My dear Sir:

I am much obliged for your letter of March 12th which enables me to see very clearly the position you hold regarding the relation of the state to society – so that if I still differ it can no longer be through misunderstanding of your view. Perhaps then you will let me answer your points briefly, not necessarily in view of a rejoinder, for I recognise sufficiently the difficulty of sparing any time for such correspondence and your kindness in replying to my previous criticism.

You "define the state against society mainly by two things": (1) its end, the end of Ethics, the good for man; (2) its means, "in the main external." My position would be that the state has for its end the good for man *so far as* that can be furthered by the external means at its command, but that the limitation involved is so great that we can no longer say that the state secures or controls *the* ethical end. If there are societies which can use other than external means how can they *so far* be controlled by a society limited to such means? These other societies have qualities of operation beyond the political sphere. Further, since external means can never really secure any ethical end itself, but at most the conditions required for its fulfilment, we have the anomaly – which I think you admit – of means being totally inadequate to end. If the state cannot directly secure the ethical end how can it control *in every aspect* those societies which directly secure some part of that end, the family, for instance?

I am not for a moment denying that the state is the supreme society. I believe it is, but still I think "society" is greater than the state. You reply,

"Society as a whole does not exist." But by society I do not mean any one society or even any union of societies. It is obvious that a great part of our social intercourse is conducted not on the basis of our membership of any particular society but in virtue of a social nature which is constantly creating and recreating social media. We may take, though it is an unnecessarily extreme case, the instance of an Englishman travelling on the continent. He is "in society" all the time but if you ask, what society? – it is difficult to answer. So far in fact as there is community of nature between fellow beings, so far there is continual social adaptation. If so, no one state can limit and completely determine the social conduct of any of its members. His membership of his state does not sum up his social individuality, either extensively or intensively – not extensively [because] he enters into social relations with nonmembers of his state; not intensively, because his intercourse with his fellow citizens cannot possibly be limited by merely external conditions such as alone a political institution can lay down. Certainly I would grant that the state is the "institution of institutions," but society is not an institution at all. It is a life continuous and progressive, the creator of institutions however supreme. Might we not say that just as Government rests on the political will, the will of citizens who recognise each other as such, so does the state rest on the social will, the will of individuals who recognise in each other a large community of interest, nature or ideal, in virtue of which they establish or maintain a society of which they are all members. Their membership binds them to one another in certain definite ways – an institution with supreme external control is absolutely necessary – but surely even here there is a "limited liability." It would be regarded as wrong, e.g., if a state were to attempt to force religion on any minority of its members. But if so, how can you say that "the state is conscious of the *whole* social end, surveys it all, and adjusts all details to it"?

I feel that this statement is inadequate but perhaps it may help to make my views also clearer. If you have time to answer, I shall be grateful.

Yours sincerely,
R.M. MacIver

BOSANQUET TO MACIVER

June 19, 1911

Dear Mr MacIver:

Just a line in answer to your very interesting letter of April 24. I think that what we are confronting is at bottom the relation of "outer" to "inner." In a great part of my book I consciously addressed myself to that problem, and I hold, on the whole, by my treatment. I will write down some propositions which seem to me to go to the heart of the matter. To take arguments to pieces, and work out each one, is such a very lengthy procedure, and I, like you no doubt, am full of business.

Every "inner" has an "outer" and there is no real existence which is wholly either the one or the other. Every "inner" is greatly affected by and affects its outer and through it all other "outers." The problem of the mode and degree of this influence is the most interesting, difficult, and dangerous, of human life. The entire "outer" of human life is institutional; birth, death, sickness, the mealtime, the family, the house and home, the place of business and conditions of the vocation, the church in all its forms, are institutional expressions of an inner life. The centrality and focus of all this outer world is naturally and necessarily the state, which is the result of the whole (not a prior cause which determined it) but also in reaction upon every part. For every individual there must be one such supreme focus of the outer life, and one only. The adjustment of outer and inner together, starting from the side of the outer, to the best life, is the problem of politics, which is the concentrated expression of the social "outer." It is an interesting paradox that the freedom of external sociality is greatest where the force and recognition of the state are greatest and deepest. This is really very natural and obvious. It is just as the best-built house gives you the great capacity of effective life. But in detail the reaction of outer upon inner is a very delicate problem – really, I think, *the* test of a statesman. It is enormously powerful, although, as I maintain, mainly indirect. Take the relation of the State to Art and Religion – the things most out of its apparent sphere. How it ought to deal with them for the best at any given epoch is a fearful problem; but if it, prima facie, lets them alone it is none the less dealing with them. It only lets them alone in a certain way and on certain terms, conceived in the interest of the best life. I must stop now but I think the crux is here.

Yours very sincerely,

B. Bosanquet

BOSANQUET TO MACIVER

March 23, 1912

Dear Mr MacIver:

You must have thought me very uncourteous to take no notice of your letter of Jan. 29 accompanying a number of the *International Journal of Ethics*.[9] The fact is, your letter actually reached me in a nursing home; and I am only now making up the arrears of correspondence.

I am much interested by your paper, and feel, as one so often does, that the difference between us is one of proportion, and angle of vision, and that there is very much on which we are in substance agreed. But just because it is a difference of this kind, to go into it further would need a treatise of some length. For though I agree in much of the substance of your contention, I think there is no statement in the article which I should not from my point of view desire to criticise and rewrite. Much of my life has been passed in the exact study and teaching of ancient history, and I could not subscribe I think to any of your statements, e.g., about Greek civilisation. The Mediterranean and Black Sea coasts from Trebizond to Marseilles were in my view much more socially one in the 5th century BC than they ever have been since, though not of course over an area extending so far from the sea as the civilised area now extends. The inhabitants of the several hundred cities or counties (not towns of course, they were large territories) met as the English speaking race meet today, as members of the same civilisation, and with some recognition of common institutions.

---

[9][Vol. 22 (1911–12), containing MacIver's article, "War and Civilization," pp. 127–145.]

So with the 18th century compared with today. France and Germany, e.g. have grown and are growing apart. No French writer, it has been remarked, could possibly have the influence in Germany today which Rousseau had from 1760 to 1810.

There is heaps and heaps more of the same kind to say. I do not think there is anything in the theoretical contention which is not thoroughly answered in my introduction to ed[n]. 2 of the [*Philosophical*] *Theory of the State.*

As to what you say about peace, of course I wish it might be so, and would do anything to promote it; and would not *in public* insist very much on the difficulties. But it worries me that you do not seem, to me, to appreciate the facts, and therefore do not really prepare yourself to deal with the problems which must arise. As to leaving national honour to honourable third parties – in private matters there are thousands of disinterested men of honour. In a dispute between England, say, and Germany, there is no disinterested party on the surface of this globe. Or substitute for "honour," what I see coming between us and Germany, an honest and fundamental difference of conviction as to the course of history in the future desirable in the interests of humanity, such as to produce collision. You may reconcile a difference like that by reason and discussion; but you can't arbitrate on it; it is too deep in men's hearts. You can't arbitrate on your religion, and these convictions *are* men's religions. One must go to work in a deeper way. At least that is my view.

Yours sincerely,

B. Bosanquet

MacIver To Bosanquet

25 April, 1912

Dear Mr Bosanquet:

Your criticism always stimulates me into replying, though I have allowed an interval to elapse in order not to bore you with my correspondence. I should like now to defend two points which you attack in my article. First as to the general issue of war and peace. You say there are differences between nations too deep to suffer arbitration. "You can't arbitrate on your religion, and these convictions *are* men's religions. One must go to work in a deeper way." True, but there is never really need to arbitrate on these things, or at any rate there would not be were it not for the existence of armaments and the possibility of violence. You need only fight with arms for your religion if someone is foolish enough to attack your religion with arms. The actual causes of war today are not these inexpugnable convictions, but some incidental dispute over territory, some encroachment by a petty official (less often by a high official or statesman acting under his executive power, i.e., without special national authorisation for the offending act), at most some overt wrong done it may be under the stimulus of a strong conviction but itself, unlike the conviction, "justiciable." Can you give a single instance in modern history where the honour or convictions of a nation have been violated, except by armed aggression of some sort, in a way itself precluding by its very nature justiciable remedy?

I am quite conscious of the difficulties of arbitration, but I think you add unnecessarily to them. You say – "In a dispute between England, say, and Germany, there is no disinterested (third) party on the surface of the globe." But arbitration doesn't mean that when England and Germany dispute say about territorial rights in Morocco, Italy or Austria or U.S.A. will be called in to settle the case. It means an arbitral international court, composed not of nations but of representatives, representatives chosen for their high judicial capacity and sense of honour. It is surely possible to find in every civilised nation on earth representatives of this high character and integrity.

"One must go to work in a deeper way." But the whole issue hinges on the truth that war is not a deeper but a shallower way. Arbitration may go wrong, accidentally; but if war does decide right, it is *only* accidentally. And everyone who values his convictions hates the idea of trusting them to a kind of arbitration which is actually – since superior might can surely never be the test of conviction – as accidental as the turning of a coin.

The difficulties of arbitration are the difficulties of every development not yet matured. I honestly believe that the only ultimate difficulty is the slowness of the dispersal of certain prejudices as to the essential alienation of nations from one another, prejudices which the growing intercommunity of peoples has indeed begun to disperse, and notably among the labour classes of the Western world.

You deny this growth of intercommunity, at least in certain cases. To me it seems obvious. Even your extreme case – the case of France and Germany – supports that view. There was in the 18th century, to which you refer, no such intercommunication between the working classes of these two countries – the bulk of the peoples – as there is just now. There was in the 18th century no such financial and commercial interdependence between France and Germany as the recent threat of war proved clearly enough that there is just now. Nor do I even see any authority in the remark you quote that "no French writer could possibly have the influence in Germany today which Rousseau had from 1760–1810." Political alienation there may be, but since I base my argument on the distinction of society and state I can hardly admit, in view of the above and other connecting facts I could quote, that there is growing social alienation. And here is an extreme case.

Lastly, as to my Greek history, you take the case of the "Mediterranean and Black Sea coasts from Trebizond to Marseilles" in the 5th century BC and say the intercommunity then was greater than it has been ever since. Well, in the first place you had throughout Greek cities then, while now you have different *peoples* along these coasts, whose difference complicates the general comparison of past and present. But further the fact of common civilisation does not involve intercommunity in the series of colonies sprung from the source of the common civilisation. The wars of the Greek colonies prove this. So does the fact expressed in the words of Freeman[10] that "in old Greece the amount of hatred between city and city seems to depend almost mathematically upon their distance from one another"! In any case I should think Thucydides III 82–3 a sufficient answer to your statement as to the 5th century BC.[11]

---

[10][Presumably MacIver is referring here to Edward Augustus Freeman's *History of Federal Government in Greece and Italy*, 2nd edn (London: Macmillan, 1893).]

[11][In these sections of Book III Thucydides is describing the outbreak of revolution throughout the Hellenic world: "So revolutions broke out in city after city.... Revenge was more important than self-preservation.... When the chance came, the one who seized it boldly, catching his enemy off his guard, enjoyed revenge that was all the sweeter from having been taken, not openly, but because of a breech of faith. Love of power, operating

I do not know what authority you have for affirming actual social intercourse of an intimate character between the Greek cities from Trebizond to Marseilles but I fancy that in an age when the rate of bottomry was something like 33¹/₃% actual social intercourse was at a minimum!

I was very sorry to hear of your illness and earnestly hope you are quite recovered. I am looking forward to reading, after my work of the term is over, your published Hibbert lectures. [12]

Yours very sincerely,

R.M. MacIver

---

through greed and personal ambition, was the cause of all these evils. To this must be added violent fanaticism...." (pp. 242–43). *Peloponnesian War*, trans., Rex Warner (Harmondsworth: Penguin, 1972).]

[12][MacIver must be referring here to the first series of *Gifford* lectures, *The Principle of Individuality and Value*, which appeared in early 1912. Bosanquet never gave the Hibbert Lectures. The 1911 Hibbert lectures were given by Lewis Richard Farnell (1856–1934) who spoke on *The Higher Aspects of Greek Religion* (London: Williams and Norgate, 1912) and, in 1912, by James Hope Moulton (1863–1917), who spoke on *Early Zoroastrianism* (London: Williams and Norgate, 1913).]

THE ANTITHESIS BETWEEN INDIVIDUALISM AND SOCIALISM PHILOSOPHICALLY CONSIDERED[1]

Editors' Introduction:

In this paper read to the Fabian Society, Bosanquet distinguishes two types of individualism and two types of socialism: moral individualism and economic individualism, moral socialism and economic socialism. Bosanquet's idealism and organic conception of society leads him to be critical of "moral individualism" – what he sees as a "materialistic or Epicurean view of life" – and so favours "moral socialism" – "which makes Society the moral essence of the individual." However, he advances a unique thesis: moral socialism supports economic individualism and a regime of private property. Indeed, he indicates that economic socialists such as the Fabians do not really have faith in the social nature of individuals and the general will, and so seek to "mechanically" impose a conception of the good life. Paradoxically, perhaps, he argues that economic socialism is based on moral individualism. This paper is important, then, in articulating an idealist-communitarian defence of economic individualism.

The purpose which I have set before myself this evening is a very humble and limited one. I have not come here to instruct skilled economists and statisticians in political economy and the use of statistics; I have not come here to attempt an analysis of the probable working of Economic Socialism. I am not going to deny, so far as I am aware, any of the fundamental principles which are really involved in the Socialist contention. What I want to be allowed to attempt is simply to state a question, to emphasise a distinction. And the good which I should hope to effect, if I had the power to effect it, would be to help in refocusing the Socialist picture of social phenomena, not obliterating its details, but perhaps taking in a little more at both sides, and altering the light and shade, and

---

[1] A paper read by invitation at a meeting of the Fabian Society on February 21, 1890. [From Bosanquet's *The Civilization of Christendom* (London: Swan Sonnenschein, 1893), pp. 304–57.]

putting some things in the foreground that are now in the background, and vice versa. Or, to change the metaphor, the Socialist express seems to me to be at present approaching a junction. I do not want it to shut off steam, but I wish I could be pointsman when it comes up; for I think that one line of rails will take it to a very barren country, and the other to a very fruitful country.

I think it only fair to myself to say that I suppose I was asked to come here on purpose to try and criticise, and I mean to do so. But if I had before me an audience of plutocratic sympathies, then I should have the pleasure of speaking much more than I shall to-night in the language of the *Fabian Essays*.[2]

(α) Individualism and Socialism may be considered as names which designate different conditions or organisations of the productive and distributive work of Society: Individualism meaning a competitive system based on private property, such as under certain limitations exists to-day in Europe; and Socialism meaning a collective organisation of these same functions. Simply for the sake of clearness I shall call these systems and the advocacy of them by the names of Economic Individualism and Economic Socialism respectively.

But (β) the two generic names in question carry with them associations belonging to pregnant views of life as a whole; and Individualism at least may be used to represent a recognised philosophical doctrine of human relations analogous to the theory of matter indicated by the equivalent Greek term Atomism. And by opposition to this pregnant use of Individualism, and also in virtue of its own obvious derivation, the

---

[2][*Fabian Essays in Socialism*, ed., George Bernard Shaw (London: The Fabian Society, 1889). Contributing were: George Bernard Shaw; Sidney Webb; William Clarke; Sydney Oliver; Annie Besant; Graham Wallas and Hubert Bland. This collection was published a number of times throughout the last decade of the nineteenth century and the first half of the twentieth. The Fabian Society, founded in 1884, supported a non-Marxist socialism. Its leading figures were the Webbs, Sidney (1859–1947) and Beatrice (1858–1943). The Bosanquets (Bernard and Helen) and the Webbs were leaders of opposed approaches to poor relief and welfare policy. The Bosanquets put great stress on non-governmental social work; see the essay in this volume on "Idealism and Social Work," pp. 358–69. For a study of the Bosanquets and Webbs, see A.M. McBriar, *An Edwardian Mixed Doubles: The Bosanquets Versus the Webbs: A Study in British Social Policy 1890–1929* (Oxford: Clarendon Press, 1987).]

term Socialism is acquiring, if it did not at first possess, a deeper meaning as a name for a human tendency or aspiration that is operative throughout history, in contrast, we have been told, with "Unsocialism." To distinguish this more human signification of the words we are discussing from their purely economic usage, I shall specify them when thus employed as Moral Individualism and Moral Socialism respectively, everything being moral, in the philosophical sense, which deals with the value of life as a whole.

Moral Individualism, then, is the materialistic or Epicurean view of life (which, when reasonably interpreted, has a good deal to be said for it);[3] and moral Socialism is the opposite view to this, the view which makes Society the moral essence of the Individual. And I may say at once that for practical purposes of discussion I shall assume this second view to be the right view. In strict philosophy neither of them is right, but only a rational conception which satisfies the demands of both. But there is this great difference between them, that the individual or atomic animal man has a visible body, and therefore we are already quite certain not to deny *his* reality, and we need not further insist upon it by help of a theory; while the moral being of man as a centre of social functions and relations is not visible to the bodily eye, and therefore we do need a theory to insist upon *it*. This shows the ground of philosophical connection between Materialism and Moral Individualism in the tendency to start from what you can most easily see.[4]

For convenience of antithesis, then, I shall speak of Moral Individualism in the sense of actual or theoretical egoism, and Moral Socialism (though this latter is not an accepted expression) in the sense of actual or theoretical recognition that man's moral being lies in his social being. I do not assume that Moral Socialism is the view of morality entertained by Economic Socialists. My object this evening is rather to put the question whether it is so either most naturally, or as a matter of fact. Therefore, what I wish to discuss is the relation between two antitheses:

---

[3] See Professor [William] Wallace's *Epicureanism* [(London: Society for Promoting Christian Knowledge, 1880)], a beautiful book.

[4] [On "theories of the first look," see below pp. 104ff.]

between the antithesis of Economic Individualism to Economic Socialism, and the antithesis of Moral Individualism to Moral Socialism.

There is, I think, a widespread tendency simply to confuse these two distinctions with one another. The mere name of Socialism evokes an enthusiasm and devotion which show that it is not felt to be merely one system of property-holding, though it is seldom distinctly announced to be anything more; and still less is the question raised, which I am trying to raise just now, *what* more it is. Mr Kirkup, in the article "Socialism" of the *Encyclopaedia Britannica*,[5] has a curiously suggestive passage. He says, "Most of the prevailing Socialism of to-day is based on the frankest and most outspoken revolutionary materialism." Well! Materialism going along with Moral Individualism, this is to say that the two antitheses which we are discussing are *cross-connected,* or at least that Economic Socialism is based on Moral Individualism. But then he continues, "The ethics of Socialism are closely akin to the ethics of Christianity, if not identical with them." This, again is to say that the two antitheses which I am discussing correspond term for term, or at least that Economic Socialism is based on Moral Socialism. But the question is not pursued after this very suggestive contradiction, which might, one would have thought, have led up to an inquiry how there comes to be this very decided right and left wing in Socialist morality. Even in the *Fabian Essays* I cannot think that the distinction between Economic and Moral Socialism, with the questions that arise out of it, is quite plainly faced. The sentence on page 148, "The system of property-holding which we call Socialism is not in itself such a life," etc., is therefore refreshing to a philosopher, who has found himself a little bewildered by an implied assumption that two things are the same, about which he wants to know whether they have any connection at all, and if so, what. The "moral ideas appropriate to Socialism,"[6] or "Socialism" as an object of moral judgment,[7] are in another paper rather assumed to be of the nature of what I call Moral Socialism, than shown to be so; nor do I feel absolutely sure that the author of this paper has made a final choice be-

---

[5][Thomas Kirkup (1844–1912), in 9th edn, vol. xxii, pp. 205–21.]

[6][*Fabian Essays,*] p. 127.

[7][Ibid.,] p. 104.

tween the ethical right and left wing. We all see, indeed, that more general comfort would give morality a better chance, and that industrial co-operation is a good ethical training; but the statement of these two points hardly amounts to a recognition and treatment of the distinction and connection between Economic Socialism and Moral Socialism. The pages of this volume, with which, speaking as an ethical student, I feel most at home, are the concluding page and a half of the Essay on "Industry under Socialism."[8] And I do not at all maintain that the connection between economic and moral Socialism, which is there indicated, need be visionary. Even if I am betrayed into a little polemic, illustrative of what I consider the risks of a false perspective, it is not my object to make an attack. My object is to get the question recognised in its full difficulty and importance. I begin, therefore, by stating the prima facie case against a connection between Moral and Economic Socialism.[9]

Morality consists in the presence of some element of the social purpose as a moving idea before the individual mind; that is, in short, in the social constitution of the individual will. This has been the recognised morality of the Western nations for more than two thousand years, without any essential or fundamental change whatever, the deepening of the individual spirit and intelligence, which has sometimes seemed to tear society apart, having been in every case the germination of a membership in a new social order, sometimes, by illusion, taken for a time to be invisible as well as visible. Able writers (Mr Belfort Bax and Mr Mackay)[10] have absolutely and utterly misunderstood this phenomenon, which they take for a growth of Individualism.

---

[8][Ibid.,] pp. 168–9.

[9]The Author of the paper on "The Moral Basis of Socialism" [Sydney Oliver] says there is no special Socialistic view of the basis of morals. This may be so, but then I hardly think you could speak of moral ideas appropriate to Socialism. At least, you would have to *make* the connection.

[10][E. Belfort Bax (1854–1926) was known for his attack on ethical individualism in favour of a socialistic morality; see his *The Religion of Socialism: Being Essays in Modern Socialist Criticism*, 6th edn (London: Swan Sonnenschein, [1887], 1902: *The Ethics of Socialism: Being Further Essays in Modern Socialist Criticism*, 3rd edn, (London, S. Sonnenschein, 1893). In contrast, Thomas Mackay (1849–1912) was an advocate of individualism and a critic of socialism. See his *The English Poor* (London: J. Murray, 1889) and his most famous book, *A Plea for Liberty: An Argument Against Socialism and So-*

Now, why should Economic Socialism not be favourable to a developed morality of this kind? Stated in the abstract, the reason is that it is the same thing in a quite different form, and the general rule is that different forms of the same thing are hostile. A regular Gallio has no objection to a State Church. Like Mr M. Arnold, he thinks that it saves people from becoming too religious.[11] But a man who thinks that the State is itself spiritual is apt to be fanatically opposed to an Establishment. The one form is always seeming to claim the functions of the other, and two different things cannot occupy the same place. It may be answered that all is well so long as they do not claim to occupy the same place, but simply to assist one another as distinct means to the same end. That may be, but then the distinction and the mode of assistance must be very precisely defined.

Morality, as I said, consists in the social purpose working by its own force on the individual will. Economic Socialism is an arrangement for getting the social purpose carried out just not by its own force, but by the force of those compulsory motives or sanctions which are at the command of the public power.

Therefore, prima facie, the normal relation of the two antitheses of which I spoke would be that of cross-correspondence. Economic Individualism would go with Moral Socialism, and Moral Individualism (or Egoism) with Economic Socialism. If you want to treat your social units as bricks in a wall or wheels in a machine, you cannot also and at the same time treat them as elements in an organism. Or, it is truer to say, if you can treat them in these two ways at once, you have solved an exceedingly difficult problem. Prima facie, machinery and morality are

---

cialistic Legislation: Consisting of An Introduction by Herbert Spencer and Essays by Various Writers, ed., Thomas Mackay (Indianapolis: Liberty Classics, 1981).]

[11] [Matthew Arnold (1822–1888) is known as a great Victorian poet, but spent a considerable part of life as a school inspector, where he had sustained contact with nonconformists. He insisted that their "idea of human perfection is narrow and inadequate, and that the Dissidence of Dissent and The Protestantism of the Protestant religion will never bring humanity to its true goal.... Look at the life imagined by a newspaper such as the *Nonconformist* – a life of jealousy of the establishment, disputes, tea-meetings, openings of chapels, sermons...." *Anarchy and Culture*, ed., J. Dover Wilson (Cambridge: Cambridge University Press, 1963), p. 58.]

quite different things, and if you are trying to model your machinery directly upon your morality, it is long odds that you are guided simply by a confusion. Economic Socialism need not presuppose the social organism. It is, in appearance, a *substitute for* the life of that organism, intended to operate on the egoistic motives of individuals for the good of the whole, which cannot, it is assumed, be attained by the moral power of the social purpose. In this point of view at least it naturally rests on Moral Individualism. All compulsion through the material necessities of individuals is morally individualistic. But Economic Individualism does presuppose the social organism, and without it would be the dissolution of society. It is often alleged that the time of the factory development a hundred years ago was a time of unmixed Economic Individualism. But this is not so; perhaps the worst evils of that time arose directly from the intentionally lax or "socialistic" Poor Law. It was the public institutions that for the most part supplied the children who were ill-treated. Owen's life shows us that by sheer competitive attraction you could *not* get the respectable country people to work under factory conditions. This suggests a different moral. Economic Individualism assumes that the moral purpose has power to take care of itself throughout the general life of society, and only embodies that purpose in acts of the public power when such acts appear definitely necessary on specific grounds for the support of the private moral will. The Economic Individualist, indeed, who thinks the State to be unconcerned with morality, and to be unjustified in any interference on moral grounds, is a fanatic and doctrinaire, and is the precise counterpart of the Economic Socialist who assumes straight away that collectivism in property naturally implies socialisation of the will. Each of these doctrinaires imagines that the economic and the moral forms of his principle are necessarily coherent with each other, whereas it is much more natural that they should be antagonistic.

If I am asked, "Does this apparent antagonism between Moral and Economic Socialism represent what I believe to be the fact?" I reply, "It represents to me the reality of certain conditions, and my own judgment of any existing or proposed economical machinery would depend upon the degree in which, at the time of its proposal, it should satisfy those conditions." And these conditions, in accordance with what has been said, may be summed up as the necessity of avoiding the confusion of machinery with morality, on the ground that the moment this confusion begins your Moral Socialism turns automatically into Moral Individualism.

It is therefore the second antithesis – and not the first – the economical antithesis – that dominates the question. Our joint purpose is, as I understand, to find a machinery which will assist morality and not be confounded with it. To my own mind the great requisite is to acknowledge that all these problems are matters of contrivance and matters of degree. I was electrified, but also edified, not long ago, to find an able writer of the extreme school of doctrinaire Individualists talking about devising new tenures of private property, and about an admirable *substitute for* private property. (He was speaking of Insurance.) This latter phrase is one with which I do not think an Economic Socialist need quarrel. It is perfectly plain and undeniable, I think, that liberty and regulation are increasing side by side as the whole range of life becomes larger, and that what is important is not the relative amount of regulation and of liberty, but the adaptation of both with delicacy and flexibility to the shape and growth of life.

Thus the question assumes the form, not of choosing between two ready-made economic systems, but of developing a specific system to suit the necessities of our life.

From this point of view it is plain that the spirit in which we go to work, the focussing of our picture, the precise line of rail on which we progress, will be simply decisive of the all-important question which I am trying to put before you: "Does Economic Socialism carry with it Moral Socialism or Moral Individualism?" In the former case it is heaven, and in the latter case it is hell. What I now propose to attempt is to insist further, by help of details both of opinion and of practice, upon the dangerous conditions which I have endeavoured to set out in the above abstract deduction – upon the danger, that is, which lies in the facility of connection between Economic Socialism and Moral Individualism. I want to show, if I can, at how important a parting of the ways Modern Socialism is about to arrive.

1. I quoted from Mr Kirkup to the effect that there is a great deal of materialism – which means Moral Individualism – in modern Socialism.

Much of this is inherited, no doubt, though not from Robert Owen,[12] and may be passing away. But much remains, and is inherent – as a *tendency* is inherent – in Economic Socialism.

Take the case in which Economic Socialism frequently appeals to moral considerations; the polemic against private property.

As a matter of the history of opinion, to begin with, this cuts off Economic Socialism at once from the two greatest expounders of the social organism that the world has ever seen – I mean Aristotle[13] and Hegel. I do not mention this as if their authority was decisive on practical questions of to-day, because the nature of property has changed and is continually changing. But it is important, when Economic Socialists begin – as I am glad to see they are beginning – to speak about the social organism, to bear in mind that a radical and fundamental polemic against private property is quite incompatible with any legitimate affiliation to those who have us this spiritual principle. What about Plato? it may be asked. Well! Aristotle's complaint against him, reduced to modern terms, is that Plato had needlessly destroyed the social organism by trusting to machinery, instead of morality. On the other hand, I grant that private property, as Aristotle would have it, is a different thing from ours. Now, with reference to Hegel, one notices at times a tendency in Economic Socialism to be a little proud of a somewhat doubtful affiliation to him. It is quite true that Karl Marx used the forms of the dialectic with extraordinary ingenuity, and one hopes that the deeper spiritual ideas of Hegel's teaching are passing, and will pass, more and more into the temper of nineteenth-century reformers. It is, moreover, true that Hegel denounced as a blunder the idea which I have stigmatised as characteristic of doctrinaire Individualism: the idea that the public recognition of moral purposes is necessarily fatal to individual moral freedom. So far, an Economic Socialist can count upon Hegel as against a doctrinaire Individualist. But when you read Hegel's treatment of private property, and realize the depth and complexity of the moral problem to

---

[12][Robert Owen (1771–1858) was a social and industrial reformer. Bosanquet seems to be referring here especially to Owen's attempts to found agricultural-industrial communities, such as New Harmony in Indiana; these cooperative communities were short-lived.]

[13][William Lambert] Newman, *Introduction to Aristotle's Politics* [(Oxford, Clarendon Press, 1887–1902)], pp. 164 and 178.

which he regards it as the answer, and then pass from that treatment to the view which regards it as the embodiment of the individual cupidity and indolence, I think every one must be aware that one has passed to another and not a higher moral atmosphere. I hope I shall not weary you too much if I quote a characteristic page from Hegel's *Philosophy of Right*:[14]

As, in property, my will is made real for me as a personal will – that is, as the will of an individual – property is characteristically *private* property; while common property, such as in its nature can be generally possessed, bears the character of a dissoluble combination, in which I can choose or not choose to leave my share.

The use of the elements [I suppose he means air and water – he might have meant land but for the next sentence] is incapable of being made a private possession. The agrarian laws at Rome contain a conflict between collectivism and private property in land; the latter necessarily gained the day, as the more reasonable factor in the social system, although at the expense of other rights. Family property contains a factor which is opposed to the right of personality, and therefore to that of private property. But the rules which deal with private property may be subordinated to higher spheres of right, to a corporation or to the State, as in the case when ownership is vested in a so-called moral person – property in mortmain. However, such exceptions must not be founded in caprice or private interest but only in the rational organisation of the State.

The idea of Plato's Republic contains as a general principle the injustice against the person of making him incapable of holding private property. The idea of a pious or friendly or even compulsory fraternity of human beings with community of goods, and the banishment of the principle of private property, may easily occur to a habit of thought which mistakes the nature of spiritual freedom and of right, and does not apprehend them in their definite factors. As for the moral or religious point of view, Epicurus deterred his friends from organising such a community of goods, when they thought of doing so, precisely on the ground that to do so would indicate mistrust, and that people who mistrust one another are not friends.[15]

---

[14][Hegel,] *Rechtsphil.*, p. 81. [See Hegel, *The Philosophy of Right*, trans. T.M. Knox (Oxford: Clarendon Press, 1942), sect. 46 and additions.]

[15][Hegel cites Laertius Diogenes X. 6. For an English translation see Laertius Diogenes

Note. In property my will takes the shape of a person. Now a person is something in particular; therefore the property is the personification of this will. As I give my will existence by means of property, property in its turn must have the attribute of being this in particular, i.e. mine. This is the important doctrine of the necessity of private property. If exceptions are made by the State, it is it alone that can make them; and often in our own days it has *restored* private property. So, for example, many nations have rightly abolished the monasteries, because in the last resort a collective institution has no such right to property as the person has.

Now if it is maintained that the reasonable necessity which in Hegel's view demanded the existence of private property can now be met by a modification of the private ownership system, or even by some different system, that might fairly be urged without breaking your line of descent from idealistic or organic philosophy which is one with moral Socialism. But if you say that private ownership is, and always has been, simply the expression of individual greed, and the desire to be indolent and incompetent, then, by a phenomenon very common in controversy, you arouse a well-grounded suspicion that you are ascribing this foundation – the foundation of Moral Individualism – to the normal life of humanity, simply because it is the foundation on which your own views ultimately rest, and you are aware of no other. It appears to me that Economic Socialism wavers between these two attitudes, and that the latter, the polemic against private ownership, altogether and as such, betrays, as Hegel implies, an entire blindness to the essential elements of the social organism, which can only exist as a structure of free individual wills, each entertaining the social purpose in an individual form appropriate to its structural position and organic functions. It is perhaps a platitude, but one which we all of us are perpetually failing to apply, that throughout life the attempt to realise an abstraction as an abstraction is self-contradictory and a ruinous failure. To aim directly at pleasure for pleasure's sake means failure in happiness; to aim at duty for duty's

---

(third century AD) *Lives of Eminent Philosophers*, trans. Robert Drew Hicks, (Cambridge, Mass.: Harvard University Press, 1959), vol. II, Book X. Epicurus (approx. 342–270 BC) opened a school outside of Athens around 306 BC. The property contained a garden, and the community became known as "The Garden." His association with his students was unusually close; after his death the garden was left to his disciples.]

sake means failure in morality; to aim at beauty for beauty's sake means failure in fine art; to aim at truth for truth's sake (the net result) means failure in science; to aim at the general purpose for the sake of the purpose as general means failure in social reform. I confess that I believe modern Economic Socialism to rest *in part* on this ineradicable confusion. "We want a general good life; let us make a law that there shall be a general good life." But, precisely as other-worldliness arises from the religious impulse when embodied in a mechanical form, so, and for identically the same reasons, does Moral Individualism arise automatically from the impulse of Moral Socialism when embodied in a mechanical form. You must let the individual make his will a reality in the conduct of his life, in order that it may be possible for him consciously to entertain the social purpose as a constituent of his will. Without these conditions there is no social organism and no Moral Socialism. This is the meaning of the doctrines of Aristotle and Hegel, and this it is which the ethical left wing of the Socialists, alluded to by Mr Kirkup,[16] appears to me wholly to ignore.

2. But the question is not one merely of the history of opinion or of ethical formulas. If it were, it would be too purely academic for even a philosophical discussion before the Fabian Society. It is one also of practical tendency – a difficult thing to grasp and bring home in detail; but I propose to indicate by one or two instances what I mean.

(α) I have spoken of the theory of private property. Now, theoretical attitude communicates a bias, as every one knows, to particular perceptions. I do not think I ever noticed a Socialist alluding, except with derision, to the duties of property. Of course you may maintain that you are right in fact – that these duties are a negligible quantity, or a ridiculous pretence. Time forbids me to argue upon the proper interpretation of this state of things which indisputably exists in great measure. But, however this attitude may be justified, I want to point out what it amounts to. The long and short of it is that those who speak in this way do not really believe in Moral Socialism. To those who believe in Moral Socialism the source of a payment makes no difference to the duty it involves. So long as one can live, the duty of working for Society is imperative; if one has

---

[16][See note 5 above.]

more than enough to live on, that is a charge – something to work with, to organise, to direct. Property is mediate payment with responsibility; salary is immediate payment. I never saw it recognised by a Socialist that property could be a burden. I wish to avoid overstraining, and I will admit against myself that my own class is probably the most selfish of all; that is, the class which has enough to tempt it into a little luxury, but not enough to constitute a notable responsibility and public charge. But this defect of a limited class does not justify a want of faith which misconstrues a fundamental factor of human morality. And this defect of faith is radical, and is connected directly with Economic Socialism. It means that the reason for equalising opportunity is not merely that you want to give nine-tenths of the people a better chance than they have now – to level up to the highest standard to which you may in practice be able to level up – but that you do not believe any one will work unless his livelihood depends upon it. Now I cannot fight the battle of all human nature in five minutes; but I will lay down one principle as tolerably certain, and it is this: a man who will not work if his livelihood is secure without it will be an uncommonly bad workman if his livelihood depends upon it. Practically speaking, this whole view is to my observation false; and, technically speaking, it unquestionably is Moral Individualism. Here I am glad to have on my side the concluding pages of the Essay on "Industry under Socialism,"[17] which represents the ethical right wing, and, as I hope, the future of Socialistic ideas.

(β) I have said that many Socialists speak as if they did not *believe in* the socialisation of the will. It is a corollary from this that they should not care about the socialisation of the will.

There are indications that the natural connection of Economic Socialism with Moral Individualism tends to realise itself in this respect also. I will adduce some instances which may at least explain my meaning.

(i) I admit that I have not found in the *Fabian Essays* the direct disparagement of *thrift* which I anticipated that I should find. The only allu-

---

[17][Written by Annie (Wood) Besant (1847–1933) theosophist, labour organiser, early champion of birth control, and (briefly) Fabian socialist. She left the Fabians in 1889 to join Madame Helena Blavatsky's (1831–1891) Theosophical Society. In 1895 Besant moved to India, which had become the centre of the Theosophists, and was active in educational reform and the "Home Rule for India League."]

sion to the subject which I have observed is the remark that thrift is preached by extravagant people, which doubtless is true. Otherwise, I think, the subject is somewhat severely let alone. I believe that am not mistaken in saying that the inculcation of thrift is looked upon with coldness, if not with aversion, by modern Economic Socialism. It is said, and I do not know that Socialists would desire to deny it, that the introduction of Post Office Savings Banks into Prussia was prevented by the influence of Lassalle's movement upon the Government, the then Director of the Post Office being anxious to introduce them.[18]

Now I am well aware of two things: first, that there are different kinds of thrift – speaking roughly, the selfish kind and the unselfish kind; and secondly, I am aware that there is no greater deterrent against saving than the impossibility of saving enough to be of any use. This is an every-day experience among the less wealthy class of professional men. But yet I appeal with confidence to any one who has practical familiarity with the character and distresses of the working class, to say whether experience does not show that thrift among them goes with unselfishness and a sense of duty, and unthrift with selfishness and self-indulgence. I would rather, I think, have on my soul the sin which has been committed by Englishmen in high places, of speaking lightly of intemperance, than the sin of having let fall a word of discouragement for that foresight and self-control which is, and always must be, the ground and medium of all Moral Socialism. I see no ultimate discrepancy between the purposes of Economic Socialism and this elementary factor of morality. I do see a prima facie antagonism between the two, in so far as Economic Socialism rests upon the individualistic fallacy of thinking that you can maintain a moral structure without maintaining the morality which is the cohesion of its units. It should be clearly understood that thrift, in the shape of a resolution to bear at least your own burdens, is not a selfish but an unselfish quality, and is the first foundation and the well-known symptom of a tendency, not to Moral Individualism, but to Moral Socialism. This point is not met by saying that it is hard to save on 19*s*. a week. We are speaking of a quality in moral char-

---

[18][Ferdinand Lassalle (1825–1864) was a German socialist, critical to the founding of Germany's first socialist party, The General Union of German Workers.]

acter, which determines the happiness or misery of those who possess or do not possess it, in a way that goes far deeper into life than by mere success or failure in laying by a sum of money. The man who looks ahead and tries to provide for bearing his own burden is the man who can appreciate a social purpose, and who cares for the happiness of those dependent on him. Him, if he fails in part you may safely help for a time; if he fails altogether by exceptional misfortune you should, I incline to think, distinguish him in your Poor Law treatment from the man who shows no signs of such a disposition. But to try and take away from him the one thing on which his manliness and his chance of happiness depend by speaking lightly of the duty of carrying at least one's own burden, betrays a standpoint which is not that of Moral Socialism.

(ii) I turn from a question of feeling and mode of speech to a question more directly practical. In speaking of the present Poor Law system, a chief fault to which a Socialist calls attention is harshness of administration and desire to save the rates. Now, that there was great brutality in Poor Law administration not very long ago, that signs of such brutality appear to crop up still from time to time, that defects arising from foolish economy are alleged against some Poor Law schools, and that the system of large district schools may require reconsideration – all this appears to me to be true. And it is plain that sensible kindliness, the greatest possible care for education, and a differential treatment of those whose misfortunes are special and unavoidable, should be principles pervading the administration of the Poor Law.[19]

Nevertheless, after all these allowances are made in justification of the Socialist criticism, I should say that it points in precisely the wrong direction. These matters, indeed, cannot really be discussed on a quantitative basis; nothing in actual life can be so treated. In all these social problems it is not really either a less or a more that is wanted; it is something *different*; something which would be more in some cases, and less in others. But if I must use roughly approximate terms of quantity, to which popular treatment always inclines, I should say that what is wanted is to lessen the amount of Poor Law assistance; to make the administration not more lax, but more strict; not more lenient, but more

---

[19]See Preface [to *The Civilization of Christendom*, loc. cit., note 1].

harsh. I observe that in the Essay on "Industry under Socialism" it is contemplated without a shudder that those who, in a reformed social system, and with a fair chance of work before them, deliberately refuse to support themselves, might without injustice be left to starve. Now the complication of deserved and undeserved calamity represented by our pauperism to-day cannot be thus regarded as meriting strictly penal treatment. On the other hand, the moral requirement suggested by the passage seems to me too low. We require more of a man than the willingness to work as an alternative to bare starvation. We require that in laying his plan of life, and not simply with a view to his own possible disaster, he should be guided by the principle that he will never become a burden to others like himself. Therefore you must judge these cases not merely by their present misery, but by their past selfish folly. And therefore we must treat the failure in self-support as something which, though we dare not now bring it, as the more socialistic Athenians did, within the compass of the penal law, yet demands not only the pity but also the reprobation of society. I look upon the exceptional case of destitution by pure misfortune in a manner analogous to that in which I regard a legal offender who is free, by some accident, from moral culpability. These cases there partly is, and more completely might be, a mode of hindering or of alleviating. Here is the sphere of individual kindliness and skill.

What do I want, then, to bring the thing to an issue? I want all ordinary cases of destitution to be treated in the workhouse, with gentleness and human care, but under strict regulation and not on a high scale of comfort. I want all cases of exceptional misfortune, which has finally frustrated foresight and persistent effort, to be treated by private skill and judgment, apart from the Poor Law, through the dutiful care of relatives or neighbours. I want the State supplementation of the resources of those who are poor but not destitute, known as out-relief, to cease altogether. Here I must add a word to show the special bearing of this on my philosophical contention. You cannot restore a broken life by mechanical support. This deep and subtle relation between the character and circumstances solves itself not in one form but in many forms of evil which arise from the attempt. There is physical evil – this supplementation of resources, owing to the constant fear of deception, is never adequate, and actually causes the partial or entire starvation which it is intended to avert. There is economical evil – the rate in aid of wages; I need not enlarge on this. There is moral evil – the confusion of responsibility between the individual and Society as a whole. "I have paid rates for many years," a labourer out of work, once said to me – "why should I not have my relief simply by asking for it?" The Economic Socialism of out-relief had driven this poor man into Moral Individualism; seeing the fund to which he contributed used to tide over the difficulties of the improvident, he thought that the State intended, in part at least, to take the duty of providence off his shoulders; his will was confused, and his life very probably ruined. No money will make up to a man for a broken mainspring in his social will.

There is one fundamental objection – or, rather, one incisive retort, for I cannot admit that it is an objection – which a Socialist may make to all this argument. He may say, "Is not, at least, inherited or unearned property an equally pernicious subvention to the rich as out-relief to the poor?"

I point out one distinction, and then, give my general answer. Property is within the owner's control and is a permission to him, to choose his work – of course an enormous indulgence. But Poor Law relief is not in the recipient's control, is a payment for idleness, and is not sufficient to set the life free to choose work. A large pension or gift of property to a man not yet demoralised would probably do no harm. This is the paradox about doles already known to Aristotle, and recognised by expert philanthropists to-day. Great expenditure which "sets a man up" does not as a rule demoralise; it is the little chronic subventions, which give no freedom and are actually consequent upon the failure of the social will, that cause demoralisation.

I do not think it can be denied that property *may* have a similar effect. Wherever it distracts from one social vocation, without forming the basis of another, there it operates as out-relief pure and simple, and there the strictures of the *Fabian Essays* have full application. With this concession, I pass from the distinction which I had to draw between property and out-relief, to the general answer which I make to the retort which consists in comparing them.

The answer is simply this: that two blacks do not make a white, and that the identification of property with out-relief, if established, might be a good argument for abolishing property, but could not possibly be a plea in favour of out-relief.

(iii) And with out-relief I class all inadequate treatment of the symptom of social evil which is known as poverty. I mention especially large-scale organisations for free dinners at popular schools, and large-scale arrangements for giving employment to the casual unemployed.

In all these matters the same tendency is traceable – the tendency to adapt machinery to dealing with a large effect, superficially apparent, without distinguishing the very different classes of cause, demanding different means for their neutralisation, which concur in producing this large apparent effect. Especially in the problem of feeding the children who attend school every case needs special and separate investigation. It is certainly sometimes possible to persuade parents to pay for food supplied to their children, who before permitted it to be given to them for nothing. I have seen this done, on a very small scale indeed, and in this case there has been not only a physical gain to the child, but also a moral gain to the parents. I cannot strongly enough protest that to us who believe in the socialisation of the will, the treatment of these questions by large-scale machinery assumes the aspect, not of sympathy and charity, but of negligence and cruelty. Discrimination, if guided merely by the test of the child's immediate need, means on the whole that the wrong people are helped and the right people are not helped. To this I should prefer, if it were the only alternative, that all children should be given a free meal without discrimination; in which case there would not be the peculiar extra aggravation that just precisely in proportion as people fail to do their duty, the public does it for them. I may add, that under the present social system these advantages probably send up the rents in the neighbourhoods where they are provided, so that the happy landlord pockets the weekly value of the child's dinner. This, however, is not an argument that can ultimately carry weight with Socialists. It should weigh with everybody for the present, I think.

(iv) It is plain, moreover, that Economic Socialism is anything but warmly disposed towards productive co-operation, the existence of which, as distinct from joint-stock shopkeeping, would hardly be gath-

ered from the reference to the subject in the *Fabian Essay* on "The Industrial Basis of Socialism." Although Dr Ingram's opinion[20] is evi-
dently, like the Fabian Essayist's, that no great importance belongs even
to productive co-operation, yet it is worth observing that in the passage
to which the Fabian Essay alludes he is discussing Cairnes[21] view to the
contrary, and the modern economists whom he quotes against Cairnes
are not quite spoken of as "modern economists in general." This is a
matter of no real importance, except as an indication of a well-known
Socialistic attitude of mind – of what almost amounts to a dread of all
processes that chiefly depend on the socialisation of the will; because, I
suppose, the primary antagonism between Economic and Moral Socialism is instinctively felt, without being theoretically demonstrated. The
success of productive co-operation, I take it, in view of the modern successful management of joint-stock companies, is simply and solely an
affair of the workman's industrial and moral education.[22]

(v) The word education brings me to my last set of illustrations, which
are on ground more familiar to me. The Economic Socialist is willing, as

---

[20][J.K. Ingram,] "Political Economy," *Encyclopaedia Britannica* [9th edn, vol. xix].

[21][John Elliott Cairnes (1823–1875) was a classical political economist, upholding the
wage fund theory and other controversial views. Many of his positions are akin to J.S.
Mill's: both, for example, allow that there are important exceptions to the laissez-faire
maxim, and that the ownership of land raises very different problems than other types of
wealth. For his main work, see *Some Leading Principles of Political Economy Newly Ex-
pounded* (London, Macmillan, 1874). For his views on Mill's political economy, see his
contribution to *John Stuart Mill: His Life and Works, Twelve Sketches by Herbert
Spencer, Henry Fawcett, Frederic Harrison, and Other Distinguished Authors* (Folcroft,
PA: Folcroft Library Editions, [1873] 1977). John Stuart Mill was an enthusiastic proponent of worker cooperatives; see his *Principles of Political Economy*, ed., Sir William
Ashley (Fairfield, NJ: Kelley, [1909], 1976), pp. 768–70 (Book IV, ch. vii, sect. 5). Interestingly, both Mill and Bosanquet focus on the same example of a cooperative – the
house painting venture of M. Leclaire. For Bosanquet's treatment see his essay on "Two
Modern Philanthropists" in his *Essays and Addresses* (London: Swan Sonnenschein,
1891), pp. 1–23.]

[22]I leave this passage as it was delivered. Miss Potter's work on "The Co-operative
Movement" has probably intensified the attitude towards "Productive" Co-operation,
which I refer to, but at the same time assigns ethical motives for the view which she
adopts. [Miss Potter is Beatrice (Potter) Webb (see above, note 2). See her *The Co-
operative Movement in Great Britain* (London: Swan Sonnenschein, 1891).]

I rejoice to see, to spend money on the children, but I do not see that, since the time of Robert Owen, his eyes have been very sharp to detect the real needs of education. Owen proposed that there should be national training colleges for teachers – a truly statesman like proposal, which I wish was included in the platform of some party to-day. Probably, in his sympathy with Lancaster, Owen may have been careless about the size of the division entrusted to a single teacher, on which both Bell and Lancaster had absurd ideas.[23] On this question experience has taught us much, and to double the present staff of teachers, at least in our infant schools, is a very moderate proposal. It would be much more important to give a piano to every Board School than to give "free dinners" to the children.[24] It is heartbreaking to see the children marching to the mere clapping of hands.

And one thing more is necessary to sound education. You must carry the parents along with you. There is nothing in this contrary to Economic Socialism; it seems to be successfully attempted in Godin's Familistère at Guise.[25] But, like the other matters I have referred to, you can only do it by real enthusiasm for the socialisation of the individual will. No machinery can effect it. You must make it your duty, and inspire your managers with the zeal for this duty, to get the parents interested, until at last they come to know and care and act effectively in

---

[23] [Joseph Lancaster (1778–1838) and Andrew Bell (1753–1832) are both credited with developing the monitorial system of education; teachers instructed the monitors, typically the outstanding students, who in turn instructed about ten other students. The system could include several levels of monitors – hence Bosanquet's complaint.]

[24] I must insist that this sentence does *not* mean that pianos, which I rejoice to see are to be given, are more important than the proper care and nourishment of school children. If I said that to pay for making school life happier is better than to pay parents to neglect their children, the saying might seem less hard.

[25] [Jean-Baptiste André Godin (1817–1888) was a major French industrialist and follower of Charles Fourier. In 1859, inspired by Fourier's *Phalanstère*, he founded the Familistère – a 3 storey building that could house, in 300 rooms, some 1500 people. For Godin's "societarian" views see his *Mutualité sociale et association du capital et du travail* (Paris: Guillaumin & Co., 1880) English translation: *The Association of Capital with Labor: Being the Laws and Regulations of Mutual Assurance Regulating the Social Palace*, trans., Louis Bristol (New York: Evening Post, 1881).]

controlling the education of their children. The thing can be done. I have seen a beginning made – a very trifling one.

(vi) And as a final instance, I would say one word upon the ideal, often connected with Economic Socialism, of beautiful surroundings of life and the interchangeability of labour. Here I believe, we find, mingled with much sound insight, a theoretical confusion, the pursuit of an abstraction. Socialists always say, and quite rightly, that you cannot go back. Well, for that reason I think that you can never again be free from the intellectuality of modern life; and therefore I think that material beauty and splendour will never again have their old importance in our lives. We shall have, I trust, a devotion to beauty – probably a deeper beauty than before – and shall learn to avoid the sordid and hideous; but when a lad can buy Shakespeare for a shilling and read him in a garret, it is impossible that we should ever again absolutely depend for our chief spiritual nutriment on the beauty of the more sensuous arts and crafts. I do not underrate these great goods of life; I am often accused of valuing them too highly. I only want to point out that the whole basis of mind and society is now definitely intellectual and ideal, and in the historical idea we have explicitly what the artistic tradition used to represent implicitly. "Literature is dirt-cheap,"[26] and every one can read it; and though I cannot doubt that the fine arts of sense-perception have a future, yet the modern mind is so deep and so strong that it can bear, and to some extent must bear, the divorce from sensuous beauty, which would have killed the ancient Greek or medieval Italian.

This brings me to the question of the interchangeability of labour. Here, as elsewhere, I do not think that Economic Socialism appreciates the depth of individuality which is necessary in order to contain, in a moral form, the modern social purpose. Each unit of the social organism has to embody his relations with the whole in his own particular work and will; and in order to do this the individual must have a strength and depth in himself proportional to and consisting of the relations which he has to embody. Thus, if the individual in ancient Greece was like a centre to which a thousand threads of relation were attached, the individual

---

[26] *Fabian Essays* [*in Socialism*, ed. G. Bernard Shaw (London: The Fabian Society, 1889)].

in modern Europe might be compared to a centre on which there may hang many millions. You cannot go back to a simple world, in which the same man can conquer all knowledge, or be versed in all practice. If all are, as we hope, to share in the aims achieved by each, it can only be through the gigantic and ever-increasing labour by which every worker takes account, in his work, of its import for all. There should not be castes of workers, if caste means a social division; there must be classes of workers, because the increasing material of human knowledge and endeavour will more and more consume the entire lives and thoughts of those upon whom its burden falls.

This argument is not directed against rational provisions for doing away with unskilled labour, or for imposing some public activity on every citizen in excess of his normal vocation. It is directed against the idea that work becomes useful by being popular in the sense of being unspecialised and superficial; whereas it is plain to all who know, that only thoroughness can impart universal significance, and that the claim upon the student, and artist, and scientist will more and more take the form, "It is expedient that one man should die for the people."[27] This is very far from being a selfish contention on the student's part. In an age of universal education, the student's services, more than those of any one else, will be obtainable, should society so choose, at starvation wages.

I need not multiply these illustrations. I have said enough to make my meaning clear. Economic Individualism and Economic Socialism are both obviously on the move, each of them desiring to make good its differently-founded claims to harmonise with Moral Socialism, which is the only thing for which any healthy human being, at the bottom of his heart, cares a single straw. The Moral Socialist looks on, confident that the forces of human nature will make the reality prevail, but not all unwilling to co-operate with those forces wherever he can find a purchase. And such a purchase would be found if it were possible to convince the Economic Socialist that in dealing with the social organism he is dealing with a structure whose units are the characters of men and women; and that in so far as he neglects to base his arrangements on the essence of

---

[27]["It is expedient for us, that one man should die for the people." John: II: 50.]

character – that is, on the social or moral will – so far he is not dealing with the social organism as an organism, but rather as a machine – that is to say, from the point of view, not of Moral Socialism, but of Moral Individualism.

THE PRINCIPLE OF PRIVATE PROPERTY[1]

Editors' Introduction:

In the following essay Bosanquet defends the idea of private property. In this account, influenced by Hegel, Bosanquet tells us that private property is necessary to express and realize the self – it provides a means for realizing the individual will. In order for property to serve this function, it must, first, be "very responsive to the character and capacity of the owner" – it must be up to you to decide what you are going to do with it – and, secondly, it must allow for planning and reflect the unity of a life. Bosanquet insists that "limited ownership is objectionable *per se.*" Bosanquet then criticises socialist and welfarist schemes that seek to ensure that everyone gets what he or she needs: this relegates citizens to the status of children and creates a "slavish dependence." This essay forms a crucial part of Bosanquet's argument against the rise of the modern welfare state.

1. There is apt to be a confusion between the history of property and the reason of its existence.[2] "Property," it has been said, "originates in 'first occupancy' or 'appropriation'." But this amounts to the truism that there must be appropriation if there is to be property, and assigns no reason either why there is or why there ought to be property. So with "force," or "enactment by the sovereign"; the right of property, like all rights, depends on social recognition, and no right can be explained by force, though society must be possessed of force to repress encroachments upon rights. "Contract" again presupposes "property," and does not account for it. One cannot acquire a thing by contract unless it already is

---

[1] [From *Aspects of the Social Problem*, ed., Bernard Bosanquet (London: Macmillan, 1895), pp. 308–318.]

[2] [In this opening paragraph, Bosanquet is following T.H. Green's analysis of the "two questions" about the "origin of property" that "are apt to be mixed up.... One is the question how men have come to appropriate; the other is the question how the idea of a right has come to be associated with their appropriations." *Lectures on the Principles of Political Obligation*, with preface by Bernard Bosanquet. (London: Longmans, Green, 1895), pp. 211ff (sects. 211ff.).]

property, nor contract that there shall be property unless social recognition already exists. Or, it is said, "Property arises from labour,"[3] i.e. because a man's person is his property, therefore the work of his hands is his property. But this, again, is no explanation. It suggests that property is recognised on the same ground as a man's right to be his own master, but does not say what that ground is.

The true reason is the recognition of a common good by the members of a society, as realised in each other's lives, for this is the foundation of all rights.

This common good has its existence in the lives of members, each of whom has a conception of himself and of his wellbeing through participation in an organised whole, apart from his particular momentary wants. This permanent conception demands a provision for possible self-satisfaction and possible self-expression, "the means of realising a will, which is, in possibility, a will for social good."[4] This is quite a different thing from the mere successive removal of wants successively arising, such as satisfies an animal. And in the social institution of property, beginning with the clan, and completed by the developed State, this "realised will," or permanent conception of wellbeing, takes its place as a right – that is to say, as a want socially recognised as demanding fulfilment. Man can only be fully realised as social when he is fully distinguished as individual. In the mere clan he is relatively unfree and unsocial.

2. We may illustrate this point by contrast with the position of a child in the family, or even of an animal. Removal of wants as they arise is the principle of our treatment of animals – no provision is needed in their case for possible self-expression demanded by the nature of their self in consequence of an idea of its own wellbeing as a whole. The same principle is applied in human life to a child in the family, and is sometimes

---

[3] Locke. [*See Second Treatise of Government*, ch. 5, sects. 27–51; ch. 16, sect. 194.]

[4] T.H. Green, *The Right of Private Property, Works*, Vol. ii. [Bosanquet is referring here to the Lecture N, on "The Right of the State in Regard to Property" in Green's *Lectures on the Principles of Political Obligation*, sect. 221. Bosanquet slightly misquotes Green; the sentence reads "The rationale of property, as we have seen, is that everyone should be secured by society in the power of getting and keeping the means of realising a will, which in possibility is a will directed to a social good."]

the ideal, or gives the general type of the ideal, proposed for man in general. Approximating to this is the ideal suggested by Plato, which either denies property, like family life, to individuals (where he permits the one he permits the other), or regards it as a mere apparatus of social function in the narrowest sense – the tools of a man's trade, which, if this was all, need not be his own property. This is connected with the whole position of the individual and the family in Plato's view. The essence of this whole position is to think it enough if momentary needs of work and life are temporarily and successively met as they arise. They may be as liberally met as we please to imagine; that is not the essential point.

Let us take the child in the family as the extreme type, and leave out any imitation of grown-up life which his parents may introduce by way of discipline, by taking away what he wastes or spoils, and so forth. His relation to things has no unity corresponding to his moral nature. No nerve of connection runs through his acts in dealing with the external world. So with his food; he may waste or throw away his food at one meal, he gets none the less at the next (unless by way of discipline). He gets what is thought necessary quite apart from all his previous action. So too with his dress. The dress of a young child does not express his own character at all, but that of his mother. If he spoils his things, that makes no difference to him (unless as a punishment); he has what is thought proper for him at every given moment. So with travel, enjoyments and education up to a certain point. What he is enabled to have and do in no way expresses his own previous action or character, except in as far as he is put in training by his parents for grown-up life. The essence of this position is, that the dealings of such an agent with the world of things do not affect each other, nor form an interdependent whole. He may eat his cake and have it; or he may not eat it and yet not have it. To such an agent the world is miraculous; things are not for him adjusted, organised, contrived; things simply *come* as in a fairy tale. The same is the case with a slave. Life is from hand to mouth; it has as such no totality, no future, and no past.

Now, private property is not simply an arrangement for meeting successive momentary wants as they arise on such a footing as this. It is wholly different in principle, as adult or responsible life differs from child-life, which is irresponsible. It rests on the principle that the inward or moral life cannot be a unity unless the outward life – the dealing with things – is also a unity. In dealing with things this means a causal unity, i.e. that what we do at one time, or in one relation, should effect what we are able to do at another time, or in another relation. I suspect that the difficulty in accepting this principle is largely due to a mistake about inward morality – to treating the pure will for good as if it could exist and constitute a moral being without capacity for external expression. This is a blunder in principle. If all power of dealing effectively with things is conceived absent, inward morality, or the good will, vanishes with it. I will return to this point in dealing with the "no margin" doctrine.

Private property, then, is the unity of life in its external or material form; the result of past dealing with the material world, and the possibility of future dealing with it; the general or universal means of possible action and expression corresponding to the moral self that looks before and after, as opposed to the momentary wants of a child or of an animal. A grown man knows that if he does this he will not be able to do that, and his humanity, his power of organisation, and intelligent self-assertion, depend on his knowing it. If he wants to do something in particular ten years hence he must act accordingly to-day; he must be able in some degree to measure his resources. If he wants to marry he must fit himself to maintain a family; he must look ahead and count the cost, must estimate his competence and his character. That is what makes man different from an animal or a child; he considers his life as a whole, and organises it as such – that is, with a view to reasonable possibilities, not merely to the passing moment.

3. Certain limitations follow from this principle. Not all property or absence of property, as existing at a given time, is the pure expression of this social or spiritual necessity. In all actual social arrangements spiritual expression is thus obstructed. There is confusion, and therefore distortion. Seeking the self, man's true purpose and calling are metamorphosed into self-seeking. The means of complete life catch the eye, are noted as undeniably important, and from an absolutely relative end become a relatively absolute end. Against this blunder the mind violently reacts, and because the means falsely pretended it was an end, the mind

in return will pronounce it not even a means, and thereby enormously aggravate the evil which the former fallacy had initiated.

Clearly the principle does not demand unlimited acquisition of wealth, if we disregard the definite mischief which may attach to the means adopted to limit it. It rests on the conception of a common good, to be realised in individuals as moral and rational agents, and subject to this, all means for its realisation must be treated as a practical problem, turning on what is best in the long run for society as the external embodiment of character.

Are powers of bequest and alienation necessary to the idea of private property? At the dawn of history both in Greece and Rome the State is found introducing these, in its own interest, as against the family or clan, which it regarded as a dangerous competitor with itself. The opposition was then between power of bequest, and unalterable family succession; now it is between power of bequest, usually to the family, and property not devolving at all, so that maintenance of bequest within limits is now in favour of the family. That ground must have full weight. A reason against compulsory devolution by equal division or the like is that it makes the several children's shares independent of character or capacity. But all these points are arguable; it should be noted, however, that limited ownership is objectionable *per se.*[5] The social need is to make possession of property very responsive to the character and capacity of the owner. Thus prohibition of alienation is objectionable as tending to keep property in the hands of incompetent holders. It is quite reasonable to treat land differently from other materials, and differently in different countries, according to the supply of it and the demand for it, as conditioned by the nature of the chief industries and so forth.

In face of Collectivist ideals, what does our principle suggest? Society is to-day largely on a basis of wages and salaries; these may and do fulfil the principle of private property so long as we keep well away from the ideal of the child or slave. Salaries, to fulfil the postulate, must be, I should say, in some decree pertinent and calculable – capable of being foreseen with probability, and capable of being dealt with by investment or some analogous process; if not, we approach the ideal of child or

---

[5][*per se*: in itself, intrinsically.]

slave life by cutting the strings of continuity between all material dealings of the same person and making it impossible for his life to be regarded as a whole; in plain language, we shall prevent his making plans.

I do not speak of wages being apportioned to service or to demand, because that is not the point of private property, though perhaps necessary or advisable on other grounds. The point of private property is that things should not come miraculously and be unaffected by your dealings with them, but that you should be in contact with something which in the external world is the definite material representation of yourself. If it were the case that self-utterance were becoming impossible in industry and regimented routine production were to be in future the only possible method of work, it would be still more important to maintain a unity in the material management of private life; but the question of the organisation of industry is really a separate question. Is it not enough, we may be asked, to know that one can have what is necessary and reasonable? No; that makes one a child. A man must know what he can count on and judge what to do with it. It is a question of initiation, plan, design, not of a more or less in enjoyment.

4. In alluding to objections, I do not speak of mere practical difficulties such as a growingly large scale organisation of industry. The London and North-Western Railway cannot be effectively private property in the sense in which a wheelbarrow can be; whether it is managed by the State or not makes but little practical difference in this impossibility. The principle of the unity of life on its external or material side does not ultimately depend upon the scale of industrial production. Rather it is a requirement which could be satisfied in very various ways. But I do not say that the destruction of small industries managed by individuals would be without a bad influence, especially in the minor arts.

Objections of principle all amount to preferring the ideal of the child in the family. The most plausible perhaps is the "no margin" argument. "You either have enough for your full wants at the moment, or you have not enough. If you have enough, you ought not to have more; if you have not enough, then plainly it ought all to be expended on your momentary necessities." Thus, in either case, a permanent definite provision for possible self-expression is in principle objected to. By the hypothesis, life is cut down to the passing moment. This always strikes me as analogous to Plato's argument somewhere to show that one cannot make a mistake. "Either you know a thing, and then you cannot be wrong; or you do not, and then you can say nothing."[6] The answer is, I suppose, in both cases, that human life is situated on the progressive margin, and its object and interest is to organise further the partly organised, not simply to rest at a given level. Man never has enough so long as his capacity for foresight and management, for treating life as a unity with a past and future, is not tasked to the full; and he never has too little to give effect to this capacity in some degree, so long as he is able to live a human life at all. The need for possessing a permanent nucleus in the material world is not subsequent to, nor accrues, so to speak, on the top of, all immediate needs, but is as deeply rooted in the mind as they are, and acts in all of them, and begins to form itself within them and against them, long before the current standard of comfort of any human society is attained. And this want is essential to humanity, and is itself a condition without which *human* comfort cannot exist. That, I suspect, is why the Workhouse is miserable, except in extreme cases of semi-imbecile dullness or of ascetic resignation.[7] The forward look to the unity of life is abandoned, and an adult has accepted the status of a

---

[6][On the nature of knowledge, see e.g., Plato's *Theaitetos*, trans. John Warrington, (London: Dent, 1961). The paradox in seeking knowledge is summed up by Meno: "And how will you inquire, Socrates, into that which you do not know? What will you put forth as the subject of your inquiry? And if you find what you want, how will you ever know that this is the thing which you did not know?" *Meno*, trans. Benjamin Jowett (Indianapolis: Bobbs-Merrill, 1949), p. 36 (80^b–81^a).]

[7][From around 1700 the Poor Law in the United Kingdom was administered partly though Workhouses, in which the poor receiving assistance were expected to support themselves. The poor law of the eighteenth century was a mixture of Workhouse and "outdoor" (or "home") relief – assistance to the poor outside Workhouses. The poor law reform of the 1830s sought a uniform national system, restricting "outdoor" relief and seeking to confine assistance to the Workhouse. The Workhouses were places of last resort, an option only to be considered as an alternative to starvation. In the Workhouse system families were separated by age and sex. The philosophy of the Workhouse system was that life should be unpleasant for the inmates: harsh conditions, hard work and meagre diet were typical. Workhouses were built by Poor Law Unions; a tax area comprising a major town and its catchment region, supervised by a committee of local gentry, clergymen and notables. Bosanquet supported the Workhouse system.]

child. So much the greater is the need to narrow, instead of widening, the sphere of such slavish dependence. To deny, in principle, the need for a permanent provision for possible work and self-expression is to ignore the root-principle of human nature, and the connection of inward and outward morality, or of character and competence. It is also most important to note that the denial of property gives an enormous impulse to animal selfishness. It declares that my share is not for me to work with, to contrive and organise with, to express myself completely with, but simply to meet my wants from day to day. The surplus over the necessary is therefore earmarked to be spent on passing enjoyment – a horrible result.

The real cause of complaint to-day, I take it, is not the presence but the absence of property, together with the suggestion that its presence may be the cause of its absence. This does not immediately concern my argument, which is directed to showing what element in human life it represents; I am speaking, as Ruskin once said, not of what is possible, but of what is necessary.[8] That society should to a great extent fail in satisfying a need of man's nature is nothing new, and the remedy for its failure is a practical problem; but no solution will be found in simply ignoring the need. All our work towards permanent organisation and improvement of conditions is to the good, as assisting the treatment of life as a whole, so long as we do not artificially introduce the ideal of the child or slave – of a life forbidden to organise its future, and restricted to receiving what is deemed necessary from day to day. I add one comparison, which strikes me as interesting. Property is no doubt liable to be stereotyped and transferred and accumulated, so that it loses all proportion to earnings or capacity. The advocates of the child-ideal cannot complain on this ground, because they disclaim all idea of apportionment to services, which disclaimer is a meeting-point of absolute communism and the extreme private property theory. But those who wish for an arrangement that should retain the idea of *earning*, by some quasi-competitive relation of salary to value or energy of service, so as to avoid in apportionment of advantages a total disregard of capacity to fulfil a social demand, should reflect on this, that the same sort of chance

---

[8][See above p. 118, note 28.]

which transfers property to persons who have not earned it, asserts itself strongly now in salaried work, and would probably do so much more intensely if all work was salaried. The fact is, that much discharge of function – that which is in any way new or original – cannot be provided for in a scheme of salaries, because it is not antecedently known to exist; so that in every large organisation by salaries we get a number of people who are doing possibly very good work, but not the work they are paid to do. The classical example is Burns (not John but Robert) as an exciseman.[9] Every institution, an experienced head of institutions once said to me, carries some dead weight so far as its immediate purpose is concerned. This may be good enough for the whole community (or not), but such persons are not paid in respect of the services which they really discharge. They may have created a new function which none of the social managers have ever thought of or wanted, or they may be discharging one which really belongs to some other branch of the social service. In a complete social organisation by salaries for function there would be a great deal of this misplacing; and it might be rather demoralising. It would be analogous to the leisure class existing on unearned property; only its existence, while generally known, would be officially denied. It is well known that positions in our Civil Service have given and do give a substantial standing ground to eminent men of letters, from Robert Burns downwards. I do not suppose for a moment that they have proved other than exceedingly valuable servants of the State, but as a matter of principle their position would probably be defended in any case by the general voice on the ground that it is proper, and is creditable to maintain in the public service men eminent in other fields, so long as their official duty is reasonably well discharged. They can hardly, I imagine, as a rule, be those devoted officials on whose shoulders the public departments really rest. What I desire to point out is that in such a feeling the principle of unearned private property as contrasted with salary for services is in some degree asserting itself. Salary is, so to speak, subse-

---

[9] [Robert Burns (1759–96), author of "Auld Lang Syne," was a Scottish poet, who held the position of exciseman at Dunfries from 1791. Bosanquet's point is that his excellent work was as a poet, not as an exciseman. John Burns (1858–1943) was a British labour leader and political figure, first with the Labour, and later with the Liberal, Party.]

quent and relative to its justification by work; unearned property is antecedent, and leaves the justification to follow. Where salary is the basis of
an unanticipated social service, to which it is not intentionally relative, it
takes on the character of private property obtained by chance, and is
similarly antecedent to its justification. In a complete salaried scheme of
society there would be a good deal more of this chance-medley. Places
would have to be found, and quite undoubtedly would be found, for
good men, and would not always represent their true services to society.
Men put into positions with one set of duties would employ them for another. In proportion as this is met by requiring only a minimum amount
of service, and taking it to free the official for his whole leisure-time, the
principle of true communism and of private property is in some degree
approached. The man is entirely supported in return for a portion of his
work, and, therefore, in part not for what he does, but because he has the
good luck to be there. Among the working classes, it must be remembered, this principle is already causing difficulty where the short-hour
men compete in other industries; and from an extension of it serious
confusion might result; every one might be doing some one else's work.
Now, if this principle of antecedent provision for chance cases of undetermined function is certain to break in, by wresting predetermined
function from its avowed and organised vocation, it may be well to recognise it as inevitable by permitting the transference of property to those
who have not earned it, rather than to commit oneself to a system which
pretends to exclude what it necessarily admits. The affinity between
communism and the effects of such transferable property, in so far as
both of them leave undetermined the special adjustment of share to
function, appears to me to be curious and interesting. It suggests that a
private property system, perhaps in addition to a wage system, is the
natural development out of the perfect communism of the family, a certain affinity between the two being retained, and their difference arising
simply from the difference between the child who is unable to deal with
his material surroundings on his own responsibility, and the man whose
manhood consists in his power and need so to deal with them.

The transference of property to those who have not earned it, however,
is quite a matter for regulation in the general interest, subject to the fact
that a total prohibition of transference would seriously maim the central

principle of property, viz. the right and need to realise a conception of wellbeing relevant to the relation which makes the individual in society what he is. A man who could do nothing for his friends or for his family would have the heart cut out of his dealings with the material conditions of his life as a whole. The true principle of State interference with acquisition or alienation would refer to their tendency, if any, to prevent acquisition of property on the part of other members of society. In a small country especially this principle may well demand exceptional regulation of land tenure. On the other hand, the probable or demonstrated bad rise of property is not by itself an adequate reason against the institution, though it may be a reason for restrictive legislation. The possible bad use is a condition of the possible good use, and the social mind cannot be realised in human individuals who are not at liberty to deal with the external conditions of life as instruments of permanent self-satisfaction and self-expression. For as far as the true human self is social, or is identified with a common good, it necessarily and inevitably is incapable of being satisfied, like that of a child or animal, with the removal of wants or needs from hour to hour, or from day to day. The principle, I hope, is clear; its practical application may take many forms in the future, as it has taken many in the past.

IDEALISM IN SOCIAL WORK[1]

AN ADDRESS TO SOME SOCIAL WORKERS

Editors' Introduction:

In this lecture to social workers, given shortly after the release of the
Majority and Minority Reports of the Poor Law Commission (1905–
1909), Bosanquet provides a clear statement of his understanding of
the nature of idealism and its relation to social practice. Though he
does not directly address the arguments of the authors of the Minority
Report, he reminds his audience that poverty is not due purely to problems of individual character, and that those involved in social work
should "look before deciding what to do" – an obvious allusion to the
Fabian socialist tendency to deal with social problems by reference to
a prearranged blueprint.

Idealism, Bosanquet notes, is rooted in experience, and is neither an
escape from, nor a raising of oneself above, reality. Attentiveness to
particular experience allows, he argues, one's insight into social conditions to expand; he refers to this as "the penetrative imagination."
Facts do not support a pessimistic view of social problems, and Bosanquet encourages his audience to have faith in, and not to lose sight
of, "the reality beneath appearance."

I have not come here to lecture social workers on the details of their
work. I do not doubt that the science of social help has advanced since
I was practically concerned with it. All that I wished or hoped to do
was to give assistance, perhaps, against some general difficulties, by
returning, in a general form, to social workers some ideas that I had
gathered from them in particular experiences. In these matters this is
really the student's function: to interpret back to others what he has
first learned from them. If he has good luck, his doing so may be suggestive; it may put matters in some new light or new connection.

---

[1][From: *Charity Organisation Review*, No. XXVIII (1910), pp. 146–156. Also published as "True and False Idealism" in Bosanquet's *Social and International Ideals*
(London: Macmillan, 1917), pp. 84–96.]

1. The word "idealism" is something of a spell. It possesses the magic of a spell, and its danger. All these great watchwords of humanity, that represent predominant leanings and accumulating histories of man's mind, have in them something of an enchantment. When we use them we are drawing upon powers that are greater than our own, and we are liable to the fate of the wizard's apprentice, who roused immense forces which he could not direct or control. Idealism is a word to conjure with; but a wizard who does not know what he is about is dangerous to himself and others.

The magic of idealism lies, I suppose, in its promise of victory for the human mind. Somehow mind is to triumph; to subdue the "real" or the "actual." It is to achieve the best we can think, to make a new world.

But danger lies in all these expressions which indicate a contrast: good and evil, beautiful and ugly, true and false. They seem to indicate a battle, but they may indicate a flight, and often there is really a flight where the victory seems to be surest. Take, for instance, a "truth" that leaves outside it, standing and unexplained, all the false-hood in the world. Such a truth may seem militant and triumphant, but really it can have very little range and very little strength.

2. May I illustrate this point in a way that might seem far-fetched? We all know Wordsworth's splendid lines:

> The gleam,
> The light that never was on sea or land,
> The consecration and the poet's dream.[2]

I wonder if others, like myself, have felt uneasy in them, supposing, that is, that they were meant to describe the poet's inspiration at its best. It was only the other day, in reading Professor Raleigh's book on Wordsworth,[3] that I really came to understand what is their true content and bearing. (What a penalty one pays for neglect and inaccuracy in reading a poet! This observation bears on the main moral of what I am saying.) One only needed to read the poem through and the thing was plain at once.

---

[2][From "Elegaic Stanzas," first published in 1807, see next paragraph.]

[3][Walter Alexander Raleigh, *Wordsworth* (London: E. Arnold, 1903).]

The poem is called "Elegaic Stanzas: Suggested by a Picture[4] of Peele Castle in a Storm." It refers to the death of the poet's brother, who was drowned at sea. It opens by alluding to a time when Wordsworth had lived near Peele Castle in calm summer weather, and here occur the famous lines, which must be given with their context:

Ah, then, if mine had been the Painter's hand
To express what then I saw; and add the gleam,
The light that never was on sea or land,
The consecration and the poet's dream;

I would have planted thee, thou hoary Pile,
Amid a world how different from this;
Beside a sea, that could not cease to smile,
On tranquil land, beneath a sky of bliss.

This is the idealism that escapes – a "fugitive and cloistered virtue." But after the deeper experience, the poet goes on to say he has won a stronger standpoint, and that a more human one, from which he cannot go back:

Such in the fond illusion of my heart,
Such Picture would I at that time have made,
And seen the soul of truth in every part,
A stedfast peace that could not be betrayed.

So once it would have been – 'tis so no more;
I have submitted to a new control:
A power is gone which nothing can restore;
A deep distress hath humanised my soul....

Farewell, farewell the heart that lives alone,
Housed in a dream, at distance from the Kind.
Such happiness, wherever it be known,
Is to be pitied; for 'tis surely blind.

But welcome fortitude and patient cheer,
And frequent sights of what is to be borne;
Such sights or worse, as are before me here;
Not without hope we suffer and we mourn.

---

[4][Painted by Sir George Beaumont.]

Here we have the idealism not of escape but of comprehension, and so of conquest.

3. I will give another instance of the spirit of true idealism, this time coming nearer home.

Have we ever noted the stages of our "comprehension" of a great city? When I was a boy I was taken to hear Lord Shaftesbury[5] speak, and, like a boy, I remembered only one thing he said, an anecdote.

He said that when he first came to London a thing which soon struck him was that there were parts of the pavement that dried after rain much sooner than the rest. These were mainly, he soon noticed, at street corners, and then he saw that they were before the bakers' shops. This put him on inquiring into the conditions of the underground bakeries and of the people who worked in them. That was one route which took him into the heart of things. And all of us have in our own way passed through a similar training. Everyone must, more or less, I suppose; though the interests that guide it must be different in kind and intensity. When they are wide and intense they lead to a true idealism. I mean that when we first begin to take notice, the great city is perhaps just the frame of our business and pleasure. The streets that take us from one to the other are meaningless, insignificant to us, but then gradually – from one suggestion or another, from one starting-point or another – our insight is awakened and our interest expands. We become able, more or less, to interpret the look of the streets, and of the people. The walls become transparent to us; we see through them into the homes, or no homes, and become alive with the great life around us. We see the weakness of the poor and their strength; their goodness and courage and fun. I don't think I ever knew a really good social worker who had not the gift of sympathetic humour.

The life which we have learned to respond to, and to feel ourselves a part of, imposes its purposes and standards upon us; we are united with it in its dangers and in its hopefulness.

---

[5][Bosanquet is referring to the seventh earl of Shaftsbury (1801–1885), Lord Ashley until he assumed the title of earl of Shaftsbury in 1851. The seventh earl of Shaftsbury was known as an advocate of legislation seeking to regulate industrialisation and its effects; he introduced bills prohibiting the employment of children and women in coal mines and mandating the ten-hour factory workday.]

Now it is a feeling of this kind which suggests itself to me as the path towards a true idealism of social work. Note how Mr Stephen Reynolds[6] has recently spoken of the cruelty of intellectual people. The best which we hope for must spring out of the life we are learning to know; it must not be brought to it or stuck upon it from without. We must learn from the people before we can teach, and as a condition of teaching. More especially we should know the life of the working people at their best and strongest, or else we can have no conception of what it is that we want them to be.

This is what I call idealism; when, instead of turning away from the life around us, we have so learned it that it speaks to us at every point, and the streets, and the houses, and shops, and people have all "come alive" to us, and indicate human wants, and hopes, and powers.

Our main point is, then, that idealism is not an escape from reality; but, first, a faith in the reality beneath appearances, which, secondly works by "comprehension" and not by opposition, and confers, thirdly, a power of transforming the appearance in the direction of the real reality.

You often begin, I suppose, by remarking a pale child at school. Then you try to pierce beneath this surface fact and work the matter out, till you have a whole network of conditions before you, by dealing with which you may be able to rescue a whole family from some misfortune which is affecting them all, or from some foolish habit; and to help them to do what you find they really want. A man must be saved, some wise writer has said, on his own decalogue, and not on somebody else's.[7]

We should observe that true idealism is optimistic, because it grasps things, and does not leave them outside to become a terror. False ide-

---

[6][Stephen Sydney Reynolds (1881–1919) lived and worked with the working class; he insisted that middle-class driven social reform was inevitably seen – and rightly so – by the workers as entailing increasing regulation of their lives in the name of middle-class ideas; his prescription was a lessening of state regulations and programs, and support for increasing worker's incomes. See his "What the Poor Really Want," *Quarterly Review* (Jan., 1910).]

[7][In the spirit of Matthew Arnold: "Be neither saint nor sophist-led, but be a man. "Empedocles on Etna" (1852) act 1, sc. 2, 1.136.]

alism, sometimes called "pure," "lofty," "exalted," is pessimistic, because it is conscious of something which it has not the courage to face and overcome. Plato has a joke against this kind of idealism, which, oddly enough, people are for ever ascribing to him. He depicts an over-zealous disciple chiming in to Socrates' praise of astronomy, with the addition that it is a study which leads the mind upwards – to a higher world. Socrates answers that the question is whether you use your intelligence or not; and if you do not do this, your mind will not be looking upward, even if you float on your back in the sea.[8]

So, with this incomplete idealism, we have a wave of pessimism in England to-day – almost always in people who are not active social workers. All through life the weaker mind recoils from what it will not grasp. It is so much easier to condemn than to comprehend. We have an output of pessimistic fiction, and then a description of the state of England founded upon it; what Plato would call, I think, two removes from the facts.

One point in this prevailing temper is well worth reflecting upon – the use made of the idea of justice.[9] Almost all pessimism rests on the thoroughly individualistic question: Why this particular suffering? in the sense of asking, Is this man's suffering due to this man's fault? The novels are quite full of it; after the manner of "Did this man sin, or his parents, that he was born blind?" We should note the answer, which they do not give. It was that love should be revealed in him.

---

[8]["You, I replied, have in your mind a truly sublime conception of our knowledge of the things above. And I dare say that if a person were to throw his head back and study the fretted ceiling, you would still think that his mind was the percipient, and not his eyes. And you are very likely right, and I may be a simpleton: but, in my opinion, that knowledge only which is of being and of the unseen can make the soul look upwards, and whether a man gapes at the heavens or blinks on the ground, seeking to learn some particular of sense, I would deny that he can learn, for nothing of that sort is matter of science; his soul is looking downwards, not upwards, whether his way to knowledge is by water or by land, whether he floats, or only lies on his back." Plato's *Republic*, trans. Benjamin Jowett (New York: Vintage Books, [1894] 1991), Book V (vii, 528).]

[9][Bosanquet considers in more depth the appeal for "Justice" in his "Three Lectures on Social Ideals" in his *Social and International Ideals* (London: Macmillan, 1917), Lecture (I) – Justice, pp. 195–210.]

Justice, of course, may mean that the best should be done for every body and soul that they can receive; and, as a rule for our action, is in this sense obviously right. But to the popular pessimist it means: "The world is all askew if anyone suffers, except by his own fault"; and this principle, the root of bad individualism, would make man's life as cheap as beast's – nay, very much cheaper; for the beasts will on occasion suffer for each other. We should rather think of the great idea which, as Professor Bradley tells us, occupied the mind of Keats, that the world is a place for the making of souls; and consider what part the suffering not by one's own fault may play in that.[10]

Our conclusion, then, so far, is this: Idealism is not the power or habit of escaping from, or, in a customary sense of the words, raising oneself above reality. It is the power and habit of diving into the core of appearance, until the real reality discloses itself. Its appropriate epithets are not so much "pure," "lofty," as "thorough," "comprehensive" – the latter word in its double sense of inclusion and understanding.

This idealism is not a matter of the dreaming imagination; but of what Ruskin[11] once called the penetrative imagination[12] what Wordsworth was unmatched in. "Love had he seen in huts where poor men lie."[13]

---

[10][Andrew Cecil Bradley (1851–1935), younger brother of F.H. Bradley, published widely in both philosophy and literary studies. He was fellow and tutor at Balliol College until 1881 and later Professor of English Language and Literature at Glasgow. He was an eminent Shakespearean critic, and author of *Shakespearean Tragedy* (1904), *English Poetry and German Philosophy in the Age of Wordsworth* (1909), and *Oxford Lectures on Poetry* (London: Macmillan, 1909). In these latter lectures, Bradley refers extensively to the letters of the English poet, John Keats (1795–1821). See *The Letters of John Keats*, ed., H. Buxton Forman. (London: Reeves & Turner, 1895). Bosanquet develops this theme of "soul-building" in his second set of Gifford lectures, *The Value and Destiny of the Individual* (London: Macmillan, 1913), Lectures III and IV (pp. 63–130).]

[11][See chapter iv, note 28, p. 118.]

[12][See *Modern Painters*, Vol. II, Part III, in particular sect. II, ch. iii, "Of Imagination Penetrative," pp. 158–185.]

[13]["Love had he found in huts where poor men lie." Wordsworth, *Song at the Feast of Brougham Castle*, published 1807.]

4. A word about the kind of emotion, the passion or enthusiasm, that goes with true idealism.

Notice that we are quite right to be modest about our personal work, our own performance; but we are not right if we entertain a discouraging idea of the rank and quality of our work. In fact, the higher the idea of it that we cherish, the more personally modest we shall tend to be. But it is not right to admit, or to pass without protest, any notion that our work goes along with a cold heart and a lack of human love. There is really a point here in which explanation may be of use.

There is a vulgar prejudice, which appeals to all of us in our weaker moments, that it is one thing to be reasonable, and quite another thing to be full of love or devotion. This is wholly false. It arises from taking the terms compared at their most commonplace level; reason, perhaps, as addition and subtraction, which really have only a little emotion, because they have only a little reason; love or devotion as blind desire or foolish sentiment, which again have only a little reason, because as emotion they awaken none of the depths of our nature. Foolish sentiment goes very well with false idealism. Neither of them need any strength or effort; they have nothing to comprehend, nothing which feeds their ardour by being overcome. But what is so cheap cannot be really dear.

If you go to any of the world's great men, you do not find them talking like that. What you find is that they bring together reason and love in a way that puzzles us; though we find it true in proportion as we are anywhere near doing our best. The two moods come together in the yearning for completeness, for the escape from contradiction; the longing to find something which achieves or expresses the consummation which we want. We do not know, indeed, what it is we want. But the working of reason is just the way we build it up or track it out; and feeling is the response of the whole mind and body – the joy or depression, the sense of life or of failure to live, which goes along with this seeking and with the expansion of finding or the privation of failing to find. And this feeling, this aspiration, is good and valuable in proportion as it means a vitality of our entire soul, an utterance of all that we want. The yearning for completeness, in a word, is at once the spur of logic and the wings of love. Plato called it, in both senses, "Passion" (*Eros*). But there is something more, and it bears on our practical difficulties. To do or to feel things thus completely is exacting work. We are not always up to it. And then it may seem rather flat; that is to say, we may feel rather flat in presence of it. Mountain climbing is a fine thing, but we are not always in the mood for it. And this is why we may find ourselves dull and cold, not merely in presence of addition and subtraction, but in presence of very great works of reason and of passion. We cannot get at them. We are like the people who mock at classical music – so dull, they say. That is literally because it has more emotion in it than they are able to receive. Give them a music-hall tune and they would be happy. But, of course, in a great work of a great master there is actually present immensely more of what they want; but it is like a food that a man cannot digest, it is too much for them and they cannot receive it.

So people are always telling you that primitive language, or primitive songs or primitive sketches, are so much more "expressive," or have so much more feeling in them, than the language, or music, or art of civilisation. Or a savage blind desire seems so much more passionate than the devotion of an educated mind. It is the old story of preferring the noble savage to the civilised man. Such things are easier to get hold of because there is so much less in them.

The whole problem may best be explained by a comparison with fine art. Many years ago (I have used the incident before in this *Review*)[14] a friend told me that I could not think of Charity Organisation Society work in an artistic light. The remark cut so wholly at the root of all my convictions that I could never forget it.

What it meant, I take it, was that first-rate social work seems to some people (and perhaps to ourselves when we are feeling flat) cold and dull, hard and austere, dirty and ugly. It is so full of planning, contriving, carefully observing, sticking to the point, severity, exploring unlikely corners for a ray of light or hope.

But all this is just like the austere demand of great art. It springs from the same cause; which is, that a great eagerness or a great vitality demands to construct something which is careful and complete, and

---

[14][See the next note.]

precise and well-ordered throughout. A blind desire smothers and chokes utterance; a loose sentimentalism issues in nerveless and sloppy productions. But a really strong and healthy emotion demands for its embodiment an orderly variety, a precise and careful fitting of part to part, the accurate and living logic that constitutes the austerity, which is an aspect of all great beauty. Let me read a passage from a writer who stated all this far better than anyone else could state it.[15]

What seems to me to be true...is that feeling is worthless or precious in proportion as it is not or is translated into something which by an extension might be called action. The ordinary form of trouble about it...is that *either* I feel, and nothing comes of it, *or* I do, and there is no self, no life, in what is done.... But it is true – isn't it? – that action is good just according to the amount of feeling, which, speaking chemically, is set free in it. The most perfect illustration seems to me to be art. In any art, the more artistic the work is, the more form is there – i.e. the more measurable, definable, calculable is it – the more rational or intellectual. Yet, on the other hand, everybody, since the world began has associated with art, strength of feeling and unconsciousness of effort. A great piece of music can be taken to pieces like a clock; a great poem, compared with any other piece of language, is intensely artificial; and yet the amount of feeling which they represent is stupendous when compared with the song of a bird or a simple story. And this relation of feeling seems to hold good both of the artist and of his public. Nobody doubts that artists are more emotional than other men; nobody thought to doubt that they apply more intellect than other men. And as to the audience, I think what you say is frightfully true, that if you go to art to get your own feeling reproduced, you find it useless and flat, just because mere feeling can't find expression, and your feeling must be, at any rate potentially, endowed with form before you can be emotionally receptive of real form.

Doesn't the same apply to action in the ordinary sense? A strong man is always a man who feels strongly, *and* who can get his feeling out;

---

[15]This quotation was printed in the *Charity Organisation Review* for March 1898, in a paper with the same title as the present. I have ventured to treat the subject again and to reprint the quotation in compliance with a request which reached me. [This quotation is taken from R.L.] Nettleship, *Philosophical Lectures and Remains* [A.C. Bradley and G.R. Benson, eds. (London: Macmillan, 1897), vol. I, p. 60.]

and it may seem fanciful, but as far as I can see, if you are asked to *describe* action, you have to do it in some such way as you would do in the case of art. I mean any act, like any work of art, is measurable in time and space, and the more of an act it is, the more measurable is it, the more form there is in it.

Does all this sound mere pedantry? I do not know; but it seemed to me that it might help to cut up by the root a dangerous and recurrent fallacy, that which arouses the fear of measurableness and co-ordination and precision in social work.

This fallacy is a great danger. For our social work only lives in the doing, and changes if and as our faith and courage change. If a reader thinks George Meredith[16] dull, or prefers Ouida's tales to *Antony and Cleopatra*,[17] he can do little harm, except to himself. Fortunately, so far, Meredith and Shakespeare are dead, and he cannot get at their works to put his own faint-heartedness into them. But with our social work, if we let ourselves be over-persuaded that it is hard, and cold, and dull, because it is precise and systematic; why, then we shall make it so. Wordsworth, we are told, spoilt several passages in his poems by changing them to meet his friends' objections; because his friends could not understand the poetry of them. That is what we are being constantly urged to do; to change something essential in our work, not in the way of growth, to remedy any defect exhibited to us, but to bring it down to the minds of people who will not take the trouble to get abreast of it.

"Precision," you know; "you can't have feeling and the passion for humanity if you will be so precise." Why, what is the precision of our case papers, say, to the precision of the rhythm of a great poem, or to the adjustments of the parts of a flower? No great feeling can be uttered, nothing can really live and be strong, without extreme precision of adjustment. This is the simple secret of Aristotle's doctrine that virtue lies in an adjustment governed by a right ratio.[18] We all know it

---

[16][George Meredith (1828–1909) is considered one of the great English novelists, and is known for his complex, intellectual works].

[17][Ouida, a pseudonym of Louise de le Ramèe (1839–1908), was a romantic novelist.]

[18][See Aristotle, *Nicomachean Ethics*, trans. Sir David Ross, (Oxford: Oxford Univer-

– we know how a secret stinginess or jealousy spoils the act of generosity, or ostentation or evil temper the act of courage. In some one of its numerous adjustments to external circumstance the imperfect motive betrays itself and the act breaks down, rings false; we give, for instance, too much or too little, or in the wrong way, or at the wrong time, or to the wrong person. You only get the perfect act when it is "the flower and native growth of noble mind."

A distinguished speaker said the other day that St. Paul, if he were now alive, would add another verse to 1 Corinthians xiii., to say that "Charity cannot be organised." Did the speaker not perceive that he was putting in the mouth of St. Paul the assertion that Charity could never be a living thing? Anything that is not organised must be dead; anything that cannot be organised must be more brute than the brutest matter.

What we have to do is just to go on, perfecting the adjustments of our work as occasion arises or as defects appear, in the confidence that that is the way to find utterance for all the poetry and all the religion that are possible to social feeling.

---

sity Press, 1954), pp. 36–43 (1106^{a}17–1108^{b}12), 106–25 (1129^{a}23–1135^{a}25).]

INDEX

A

Absolute · xx, xxii, xxiii
Absolutism, administrative · 89
Acts of Parliament · 215, 309
Actual will · 132; contrasted
  with real will · xxvi, 136
Albion, launch of · 116
Alexander, Prof. · 173
All and each: as society and
  individual · 104, 173; will of
  all distinguished from general
  will · 128
Allness, judgment of · 129
Altruism · 80; and egoism · 79,
  105, 107; in Spencer · 63
Amiel, H.F. · 218
Analysis of motive, fallacy of ·
  260
Analytic Psychology · 82, 166,
  299
Anderson, John · xxxii
Anglo-Saxon race · 269
Anthropology · 232; in Hegel ·
  232
Apperception · 294, 298, 299,
  302
Appercipient masses · xxv, 167,
  301; being entirely active ·
  299; compared to persons ·
  302; compared with
  commonwealth · 301;
  compared with social groups
  · 169

Aristocracy, monarchy and
  democracy · 254
Aristotle · ix, xxiv, 1, 7, 22, 50,
  52, 174, 226, 283, 303, 333,
  336, 341, 369; community of
  minds · 50; *Ethics* · 141;
  good life · 263; manuscripts
  of · 53; on the poor · 283; on
  the state · 68; religion as aim
  of civic life · 46
Aristotle's Ethical Theory ·
  W.F.R. Hardie · 22
Armour, Leslie · xxxii
Army: opposed to crowd · 163
Art · 233, 293; how far a social
  good · 293
Artisan, or public worker · 278
Assimilation · 294, 295; and
  discrimination · 294
Association (*See also*
  Organisation) · x, 70, 161,
  302, 303; belonging to
  reproduction · 294; between
  colours, sounds, smells · 297;
  of persons and ideas · 161
Association: laws of
  resemblance, contrast,
  contiguity · 303
Assyria · 49
Athens · 54, 69, 131, 241, 283,
  335
Atomism, psychological · 303
Atomists · 141
Attention (*See also* Automatism,
  Appercipient) · 165, 299.
Austen, Jane · *Emma* · 165

F

H

S

T